A Practitioner's Guide to Ancillary Orders in Criminal Courts

The University of Law
14 Store Street
London
WC1E 7DE

A Practitioner's Guide to Ancillary Orders in Criminal Courts

Dr Elaine Freer,
Barrister, 5 Paper Buildings

Bloomsbury Professional

LONDON · DUBLIN · EDINBURGH · NEW YORK · NEW DELHI · SYDNEY

BLOOMSBURY PROFESSIONAL

Bloomsbury Publishing Plc
41–43 Boltro Road, Haywards Heath, RH16 1BJ, UK

BLOOMSBURY and the Diana logo are trademarks of

Bloomsbury Publishing Plc

First published in Great Britain 2019

British Library Cataloguing-in-Publication Data

A catalogue record for this book is available from the British Library.

ISBN:	PB:	978-1-52650-872-0
	ePDF:	978-1-52650-874-4
	ePub:	978-1-52650-873-7

Typeset by Evolution Design & Digital Ltd (Kent)
Printed and bound by CPI Group (UK) Ltd, Croydon, CRO 4YY

To find out more about our authors and books visit
www.bloomsburyprofessional.com. Here you will find extracts, author
information, details of forthcoming events and the option to sign up for
our newsletters

For Bob,

who cannot write a three-line email without multiple typos, but who meticulously proofread every word of this book without complaint, and made it all the better by doing so.

Thank you.

Foreword

I am very pleased to be able to write a foreword to this practitioner's guide to ancillary orders in criminal courts. When I started practising criminal law, almost 50 years ago, there were very few sentencing options and few ancillary orders. Over the years, these orders have multiplied and present a bewildering array of possibilities to judges responsible for passing sentence. This book provides a clear analysis of those possibilities and is to be welcomed: it will help judges and practitioners navigate the complex landscape that the law has created. Dr Freer's book sets out the criteria and law surrounding orders and explains them clearly and in detail: it addresses an often overlooked area of the law but one that it is essential we understand and apply correctly.

Sir Brian Leveson
President of the Queen's Bench Division
Head of Criminal Justice

Preface

This book was the product of my first (and so far, only) trip to the Court of Appeal. My case had been conjoined with another which raised the same point of law. The advocate in that case, whom I had never met before, was exceptionally kind and supportive of me, but the fact that her case had ended up there for the same reason as mine illustrated to me how very easy it was for advocates and judges to become so focussed on the main part of the sentence, such as whether someone receives immediate custody or not, that ancillary orders easily end in confusion and appeal. She was much senior to me; a Recorder, an experienced and highly-regarded advocate. The Court that heard those appeals was also the epitome of fairness and thoroughness. The error made by the respective first instance judges was corrected by Hickinbottom LJ, O'Farrell J and Sir John Royce. A then-pupil, now tenant, at my chambers, Christopher Jenkins, had been sent with me to the Royal Courts of Justice, and smiled politely as I came out muttering about how somebody should write a book where all these orders were set out, to help stop this sort of thing happening.

I could not shake the feeling that if there was a book – a one-stop shop – where advocates who knew they might face an ancillary order in the course of a sentencing hearing could go, and find all the legislation and cases in one place, that it might make errors like that less common, as advocates had what they needed to deploy before the judge easily available. Working on the Bar Council Law Reform Committee's response to the Law Commission's consultation on the Sentencing Code further illustrated to me the enormous complexities that arise from orders traditionally seen as 'afterthoughts' to the main event of the sentence. For getting me involved in that project, Dominic Lewis must take some of the blame for this book.

I am very grateful to Bloomsbury Professional for their positive response to my proposal for this book, and particularly to my editor, Kiran Goss, for all her support along the way. The reviews of the proposal by anonymous practitioners gave me valuable direction and helped to strengthen the final product. Sir Brian Leveson has generously given his time to write a foreword, for which I am indebted to him. Having started this book only a few months after publishing a research monograph, I owe particular thanks to everyone at both Robinson College, Cambridge, and 5 Paper Buildings, who has not rolled their eyes or put their head in their hands when the answer to 'what are you doing at the moment?' has now been 'writing a book' for 20 of the last 24 months. They can all be assured it will be a while before I even think about writing another one.

I owe especial thanks to Robert O'Sullivan QC and Andrew Johnson for their assiduous proofreading, and to my parents for their tolerance of my determination to do (too) many things at once. My love of criminal justice is probably genetic, and I am deeply grateful to them both for that, and their support.

Elaine Freer
5 Paper Buildings, Temple
Robinson College, Cambridge
28 January 2019

Contents

Table of Statutes

[All references are to paragraph number]

Table of Statutory Instruments

Table of Cases

S

List of Abbreviations

ABD	application for benefit deductions
ABCPA 2014	Anti-social Behaviour, Crime and Policing Act 2014
AEO	attachment of earnings order
ASBO	anti-social behaviour order
AWA 2006	Animal Welfare Act 2006
CA 1971	Courts Act 1971
CBO	criminal behaviour order
CDDA 1986	Company Directors Disqualification Act 1986
CDPA 1988	Copyright, Designs and Patents Act 1988
CEMA 1979	Customs and Excise Management Act 1979
CICA 2003	Crime (International Co-operation) Act 2003
CJA 1967	Criminal Justice Act 1967
CJA 1988	Criminal Justice Act 1988
CJA 2003	Criminal Justice Act 2003
CJEU	Court of Justice of the European Union
CJIA 2008	Criminal Justice and Immigration Act 2008
CJPA 2001	Criminal Justice and Police Act 2001
CPS	Crown Prosecution Service
CrimPR	Criminal Procedure Rules
DCO	defence costs order
DDA 1991	Dangerous Dogs Act 1991
ECHR	European Convention on Human Rights
EPA 1990	Environmental Protection Act 1990
EPR 2016	Environmental Permitting (England and Wales) Regulations 2016
FA 1968	Firearms Act 1968
FBO	football banning order
FSA 1989	Football Spectators Act 1989
HSWA 1974	Health and Safety at Work etc Act 1974
LASPOA 2012	Legal Aid, Sentencing and Punishment of Offenders Act 2012
MCA 1980	Magistrates' Courts Act 1980

MDA 1971	Misuse of Drugs Act 1971
MSA 2015	Modern Slavery Act 2015
NCA	National Crime Agency
OAPA 1861	Offences Against the Person Act 1861
OPA 1959	Obscene Publications Act 1959
OPA 1964	Obscene Publications Act 1964
PCC(S)A 2000	Powers of Criminal Courts (Sentencing) Act 2000
PHA 1997	Protection from Harassment Act 1997
POA 1985	Prosecution of Offences Act 1985
POA 1986	Public Order Act 1986
POCA 2002	Proceeds of Crime Act 2002
PSA 2016	Psychoactive Substances Act 2016
PSHFA 2013	Prevention of Social Housing Fraud Act 2013
RSHO	risk of sexual harm order
RTA 1988	Road Traffic Act 1988
RTOA 1988	Road Traffic Offenders Act 1988
RTRA 1984	Road Traffic Regulation Act 1984
SCA 2007	Serious Crime Act 2007
SCPO	serious crime prevention order
SHPO	sexual harm prevention order
SOA 1997	Sexual Offences Act 1997
SOA 2003	Sexual Offences Act 2003
SOPO	sexual offence prevention order
SRO	sexual risk order
STPO	slavery and trafficking prevention order
STRO	slavery and trafficking risk order
TA 2000	Terrorism Act 2000
TA 2006	Terrorism Act 2006
TMA 1994	Trade Marks Act 1994
TRO	travel restriction order
UPO	unlawful profits order
VOO	violent offender order
YJCEA 1999	Youth Justice and Criminal Evidence Act 1999
YOT	youth offending team
YRO	youth rehabilitation order

Introduction

This book does not pretend to cover every possible order that a practitioner could ever come across in the criminal courts. What it does aim to do is set out a summary of the legislation, and the case law which has clarified its operation, of the ancillary orders that are most commonly sought in criminal proceedings in magistrates' courts and the Crown Court.

Specialist orders, or those that are purely civil, are not covered. However, where a civil notice can lead to an order made by the court, breach of which is a criminal offence, such as Closure Notices, the corresponding order is covered.

Costs are an increasingly specialist matter. This book deals with applications for prosecution and defence costs. It does not deal with wasted costs orders, these being properly covered in books that deal specifically with questions of costs. Applications for wasted costs orders are usually heard separately, and on notice, allowing advocates time to properly prepare with reference to specialist texts.

One thing that almost all of these orders have in common is that breach of them is an offence. Practitioners representing a client for breach of an order found in this book should arm themselves with the Sentencing Council's Definitive Guideline for Breach Offences.[1]

The Court of Appeal has made clear that ancillary orders should not be sidelined in busy lists where judges and counsel are under immense pressure to get matters agreed and dealt with. All parties must remember that these 'simple pieces of paper' often set out conditions by which D must abide, on pain of conviction and imprisonment if they do not. The Court in *Connor*[2] concluded their judgment with two paragraphs which sharply illustrate the damage which minimising the importance of ancillary orders can cause:[3]

> 'We cannot leave this case without commenting on the quality of the order which was produced by the court and which forms part of the official court record. It does not accurately reflect the content of the order made by the judge. It has been prepared from a proforma, with no thought given to whether the resulting document makes sense. As a result a number of double negatives appear which, if read literally, would have the opposite effect to that intended. It also contains spelling and typographical errors. In the event no one was misled and the appellant has not sought to make anything of the mistakes made. This should

---

1   Effective from 1 October 2018: https://www.sentencingcouncil.org.uk/wp-content/uploads/BreachOffencesDefinitiveGuideline_WEB.pdf.
2   [2019] EWCA Crim 234.
3   *Connor* [2019] EWCA Crim 234, at [31]–[32].

not happen. All orders sent out from the Crown Court must be in proper form and reflect the order made by the judge. They should be produced by suitably trained staff who understand the importance of the order and the consequences of a failure to comply with it. If there is any doubt the order must be brought back to the judge.

It is plain that most of the problems with this order would have been avoided had proper time been allocated to it in the courtroom and afterwards. The funds wasted on applications (4 in this case) and this appeal with the consequent pressures on the lists far outweigh the costs saved by dealing with the matter in haste. Listing is a judicial function. Resident judges and listing officers should ensure that in every case which may require an ancillary order the list reflects the time needed to deal effectively with all the issues.'

Similarly, as with any sentencing disposal, any variation to ancillary orders that is more than merely technical should be dealt with in open court.[4] Whilst a correction to the time to count towards sentence from a qualifying curfew could properly be dealt with administratively, imposing a disqualification via the 'totting up' procedure could not. Even where there has been an opportunity for the defendant and prosecution to make written representations on the question, transparency requires such:[5]

'However, the other variation which was made administratively on the papers in this particular case, namely the adoption of the totting-up procedure and the consequent imposition of a period of disqualification from driving of ten months pursuant to that totting-up procedure, is altogether a different matter. In our view, such a matter should not have been done "administratively" on the papers. It is clear that all concerned were trying to avoid the expense and inconvenience involved in a further court hearing. Further, both sides were afforded the opportunity to put in written representations and did so: the appellant by his counsel opposing the making of a disqualification order. Both sides were content to proceed on such a footing. Nevertheless, potential disqualification from driving in itself is a serious matter. It will also potentially involve an increase in the overall sentence. Accordingly, such matter should in our judgment have been dealt with in the ordinary way in open court, with the appellant having the opportunity to be present, if need be by video-link.'

Courts and advocates must thus work together to ensure that ancillary orders are made in their proper form, in open court, and with proper regard had to their terms and practical implications.

---

4   *Cox* [2019] EWCA Crim 71.
5   *Cox*, at [15].

PART 1

ORDERS ON CONVICTION

1 Forfeiture I – General Powers

1.01

There are a number of different powers available to the courts where it is appropriate to remove an item from the possession of the defendant (D) due to its use or involvement in criminal behaviour. Those powers are considered over this and the following two chapters. Anyone appearing in cases where weapons or cars have been used in the commission of the offence, or where money or drugs were found in D's possession, must be alive to the potential orders on conviction. It should be clear to everyone in court which power the prosecution are inviting the court to use when they apply for an order to remove property from a person on conviction.[1]

Deprivation of property

1.02

Section 143 of the Powers of Criminal Courts (Sentencing) Act (PCC(S)A) 2000 governs the powers of the convicting court[2] to deprive[3] an offender of any property,[4] which will be surrendered to the police if not already in their possession,[5] in the following circumstances:

1.03

Circumstance 1 – s 143(1) – conviction or plea:

- property which was lawfully seized from D;[6] or

- which was in his possession or under his control when he was arrested[7] or summonsed for the offence; or

---

1   *Jones* [2017] EWCA Crim 2192, at [5]–[6].
2   PCC(S)A 2000, s 143(1).
3   It cannot be used to order the destruction of property – *Williams* [2005] EWCA Crim 3585, at [8].
4   Including dogs – *Haynes* [2003] EWCA Civ 3247; and indecent images of children – *Fillary* [2003] EWCA Crim 2682, at [2].
5   PCC(S)A 2000, s 143(3).
6   It need not have been seized by the police at the time that the order is made, providing it was in his possession when he was apprehended, and is still owned by him – *Hall* [2014] EWCA Crim 2413, at [11].
7   The term in the legislation is 'apprehended', but case law tells us that this means arrested – *Hinde* (1977) 64 Cr App R 213, at 215–216.

- which was used, or intended to be used, to commit or facilitate[8] the commission of any offence (not only the offence of which the offender has been convicted).[9]

1.04

It should be noted that profit from illegal activity does not come under the definition of 'used, or intended to be used, to commit or facilitate'.[10]

1.05

Circumstance 2 – s 143(2) – offence or offence taken into consideration (TiC) consists of unlawful possession of property:

- the unlawfully possessed property has been lawfully seized from D;[11] or

- was in his possession or under his control at the time of arrest or summons in respect of the offence for which he was convicted.

1.06

The terms 'seized' and 'in possession' are to have their natural meanings: in *Robinson*,[12] the Court of Appeal held that there was no jurisdiction to order the deprivation of money that D gave to an undercover police officer who was posing as a hitman, when hiring him to murder her ex-partner, following her conviction for inciting murder. D had not been in possession of the money when apprehended,[13] and it was not 'seized' from her.[14] The Court, however, expressed its disapproval of any notion of her being entitled to the money,[15] and concluded that under civil law, as it had been paid in pursuance of a criminal agreement, D could no longer claim ownership of the money.[16] Likewise, a part of the human body cannot be subject to an order under s 143.[17] By analogy with its predecessor power under s 43 of the Powers of Criminal Courts Act 1973, such an order cannot be made in relation to real property.[18]

---

8   According to s 143(8), facilitating the commission of an offence includes the taking of any steps after it has been committed for the purpose of disposing of any property to which it relates or of avoiding apprehension or detection.
9   PCC(S)A 2000, s 143(1)(a) and (b). This includes 'working capital' that it is intended will fund drug dealing in the future: *O'Farrell* (1988) 10 Cr App R (S) 74.
10   *Slater* [1986] 1 WLR 1340 – a decision under the predecessor 1973 Act.
11   PCC(S)A 2000, s 143(2)(a).
12   [2002] EWCA Crim 2812.
13   *Robinson*, at [28].
14   *Robinson*, at [29].
15   *Robinson*, at [30].
16   *Robinson*, at [29].
17   *Bentham* [2005] UKHL 18, at [8].
18   *Khan* (1983) 76 Cr App R 29, at 32.

1.07

The powers of a court under circumstances 1 and 2 above may be exercised:[19]

- whether or not the court also deals with the offender in any other way in respect of the offence of which he has been convicted;[20] and

- without regard to any restrictions on forfeiture in any enactment contained in an Act passed before 29 July 1988.[21]

Vehicles

1.08

Any vehicle which is used in the course of:

- driving, attempting to drive, or being in charge of a vehicle;[22] or

- failing to comply with a requirement made under Road Traffic Act (RTA) 1988, s 7 or 7A (failure to provide specimen for analysis or laboratory test or to give permission for such a test in the course of an investigation into whether the offender had committed an offence while driving, attempting to drive or being in charge of a vehicle); or

- failing, as the driver of a vehicle, to comply with RTA 1988, s 170(2) and (3) (duty to stop and give information or report accident); or

- an offence under RTA 1988 which is punishable with imprisonment;[23] or

- an offence of manslaughter;[24] or

- an offence under s 35 of the Offences Against the Person Act (OAPA) 1861 (wanton and furious driving),[25]

shall be regarded as being used for the purpose of committing the offence (and for the purpose of committing any offence of aiding, abetting, counselling or procuring the commission of the offence).[26]

---

19 PCC(S)A 2000, s 143(4).
20 PCC(S)A 2000, s 143(1)(a).
21 PCC(S)A 2000, s 143(1)(b).
22 PCC(S)A 2000, s 143(6)(a).
23 PCC(S)A 2000, s 143(7)(a).
24 PCC(S)A 2000, s 143(7)(b).
25 PCC(S)A 2000, s 143(7)(c).
26 PCC(S)A 2000, s 143(6)(c).

Procedure

1.09

As will be seen in later chapters, the Court of Appeal is often critical of both counsel and judges: judges for not properly considering the requirements before an order can be made, and the effect on the totality of the sentence when a deprivation order is included, and counsel for failing to provide and thoroughly address in their submissions evidence which would affect the judge's decision as to whether it is appropriate in a particular case to make an order:[27]

> 'We are bound to observe that the whole procedure which was followed in relation to this aspect of the sentencing process seems to have been extremely lax. If we may say so, not only should the judge have taken a much firmer and more formal grip on the way matters were being dealt with, but counsel too were under an obligation to ensure that any order the judge made was made on a proper basis and in accordance with proper process.'

1.10

It should be noted that a deprivation order, in line with its characterisation as a 'punishment', cannot be imposed alongside an absolute or conditional discharge, which themselves indicate that the court thought that no punishment was appropriate.[28]

Value of the property

1.11

The making of orders in both circumstances 1 and 2 above (see 1.3 and 1.5) is subject to s 143(5), which requires that the court must have regard to the value of the property[29] and the likely financial and other effects of the making of the order (taken together with any other orders that the court is considering) on the offender.[30] Any forfeiture of property must be considered in the context of the totality of the sentence, especially if D is of modest means. However, there can be no objection to taking a notional value for an item if both parties agree that it is a broadly accurate value.[31]

---

27 *Jones* [2017] EWCA Crim 2192, at [11].
28 *Savage* (1983) 5 Cr App R (S) 216.
29 PCC(S)A 2000, s 143(5)(a).
30 PCC(S)A 2000, s 143(5)(b).
31 *Norman* [2007] EWCA Crim 624, at [7].

1.12

An order of this kind is to be considered akin to a financial penalty and should thus be reflected in the length of any term of imprisonment or other disposal.[32] For this reason, it is desirable that any order for deprivation is considered and made at the same time as the sentencing disposal, to minimise the risk of totality being neglected.[33]

1.13

The sentencing court should also bear in mind that the deprivation of the specific item of property does not prevent D replacing that property and carrying on any lawful activities, as a sexual harm prevention order (SHPO), for example, could.[34] Thus, deprivation with the intention of preventing him committing further offences is likely to be misconceived if the item is not in and of itself illegal, or illegally possessed.

1.14

A sentencing judge who is considering making a deprivation order should warn counsel, or a self-representing defendant, that s/he is considering making such an order, so that appropriate submissions can be made.[35] The proper value of any items should be established before an order under s 143 can be made.[36] The prosecution cannot satisfy this requirement by stating 'baldly, without any supporting evidence, that they seek an order for forfeiture. It is incumbent on the trial judge to put the prosecution to proof'.[37] The prosecution must also produce evidence that the seizure of the item was done lawfully,[38] or risk the order being quashed.[39]

1.15

Where a defendant wishes to contest the making of a deprivation order, defence counsel would be well advised to obtain as much paperwork as possible showing the use and value in terms of earning potential of the item. In *Lee*,[40] the Court of Appeal noted that paperwork showing that the van in question, used by the appellant to drive his sons to administer a kidnap and punishment beating, was being used for self-employed work, or had increased the appellant's

---

32 *Ling* [2007] EWCA Crim 1413, at [13], quoting Bingham LJ in *Joyce* (1989) 11 Crim App R 253, referring to the predecessor power to PCC(S)A 2000, s 143 (Powers of Criminal Courts Act 1973, s 43).

33 *Townsend-Johnson* [2010] EWCA Crim 1027, at [8]. The importance of totality is highlighted in the case of *R v Highbury Corner Magistrates' Court, ex p Di Matteo* (1990) 12 Cr App R (S) 594.

34 *Townsend-Johnson*, at [10].

35 *Ball* [2002] EWCA Crim 2777, at [8].

36 *Ball*, at [9].

37 *Pemberton* (1982) 4 Cr App R (S) 328; although decided under previous legislation (Powers of Criminal Courts Act 1973, s 43), this case was cited with approval in relation to the 2000 Act in *Ball*.

38 *Brookes* [2003] EWCA Crim 3037, at [8].

39 *Brookes*, at [11].

40 [2012] EWCA Crim 2658.

earning capacity in such work, might have assisted him.[41] However, where a car was someone's only real asset, it has been held that a deprivation order for it could be disproportionate when totality was considered.[42] The additional penalty that a defendant will experience in being deprived of his car led to the quashing of a deprivation order in *Slater*,[43] in circumstances where he was 'not employed and was on benefits at the time of the offence. He had family responsibilities. He had large debts'.[44] Similarly, where a car that was to be forfeited had been bought with the help of an informal loan, the possible effect of depriving the defendant of the car (in circumstances where he would nonetheless have to repay the loan and so be put into debt) would be a relevant consideration, but in no way conclusive.[45]

1.16

When trying to assess proportionality in *De Jesus*,[46] the court considered the value of the car, and what the period in default would have been if the value of the car had been imposed by way of a fine. When quashing the deprivation order, they stated explicitly that this had the effect of 'reducing the sentence'.[47]

1.17

Where items have had both a legitimate and illegitimate purpose (such as computer equipment used both to print racially inflammatory material and to run a legitimate publishing business), forfeiture is appropriate.[48] Similarly, where a judge cannot identify which specific items from an assortment have been used in the criminal conduct, but is satisfied that if they had not been used they were intended to be used for such a purpose, the judge is entitled to draw an inference of intended use.[49] If the judge is not satisfied of this on the evidence before him/her (considering the likely or proven location of the items at the time of the offending, and any other available evidence) then no order can be made.[50] Any evidence tending to support an innocent account for possession of large sums of money, for example, must be wholly ruled out before an order for deprivation of it can be made.[51]

1.18

Where a defendant has used his computer for the downloading of indecent images, but also has a large amount of wholly innocent personal family

---

41 *Lee*, at [15].
42 *Kent* [2013] EWCA Crim 448, at [21].
43 [2013] EWCA Crim 2715.
44 *Slater*, at [16].
45 *Hamlett* [2015] EWCA Crim 1412, at [10], [17].
46 [2015] EWCA Crim 1118, at [19].
47 *De Jesus*, at [20].
48 *Sheppard* [2010] EWCA Crim 65, at [46].
49 *Sheppard*, at [47].
50 *Harrison* [2017] EWCA Crim 1209, at [33]–[35].
51 *Jones* [2017] EWCA Crim 2192, at [18].

photographs stored on the computer, a deprivation order for the computer may be disproportionate – a more appropriate response being to have the item cleansed of the illegal material and then returned – it was 'not just [...] a computer, [but] an item of some value and importance'.[52] This assumed, however, that on the facts there was not a real and immediate risk that the defendant would seek to use sophisticated software to retrieve the images.[53]

Complex ownership

1.19

Where the ownership of the item is not straightforward the court should not make a deprivation order.[54] This will include circumstances such as ordering the deprivation of a car that is on a hire-purchase arrangement. In *Kearney*,[55] the judge ordered that a car used in offences of making off without payment be forfeited, sold, and some of the proceeds used to pay compensation. The Court of Appeal found that as there was significant loan finance outstanding, and on an application to the magistrates' court under the Police Property Act 1897, s 1(1) (see 1.32) the finance company would be bound to succeed, the vehicle could not have been sold by the appellant, who would therefore have needed to pay the compensation out of other funds.[56] Under these complications, the judge had been wrong to make such an order.[57] In *Thomas*,[58] the Court went further, holding that it would rarely be appropriate to make a deprivation order where there was a hire-purchase agreement, as it was not possible to calculate the precise financial effect on the defendant.[59] Thus, where the first instance judge makes an order in ignorance of the existence of a hire-purchase agreement, it will be quashed – a further warning to defence counsel to ensure that they have fully investigated the ownership position of cars that might be subject to such an order.

1.20

A deprivation order operates to deny D his right in the property. It does not remove the rights of any other person in the property,[60] and it does not determine ownership of the property.[61] It is also likely that it cannot be used to order that an asset should be sold so that resultant funds can be used to pay

---

52 *Connolly* [2012] EWCA Crim 2049, at [9]–[10].
53 *Connolly*, at [10].
54 *Troth* (1979) 1 Cr App R (S) 341 – in that case, under the Powers of Criminal Courts Act 1973, the property belonged to a partnership.
55 [2011] EWCA Crim 826.
56 *Kearney*, at [12].
57 *Kearney*, at [8] and [16].
58 [2012] EWCA Crim 1159.
59 *Thomas*, at [10]–[11].
60 *Brookes*, at [5]
61 *R v Chester Justices, ex p Smith (Kenneth)* (1978) 67 Cr App R 133.

costs or compensation, though in *Bye*,[62] when the matter caused the Court 'some anxiety', it managed to avoid having to resolve this question by simply quashing the order.[63]

1.21

Deprivation orders should not be made to punish a third party – ie an order made against an employee who committed an offence, with the intention of punishing his employer, whose previous employees had been convicted of similar offences.[64] However, where a number of defendants commit an offence together, using the car of one of them, a deprivation order for the car will not be quashed for causing disparity simply because it meant that one of them was being punished additionally through being deprived of the car.[65]

Interaction with other orders

Restraint

1.22

For the purposes of restraint anything under a deprivation order is not to be regarded as 'free property'.[66]

Confiscation

1.23

Section 13 of the Proceeds of Crime Act (POCA) 2002 states clearly that if the court makes a confiscation order it must take account of the confiscation order before it imposes a deprivation order under s 143 of the 2000 Act.[67] Thus there should be no s 143 order made before confiscation takes place.

1.24

If a confiscation order including a sum of money gained as a result of, or intended for use in, a criminal enterprise is quashed, the Crown cannot automatically seek a deprivation order in respect of that money instead.[68] It would be necessary for the appropriate findings of fact to satisfy an application for a deprivation order to have been made in the court below, and the potentially difficult technical

---

62 [2005] EWCA Crim 1230, at [2], [9]–[10].

63 *Bye*, at [10] and [12].

64 *R (Trans Berckx BVBA) v North Avon Magistrates' Court* [2011] EWHC 2605 (Admin), at [13].

65 *Burgess* (2001) 2 Cr App R (S) 2, at [8]–[10] (decided under the Powers of Criminal Courts Act 1973).

66 Proceeds of Crime Act (POCA) 2002, s 82(1)(d).

67 POCA 2002, s 13(2)(b) and (3)(c).

68 *Bajwa* [2011] EWCA Crim 1093.

issues concerning POCA 2002, ss 13–15 and the Criminal Appeals Act 1968, s 11(3A) as amended, to be resolved.[69]

Application of proceeds of forfeited property

1.25

Section 145 provides that where a court makes an order under s 143 in a case where:

- the offender has been convicted of an offence which has resulted in a person suffering personal injury, loss or damage;[70] or

- any such offence is taken into consideration by the court in determining sentence,[71]

the court may also make an order that any proceeds which arise from the disposal of the property and which do not exceed a sum specified by the court shall be paid to that person.

1.26

Such an order can only be made if, but for the inadequacy of the offender's means, the court would have made a compensation order under which the offender would have been required to pay compensation of an amount not less than the specified amount.[72]

1.27

An order under this section has no effect:

- before the end of the period specified in s 144(1)(a);[73] or

- if a successful application under the Police (Property) Act 1897, s 1(1) has been made.[74]

---

69 *Bajwa*, at [100]–[104].
70 PCC(S)A 2000, s 143(1)(a).
71 PCC(S)A 2000, s 145(1)(b).
72 PCC(S)A 2000, s 145(2).
73 PCC(S)A 2000, s 145(3)(a).
74 PCC(S)A 2000, s 145(3)(b).

Recovery of property

PCC(S)A 2000, s 14

1.28

When making an order under s 143 the judge is not required to give any consideration to the rights of third parties.[75] Such third parties have no right to appear or be heard when the s 143 order is being made.[76]

1.29

This is because the procedure for someone other than D who claims to have an interest in property seized under s 143 is laid down under the Police Property Act 1897, s 1 (see 1.32). This is subject to an important proviso introduced by PCC(S)A 2000, s 144(1)(b) that the third party must satisfy the court that they had not consented to D having the item or that they did not know and had no reason to suspect that the item was likely to be used for the purposes of crime. Sometimes such satisfaction might come from rejecting the evidence of the defendant during the trial on this point.[77]

1.30

The exercise of the s 144 power is judicially reviewable.[78] An application under s 144 by an owner who was not the defendant against whom the deprivation order was made confers an additional jurisdiction. It does not provide an exclusive remedy that bars the bringing of a civil claim,[79] and often in such a civil claim there will be no defence available to the police against the non-defendant owner of the items.[80] In case this conclusion was in any way incorrect, the Court in *O'Leary* did consider the applicant's submission that s 144 required to be read down in accordance with the Human Rights Act 1998.

1.31

The Divisional Court concluded that, considering the requirement under s 143(5) for a court to take into account the value of the item and the financial effect of the order on the *defendant*, it would not be logical if, in exercising the s 144 power, those considerations were not taken into account in relation to the *non-defendant owner*. There, the Court held, unless s 144 was read down to include that consideration, and a consideration of whether deprivation would be disproportionate, the rights of the owner of the goods would be violated.[81]

---

75 *Brookes*, at [9].
76 *O'Leary International v Chief Constable of North Wales Police* [2012] EWHC 1516 (Admin), at [22] and [27].
77 *Hall* [2014] EWCA Crim 2413.
78 *R (Trans Berckx BVBA) v North Avon Magistrates' Court* [2011] EWHC 2605 (Admin), at [2]–[3].
79 *O'Leary*, at [26].
80 *O'Leary*, at [28].
81 *O'Leary*, at [36]–[37].

Police Property Act 1897, s 1

1.32

Under s 1(1) of the 1897 Act:

- Where any property has come into the possession of the police through their investigation of a suspected offence the magistrates' court may hear an application in respect of that property.

- The application may be made by either a police officer or someone claiming to have a right to the property. They may seek an order for delivery of the property to the person the court holds to be the owner of it. If the owner cannot be identified, then the court is to make such order with respect to the property as 'may seem meet'.

1.33

Subsection (2) provides that an order under s 1 shall not affect the right of any person to take legal proceedings against any person in possession of property delivered as a result of an order under s 1 within six months from the date of the order. On the expiration of those six months the right shall cease and the order is final (save, presumably, if it is made *ultra vires* or in other legal error).

1.34

The operation of the section is confined to the police – it does not extend to customs' officers.[82] The word 'owner' is to be given its usual meaning of a person entitled by law to the item, not merely a possessor.[83]

1.35

Where an officer seizes property and the defendant is acquitted (or no evidence offered) of the offence in relation to which the item was seized, the police must return it, or if it cannot be returned *in specie*, be liable for its value.[84] The effect of s 1 is to shift the burden on to the claimant to prove title, not mere prior possession, in order to claim the property – an order under s 1 removes any possessory title from the defendant and gives the claimant title (subject to defeat only by the true owner for six months, and thereafter, good against everyone).[85] The police may only retain the property for the period of time it takes to establish the owner's identity, and this may be the defendant, as title can pass even under an illegal contract.[86] It is thus no defence to the police's continued holding of money under s 1(1) that, on the balance of probabilities,

---

82 *R v Southampton Magistrates' Court, ex p Newman* (1989) 88 Cr App R 202, at 205.
83 *Raymond Lyons & Co Ltd v Metropolitan Police Commissioner* [1975] QB 321.
84 *Stowe v Benstead* [1909] 2 KB 415.
85 *Irving v National Provincial Bank* [1962] 2 QB 73.
86 *Chief Constable of the West Midlands v White* [1992] 3 WLUK 173.

it came from the drug dealing of which the claimant's sons had been convicted, but of which charges had been dropped as against her.[87]

1.36

Once the police's statutory power under s 1(1) to retain the property is exhausted, the right to possession of the person from whom it was seized revives,[88] as it acts to suppress the right, not extinguish it. Thus, possessory title is protected equally whether it is obtained by legal means or not, and moral disapprobation or public policy does not give sufficient grounds to remove that protection.[89] Where a bona fides buyer has purchased previously stolen items, if the original owner cannot be traced, the more recent purchaser will have good title.[90] However, such cases are not suited to the summary procedure under s 1(1), and would be better heard in the civil courts.[91]

1.37

When considering any application made by the defendant under s 1(1), the provisions of s 11(1) of the Civil Evidence Act 1968 apply, meaning that the conviction is admissible in evidence for the purpose of proving that he committed that offence (whether convicted on plea or after trial) unless he can prove, to the civil standard of proof, that he did not commit the offence and the conviction was wrongful.[92]

1.38

The court has made clear that, in common with the provisions on forfeiture, s 1(1) is not appropriate for resolving disputes where there are real issues of law, or real difficulty in determining who is the owner.[93] Where the potential ownership is complex, more appropriate civil remedies are available in the county court and High Court.[94] An example is where the police deny that the items were ever in their possession, and could possibly have been removed by an unknown third party.[95] Although it is open to the magistrates to find as a fact that the property did come into the possession of the police, in order to do so they would need to be satisfied that it had.

1.39

Where the identity of the owner is clear, it is not for the magistrates to conduct an enquiry into how that person came to own it if there has been no relevant

---

87 *Porter v Chief Constable of Merseyside* [2000] QB 427 (conjoined appeal with *Webb*, below).
88 *Webb v Chief Constable of Merseyside* [2000] QB 427, at 448.
89 *Costello v Chief Constable of Derbyshire* [2001] EWCA Civ 381.
90 *Haley and Whitup v Chief Constable of Northumbria* [2002] EWHC 1942 (Admin), at [15].
91 *Haley and Whitup v CC Northumbria*, at [17].
92 *Stupple v Royal Insurance Company* [1971] 1 QB 50.
93 *Raymond Lyons & Co Ltd v Metropolitan Police Commissioner* [1975] QB 321; *Troth* (see n 54 above).
94 *R v Basildon Justices, ex p Holding & Barnes Plc* [1994] 4 WLUK 33.
95 *Chief Constable of Nottingham v Parkin* [2000] 2 WLUK 888.

conviction of the person claiming the item.[96] If the police have ceased seeking the true owner of property recovered, then it will not be a defence to civil proceedings or a claim under s 1(1) that they are detaining the items to establish their true owner under the Police and Criminal Evidence Act 1984, s 22(2)(b).[97] It will no longer be 'necessary' under s 22(1) of the 1984 Act once there is no longer any enforcement reason for the police to keep the items – this includes waiting on the outcome of a civil action.[98] Although not relevant under s 1(1), where a claimant has delayed taking civil action against the police for return of items inexplicably, this should be reflected in the amount of damages awarded in any civil suit.[99]

1.40

In *Chief Constable of Merseyside v Owens*,[100] the Court was 'prepared to assume [that] in a Magistrates' Court under the 1897 Act, the court could refuse to grant relief and refuse to order the return if on the facts it could be established that the return of the property would indirectly encourage or assist a person in his criminal act'.[101]

1.41

When considering an application under s 1(1), a summons must be served on the police who have the property, and they are entitled to be heard at a hearing to decide the ownership of the property – it is a breach of natural justice not to permit such an opportunity.[102]

1.42

Although s 1(1) states that the magistrates have a discretion as to whether to make the order, through the use of the word 'may', it is clear that if they accept jurisdiction, embark upon a hearing and make findings of fact, there will be very limited situations in which they can then lawfully refuse to make an order.[103] Either they will find that the property has an owner (even if one of whom they do not approve) or it has no identifiable owner, and thus the police lawfully retain possession.

---

96 *R (Morgan) v Dyfed Powys Magistrates* [2003] EWHC 1568 (Admin), at [11].
97 *Gough v Chief Constable of the West Midlands* [2004] EWCA Civ 206.
98 *Gough v CC West Midlands,* at [26]–[27].
99 *Gough v CC West Midlands,* at [36]–[40].
100 [2012] EWHC 1515 (Admin).
101 *Owens,* at [28].
102 *R v Durham Magistrates' Court, ex p Chief Constable of Durham* [2000] 4 WLUK 206.
103 *R (Carter) v Ipswich Magistrates' Court* [2002] EWHC 332 (Admin).

Unlawful items

1.43

When considering the Northern Irish equivalent of s 1(1), the Court of Appeal (Northern Ireland) upheld the district judge's decision not to allow the return to D of 'legal highs'; the Court set out three public policy bases upon which it could be proper to refuse to return goods to someone who was clearly the owner:[104]

- It would be unlawful for the claimant to be in possession of the goods or for the police to give up possession.

- The return of the goods would directly or indirectly assist or encourage the commission of a crime.

- The return of the goods would be contrary to the policy of Parliament as contained in legislation.

1.44

Although not binding on the England and Wales Court of Appeal, in the light of decided cases discussed above, it seems likely that the same considerations would apply.

Costs on applications under s 1(1)

1.45

Power to award costs against a chief constable under the 1897 Act stems from the Magistrates' Courts Act (MCA) 1980, s 64(1), and by s 64(1)(b) is limited to when a complaint was dismissed.[105] See Chapters 15 and 18 for more on powers to award costs.

1.46

If the hearing is instigated by way of a complaint instead of an application, then the magistrates have a power under the Magistrates' Courts Act 1952, s 55(1) to make an order for costs.[106] It seems that rarely will an application for costs against the police be appropriate in these cases. As Sir Stanley Rees stated:[107]

> '[the police's] discretion must be exercised having regard to the exceptional and perhaps unique nature of the order sought and to the respective roles of the parties concerned. In a case in which the police

---

104 *McCarthy v Chief Constable of Northern Ireland* [2016] NICA 36.
105 *R (Chief Constable of Northamptonshire) v Daventry Justices* [2001] EWHC 446 (Admin).
106 *R v Uxbridge Justices, ex p Commissioner of Police for the Metropolis* [1981] QB 829.
107 *R v Uxbridge Justices*, at 848.

have clearly indicated that they do not oppose the making of the order sought and are merely attending before the justices to confirm their attitude and to ensure that an appropriate order is made before the property is delivered to the complainant, it would indeed be difficult to justify any order for costs against the police. Even in a case in which the police do not consent to the order sought by the claimant or claimants but attend the hearing and the justices are satisfied that it was reasonable for them to do so in order to assist the court to assess the validity of the claim or claims made to the ownership of the property, it would be proper for no order for costs to be made against the police, even if the order for delivery of the property sought by a claimant were made.'

2 Forfeiture II – Drugs, Terrorism and Weapons

Drugs

Qualifying offences

2.01

Section 27(1) of the Misuse of Drugs Act (MDA) 1971 allows the court to order forfeiture of anything shown to the satisfaction of the court to relate to an offence of which an offender is convicted under:

- any provision of the MDA 1971;

- any offence listed in the Proceeds of Crime Act (POCA) 2002, Sch 2, para 1,[1] which additionally consists of:

  - an offence under any of the following provisions of the Customs and Excise Management Act 1979 if committed in connection with a prohibition or restriction on importation or exportation under MDA 1971, s 3:[2]

    (a) s 50(2) or (3) (improper importation of goods);

    (b) s 68(2) (exportation of prohibited or restricted goods);

    (c) s 170 (fraudulent evasion);

  - an offence under either of the following provisions of the Criminal Justice (International Co-operation) Act 1990:[3]

    (a) s 12 (manufacture or supply of a substance for the time being specified in Sch 2 to that Act);

    (b) s 19 (using a ship for illicit traffic in controlled drugs);

---

1   MDA 1971, s 27(3)(a).
2   POCA 2002, Sch 2, para 1(2).
3   POCA 2002, Sch 2, para 1(3).

- any offence of attempting, conspiring or inciting;[4] doing an act capable of encouraging or assisting;[5] or aiding, abetting, counselling or procuring,[6] the commission of an offence found in POCA 2002, Sch 2, para 1.[7]

2.02

In reality, it is common in drugs supply cases that, rather than embarking upon confiscation proceedings in respect of cash which has been recovered, an order is made (usually by consent) under s 143 of the Powers of Criminal Court (Sentencing Act) 2000 Act (see Chapter 1), or MDA 1971, s 27, with a direction that the money be paid to a relevant organisation tasked with combatting drug crime or the rehabilitation of offenders for drugs offences. The Court of Appeal has been clear that although there is nothing wrong in law with adopting this course, it should nonetheless be undertaken scrupulously, with clarity about the provision under which any application is being made, so that its lawfulness can be scrutinised.[8]

2.03

It should be noted, however, that this section is equipped to deal only with relatively low-level offenders – indeed its insufficiency for depriving professional drug dealers of the gains from their conduct was the inspiration behind the confiscation regime,[9] which is written about extensively in other texts.

2.04

In *Cuthbertson*,[10] the House of Lords held that the forfeiture powers under MDA 1971, s 27 did not apply to offences of common law conspiracy to commit an offence contrary to MDA 1971, s 4, since conspiracies were not 'offences under the Act' within s 27(1), not being offences defined by any specific provision of the Act. Further (though not supported by Lord Scarman) the subsection envisaged dealings with tangible objects. Therefore, when it was possible to relate a transaction to tangible things such as drugs, apparatus, vehicles or cash, that transaction had to be made the subject of a charge of a specific offence before a forfeiture order could be made in respect of them. If such a circumstance arose now confiscation under POCA 2002 would be available to the Crown.

---

4   POCA 2002, Sch 1, para 10(1).
5   POCA 2002, Sch 1, para 10(1A).
6   POCA 2002, Sch 1, para 10(2).
7   MDA 1971, s 27(3)(b).
8   *Jones* [2017] EWCA Crim 2192, at [12].
9   In *Cuthbertson* [1981] AC 470 the House of Lords held, with an expression of 'considerable regret' (at 479), that the power of forfeiture and destruction under s 27 did not provide a means of stripping professional drug traffickers of the whole of their ill-gotten gains or the total profits of their unlawful enterprises.
10   [1981] AC 470, at 481–484.

Basis for making order

2.05

Having been convicted of one of the qualifying offences above, the court must then be satisfied that the item of which forfeiture is sought relates to the offences before the court.[11] Its mere presence in the house in which someone who was arrested for a qualifying offence lives will not suffice to show this nexus.[12] In the Northern Irish case of *Fenton*,[13] the Court confirmed that when deciding whether the items to be forfeited were related to the offence, the standard of proof was the criminal standard.

2.06

It has been held that 'anything' includes money,[14] but it does not include real property.[15] This was confirmed in *Cuthbertson*, where it was held that the forfeiture power applied only to tangible property (including drugs, apparatus, vehicles and 'cash ready to be, or having just been, handed over for them'). It also does not apply to intangible property ('anything incapable of being taken into physical possession'), or to property situated abroad, and it does not authorise the court to follow or trace assets, and so forfeit other assets for which they had been exchanged.[16] Having confirmed this, the Court of Appeal in *Pearce* observed that one way of dealing with the lack of power to forfeit a house was to include in the sentence a fine of the value, or a proportion of the value, of the house.[17] Money in a bank account of the defendant's at the point of arrest is a chose in action, and thus not susceptible to a forfeiture order.[18]

2.07

If, however, the police have seized money in the form of cash (in any currency) at the time of the arrest, but then pay that money into an account so that it can earn interest and be kept safely pending the outcome of the proceedings, that has not put it beyond the reach of forfeiture, as it was not a chose in action at the time the defendant was apprehended and his property seized.[19]

---

11 MDA 1971, s 27(1).
12 *Askew* [1987] 3 WLUK 337; [1987] Crim LR 584.
13 [2001] NI 65.
14 *Beard* [1974] 1 WLR 1549.
15 *Khan* (1983) 76 Cr App R 29, at 32 – indicated by the fact that the Police Property Act 1897 is applicable, which is restricted to property that can be taken into the possession of the police.
16 *Cuthbertson* (n 9 above).
17 (1996) 2 Cr App R (S) 316.
18 *Marland* (1986) 82 Cr App R 134, at 138.
19 *Marland*, at 140.

2.08

Where money is found at the house of someone who is convicted of possession with intent to supply a drug of Class A, if that money is to be used, or possibly to be used, to buy drugs in the future, it does not 'relate' to an offence of supplying.[20] Where a defendant had been charged with possession with intent to supply rather than actual supply, and the judge's observations that the cash came possibly from the sale of drugs were inconsistent with the accepted basis of plea, the order would also be quashed.[21]

2.09

It has been suggested by the Court of Appeal that certain enquiries should be conducted before an order under s 27 is made.[22] Sadly, in a two-paragraph judgment, the Court set out neither the facts of the offence, nor the procedures that were lacking in the lower court, the flaws being so grave that the Crown did not contest the appeal. Similarly, in *Haggard v Mason*,[23] the Court of Appeal upheld a conviction under MDA 1971, s 4(1) and (3). D thought he was selling a controlled drug (LSD) but in fact was selling Bromo STP, which was not controlled. However, the Court quashed the forfeiture order for the money found on D that represented the profits from him selling the substance (£146). No reason was given for quashing the forfeiture order, so it cannot be ascertained whether this was because the offence was committed on the basis of mistake, or for some other reason.

2.10

Where a count is left to lie on the file as other counts are disposed of by guilty plea, it will not be appropriate to seek forfeiture of goods seized which relate only to the offence left on the file.[24]

2.11

Where the money found on a defendant is the proceeds of previous drug dealing (often referred to as 'working capital'), it is not money that is related to the offence for which the defendant is before the court – it is axiomatically related to previous offences.[25] It is not necessary for the activity of selling the drugs that are the subject of the present charge.[26] Therefore it cannot be the

---

20 *Cox* (1986) 8 Cr App R (S) 384, at 385.
21 *Johnson* [2008] EWCA Crim 2427, at [10].
22 *Wilburn* [2003] EWCA Crim 2914, at [2].
23 [1976] 1 WLR 187, at 191.
24 *R v Maidstone Crown Court, ex p Gill* [1986] 1 WLR 1405, at 1410–1411.
25 *Boothe* (1987) 9 Cr App R (S) 8.
26 *Llewellyn* (1985) 7 Cr App R (S) 225.

subject of a s 27 forfeiture order.[27] Similarly, in *Johnson*,[28] whilst the Court expressed great scepticism at the notion that the money found on an appellant selling drugs, and without identifiable lawful income, was not the proceeds of earlier dealing, they had to proceed on the basis that it was not. In that case, the Crown had accepted a guilty plea to possession and not pursued a count of supplying. The Court held that therefore 'it would not be right to treat the appellant as though he had been a previous supplier and therefore, in effect, to require him to forfeit the £400 as being part of the proceeds of the previous illegal activity'.[29]

2.12

A forfeiture order made against a car used in the offence that had been bought with money provided by A's elderly mother and which caused hardship as the appellant used it to take his mother to visit his mentally handicapped brother was not appealable – the criteria for forfeiture were clearly established and it could not be said that the court had wrongly exercised its discretion.[30] There thus seems to be no allowance for an 'exceptional hardship'-style argument.

Procedural matters

2.13

When a judge is minded to make an order under s 27, s/he should give the defendant an opportunity to produce evidence showing that the money or items are not related to the present offence(s).[31]

2.14

If a forfeiture order is wrongly made, it is not appropriate for the Court of Appeal to substitute such an order for a fine in the same amount, as a fine would have a default term attached, and thus is technically a more severe punishment.[32]

2.15

The making of a forfeiture order is susceptible to judicial review, as it is not a sentence, nor an order dealing with the offender in relation to a trial on indictment.[33]

---

27   *Ribeyre* (1982) 4 Cr App R (S) 165, at 167; *Morgan* [1977] Crim LR 488.
28   (1984) 6 Cr App R (S) 227.
29   *Johnson*, at 230.
30   *Bowers (Christopher)* (1994) 15 Cr App R (S) 315.
31   *Churcher* (1986) 8 Cr App R (S) 94.
32   *Marland* (1986) 82 Cr App R 134, at 139.
33   *R v Maidstone Crown Court, ex p Gill* [1986] 1 WLR 1405 at 1409–1410.

Effect of an order

2.16

Anything that is so forfeited can be ordered to be destroyed, or dealt with in any manner that the court orders.[34] What happens to it is for the judge to decide, though this must be having adopted a judicial approach, and 'not a whimsical one'.[35] This can include splitting money between different recipients, and its use as a reward for an officer who had acted bravely in the course of arresting the defendant.[36]

2.17

This power is subject to the court allowing representations from any third party claiming to be the owner, or to have an interest in it, as to why an order should not be made.[37]

2.18

Where the property belongs to a third party who willingly lent it to the offender, whether an order forfeiting it should be made will turn on whether the lender should have been put on notice or on suspicion that it was going to be used for some illegal purpose. If the third party is on notice, it may be perfectly proper for a judge to order forfeiture 'to mark disapproval of the failure to take the necessary precautions'.[38] Where, however, the lender, on the judge's findings, had no reason to suppose that the property was going to be used for anything other than legitimate purposes, the order will be quashed.[39]

Restraint

2.19

For the purposes of restraint anything subject to a forfeiture order is not to be regarded as 'free property'.[40]

Confiscation

2.20

POCA 2002, s 13 states clearly that if the court makes a confiscation order it must take account of the confiscation order before it makes a forfeiture order under MDA 1971, s 27.[41] Where a judge fails to do this, and makes an order for

---

34 MDA 1971, s 27(1).
35 *Beard*, at 1551.
36 *Beard*, at 1551–1552.
37 MDA 1971, s 27(2)
38 *R v Maidstone Crown Court, ex p Gill* [1986] 1 WLR 1405 at 1411.
39 *R v Maidstone Crown Court, ex p Gill*, at 1411–1412.
40 POCA 2002, s 82(1)(a).
41 POCA 2002, s 13(2)(b) and (3)(b).

forfeiture under s 27 where confiscation proceedings have been instituted, but then validly postponed and not yet completed, this will not invalidate the making of the confiscation order, as to do so would frustrate the statutory scheme of POCA 2002 on a technicality.[42] POCA 2002, s 14(11), which requires that a confiscation order must not be quashed only on the ground that there was a defect or omission in the procedure connected with the application for or the granting of a postponement does not apply if before it made the confiscation order the court had made an order listed in s 13(3), which includes orders made under s 27 of the 1971 Act.[43]

2.21

Under the Criminal Justice Act (CJA) 1988, the court is prohibited from making an order under s 27 before dealing with confiscation.[44] A similar provision is made by POCA 2002, s 15(2). Section 72A(9) of CJA 1988 says 'in sentencing, or otherwise dealing with, the defendant in respect of the offence, or any of the offences, concerned at any time during the specified period, the court shall not (a) impose any fine on him …' or impose certain other orders. Section 15(2) of POCA 2002 says: 'in sentencing the defendant for the offence (or any of the offences) concerned in the postponement period the court must not (a) impose a fine on him' or make various other orders. Nonetheless, these restrictions have been largely ignored to stop procedural hiccups from preventing the pursuit of confiscation proceedings under either Act.[45]

2.22

Where a confiscation order had been made invalidly (out of time) it is possible (and will be appropriate) for an order under MDA 1971, s 27 to be made instead for the value of items that fulfil the criteria in s 27(1).[46]

2.23

As observed in *Islam*,[47] for confiscation purposes it is the value of the drugs on the black market which is relevant when calculating the market value of property under s 79(2).[48]

2.24

For this reason, counsel representing a client who is likely to face both confiscation and a forfeiture order should ascertain the value of those drugs on

---

42 *Donohoe* [2006] EWCA Crim 2200, at [15]–[17].
43 *Lye* [2006] EWCA Crim 1347, at [3]–[4].
44 CJA 1988, s 72A(9).
45 As observed by Thomas [2010] Crim LR, 5, 424–428, commenting on *Paivarinta-Taylor* [2010] EWCA Crim 28. Similarly, in relation to the 2002 Act, *Kakkad* [2015] EWCA Crim 385, applying *Donohoe* [2007] 1 Cr App R (S) 88.
46 *Hussain* [2000] 4 WLUK 514, at [3].
47 [2009] UKHL 30.
48 *Islam*, at [18], [25], [34].

the illegal market both at the time they were obtained by the defendant, and their current value.

2.25

Where a court makes an assumption for the purposes of confiscation that drugs found in the offender's possession have been bought with the proceeds of earlier drug trafficking, there is no principle of double jeopardy which requires the court to disregard that amount in assessing the value of the offender's proceeds of drug trafficking, if the drugs themselves are forfeited under s 27.[49] However, the court must be careful not to double count cash that has been ordered to be forfeited by also including it in the confiscation order.[50]

Psychoactive substances (on application) – Psychoactive Substances Act 2016, s 51

2.26

A relevant enforcement officer may apply to the appropriate court[51] for the forfeiture of an item retained having been seized during a search.[52] The item is to be retained while proceedings on the application are in progress.[53]

2.27

If the court is satisfied that:

- the item is a psychoactive substance which, if it had not been seized, was likely to be consumed by an individual for its psychoactive effects;[54] and

- at the time of its seizure, the item was not being used for the purposes of, or in connection with, an exempted activity[55] carried on by a person entitled to the item,[56,57]

the court must order the forfeiture of the item.

---

49   *Dore* (1997) 2 Cr App R (S) 152.
50   *Dore*, at 159.
51   As defined in the Psychoactive Substances Act (PSA) 2016, s 51(11)(a)(i)–(ii) – where the person in respect of whom the application is made is an individual who is under the age of 18, a youth court, and in any other case, a magistrates' court.
52   PSA 2016, s 51(1).
53   PSA 2016, s 51(2).
54   PSA 2016, s 51(3)(a).
55   As defined in PSA 2016, s 51(12)(a) – an activity precluded from being an offence by PSA 2016, s 11 if it is an 'exempted activity' as defined in Sch 2 to the Act.
56   As defined in PSA 2016, s 51(12)(b)(i)–(ii) – the person from whom it was seized; or (if different) any person to whom it belongs.
57   PSA 2016, s 51(3)(b).

2.28

If the item is not a psychoactive substance, the court may order the forfeiture of the item if satisfied that it has been used in the commission of an offence under this Act.[58]

2.29

Where an order for forfeiture of an item is made, the item may be disposed of in whatever way the officer who applied for the order, or another relevant enforcement officer acting on behalf of the same person as that officer, thinks is suitable.[59] However, it may not be disposed of (a) before the end of the period within which an appeal under s 52 may be made,[60] or (b) before final determination of any appeal.[61]

2.30

The court must return an item to the person entitled to it if:[62]

- The court is not satisfied that the item:

    – is a psychoactive substance;[63] or

    – has been used in the commission of an offence under the Act.[64]

- The item is a psychoactive substance,[65] and the court is satisfied that:[66]

    – if the item had not been seized, it was not likely to be consumed by any individual for its psychoactive effects;[67] or

    – at the time of its seizure, the item was being used for the purposes of, or in connection with, an exempted activity carried on by a person entitled to the item.[68]

2.31

Where an order for the return of an item is made, the item may nevertheless be retained:

- until the end of the period within which an appeal under s 52 may be made against the order,[69] (but if it is decided before the end of that period

---

58   PSA 2016, s 51(4).
59   PSA 2016, s 51(5).
60   PSA 2016, s 51(5)(a).
61   PSA 2016, s 51(5)(b).
62   PSA 2016, s 51(7).
63   PSA 2016, s 51(8)(a).
64   PSA 2016, s 51(8)(b).
65   PSA 2016, s 51(9)(a).
66   PSA 2016, s 51(9)(b).
67   PSA 2016, s 51(9)(b)(i).
68   PSA 2016, s 51(9)(b)(ii).
69   PSA 2016, s 51(10)(a).

that there is to be no appeal, the item must be returned as soon as possible after that decision is made); or

- if such an appeal is made, until the time when it is determined or otherwise dealt with.[70]

Psychoactive substances (on conviction) – Psychoactive Substances Act 2016, s 54

2.32

Where a person is convicted of:

- an offence under any of PSA 2016, ss 4–9 and 26;[71] or

- an ancillary offence in relation to any of those sections,[72] being:

  - attempting or conspiring;[73]

  - an offence under Part 2 of the Serious Crime Act 2007;[74]

  - incitement;[75]

  - aiding, abetting, counselling or procuring,[76]

the court by or before which the person is convicted of the offence,[77] unless they are committed to the Crown Court to be dealt with for that offence, in which case, the Crown Court,[78] MUST order the forfeiture of any psychoactive substance in respect of which the offence was committed.[79] The court MAY also make an order for the forfeiture of any other item that was used in the commission of the offence.[80]

2.33

Where the order is discretionary, before making the forfeiture order[81] in relation to any item, the court must give an opportunity to make representations to any person (in addition to the defendant) who claims to be the owner of the item or otherwise to have an interest in it.[82]

---

70   PSA 2016, s 51(10)(b).
71   PSA 2016, s 54(1)(a).
72   PSA 2016, s 54(1)(b).
73   PSA 2016, s 54(11)(a).
74   PSA 2016, s 54(11)(b).
75   PSA 2016, s 54(11)(c).
76   PSA 2016, s 54(11)(d).
77   PSA 2016, s 54(2)(a).
78   PSA 2016, s 54(2)(b).
79   PSA 2016, s 54(3).
80   PSA 2016, s 54(4).
81   PSA 2016, s 54(4).
82   PSA 2016, s 54(6).

2.34

A forfeiture order may not be made so as to come into force at any time before there is no further possibility (ignoring any power to appeal out of time) of the order being varied or set aside on appeal.[83]

2.35

Where the court makes a forfeiture order, it may also make such other provision as it considers to be necessary for giving effect to the forfeiture,[84] including provision relating to the retention, handling, destruction or other disposal of the item.[85] Such provision may be varied at any time by the court that made it.[86]

Firearms

2.36

The Firearms Act (FA) 1968, s 52(1) provides for the forfeiture and disposal of firearms and ammunition. This can be ordered by the court by or before which D is convicted, or by which s/he is sentenced or bound over. That court may make such order as to the forfeiture or disposal of any firearm or ammunition found in D's possession as it thinks fit, and may cancel any firearm certificate or shot gun certificate held by D.

Pre-conditions for making an order

2.37

The pre-conditions for making an order are that a person is:

- convicted of one or more offences under the Act (other than an offence relating to an air weapon); AND

- is given a custodial sentence;[87] OR

- a bind over[88] containing a requirement not to possess, use or carry a firearm; OR

- a community order[89] containing a requirement not to possess, use or carry a firearm.

---

83 PSA 2016, s 54(7).
84 PSA 2016, s 54(8).
85 PSA 2016, s 54(9).
86 PSA 2016, s 54(10).
87 FA 1968, s 51(1)(a).
88 FA 1968, s 51(1)(b).
89 FA 1968, s 51(1)(c).

2.38

Once these conditions are fulfilled, the court has a discretion to make an order – it is not under a duty to do so. However, as most guns involved in criminal offences will be held illegally, it is likely to be difficult to contest the making of such an order in most cases.

2.39

FA 1968, s 52(3) allows a constable to seize and retain any firearm or ammunition which might be the subject of an order.

2.40

It is very rare that an order under FA 1968, s 52(1) will be made where the underlying conviction is not for an offence under FA 1968, but it is permissible and does occasionally occur.[90]

2.41

In *Hyde*,[91] a commercial munitions dealer was convicted of being knowingly concerned in the movement of controlled goods with intent to evade a prohibition on actions done or arrangements made in connection with the movement of controlled goods between third countries contrary to art 9(2) of the Trade in Goods (Control) Order 2003.[92] Nearly seven months after he had been sentenced, on application by the Chief Constable of Lincolnshire Police, an order for the forfeiture and destruction of 14,231 firearms was made pursuant to FA 1968, s 52(1).[93] These weapons (primarily AK-47s and MG34 Barrels) were unconnected with the offences of which he was convicted. They remained in storage in the custody of an entirely independent private company, housed in secure premises on a former RAF base.[94]

2.42

The judge recognised that the firearms were in secure custody and that, without a licence (and paying the storage costs, which had created a lien), the applicant could not sell them himself.[95] He determined that 'possession' within the Act was to be given a very wide interpretation as the legislation was intended to be draconian.[96] The applicant challenged the order on the basis that he was not then in possession of those firearms, and also because of want of proportionality

---

90   *Hyde* [2014] EWCA Crim 713, at [37].
91   [2014] EWCA Crim 713.
92   SI 2003/2765.
93   *Hyde*, at [2].
94   *Hyde*, at [4].
95   *Hyde*, at [18].
96   *Hyde*, at [19].

and a failure properly to have regard to Article 1 of Protocol 1 to the European Convention on Human Rights.[97]

2.43

The Court of Appeal quashed the order for forfeiture. They noted that possession of the firearms passed to the storage company not least because to decide otherwise would be to impact on the potential rights of that innocent third party in respect of the lien for storage. However, the Court held that it did not need to decide the precise impact of the lien because it was quite clear that the weapons were owned by a corporate entity, Jago Ltd. (Jago Ltd had been owned by the applicant and a third party; by the time of the Court's decision, the applicant had transferred his shareholding to his wife.)[98] Jago Ltd had not been convicted of any offence and, unless the corporate veil can be pierced, there was no basis for bringing them within s 52. (As Jago Ltd was a company lawfully operating with true, openly-disclosed and regulated ownership of the weapons pre-dating any allegations of wrongdoing related to the present conviction, there was no basis for piercing the corporate veil.) Jago Ltd not having been convicted, its property could not be forfeited as part of the sentence imposed on D pursuant to s 52.[99] The order was quashed.[100]

2.44

It does not matter whether the defendant in fact had a gun – ammunition alone will be sufficient.[101]

2.45

The forfeiture of air weapons is allowed under FA 1968, Sch 6, Part II, paras 7 and 8.

2.46

An appeal against an order for forfeiture or disposal of firearms lies to the Court of Appeal.[102]

Offensive weapons

2.47

Section 1(2) of the Prevention of Crime Act 1953 provides:

---

97   *Hyde*, at [20].
98   *Hyde*, at [45].
99   *Hyde*, at [47].
100   *Hyde*, at [53].
101   *Orwin* (1999) 1 Cr App R (S) 103.
102   *Hyde*, at [38].

'Where any person is convicted of an offence under subsection (1) of this section the court may make an order for the forfeiture or disposal of any weapon in respect of which the offence was committed.'

2.48

There is no similar power in relation to offences committed under CJA 1988, ss 139 and 139A (possessing bladed or pointed article in a public place).

2.49

Due to the diverse range of items which, when adapted for nefarious purposes, are capable of being offensive weapons, eg a milk bottle filled with acid,[103] there is a wide variety of items which could fall to be forfeited under this provision. However, there is very little relevant case law. That may be because the items involved are often prima facie illegal, or are everyday items adapted or used in such a way as to make them 'offensive' under the Act, and thus easily replaceable. However, the authority of *Hyde* as set out above seems likely to apply by analogy when seeking an answer to the question of whether the weapon was 'in respect of which the offence was committed'. Thus, a person arrested for another offence who happens to have an offensive weapon on them for which they are not charged, is not liable to have the weapon declared forfeit. As other powers are available, it is a matter of ensuring that the items are forfeited under the right power, as opposed to whether they are forfeited at all.

Terrorism

2.50

The Terrorism Act 2000 provides three forfeiture provisions, and the Terrorism Act (TA) 2006 provides a further two.

Terrorism Act 2000, s 23

2.51

This section provides the court with a power of forfeiture where a defendant has pleaded guilty to, or been convicted of, an offence under TA 2000, ss 15–18.[104]

(1)   Conviction under s 15(1), 15(2), or 16

The court may order the forfeiture of money or any other property which, at the time of the offence, the defendant had in their possession or under

---

103 *Formosa* [1991] 2 QB 1, at 5–6.
104 TA 2000, s 23(1).

their control and which had been used for the purposes of terrorism,[105] or which they intended should be, or had reasonable cause to suspect might be, used for those purposes.[106]

The court may order the forfeiture of any money or other property which wholly or partly, and directly or indirectly, is received by any person as a payment or other reward in connection with the commission of the offence.[107]

(2) Conviction under s 15(3)

The court may order the forfeiture of money or any other property which, at the time of the offence, the defendant had in their possession or under their control and which had been used for the purposes of terrorism,[108] or which, at that time, they knew or had reasonable cause to suspect would or might be used for those purposes.[109]

The court may order the forfeiture of any money or other property which wholly or partly, and directly or indirectly, is received by any person as a payment or other reward in connection with the commission of the offence.[110]

(3) Conviction under s 17

The court may order the forfeiture of money or any other property which, at the time of the offence, the defendant had in their possession or under their control and which had been used for the purposes of terrorism,[111] and was, at that time, intended by them to be used for such purposes.[112]

The court may also order forfeiture of money or other property to which the arrangement in question related, and which had been used for the purposes of terrorism,[113] or at the time of the offence, the person knew or had reasonable cause to suspect that it would or might be used for those purposes.[114]

The court may order the forfeiture of any money or other property which wholly or partly, and directly or indirectly, is received by any person as a payment or other reward in connection with the commission of the offence.[115]

---

105 TA 2000, s 23(2)(a).
106 TA 2000, s 23(2)(b).
107 TA 2000, s 23(7).
108 TA 2000, s 23(3)(a).
109 TA 2000, s 23(3)(b).
110 TA 2000, s 23(7).
111 TA 2000, s 23(4)(a).
112 TA 2000, s 23(4)(b).
113 TA 2000, s 23(5)(a).
114 TA 2000, s 23(5)(b).
115 TA 2000, s 23(7).

(4)   Conviction under s 17A

The court may order the forfeiture of the amount paid under, or purportedly under, the insurance contract.[116]

The court may order the forfeiture of any money or other property which wholly or partly, and directly or indirectly, is received by any person as a payment or other reward in connection with the commission of the offence.[117]

(5)   Conviction under s 18

The court may order the forfeiture of money or any other property which, at the time of the offence, the defendant had in their possession or under their control and which had been used for the purposes of terrorism,[118] and was, at that time, intended by them to be used for such purposes.[119]

The court may also order the forfeiture of money or other property to which the arrangement related.[120]

The court may order the forfeiture of any money or other property which wholly or partly, and directly or indirectly, is received by any person as a payment or other reward in connection with the commission of the offence.[121]

Terrorism Act 2000, s 23A

2.52

Section 23A offers a more general power to cover those situations where an offence that is not necessarily terrorist in nature is done for terrorist purposes. It permits a court to order forfeiture of any money or property when sentencing an offender for particular offences:

- TA 2000 – ss 54, 57, 58, 58A, 59, 60 or 61;

- TA 2006 – ss 2, 5, 6, 9–11;

- aiding, abetting, counselling, procuring, encouraging, assisting or attempting or conspiring to commit those offences;[122] or

---

116 TA 2000, s 23(5A).
117 TA 2000, s 23(7).
118 TA 2000, s 23(4)(a).
119 TA 2000, s 23(4)(b).
120 TA 2000, s 23(6).
121 TA 2000, s 23(7).
122 TA 2000, s 23A(3) applying the provisions of s 94(a)–(c) of the Counter-Terrorism Act 2008.

- any offence specified in Sch 2 to the Counter-Terrorism Act 2008, where the court dealing with it has determined, in accordance with s 30 of that Act, that it has a terrorist connection.[123]

providing two out of the following four conditions are met:

- at the time of the offence it was in the possession or control of the person convicted;[124] AND
- it had been used for the purposes of terrorism; OR
- it was intended by that person that it should be used for the purposes of terrorism; OR
- the court believes that it will be used for the purposes of terrorism unless forfeited.

Matters generally applicable to ss 23 and 23A

2.53

Before making an order a court must give an opportunity to be heard to any person, other than the convicted person, who claims to be the owner or otherwise interested in anything which can be forfeited under that section.[125]

2.54

In considering whether to make an order in respect of any property, a court shall have regard to both the value of the property,[126] and the likely financial and other effects on the convicted person of the making of the order (taken together with any other order that the court contemplates making).[127]

2.55

TA 2000, Sch 4 applies to forfeiture orders made under s 23 or s 23A.[128] It provides that a court making a forfeiture order may make such other provision as appears to it to be necessary for giving effect to the order; in particular it may:

- require any of the forfeited property to be paid or handed over to the proper officer[129] or to a constable designated for the purpose by the chief officer of police of a police force specified in the order;[130]

---

123 TA 2000, s 23A(4)(a).
124 TA 2000, s 23A(1)(a).
125 TA 2000, s 23B(1).
126 TA 2000, s 23B(2)(a).
127 TA 2000, s 23B(2)(b).
128 TA 2000, Sch 4, para 1.
129 As defined in TA 2000, Sch 4, para 4(1).
130 TA 2000, Sch 4, para 2(1)(a).

- direct any of the forfeited property other than money or land to be sold or otherwise disposed of in such manner as the court may direct and the proceeds (if any – after deduction of the costs of sale, disposal or realisation)[131] to be paid to the proper officer;[132]

- appoint a receiver to take possession, subject to such conditions and exceptions as may be specified by the court, of any of the forfeited property, to realise it in such manner as the court may direct and to pay the proceeds to the proper officer[133] (para 3 deals fully with the role and remuneration of any such receiver);[134]

- direct a specified part of any forfeited money, or of the proceeds of the sale, disposal or realisation of any forfeited property (after deduction of the costs of sale, disposal or realisation)[135] to be paid by the proper officer to a specified person falling within s 23B(1).[136]

2.56

A forfeiture order shall not come into force until there is no further possibility of it being varied, or set aside, on appeal (disregarding any power of a court to grant leave to appeal out of time).[137]

2.57

Section 140 of the Magistrates' Courts Act 1980 does not apply.[138] That section provides that where forfeiture of property has been ordered, which may be enforced by a magistrates' court, that property shall be sold or otherwise disposed of in such manner as the court may direct; and the proceeds shall be applied as if they were a fine imposed under the enactment on which the proceedings for the forfeiture are founded.

2.58

The proper officer[139] shall issue a certificate in respect of a forfeiture order, stating the extent (if any) to which, at that date, effect has been given to the forfeiture order,[140] if an application is made by:

- the prosecutor in the proceedings in which the forfeiture order was made;[141]

---

131 TA 2000, Sch 4, para 2(3).
132 TA 2000, Sch 4, para 2(1)(b).
133 TA 2000, Sch 4, para 2(1)(c).
134 TA 2000, Sch 4, para 3.
135 TA 2000, Sch 4, para 2(3).
136 TA 2000, Sch 4, para 2(1)(d).
137 TA 2000, Sch 4, para 2(2).
138 TA 2000, Sch 4, para 2(4).
139 As defined in TA 2000, Sch 4, para 4(1).
140 TA 2000, Sch 4, para 4(3).
141 TA 2000, Sch 4, para 4(2)(a).

- the defendant in those proceedings;[142] or

- a person whom the court heard under s 23B(1) before making the order.[143]

2.59

Schedule 4, para 4A provides that where a court makes a forfeiture order in a case where:

- the offender has been convicted of an offence that has resulted in a person suffering personal injury, loss or damage;[144] or

- any such offence is taken into consideration by the court in determining sentence,[145]

the court may also order that an amount not exceeding a sum specified by the court is to be paid to that person out of the proceeds of the forfeiture.

2.60

For this purpose, the 'proceeds of the forfeiture' means the aggregate amount of:

- any forfeited money;[146] and

- the proceeds of the sale, disposal or realisation of any forfeited property, after deduction of the costs of the sale, disposal or realisation,

reduced by the amount of:

- any payment to be paid by the proper officer to a specified person falling within s 23B(1);[147] or

- the remuneration and expenses paid by the proper officer to the receiver out of the proceeds of the property realised.[148, 149]

2.61

The court may make an order under Sch 4, para 4A only if it is satisfied that, but for the inadequacy of the offender's means, it would have made a compensation order under s 130 of the Powers of Criminal Courts (Sentencing) Act 2000 under which the offender would have been required to pay compensation of not less than the amount specified in the order made under Sch 4, para 4A.[150]

---

142 TA 2000, Sch 4, para 4(2)(b).
143 TA 2000, Sch 4, para 4(2)(c).
144 TA 2000, Sch 4, para 4A(1)(a).
145 TA 2000, Sch 4, para 4A(1)(b).
146 TA 2000, Sch 4, para 4A(2)(a).
147 TA 2000, Sch 4, para 2(1)(d).
148 TA 2000, Sch 4, para 3(1).
149 TA 2000, Sch 4, para 4A(2)(b).
150 TA 2000, Sch 4, para 4A(3).

2.62

Where an order for forfeiture was made for a relevant offence under Sch 4, but the person is acquitted of the relevant offence,[151] later pardoned,[152] or has their conviction quashed,[153] a person who had an interest in any property which was subject to the order may apply to the High Court for compensation.[154]

2.63

The High Court may order compensation to be paid to the applicant if satisfied:

- that there was a serious default on the part of a person concerned in the investigation or prosecution of the offence;[155]

- that the person in default was, or was acting as, a member of a police force, or was a member of, or acting on behalf of, the Crown Prosecution Service;[156]

- that the applicant has suffered loss in consequence of anything done in relation to the property by or in pursuance of the forfeiture order or restraint order;[157] and

- that, having regard to all the circumstances, it is appropriate to order compensation to be paid.[158]

2.64

The High Court shall not order compensation to be paid where it appears to it that proceedings for the offence would have been instituted even if the serious default had not occurred.[159]

2.65

Compensation payable under this paragraph shall be paid:

- where the person in default was, or was acting as, a member of a police force, out of the police fund out of which the expenses of that police force are met;[160] and

- where the person in default was a member of, or was acting on behalf of, the Crown Prosecution Service, by the Director of Public Prosecutions.[161]

---

151 TA 2000, Sch 4, para 9(2)(a).
152 TA 2000, Sch 4, para 9(2)(b).
153 TA 2000, Sch 4, para 9(2)(c).
154 TA 2000, Sch 4, para 9(3).
155 TA 2000, Sch 4, para 9(4)(a).
156 TA 2000, Sch 4, para 9(4)(b).
157 TA 2000, Sch 4, para 9(4)(c).
158 TA 2000, Sch 4, para 9(4)(d).
159 TA 2000, Sch 4, para 9(5).
160 TA 2000, Sch 4, para 9(6)(a).
161 TA 2000, Sch 4, para 9(6)(b).

2.66

Where D is convicted of a relevant offence (involving dealings with a proscribed organisation),[162] but on appeal under TA 2000, s 5 to the Proscribed Organisations Appeal Commission, that organisation is de-proscribed, s 7(2) of the Act mandates that an appeal to the Court of Appeal shall be allowed.[163] The consequential effect on forfeiture orders in those circumstances is as set out in Sch 4, para 10.

2.67

A person who had an interest in any property which was subject to the order may apply to the High Court for compensation.[164]

2.68

The High Court may order compensation to be paid to the applicant if satisfied:

- that the applicant has suffered loss in consequence of anything done in relation to the property by or in pursuance of the forfeiture order or restraint order;[165] and

- that, having regard to all the circumstances, it is appropriate to order compensation to be paid.[166]

2.69

Compensation payable under this paragraph shall be paid by the Secretary of State.[167]

2.70

In line with POCA 2002, s 13(2)(b) and (3)(c), where a judge makes a confiscation order, they must take account of such an order BEFORE they make a deprivation order under s 23 or s 23A.

---

162 TA 2000, Sch 4, para 10(1)(a).
163 TA 2000, Sch 4, para 10(1)(b).
164 TA 2000, Sch 4, para 10(2).
165 TA 2000, Sch 4, para 10(3)(a).
166 TA 2000, Sch 4, para 10(3)(b).
167 TA 2000, Sch 4, para 10(4).

Terrorism Act 2000, s 120A

2.71

In addition to the forfeiture powers under s 23A,[168] where a person falls to be sentenced for specific offences in column 1 below, the court has the additional powers of forfeiture seen in column 2:[169]

Column 1	**Column 2**
Offence	*Items liable to forfeiture*
Section 54 (weapons training)	Anything that the court considers to have been in the possession of the person for purposes connected with the offence.
Section 57 (possession for terrorist purposes)	Any article that is the subject matter of the offence.
Section 58 (collection of information)	Any document or record containing information of the kind mentioned in sub-s (1)(a) of that section.
Section 58A (eliciting, publishing or communicating information about members of armed forces etc)	Any document or record containing information of the kind mentioned in sub-s (1)(a) of that section.

2.72

Before making an order under this section, a court must give an opportunity to be heard to any person, other than the convicted person, who claims to be the owner or otherwise interested in anything liable to be forfeited under this section.[170]

2.73

An order under this section does not come into force until there is no further possibility of it being varied, or set aside, on appeal (within time).[171]

2.74

Where a court makes an order under this section, it may also make such other provision as appears to it to be necessary for giving effect to the forfeiture, including, in particular, provision relating to the retention, handling, disposal or

---

168 TA 2000, s 120A(6).
169 TA 2000, s 120A(1).
170 TA 2000, s 120A(2).
171 TA 2000, s 120A(3).

destruction of what is forfeited.[172] Such provision may be varied at any time by the court that made it.[173]

Terrorism Act 2006, s 7

2.75

This section creates a power of forfeiture against Ds who have been convicted of an offence under TA 2006, s 6 (training for terrorism). It is in addition to any power of forfeiture under TA 2000, s 23A.[174]

2.76

The court before which D is convicted may order the forfeiture of anything the court considers to have been in D's possession for purposes connected with the offence,[175] and make any other provision as appears necessary to give effect to the forfeiture,[176] including provision relating to the retention, handling, destruction or other disposal of items forfeited.[177]

2.77

Before making such an order the court must give an opportunity of being heard to any person (in addition to the convicted person) who claims to be the owner of that thing or otherwise to have an interest in it.[178]

2.78

No order may come into force until the ordinary time for an appeal has lapsed,[179] and provision made by virtue of this section may be varied at any time by the court that made it.[180]

Terrorism Act 2006, s 11A

2.79

This section creates a power of forfeiture against Ds who have been convicted of an offence under TA 2006:

---

172 TA 2000, s 120A(4).
173 TA 2000, s 120A(5).
174 TA 2006, s 7(7).
175 TA 2006, s 7(1).
176 TA 2006, s 7(4).
177 TA 2006, s 7(5).
178 TA 2006, s 7(2).
179 TA 2006, s 7(3).
180 TA 2006, s 7(6).

(a)   s 9 – making and possessing radioactive devices or materials;

(b)   s 10 – misuse of nuclear devices or material and misuse and damage of nuclear facilities; or

(c)   s 11 – making terrorist threats relating to radioactive devices, materials or facilities.

It is in addition to any power of forfeiture under TA 2000, s 23A.[181]

2.80

A court by or before which D is convicted under TA 2006, s 9 or s 10 may order the forfeiture of any radioactive device or radioactive material, or any nuclear facility, made or used in committing the offence.[182] A court by or before which D is convicted under s 11 may order the forfeiture of any radioactive device or radioactive material, or any nuclear facility, which is the subject of:

(a)   a demand under s 11(1);[183,184] or

(b)   a threat falling within s 11(3).[185,186]

2.81

The court may also make any other provision as appears necessary to give effect to the forfeiture, including provision relating to the retention, handling, destruction or other disposal of what is forfeited.[187]

2.82

Before making an order under this section, a court must give an opportunity to be heard to any person, other than the convicted person, who claims to be the owner or otherwise interested in anything liable to be forfeited under this section.[188]

---

181 TA 2006, s 11A(7).
182 TA 2006, s 11A(1).
183 In the course of or in connection with the commission of an act of terrorism or for the purposes of terrorism D makes a demand for:
(a)   the supply to himself or to another of a radioactive device or of radioactive material;
(b)   a nuclear facility to be made available to himself or to another; or
(c)   access to such a facility to be given to himself or to another.
184 TA 2006, s 11A(2)(a).
185 A threat to:
(a)   use radioactive material;
(b)   use a radioactive device; or
(c)   use or damage a nuclear facility in a manner that releases radioactive material or creates or increases a risk that such material will be released.
186 TA 2006, s 11A(2)(b).
187 TA 2006, s 11A(5).
188 TA 2006, s 11A(3).

2.83

No order may come into force until the ordinary time for an appeal has lapsed,[189] and provision made by virtue of this section may be varied at any time by the court that made it.[190]

Crossbows Act 1987, s 6

2.84

Section 6(3) gives a power to the court by which a person is convicted of an offence under the Crossbows Act 1987 to make such order as it thinks fit as to the forfeiture or disposal of any crossbow or part of a crossbow in respect of which the offence was committed.

---

189 TA 2006, s 11A(4).
190 TA 2006, s 11A(6).

3 Forfeiture III – Miscellaneous Powers

Marketing material for knives

3.01

Section 6 of the Knives Act 1997 gives powers of forfeiture flowing from convictions for offences contrary to s 1 (unlawful marketing of knives) and s 2 (material published in connection with the marketing of knives). It should be noted that these offences relate to the marketing of, and material associated with, knives which are being portrayed as suitable for combat,[1] or in a way that is otherwise likely to encourage violent behaviour using the knife as a weapon.[2]

Section 1 offence – forfeiture power under s 6(1)

3.02

If a person (D) is convicted of an offence under s 1 in relation to a knife of a particular description, the court may make an order for forfeiture in respect of any knives of that description that are seized under a warrant issued under s 5;[3] or are in the offender's possession or under his control at the time of his arrest for the offence or the issuing of a summons in relation to it.[4]

Section 2 offence – forfeiture power under s 6(2)

3.03

If a person is convicted of an offence under s 2 in relation to particular material, the court may make an order for forfeiture in respect of any publications consisting of or containing that material which have been seized under a warrant issued under s 5;[5] or which were in the offender's possession or under

---

1   Knives Act 1997, s 1(1)(a) and 2(1)(a).
2   Knives Act 1997, s 1(1)(b) and 2(1)(b).
3   Knives Act 1997, s 6(1)(a).
4   Knives Act 1997, s 6(1)(b) with interpretation from s 6(5)(a).
5   Knives Act 1997, s 6(2)(a).

his control at the time of his arrest for the offence, or the issuing of a summons in relation to it.[6]

General

3.04

The court may make an order under either subsection whether or not it also deals with the offender in respect of the offence in any other way;[7] and without regard to any restrictions on forfeiture in any enactment.[8]

3.05

In considering whether to make an order, the court must have regard to both the value of the property[9] and the likely financial and other effects on the offender (taken together with any other order that the court contemplates making).[10]

3.06

Section 7 sets out the effect of the making of an order under s 6. It is thorough, and this might explain the absence of reported cases on the operation of the section.

3.07

A forfeiture order under s 6 operates to deprive D of any rights he has in that property,[11] which must be surrendered to the police.[12]

3.08

On an application within six months of the forfeiture order being made,[13] by a person who:

- claims property to which a forfeiture order applies;[14] but

- is not the offender from whom it was forfeited,[15]

---

6   Knives Act 1997, s 6(2)(b) with interpretation from s 6(5)(a).
7   Knives Act 1997, s 6(3)(a).
8   Knives Act 1997, s 6(3)(b).
9   Knives Act 1997, s 6(4)(a).
10   Knives Act 1997, s 6(4)(b).
11   Knives Act 1997, s 7(1).
12   Knives Act 1997, s 7(2).
13   Knives Act 1997, s 7(5).
14   Knives Act 1997, s 7(3)(a).
15   Knives Act 1997, s 7(3)(b).

and who satisfies the court that:

- s/he had not consented to the offender having possession of the property;[16] or

- s/he did not know, and had no reason to suspect, that the offence was likely to be committed,[17]

the court may make a recovery order for delivery of the property to the applicant if it appears to the court that s/he owns it.[18]

3.09

At the end of six months after the recovery order is made in favour of the applicant, ownership crystallises with him/her and cannot be challenged by a third party.[19] During the six months it can be challenged.[20]

3.10

The Secretary of State is empowered to make regulations, in relation to property forfeited under this section, for disposing of the property and dealing with the proceeds and investing money and auditing accounts,[21] in cases where:

- no application has been made before the end of the period of six months beginning with the date on which the forfeiture order was made;[22] or

- no such application has succeeded.[23]

3.11

Pursuant to this power the Secretary of State has issued the Knives (Forfeited Property) Regulations 1997.[24]

Written materials or recordings related to hate crimes

3.12

The Public Order Act (POA) 1986 contains two powers of forfeiture.

---

16   Knives Act 1997, s 7(6)(a).
17   Knives Act 1997, s 7(6)(b).
18   Knives Act 1997, s 7(3).
19   Knives Act 1997, s 7(7)(b).
20   Knives Act 1997, s 7(7)(a).
21   Knives Act 1997, s 7(9).
22   Knives Act 1997, s 7(8)(a).
23   Knives Act 1997, s 7(8)(b).
24   SI 1997/1907.

Public Order Act 1986, s 25

3.13

This section permits a court by which the offender is convicted, or before which he pleads guilty, to order forfeiture of any written material or recording produced to the court and shown to its satisfaction to be written material or a recording to which the offence relates.

3.14

'The offence' must be:

- words, behaviour or a display of written material to stir up racial hatred (under s 18);[25]

- publishing or distributing written material to stir up racial hatred (under s 19);[26]

- distributing, showing or playing a recording to stir up racial hatred (under s 21);[27]

- possession of racially inflammatory material (under s 23).[28]

3.15

Any such order only takes effect once the ordinary time limit for an appeal has expired,[29] or where proceedings at the highest court to which an appeal could be made have been concluded or abandoned.[30] This includes an application for leave to appeal, or stating a case.[31]

3.16

It is clear from the case law that forfeiture orders are often made wrongly under this section, but not necessarily corrected when conviction or other aspects of sentence are appealed.[32] However, an astute Court of Appeal in *King*[33] noted that the forfeiture power under s 25 relates only to written or recorded material, and thus where the court wished to deprive Mr King of his catapult, s 143 of the Powers of Criminal Courts (Sentencing) Act (PCC(S)A) 2000 was the appropriate legislative tool. The Court had to make a similar correction where

---

25   POA 1986, s 25(1)(a).
26   POA 1986, s 25(1)(b).
27   POA 1986, s 25(1)(b).
28   POA 1986, s 25(1)(b).
29   POA 1986, s 25(2)(a).
30   POA 1986, s 25(3)(b).
31   POA 1986, s 25(3)(a).
32   Eg *Lubban* [2002] EWCA Crim 1298; and *Ray* [2002] EWCA Crim 84, amongst others.
33   [2015] EWCA Crim 1631, at [81]–[82].

an offensive weapon had purportedly been forfeited under s 25, when s 1(2) of the Prevention of Crime Act 1953 was the correct power.[34]

Public Order Act 1986, s 29I

3.17

This section imposes a duty on a sentencing court to order forfeiture of any written material or recording produced to the court and shown to its satisfaction to be written material or a recording to which any of the following offences relate: an offence under s 29B relating to the display of written material,[35] or an offence under s 29C, s 29E or s 29G.[36]

3.18

An order made under this section shall not take effect until the expiry of the ordinary time within which the highest level[37] of appeal or application by way of case stated[38] may be brought, or before the deciding or withdrawal of such.[39]

Obscene publications

Power without conviction

3.19

Section 1(4) of the Obscene Publications Act (OPA) 1964 requires the forfeiture of articles which were seized under s 3 of the OPA 1959, and whose existence led to a conviction under s 2 of the 1959 Act of having them for publication for gain.[40, 41] Being kept for publication for gain does not require that their distribution is intended to be in the UK.[42] Where D has pornography, but there is no suggestion that s/he has been gaining from distributing it to others, the power under PCC(S)A 2000 will be more appropriate, though it appears that this has not always been noted, even on appeal.[43] 'Obscenity' is not limited to sex – material relating to drug-taking has also been held to be capable of amounting

---

34 *Byrne* [2016] EWCA Crim 2124, at [3].
35 POA 1986, s 29I(1)(a).
36 POA 1986, s 29I(1)(b).
37 POA 1986, s 29I(3)(b).
38 POA 1986, s 29I(3)(a).
39 POA 1986, s 29I(2)(a).
40 OPA 1964, s 1(4).
41 This cannot apply to films – *AG's Reference (2 of 1975)* (1976) 62 Cr App R 255.
42 *Gold Star Publications Ltd v DPP* [1981] 1 WLR 732.
43 See *Gojkovic* [2017] EWCA Crim 1025, in which there is no suggestion that D obtained any gain from having child pornography, but no comment was made by the Court of Appeal that the power under s 1 had been wrongly used.

to an 'obscene' publication due to its tendency to 'deprave and corrupt'.[44] Similarly, not all sexually explicit material will necessarily be obscene.[45]

3.20

The power under s 3 of OPA 1959 permits seizure of obscene articles possessed for gain. It also creates a separate power of forfeiture available without conviction as a pre-requisite, or even any criminal proceedings being brought.

3.21

Without prejudice to the duty of a court to make an order for the forfeiture of an article where there has been a conviction, no order for the forfeiture of the article shall be made under s 3 unless the warrant under which the article was seized was issued on an information laid by or on behalf of the Director of Public Prosecutions.[46]

3.22

Section 3(3) of OPA 1959 provides that any articles seized under s 3(1) shall be brought before a magistrate acting in the local justice area in which the articles were seized. That magistrate may then issue a summons to the occupier of the premises or the user of the stall or vehicle to appear on a day specified in the summons before a magistrates' court acting in that local justice area to show cause why the articles or any of them should not be forfeited. If the court is satisfied that at the time when any of the articles were seized they were obscene articles kept for publication for gain, the court shall order those articles to be forfeited.

3.23

In coming to a decision where there are a number of different books alleged to be obscene, each book need not be read by each of the presiding magistrates. It will be sufficient that every book is read by at least one, and that there has then been a discussion between them about each book.[47] Similarly, a judge need not view each of many pornographic images – it is sufficient if they have been split into categories and the judge views a sample including at least one from each category.[48]

3.24

If the person summonsed does not appear, the court shall not make an order unless service of the summons is proved. If it is found that the articles do not

---

44   *John Calder (Publications) Ltd v Powell* [1965] 1 QB 509.
45   *Darbo v DPP* [1991] 6 WLUK 305.
46   OPA 1959, s 3(3A).
47   *Olympia Press Ltd v Hollis* (1974) 59 Cr App R 28, at 31.
48   *R v Snaresbrook Crown Court, ex p Commissioner of the Police for the Metropolis* (1984) 79 Cr App R 184.

fall within s 3 then they shall be returned to the occupier of the premises or, as the case may be, to the user of the stall or vehicle in or on which it was found.[49]

3.25

In addition to the person summonsed, any other person being the owner, author or maker of any of the articles brought before the court, or any other person through whose hands they had passed before being seized, shall be entitled to appear before the court on the day specified in the summons to show cause why they should not be forfeited.[50]

3.26

Where an order is made for the forfeiture of any articles, any person who appeared, or was entitled to appear, to show cause against the making of the order may appeal to the Crown Court. This is not to be read as creating an exclusive avenue of appeal that prevents an appeal by way of case stated to the Divisional Court.[51]

3.27

No forfeiture order shall take effect until the expiration of the period within which notice of appeal to the Crown Court may be given against the order, or, if before the expiration thereof notice of appeal is given or application is made for the stating of a case for the opinion of the High Court, until the final determination or abandonment of the proceedings on the appeal or case stated.[52]

3.28

If the court does not order forfeiture of any of the items, the court may if it thinks fit order the person on whose information the warrant for the seizure of the articles was issued to pay such costs as the court thinks reasonable to any person who has appeared before the court to show cause why those articles should not be forfeited; and costs ordered to be paid under this subsection shall be enforceable as a civil debt.[53]

3.29

When deciding whether the articles are obscene, s 3(7) requires consideration of the nature of the publication and what manner of publication is likely, having regard to the circumstances in which the articles were found. For the purposes of this section it should be assumed that copies would be published in any

---

49   OPA 1959, s 3(3).
50   OPA 1959, s 3(4).
51   *Burke v Copper* [1962] 1 WLR 700.
52   OPA 1959, s 3(5).
53   OPA 1959, s 3(6).

manner likely having regard to the circumstances in which it was found, but in no other manner.[54] Therefore in *Morgan v Bowker*,[55] the justices were wrong in ignoring the evidence of D as regards the nature of his business and the methods employed by him in conducting it. The case was consequently remitted to the justices to determine, in the light of D's evidence, whether the articles or any of them tended to deprave or corrupt adults, whether they were likely to be published to persons under 21, and, if so, whether they tended to deprave or corrupt such persons.

3.30

It has been held that negatives of photographs cannot be subject to forfeiture under these provisions as they cannot be shown, played or projected to any member of the public and that, therefore, there is no jurisdiction to order the negatives to be forfeited, though photographs made from them could be.[56]

Power on conviction

3.31

Anything seized under s 3 MUST be forfeited (and the court is under a duty) after convictions under OPA 1964, s 1(2), as required by s 1(4) of the 1964 Act. Any such order only takes effect once the ordinary time limit for an appeal has expired,[57] or where proceedings at the highest court to which an appeal could be made have been concluded or abandoned.[58] This includes an application for leave to appeal, or stating a case.[59] The forfeiture and destruction of items under this provision deprives D of ownership, but is compliant with the right to property as protected by Article 1, Protocol 1 to the European Convention on Human Rights as they are items that have been lawfully adjudged illicit and dangerous to the general interest.[60]

3.32

Where the convictions for the relevant offences are quashed on appeal, any consequent forfeiture orders must also be quashed.[61]

---

54 OPA 1959, s 3(7).
55 [1963] 2 WLR 860.
56 *DPP v Straker* [1963] 1 QB 926.
57 OPA 1964, s 1(4).
58 OPA 1964, s 1(4)(a).
59 OPA 1964, s 1(4)(b).
60 *Handyside v UK* (1979-80) 1 EHRR 737.
61 *Levy* [2004] EWCA Crim 1141, at [13]–[14].

Children and Young Persons (Harmful Publications) Act 1955, s 3

3.33

The Children and Young Persons (Harmful Publications) Act 1955 makes it an offence to print, publish, sell or hire out[62] any book, magazine or other like work which is of a kind likely to fall into the hands of children or young persons and consists wholly or mainly of stories told in pictures (with or without the addition of words), being stories portraying:

- the commission of crimes;[63] or

- acts of violence or cruelty;[64] or

- incidents of a repulsive or horrible nature,[65]

in such a way that the work as a whole would tend to corrupt a child or young person into whose hands it might fall.

3.34

Section 3 provides a power to search for, and order the forfeiture of, any such works.

3.35

The court by or before which a person is convicted of an offence under s 2 may order forfeiture of:

- any copies of that work, and

- any plate prepared for the purpose of printing copies of that work or photographic film prepared for that purpose,

- which have been found in D's possession or under his control.[66]

3.36

No order shall take effect until the final period for appeal has expired, or any appeal has been determined or abandoned.

---

62   Children and Young Persons (Harmful Publications) Act, s 2.
63   Children and Young Persons (Harmful Publications) Act, s 1(a).
64   Children and Young Persons (Harmful Publications) Act, s 1(b).
65   Children and Young Persons (Harmful Publications) Act, s 1(c).
66   Children and Young Persons (Harmful Publications) Act, s 3(2).

Forgery and Counterfeiting Act 1981, s 24

3.37

This section permits a magistrate to order the forfeiture of counterfeited currency and items associated with the making of it.

3.38

If it appears to a magistrate, from information given on oath, that there is reasonable cause to believe that a person has in his custody or under his control:

- any counterfeit currency note or protected coin, or reproduction British currency note or coin;[67] or

- any thing which he or another has used, or intends to use, for the making of any such counterfeit or reproduction,[68]

the magistrate may issue a warrant authorising a constable to enter premises, search for and seize the object in question.

3.39

Any time after seizing any such suspected object (whether under warrant or otherwise) the police may apply to a magistrates' court for forfeiture of the object.[69] The court may make an order for forfeiture and disposal,[70] or passing of the items to an authority with power to issue, or authority to receive, such objects,[71] if it is satisfied both that the object falls within either criteria above (at 3.38), and that it is conducive to the public interest to do so.[72]

3.40

The court shall not order any thing to be forfeited where a person claiming to be the owner of or otherwise interested in it applies to be heard by the court, unless an opportunity has been given to them to show cause why the order should not be made.[73]

---

67 Forgery and Counterfeiting Act 1981, s 24(1)(a).
68 Forgery and Counterfeiting Act 1981, s 24(1)(b).
69 Forgery and Counterfeiting Act 1981, s 24(1).
70 Forgery and Counterfeiting Act 1981, s 24(3).
71 Forgery and Counterfeiting Act 1981, s 24(5).
72 Forgery and Counterfeiting Act 1981, s 24(2).
73 Forgery and Counterfeiting Act 1981, s 24(4).

Goods, materials or articles breaching consumer protection legislation – Trade Marks Act 1994

3.41

Section 97 of the Trade Marks Act (TMA) 1994 creates a power of forfeiture that is activated by the commission of a 'relevant offence'. It is a power, and not a duty requiring the court to make the order wherever there has been a relevant offence;[74] it is a matter for judicial discretion whether such an order is made.[75]

3.42

Where any person, in connection with the investigation or prosecution of a relevant offence, has come into possession of:

- goods which, or the packaging of which, bears a sign identical to or likely to be mistaken for a registered trade mark;[76]

- material bearing such a sign and intended to be used for labelling or packaging goods, as a business paper in relation to goods, or for advertising goods;[77] or

- articles specifically designed or adapted for making copies of such a sign,[78]

that person may apply under this section for an order for the forfeiture of the goods, material or articles.

3.43

As the Divisional Court in *UNIC v LB Brent & Harrow Trading Standards* observed:[79]

'There does not have to have been a prosecution to conviction, nor even an existing prosecution. An investigation will be sufficient if combined with possession. The right to apply for forfeiture conferred by s 97 is obviously of particular value to the trading standards service of a local authority, for it will, in a variety of circumstances, be a person coming into possession of goods in the circumstances envisaged by the section. Important though the power may be to a local authority it is nevertheless capable of being exercised by any person, for example the registered trademark proprietor or the licensee of the trademark, so long as the qualifying circumstances set out by the section exist.'

---

74   *R (Drain) v Birmingham Crown Court, Birmingham Trading Standards, Dept for BEIS* [2018] EWHC 1255 (Admin), at [25]
75   *R (Drain)*, at [28].
76   TMA 1994, s 97(1)(a).
77   TMA 1994, s 97(1)(b).
78   TMA 1994, s 97(1)(c).
79   [2000] 1 WLR 2112, at [11]

3.44

A 'relevant offence' is an offence under:

- s 92 of TMA 1994 (unauthorised use of trade mark, etc in relation to goods);[80]

- the Trade Descriptions Act 1968;[81]

- the Business Protection from Misleading Marketing Regulations 2008;[82]

- the Consumer Protection from Unfair Trading Regulations 2008;[83] or

- any offence involving dishonesty or deception.[84]

3.45

An application under this section may be made:

- where proceedings have been brought in any court for a relevant offence relating to some or all of the goods, material or articles, to that court;[85] or

- where no application for the forfeiture of the goods, material or articles has been made in that way, by way of complaint to a magistrates' court.[86]

3.46

On an application under this section the court shall make an order for the forfeiture of any goods, material or articles only if it is satisfied that a relevant offence has been committed in relation to them.[87]

3.47

Where the proceedings for the 'relevant offence' have ended with a hung jury and the decision by the prosecution not to seek a retrial, it was not inappropriate for the judge to have made a forfeiture order in respect of goods. The first instance judge was best placed to decide whether to exercise the discretion having heard all of the evidence during the trial. That it had ended with a hung jury and a subsequent acquittal on the offering of no evidence were held not to assist the application.[88]

---

80 TMA 1994, s 97(8)(a).
81 TMA 1994, s 97(8)(b).
82 TMA 1994, s 97(8)(c).
83 TMA 1994, s 97(8)(d).
84 TMA 1994, s 97(8)(e).
85 TMA 1994, s 97(2)(a).
86 TMA 1994, s 97(2)(b).
87 TMA 1994, s 97(3).
88 *R (Drain)*, at [30]

3.48

A court may infer for the purposes of this section that such an offence has been committed in relation to certain goods, material or articles if it is satisfied that there has been an offence committed in relation to other items which are representative of those being considered. Examples of how items would be representative would be if they were of the same design, or part of the same consignment or batch.[89]

3.49

Appeal against an order made under this section by a magistrates' court, or by a decision of such a court not to make such an order, lies to the Crown Court,[90] which may make an order containing such provision as appears to the court appropriate for delaying the coming into force of the order pending the making and determination of any appeal (including any application under s 111 of the Magistrates' Courts Act 1980).[91]

3.50

There is a presumption in favour of destruction of goods forfeited under this section, in accordance with directions of the court.[92] However, the court may, if it considers it appropriate to do so, direct that the goods, material or articles to which the order relates shall instead be released to such person as the court may specify, on condition that that person:

- causes the offending sign to be erased, removed or obliterated;[93] and

- complies with any order to pay costs which has been made against him in the proceedings for the order for forfeiture.[94]

3.51

This has been characterised as:[95] '[not] a penalty or an essential part of the prosecution of the criminal offence. The forfeiture process comprises a court procedure for working out the consequences of the commission of a criminal offence in connection with goods, having regard to the commercial and proprietary interests of persons who entered into transactions in connection with the goods.'

---

89   TMA 1994, s 97(4).
90   TMA 1994, s 97(5)(a).
91   TMA 1994, s 97(5).
92   TMA 1994, s 97(6).
93   TMA 1994, s 97(7)(a).
94   TMA 1994, s 97(7)(b).
95   *UNIC*, at [21].

3.52

Indeed, forfeiture proceedings pursuant to s 97 and an appeal by an aggrieved person to the Crown Court in respect of a forfeiture order have been held, on judicial review, to be civil proceedings.[96] In those proceedings, the Court was being asked to determine whether the proceedings were civil, criminal or administrative, on the basis that the Brussels Convention would apply only if they were civil.

Items infringing copyright – Copyright, Designs and Patents Act 1988

3.53

The Copyright, Designs and Patents Act (CDPA) 1988 provides powers to order forfeiture of:

- items infringing copyright under s 114A;

- illicit recordings under s 204A; and

- unauthorised decoders under s 297C.

3.54

This power arises in each case where a relevant offence has been committed. The definition of a 'relevant offence' is the same for all three sections, with the exception that the specific offence to which the power relates is different in each of the three:

- s 107(1), (2) or (2A) (unauthorised use of trade mark etc in relation to goods)[97]/s 198(1) or (1A) (criminal liability for making or dealing with illicit recordings)[98]/s 297A(1) (criminal liability for making, importing etc unauthorised decoders);[99]

- the Trade Descriptions Act 1968;[100]

- the Business Protection from Misleading Marketing Regulations 2008;[101]

- the Consumer Protection from Unfair Trading Regulations 2008;[102] or

- any offence involving dishonesty or deception.[103]

---

96 *UNIC*, at [40].
97 CDPA 1988, s 114A(2)(a).
98 CDPA 1988, s 204A(2).
99 CDPA 1988, s 297C(2).
100 CDPA 1988, s 114A/s 204A/s 297C(2)(b).
101 CDPA 1988, s 114A/s 204A/s 297C(2)(ba).
102 CDPA 1988, s 114A/s 204A/s 297C(2)(bb).
103 CDPA 1988, s 114A/s 204A/s 297C(2)(c).

3.55

When a 'relevant offence' can be found to have been committed the power of forfeiture is governed by the same case law as in relation to TMA 1994, s 97(3)[104] (see 3.47).

3.56

Where any person, in connection with the investigation or prosecution of such a relevant offence, has come into possession of:

- infringing copies of a copyright work;[105] or

- articles specifically designed or adapted for making copies of a particular copyright work;[106]

- illicit recordings;[107]

- unauthorised decoders,[108]

that person may apply under this section for an order for the forfeiture of them.

3.57

An application under this section may be made:

- where proceedings have been brought in any court for a relevant offence relating to some or all of the infringing copies or articles, to that court;[109] or

- where no application for the forfeiture of the items has been made in that way, by way of complaint to a magistrates' court.[110]

3.58

On an application under this section the court shall make an order for the forfeiture of any such item only if it is satisfied that a relevant offence has been committed in relation to them.[111]

3.59

A court may infer for the purposes of this section that such an offence has been committed in relation to certain such items if it is satisfied that there has been an offence committed in relation to other items which are representative of

---

104 *R (Drain)*, at [27].
105 CDPA 1988, s 114A(1)(a).
106 CDPA 1988, s 114A(1)(b).
107 CDPA 1988, s 204A(1).
108 CDPA 1988, s 297C(1).
109 CDPA 1988, s 114A/s 204A/s 297C(3)(a).
110 CDPA 1988, s 114A/s 204A/s 297C(3)(b).
111 CDPA 1988, s 114A/s 204A/s 297C(4).

those being considered. Examples of how items would be representative would be if they were of the same design, or part of the same consignment or batch.[112]

3.60

Appeal against an order made under this section by a magistrates' court, or against a decision not to make an order, lies to the Crown Court,[113] which may make an order containing such provision as appears to the court appropriate for delaying the coming into force of the order pending the making and determination of any appeal (including any application under s 111 of the Magistrates' Courts Act 1980).[114]

3.61

There is a presumption in favour of destruction of goods forfeited under this section, in accordance with direction of the court.[115] However, the court may, if it considers it appropriate to do so, direct that the infringing copies or articles to which the order relates shall instead be forfeited to the owner of the copyright in question or dealt with in such other way as the court considers appropriate.[116] If there is an illicit recording, the court may direct that it be forfeited to the person having the performer's rights or recording rights in question or dealt with in such other way as the court considers appropriate.[117] Where an unauthorised decoder has been forfeited, the court can order that instead of being destroyed it be forfeited to a person who has rights or remedies in relation to the unauthorised decoder in question under s 298, or deal with it in such other way as the court considers appropriate.[118]

Vehicle, ship or aircraft used for modern slavery

3.62

Section 11 of the Modern Slavery Act (MSA) 2015 provides a power of forfeiture on conviction of an offence of human trafficking under s 2 of that Act.[119]

3.63

The court may order the forfeiture of a land vehicle,[120] ship or aircraft[121] used or intended to be used in connection with the offence if the convicted person:

---

112 CDPA 1988, s 114A/s 204A/s 297C(5).
113 CDPA 1988, s 114A/s 204A/s 297C(6)(a).
114 CDPA 1988, s 114A/s 204A/s 297C(7).
115 CDPA 1988, s 114A/s 204A/s 297C(8).
116 CDPA 1988, s 114A(9).
117 CDPA 1988, s 204A(9).
118 CDPA 1988, s 297C(9).
119 MSA 2015, s 11(1).
120 MSA 2015, s 11(2).
121 MSA 2015, s 11(3).

- owned it at the time the offence was committed;[122]

- was at that time a director, secretary or manager of a company which owned it;[123]

- was at that time in possession of it under a hire-purchase agreement;[124]

- was at that time a director, secretary or manager of a company which was in possession of it under a hire-purchase agreement;[125]

- was at that time a charterer of the ship or aircraft;[126] or

- was driving the vehicle in the course of the commission of the offence;[127]

- committed the offence while acting as captain of the ship or aircraft.[128]

3.64

Where D was not the owner of the ship or aircraft at the time the offence was committed, or a director, secretary or manager of a company which owned the ship or aircraft, forfeiture may only be ordered if:

- in the case of a ship other than a hovercraft, its gross tonnage is less than 500 tons;[129]

- in the case of an aircraft, the maximum weight at which it may take off in accordance with its certificate of airworthiness is less than 5,700 kilogrammes;[130] or

- a person who at the time the offence was committed owned the ship or aircraft,[131] or was a director, secretary or manager of a company which owned it,[132] knew or ought to have known of the intention to use it in the course of the commission of an offence under s 2.

3.65

Where a person who claims to have an interest in a land vehicle, ship or aircraft applies to a court to make representations about its forfeiture, the court may not order its forfeiture without giving the person an opportunity to make representations.[133]

---

122 MSA 2015, s 11(2)(a), (3)(a).
123 MSA 2015, s 11(2)(b), (3)(b).
124 MSA 2015, s 11(2)(c), (3)(c).
125 MSA 2015, s 11(2)(d), (3)(d).
126 MSA 2015, s 11(3)(e).
127 MSA 2015, s 11(2)(e).
128 MSA 2015, s 11(3)(f).
129 MSA 2015, s 11(4)(a).
130 MSA 2015, s 11(4)(b).
131 MSA 2015, s 11(5)(a).
132 MSA 2015, s 11(5)(b).
133 MSA 2015, s 11(6).

Unlawful profit from unlawful subletting

3.66

Section 4 of the Prevention of Social Housing Fraud Act (PSHFA) 2013 gives the court a power to make an unlawful profit order (UPO) when D is convicted of an offence under either s 1 (unlawful sub-letting: secure tenancies) or s 2 (unlawful sub-letting: assured tenancies),[134] or an associated offence in relation to either section.[135]

3.67

A UPO requires the offender to pay the landlord under the tenancy in respect of which the offence was committed[136] an amount representing the profit made by the offender as a result of the conduct constituting the offence.[137]

3.68

The court by or before which the offender is convicted must, on application or otherwise, decide whether to make a UPO,[138] and give reasons if it does not make such an order.[139] The court may make such an order instead of or in addition to dealing with the offender in any other way.[140]

3.69

The amount payable under a UPO must be such amount as the court considers appropriate, having regard to any evidence and to any representations that are made by or on behalf of the offender or the prosecutor, but constrained by two calculations.[141] The maximum amount payable under an unlawful profit order is calculated as follows:[142]

- Step 1:

  Determine the total amount the offender received as a result of the conduct constituting the offence (or the best estimate of that amount).

- Step 2:

  Deduct from that amount the total amount, if any, paid by the offender as rent to the landlord (including service charges) over the period during which the offence was committed.

---

134 PSHFA 2013, s 4(1)(a).
135 PSHFA 2013, s 4(1)(b).
136 PSHFA 2013, s 4(13).
137 PSHFA 2013, s 4(3).
138 PSHFA 2013, s 4(2)(a).
139 PSHFA 2013, s 4(4).
140 PSHFA 2013, s 4(2)(b).
141 PSHFA 2013, s 4(5).
142 PSHFA 2013, s 4(6).

3.70

Where a UPO has been made against D in civil proceedings under PSHFA 2013, s 5, a UPO in respect of criminal proceedings pursuant to s 4 may only provide for the landlord to recover an amount equal to the aggregate of the following:

- any amount by which the amount of the offender's profit calculated under this section exceeds the amount payable under the order made under s 5;[143] and

- a sum equal to any portion of the amount payable under the order made under s 5 that the landlord fails to recover,

and the landlord may not enforce the order under this section, so far as it relates to a sum that he fails to recover without the leave of the court.

3.71

If the court thinks that both a UPO and a fine are appropriate,[144] but D has insufficient means to pay both[145] the court must give preference to a UPO.[146]

3.72

If the amount required to be paid by a person under a UPO is not paid when it is required to be paid, that person must pay interest on the amount for the period for which it remains unpaid[147] at the rate of interest for the time being specified in s 17 of the Judgments Act 1838 (interest on civil judgment debts).[148]

3.73

PCC(S)A 2000, ss 131–133 (supplementary provisions about compensation orders) apply to UPOs as if:

(a) references to compensation orders[149] were to UPOs,[150,151] subject to the reference in s 133(3)(c)(ii) to a UPO being read as a reference to a compensation order under PCC(S)A 2000, s 130;[152] and

(b) s 133(3)(a) and (b) were omitted.[153]

---

143 PSHFA 2013, s 4(7)(a).
144 PSHFA 2013, s 4(8)(a).
145 PSHFA 2013, s 4(8)(b)(i) and (ii).
146 PSHFA 2013, s 4(9).
147 PSHFA 2013, s 4(10).
148 PSHFA 2013, s 4(11).
149 PSHFA 2013, s 4(12)(b).
150 PSHFA 2013, s 4(12)(b).
151 PSHFA 2013, s 4(12)(a).
152 PSHFA 2013, s 4(12)(d).
153 PSHFA 2013, s 4(12)(c).

3.74

The Proceeds of Crime Act (POCA) 2002, s 14(12) provides that a confiscation order can be quashed on the grounds of procedural irregularities in applying for or granting a postponement if a UPO has been made before a confiscation order is made. POCA 2002, s 15(3)(d) also explicitly states that if a court is sentencing in the postponement period of confiscation proceedings, after that period ends it can impose a UPO.

Cultural Property (Armed Conflicts) Act 2017, s 18

3.75

Under s 17 of Cultural Property (Armed Conflicts) Act 2017, the court by or before which a person is convicted of an offence of dealing in unlawfully exported cultural property may order the forfeiture of the property in respect of which the offence was committed.[154]

3.76

The court may also make such provision as appears to it to be necessary for giving effect to the forfeiture.[155] That provision may include, in particular, provision relating to the retention or disposal of the property.[156]

3.77

Any provision made under this section may be varied at any time by the court that made it.[157]

Animal welfare offences

3.78

There are a variety of powers available to courts under the Animal Welfare Act (AWA) 2006 where D has been convicted of an offence under that Act.

---

154 PSHFA 2013, s 18(1).
155 Cultural Property (Armed Conflicts) Act 2017, s 18(2).
156 Cultural Property (Armed Conflicts) Act 2017, s 18(3).
157 Cultural Property (Armed Conflicts) Act 2017, s 18(4).

Section 33 – deprivation

3.79

If the person convicted of an offence under any of ss 4, 5, 6(1) and (2), 7, 8 (including an animal that took part in an animal fight[158]) or 9 is the owner of the animal victim, the court may, instead of or in addition to dealing with him in any other way, make an order depriving him of ownership of the animal (and any dependent offspring[159]) and for its disposal,[160] including by destruction.[161]

3.80

Where the owner of an animal who is convicted of ownership of the animal is in breach of a disqualification under s 34(2),[162] the court by or before which he is convicted may, instead of or in addition to dealing with him in any other way, make an order depriving him of ownership of the animal (and any dependent offspring[163]) and for its disposal.[164]

3.81

Where a court makes an order it may:

- appoint a person to carry out, or arrange for the carrying out of, the order;[165]

- require any person who has possession of an animal to which the order applies to deliver it up to enable the order to be carried out;[166]

- give directions with respect to the carrying out of the order,[167] including specifying the manner in which an animal is to be disposed of,[168] or delegating that decision to a person appointed to carry out, or arrange for the carrying out, of the order;[169]

- confer additional powers (including power to enter premises where an animal to which the order applies is being kept) for the purpose of, or in connection with, the carrying out of the order;[170]

- order the offender to reimburse the expenses of carrying out the order.[171]

---

158 AWA 2006, s 33(8).
159 AWA 2006, s 33(3).
160 AWA 2006, s 33(1).
161 AWA 2006, s 33(9).
162 An offence contrary to AWA 2006, s 34(9).
163 AWA 2006, s 33(3).
164 AWA 2006, s 33(2).
165 AWA 2006, s 33(4)(a).
166 AWA 2006, s 33(4)(b).
167 AWA 2006, s 33(4)(c).
168 AWA 2006, s 33(5)(a).
169 AWA 2006, s 33(5)(b).
170 AWA 2006, s 33(4)(d).
171 AWA 2006, s 33(4)(e).

3.82

Where a court decides not to make an order depriving D of ownership and disposing of the animal, it shall, unless it makes a disqualification order under s 34(1)[172] (see 3.85):

- give its reasons for the decision in open court;[173] and

- if it is a magistrates' court, cause them to be entered in the register of its proceedings.[174]

3.83

Where orders under s 33 have been made by the magistrates' court but suspended pending an appeal, there can be no complaint that the Crown Court does not have the jurisdiction to activate that order once the appeal has been heard, if it is unsuccessful.[175]

Section 34 – disqualification

3.84

This section provides three possible types of disqualification from keeping animals.

3.85

If a person is convicted of an offence under any of ss 4, 5, 6(1) and (2), 7, 8, 9 or 13(6) and (9),[176] the court by or before which he is convicted may, instead of or in addition to dealing with him in any other way, make an order disqualifying him in one or more of the three ways below, for such period as it thinks fit.[177]

(1)   Disqualification from:

- owning;[178]

- keeping;[179,180]

- participating in the keeping of;[181] and

---

172 AWA 2006, s 33(7).
173 AWA 2006, s 33(6)(a).
174 AWA 2006, s 33(6)(b).
175 *R (Gray) v Aylesbury Crown Court* [2013] EWHC 500 (Admin), at [42].
176 AWA 2006, s 34(10).
177 AWA 2006, s 34(1).
178 AWA 2006, s 34(2)(a).
179 AWA 2006, s 34(2)(b).
180 This includes keeping through an agent – *Wright v Reading Crown Court* [2017] EWHC 2643 (Admin), at [15]–[20].
181 AWA 2006, s 34(2)(c).

- being party to an arrangement under which he is entitled to control or influence the way in which animals generally, or animals of one or more specified kinds[182] are kept.[183]

There is no possibility, subject to human rights' arguments, to modify an order under this section so that D is disqualified from only some of the activities.[184] Likewise, an order cannot specify an individual animal, it can only specify a type of animal.[185] It is also not permissible to make requirements of the number and condition of a kind of animal that D is permitted to keep.[186]

(2)   Disqualification from dealing in animals,[187] generally, or of one or more specified kinds.[188]

(3)   Disqualification from:

- transporting;[189] and

- arranging for the transport of animals[190] generally, or animals of one or more specified kinds.[191]

3.86

The purpose of a disqualification order is to afford protection to animals, not to punish D.[192] For this reason, careful consideration will need to be given to both the length and whether to make an 'all animals' order. Even in a less serious case of a general uncaring attitude, instead of deliberate cruelty, a person's treatment of one type of animal may shed light on their likely treatment of animals of any other type, and an 'all animals' order could be appropriate.[193] Similar thinking can support a disqualification extending beyond the specific species with which the current offence was concerned where D had a previous conviction relating to the other species.[194] Likewise, previous convictions can justify a disqualification on facts where none was imposed on a co-defendant of good character.[195]

3.87

In other cases, someone may have the resources to care for one sort of animal, but not another sort which requires generally more expensive provision – for

---

182   AWA 2006, s 34(5).
183   AWA 2006, s 34(2)(d).
184   *R (RSPCA) v Guildford Crown Court* [2012] EWHC 3392 (Admin), at [9]–[11].
185   *Barker v RSPCA* [2018] EWHC 880 (Admin), at [51].
186   *RSPCA v Preston Crown Court* [2015] EWHC 4875 (Admin), at [19]–[21].
187   AWA 2006, s 34(3).
188   AWA 2006, s 34(5).
189   AWA 2006, s 34(4)(a).
190   AWA 2006, s 34(4)(b).
191   AWA 2006, s 34(5).
192   *Barker*, at [59].
193   *Barker*, at [48]
194   *Ward v RSPCA* [2010] EWHC 347 (Admin), at [17].
195   *Ward*, at [18].

example someone who can very well afford to keep a cat may not be able to afford to keep a horse.[196]

3.88

Finally, someone may need to be generally prohibited from keeping animals, except for a sort which is unlikely to be affected by the kind of harm that others have suffered – for example, in *Barker*, terrapins.[197]

3.89

The court making the order may specify a period during which the offender may not make an application under s 43(1) for termination of the order.

3.90

The court making the order may:

- suspend the operation of the order pending an appeal;[198] or

- where it appears to the court that the offender owns or keeps an animal to which the order applies, suspend the operation of the order, and of any order made under s 35 for seizure of animals in connection with the disqualification, for such period as it thinks necessary for enabling alternative arrangements to be made in respect of the animal.[199]

3.91

Where a court decides not to make an order, it shall:

- give its reasons for the decision in open court;[200] and

- if it is a magistrates' court, cause them to be entered in the register of its proceedings.[201]

3.92

A person who breaches a disqualification under this section commits an offence.[202] D does not commit an offence where s/he is in a position to be able to offer care to animals whilst disqualified (ie was living in a house with another who owned animals) unless D was responsible for, or entitled to participate in, their care.[203]

---

196 *Barker*, at [49].
197 *Barker*, at [50]–[51].
198 AWA 2006, s 34(7)(a).
199 AWA 2006, s 34(7)(b).
200 AWA 2006, s 34(8)(a).
201 AWA 2006, s 34(8)(b).
202 AWA 2006, s 34(9).
203 *Patterson v RSPCA* [2013] EWHC 4531 (Admin), at [27]–[33].

Section 35 – seizure following disqualification

3.93

Where a court disqualifies someone under s 34(1),[204] and it appears to the court that that person owns or keeps any animal forbidden by the order,[205] it may order that all animals he owns or keeps contrary to the disqualification be taken into possession.

3.94

Where a person is convicted of an offence under s 34(9) of owning or keeping an animal in breach of disqualification under s 34(2), the court by or before which he is convicted may order that all animals he owns or keeps in breach of the disqualification be taken into possession.[206]

3.95

Where an animal is seized in either of those circumstances from an owner, the animal will be ordered to be disposed of,[207] (which can include destruction)[208] providing that the court:

- has given the owner of the animal an opportunity to be heard;[209] or

- is satisfied that it is not reasonably practicable to communicate with the owner.[210]

3.96

If an order for disposal is so made, the owner may appeal in the usual ways: from the magistrates' court to the Crown Court,[211] and from the Crown Court to the Court of Appeal.[212]

3.97

Where the animal is seized from a keeper (as opposed to an owner who is disqualified) the animal 'shall be dealt with in such manner as the appropriate court may order'.[213] For these purposes, the appropriate court is either the court

---

204 AWA 2006, s 35(1)(a).
205 AWA 2006, s 35(1)(b).
206 AWA 2006, s 35(2).
207 AWA 2006, s 35(3).
208 AWA 2006, s 35(8).
209 AWA 2006, s 35(5)(a).
210 AWA 2006, s 35(5)(b).
211 AWA 2006, s 35(6)(a).
212 AWA 2006, s 35(6)(b).
213 AWA 2006, s 35(4).

that made the order,[214] or (if the order was made by a magistrates' court) any magistrates' court in the same local justice area.[215]

3.98

When a court makes an order under s 35, it may:

- appoint a person to carry out, or arrange for the carrying out of, the order;[216]

- require any person who has possession of an animal to which the order applies to deliver it up to enable the order to be carried out;[217]

- give directions with respect to the carrying out of the order,[218] (including specifying the manner of disposal,[219] or delegate the decision about the manner of disposal to the person appointed to carry out, or arrange for the carrying out, of an order[220]);

- confer additional powers (including entry to premises where an animal to which the order applies is being kept) for the purpose of, or in connection with, the carrying out of the order;[221]

- order the person subject to disqualification, or another person, to reimburse the expenses of carrying out the order.[222] If the owner of an animal ordered to be disposed of under s 35 is subject to a liability for such costs, any amount to which he is entitled from the sale of the animal may be reduced by that amount.[223]

3.99

In determining how to exercise its powers, the court (or any person acting under a delegated power from s 35(2)(b)[224]) shall have regard, amongst other things, to:

- the desirability of protecting the value of any animal to which the order applies;[225] and

- the desirability of avoiding increasing any expenses which a person may be ordered to reimburse.[226]

---

214 AWA 2006, s 35(7)(a).
215 AWA 2006, s 35(7)(b).
216 AWA 2006, s 36(1)(a).
217 AWA 2006, s 36(1)(b).
218 AWA 2006, s 36(1)(c).
219 AWA 2006, s 36(2)(a).
220 AWA 2006, s 36(2)(b).
221 AWA 2006, s 36(1)(d).
222 AWA 2006, s 36(1)(e).
223 AWA 2006, s 36(5).
224 AWA 2006, s 36(4).
225 AWA 2006, s 36(3)(a).
226 AWA 2006, s 36(3)(b).

Sections 37 and 38 – destruction

3.100

The court by or before which a person is convicted of an offence under any of ss 4, 5, 6(1) and (2), 7, 8(1) and (2) (including an animal which took part in an animal fight in relation to which the offence was committed[227]) or 9 may order the destruction of the victim animal if it is satisfied, on the basis of evidence given by a veterinary surgeon, that to do so is in the interests of the animal.[228]

3.101

Where an animal has been involved in a fighting offence under s 8(1) or (2), the court may order its destruction for reasons other than the interests of the animal.[229] It seems most likely that this would cover a situation where the animal was the aggressor in such a situation but had not itself suffered any harm.

3.102

Where a court makes such an order, it may:

- appoint a person to carry out, or arrange for the carrying out of, the order;[230]

- require a person who has possession of the animal to deliver it up to enable the order to be carried out;[231]

- give directions with respect to the carrying out of the order (including directions about how the animal is to be dealt with until it is destroyed);[232]

- confer additional powers (including power to enter premises where the animal is being kept) for the purpose of, or in connection with, the carrying out of the order;[233]

- order the offender or another person to reimburse the expenses of carrying out the order.[234]

The same powers are granted in relation to a s 38 order.[235]

---

227 AWA 2006, s 37(6).
228 AWA 2006, s 37(1).
229 AWA 2006, s 38(1).
230 AWA 2006, s 37(3)(a).
231 AWA 2006, s 37(3)(b).
232 AWA 2006, s 37(3)(c).
233 AWA 2006, s 37(3)(d).
234 AWA 2006, s 37(3)(e).
235 AWA 2006, s 38(3)(a)–(e).

3.103

A court may not make an order for destruction unless it has given the owner of the animal an opportunity to be heard,[236] or it is satisfied that it is not reasonably practicable to communicate with the owner.[237] This applies equally to an order under s 38.[238]

3.104

Where a court makes a destruction order, each defendant and the owner (if different)[239] may:

- where the order is made by a magistrates' court, appeal to the Crown Court;[240]

- where the order is made by the Crown Court, appeal to the Court of Appeal.[241]

Unless the court by which the order is made directs that it is in the interests of the animal that it should be destroyed without delay.[242]

Section 39 – reimbursement of expenses where animal involved in fighting offence

3.105

The court by or before which a person is convicted of an offence under s 8(1) or (2) may order the offender or another person to reimburse any expenses incurred by the police in connection with the keeping of an animal (including one which took part in a fight[243]) in relation to which the offence was committed.[244]

Section 40 – forfeiture of equipment

3.106

Where a person is convicted of an offence under any of ss 4, 5, 6(1) and (2), 7 or 8, the court by or before which he is convicted may order any qualifying

---

236 AWA 2006, s 37(2)(a).
237 AWA 2006, s 37(2)(b).
238 AWA 2006, s 38(2)(a) and (b).
239 Or under s 38(4), only if the animal is owned by someone other than the defendant.
240 AWA 2006, s 37(4)(a).
241 AWA 2006, s 37(4)(b).
242 AWA 2006, s 37(5) – note that this proviso does not exist under s 38 where an animal involved in a fighting offence is being destroyed for reasons other than its own interests.
243 AWA 2006, s 39(2).
244 AWA 2006, s 39(1).

item which is shown to the satisfaction of the court to relate to the offence to be forfeited,[245] and destroyed or dealt with in such manner as may be specified in the order.[246]

3.107

However, the court shall not order anything to be forfeited if a person claiming to be the owner, or otherwise interested in it, applies to be heard, unless he has been given an opportunity to show cause why the order should not be made.

3.108

Qualifying items are specified in the case of a conviction for each offence as follows:[247]

- s 4 – anything designed or adapted for causing suffering to an animal;

- s 5 – anything designed or adapted for carrying out a prohibited procedure on an animal;

- s 6(1) or (2) – anything designed or adapted for removing the whole or any part of a dog's tail;

- s 7 – anything designed or adapted for administering any drug or substance to an animal;

- s 8(1) or (2) – anything designed or adapted for use in connection with an animal fight; and

- s 8(3) – a video recording of an animal fight, including anything on or in which the recording is kept.

Vehicles – Environmental Protection Act 1990, s 33C

3.109

The Environmental Protection Act (EPA) 1990, s 33C applies where a person is convicted of:

- an offence (but not a 'relevant offence'[248] unless committed by an establishment or undertaking)[249] under s 33(1) of depositing or disposing of controlled waste;[250]

---

245 AWA 2006, s 40(1)(a).
246 AWA 2006, s 40(1)(b).
247 All expressions have the same meaning as in the provision referred to in the paragraph (EPA 1990, s 40(4)).
248 Defined under EPA 1990, s 33(10).
249 EPA 1990, s 33C(1A).
250 EPA 1990, s 33C(1)(a).

- an offence under reg 38(1) of the Environmental Permitting (England and Wales) Regulations (EPR) 2016[251] in respect of an offence under reg 12 consisting of the disposal of waste.[252]

3.110

The court by or before which the offender is convicted may make an order under this section if:

- the court is satisfied that a vehicle[253] was used in or for the purposes of the commission of the offence;[254] and

- at the time of his conviction the offender has rights in the vehicle.[255]

3.111

In considering whether to make an order under this section a court must in particular have regard to:

- the value of the vehicle;[256]

- the likely financial and other effects on the offender of the making of the order (taken together with any other order that the court contemplates making);[257]

- the offender's need to use the vehicle for lawful purposes;[258]

- whether, in a case where it appears to the court that the offender is engaged in a business which consists wholly or partly of activities which are unlawful by virtue of s 33, or EPR 2016, reg 38(1) or (2), the making of the order is likely to inhibit the offender from engaging in further such activities.[259]

3.112

Such an order operates to deprive the offender of his rights in the vehicle (including its fuel) at the time of his conviction and to vest those rights in the

---

251 SI 2016/1154.
252 EPA 1990, s 33C(1)(b).
253 As defined in EPA 1990, s 33C(10) as 'any motor vehicle or trailer within the meaning of the Road Traffic Regulation Act 1984 or any mobile plant'.
254 EPA 1990, s 33C(2)(a).
255 EPA 1990, s 33C(2)(b).
256 EPA 1990, s 33C(7)(a).
257 EPA 1990, s 33C(7)(b).
258 EPA 1990, s 33C(7)(c).
259 EPA 1990, s 33C(7)(d).

relevant enforcement authority,[260,261] which may take possession of the vehicle (if it has not already done so under s 34C).[262]

3.113

Where a vehicle has been seized under s 34B and the offender retains rights in any of the vehicle's contents, an order under this section may, to any extent it so specifies, deprive the offender of those rights and vest them in the relevant enforcement authority.[263] Where a vehicle or its contents have been seized under s 34B in connection with the offence to which s 33C applies, any transfer by D, after the seizure and before his conviction, of any of his rights in the vehicle or its contents is of no effect.[264]

3.114

The court may make an order under this section whether or not it also deals with D in any other way for the offence,[265] but PCC(S)A 2000, s 143 (power to deprive offender of property) does not apply where this section applies.[266]

Health and Safety at Work etc Act 1974, s 42

3.115

Where a person is convicted of an offence under any of the relevant statutory provisions in the Health and Safety at Work etc Act (HSWA) 1974 in respect of any matters which appear to the court to be matters which it is in his power to remedy, the court may, in addition to or instead of imposing any punishment, order him, within such time as may be fixed by the order, to take such steps as may be specified in the order for remedying those matters.[267]

3.116

The time fixed by such an order may be extended or further extended by order of the court on an application made before the end of that time as originally fixed or as extended under this subsection, as the case may be.[268]

---

260 EPA 1990, s 33C(3).
261 *'relevant enforcement authority'* means: the Environment Agency (EPA 1990, s 33C(10)(a)), or the Natural Resources Body for Wales (s 33C(10)(aa)), depending upon which body on whose behalf proceedings in respect of the offence were brought, or in any other case, the waste collection authority in whose area the offence was committed (s 33C(10)(b)).
262 EPA 1990, s 33C(5).
263 EPA 1990, s 33C(4).
264 EPA 1990, s 33C(9).
265 EPA 1990, s 33C(6).
266 EPA 1990, s 33C(8).
267 HSWA 1974, s 42(1).
268 HSWA 1974, s 42(2).

3.117

Where a person is ordered to remedy a matter, they shall not be liable under HSWA 1974 in respect of those matters during the time fixed by the order or any further time allowed.[269]

3.118

If D is convicted of an offence consisting of acquiring or attempting to acquire, possessing or using an explosive article or substance (within the meaning of any of the relevant statutory provisions) in contravention of any of the relevant statutory provisions then the court has a forfeiture power.[270]

3.119

The court by or before which D is convicted may order the article or substance in question to be forfeited and either destroyed or dealt with in such other manner as the court may order.[271] This may not happen before a person claiming to be the owner of or otherwise interested in it has been given the opportunity to be heard to show cause why the order should not be made.[272]

Any item involved in breach of a serious crime prevention order

3.120

If a person is convicted of breaching a serious crime prevention order (SCPO) under s 25 of the Serious Crime Act (SCA) 2007 the court may order forfeiture of anything in the person's possession at the time of the offence and which it considers to have been involved in the offence.[273] It must first give any person claiming to be an owner or having an interest in the thing, opportunity to make representations.[274]

3.121

Such an order can only come into force once there is no possibility of it being varied or set aside on appeal.[275] The court may order other provisions it considers necessary to give effect to the order,[276] including provision in relation to handling, destruction or other disposal of the item forfeited.[277]

---

269 HSWA 1974, s 42(3).
270 HSWA 1974, s 42(3A).
271 HSWA 1974, s 42(4).
272 HSWA 1974, s 42(5).
273 SCA 2007, s 26(1).
274 SCA 2007, s 26(2).
275 SCA 2007, s 26(3).
276 SCA 2007, s 26(4).
277 SCA 2007, s 26(5).

Forfeiture on customs and excise bases

3.122

There are various provisions allowing forfeiture of items which have been brought into the jurisdiction without the appropriate tax or fees being paid, or items that assisted in doing so. These are contained within the Customs and Excise Management Act (CEMA) 1979. There are 11 sections of that Act that contain provisions allowing forfeiture in some form. They are summarised here for brief reference, with the most common ones set out with their key cases, but practitioners undertaking a case where they arise would be best advised to refer to a specialist text on customs cases for a full exposition of the law and precedent, including matters such as lawfulness of seizure and restoration.

3.123

Schedule 3 of CEMA 1979 provides the procedural steps that must be complied with for forfeiture to be lawful.

Goods improperly imported – CEMA 1979, s 49

3.124

Where (except as provided by or under the Customs and Excise Acts 1979):[278]

- any imported goods, liable on their importation to customs or excise duty, are, without payment of that duty:
    - unshipped in any port;[279]
    - unloaded from any aircraft in the UK;[280]
    - unloaded from any vehicle in, or otherwise brought across the boundary into, Northern Ireland;[281] or
    - removed from their place of importation or from any approved wharf, examination station or transit shed;[282] or
- any goods are imported, landed or unloaded contrary to any prohibition or restriction for the time being in force with respect thereto under or by virtue of any enactment;[283] or

---

278 The reference to the Customs and Excise Acts 1979 is a conjoined reference to Customs and Excise Duties (General Reliefs) Act 1979, and Customs and Excise Management Act 1979.
279 CEMA 1979, s 49(1)(a)(i).
280 CEMA 1979, s 49(1)(a)(ii).
281 CEMA 1979, s 49(1)(a)(iii).
282 CEMA 1979, s 49(1)(a)(iv).
283 CEMA 1979, s 49(1)(b).

- any goods, being goods chargeable with any duty or goods the importation of which is for the time being prohibited or restricted by or under any enactment, are found, whether before or after their unloading, to have been concealed on board any ship or aircraft or, while in Northern Ireland, in any vehicle;[284] or

- any goods are imported concealed in a container holding goods of a different description;[285] or

- any imported goods are found, whether before or after delivery, not to correspond with the entry made thereof;[286] or

- any imported goods are concealed or packed in any manner appearing to be intended to deceive an officer,

those goods shall, subject to the following exclusion, be liable to forfeiture.[287]

3.125

Where any goods, the importation of which is for the time being prohibited or restricted by or under any enactment, are on their importation either:

- reported as intended for exportation in the same ship, aircraft or vehicle;[288] or

- entered for transit or transhipment;[289] or

- entered to be warehoused for exportation or for use as stores,[290]

the Commissioners may, if they see fit, permit the goods to be dealt with accordingly.

3.126

It was held in *Commissioners of Customs and Excise v Newbury*,[291] that liability to forfeiture did not depend upon the lawfulness of the seizure, which was dependent upon the lawfulness of the interception of the travellers.[292] The High Court further held that excise goods are liable to forfeiture in a case where they are imported without payment of duty for others who have given the importer the money to buy them.[293] When a court is deciding whether property is liable to forfeiture it needs to consider whether forfeiture would be so disproportionate as to be in breach of the particular claimant's rights under

---

284 CEMA 1979, s 49(1)(c).
285 CEMA 1979, s 49(1)(d).
286 CEMA 1979, s 49(1)(e).
287 CEMA 1979, s 49(1)(f).
288 CEMA 1979, s 49(2)(a).
289 CEMA 1979, s 49(2)(b).
290 CEMA 1979, s 49(2)(c).
291 [2003] EWHC 702 (Admin).
292 *Newbury*, at [5].
293 *Newbury*, at [6] and [35].

Article 1, Protocol 1 to the European Convention on Human Rights (ECHR) (peaceful enjoyment of possessions) and both can be resolved by the court. It is not strictly a question of discretion but a matter upon which the court is entitled to reach its own independent judgment.[294]

3.127

There need be no more than a reference, however, to the court's awareness of the requirement for proportionality in making any order that it did. If no express point is taken on proportionality at first instance, an appellant will struggle to convince the appellate court that the order was disproportionate.[295]

3.128

When considering seizure of a vehicle, the customs officer must have regard to all facts apparent once D has had an opportunity to explain his case and the circumstances of the seizure.[296]

3.129

It has been held that for importation for personal use the importer must be physically present at the moment of importation,[297] even if there is no evidence whatsoever that the goods are for commercial use, and they have been brought in by a private employee of the importer, who is unable to travel himself due to disability.[298] The High Court raised an issue that this was disproportionate, and clearly disapproved of the result of the European jurisprudence.[299]

Vehicles used in connection with goods liable to forfeiture – CEMA 1979, s 141

3.130

Without prejudice to any other provision of the Customs and Excise Acts 1979, where any thing has become liable to forfeiture under the Acts:

- any ship, aircraft, vehicle, animal, container (including any article of passengers' baggage) or other thing whatsoever which has been used for the carriage, handling, deposit or concealment of the thing so liable to forfeiture, either at a time when it was so liable or for the purposes of the commission of the offence for which it later became so liable;[300] and

---

294 *Newbury,* at [7] and [35].
295 *R (Bartholomew) v HMRC* [2005] EWHC 1666 (Admin), at [12]–[14].
296 *Staniszewski v Director of Border Revenue* [2017] UKFTT 0845 (TC), at [51]–[53].
297 *Stern v Director of Border Revenue* [2013] EWHC 553 (Admin), at [6] and [13].
298 *Stern,* at [12] and [14].
299 *Stern,* at [14].
300 CEMA 1979, s 141(1)(a).

- any other thing mixed, packed or found with the thing so liable,[301]

shall also be liable to forfeiture.

3.131

These two subsections of s 141 are to be read disjunctively, meaning that anything mixed, packed or found with material liable to forfeiture can itself be liable to forfeiture, although the Commissioners have a discretion not to require such forfeiture.[302]

3.132

Where any ship, aircraft, vehicle or animal has become liable to forfeiture under the Customs and Excise Acts under any power, all tackle, apparel or furniture thereof shall also be liable to forfeiture.[303]

3.133

Where any of the following, that is to say:

- any ship not exceeding 100 tons register;[304]

- any aircraft;[305] or

- any hovercraft,[306]

becomes liable to forfeiture under this section by reason of having been used in the importation, exportation or carriage of goods contrary to or for the purpose of contravening any prohibition or restriction for the time being in force with respect to those goods, or without payment having been made of, or security given for, any duty payable thereon, the owner and the master or commander shall each be liable on summary conviction to a penalty equal to the value of the ship/aircraft/hovercraft or £20,000, whichever is the lesser.

3.134

For the purposes of this provision, the Court of Appeal has held that the Commissioners must differentiate between those using their vehicles for commercial smuggling (ie that done for a profit),[307] and those importing goods for social distribution to family and friends, when considering whether to seek forfeiture of a vehicle. Where there is not commercial importation, each case must be considered on its facts.[308] The Court held that proportionality

---

301 CEMA 1979, s 141(1)(b).
302 *Travell v Customs and Excise Commissioner* (1998) 162 JP 181.
303 CEMA 1979, s 141(2).
304 CEMA 1979, s 141(3)(a).
305 CEMA 1979, s 141(3)(b).
306 CEMA 1979, s 141(3)(c).
307 *Lindsay v Commissioners of Customs and Excise* [2002] EWCA Civ 267, at [63].
308 *Lindsay*, at [64].

required this distinction to be drawn, and that there must be consideration of the car's value.[309]

3.135

It has been held that the court has no choice but to condemn as forfeited such a vehicle which at the material time had been used for the carriage of goods adjudged as liable to forfeiture. Taken in conjunction with CEMA 1979, Sch 3, para 6, it is clear that where the court has adjudged that the relevant thing was liable to forfeiture, the court must then condemn it as forfeited. It has no residual discretion.[310] This power of forfeiture is not dependent upon the owner of the vehicle having had any knowledge of what was being carried within it.[311]

3.136

The European Court of Human Rights later ruled that the seizure of the aircraft from the owner, Air Canada (AC), was lawful. It held that to seize an aircraft found carrying prohibited drugs and release it only in return for payment did not contravene Article 1 of the First Protocol to the ECHR on quiet enjoyment of property rights because Member States were entitled to control the use of property in so far as to do so was proportionate to enforce policy in the general public interest. In the instant case the seizure of the plane was not disproportionate to the aim of encouraging AC to improve its security, bearing in mind the way security had lapsed, the value of the drugs found and the history of security lapses by the airline.[312]

3.137

Any recourse against this comes from the restoration procedure (including appeals from and reviews of it) available to those whose vehicles are seized under CEMA 1979, s 152 (see other texts for full coverage of the restoration regime).[313]

Interaction between s 49 and s 141

3.138

Where there is a power to forfeit arising under both s 49 and s 141 (because there are dutiable goods and others mixed with them), the court need not decide and specify what fraction of the goods is to be forfeited under which provision.[314]

---

309 *Lindsay*, at [65].
310 *R (Customs and Excise Commissioners) v Helman* [2002] EWHC 2254 (Admin), at [34].
311 *Customs and Excise Commissioners v Air Canada* [1991] 2 QB 446, at 467.
312 *Air Canada v UK* (1995) 20 EHRR 150.
313 *Air Canada v UK,* at [35].
314 *R (Bartholomew) v HMRC* [2005] EWHC 1666 (Admin), at [15].

3.139

If two Ds have goods in a vehicle, and the goods belonging to one become liable to seizure only because they are mixed or packed with the goods of the other, it has been held that s 141(1)(b) only bites where the court finds as a fact in the proceedings relating to the seized goods that other goods are liable to forfeiture and that the seized goods are mixed, packed or found with those other goods:[315]

> 'As a matter of common sense and as a matter of common justice it must be open to the owner of the seized goods (in this case Mr Fox) to challenge the facts relied on to establish the liability to forfeiture of the other party's (in this case Mr Everett's) goods. It is nothing to the point that the other party (in this case Mr Everett) declines to make a claim or attend the hearing, and default decisions are accordingly mandated by the 1979 Act in respect of Mr Everett's Goods.'[316]

Ships – CEMA 1979, ss 88–91

3.140

Sections 88–91 cover the position of ships that are used to bring in dutiable goods on which no duty has been paid.

3.141

Section 88 provides that where:

- a ship is or has been in UK waters;[317] or

- an aircraft is or has been at any place, whether on land or on water, in the UK;[318] or

- a vehicle is or has been within the limits of any port or at any aerodrome or, while in Northern Ireland, within the prescribed area,[319]

while constructed, adapted, altered or fitted in any manner for the purpose of concealing goods, that ship, aircraft or vehicle shall be liable to forfeiture.

3.142

Much of the case law concerning s 88 relates to restoration of items forfeited – an area outside the scope of this text, but practitioners involved in a case where

---

315 *Fox v HM Customs and Excise* [2002] EWHC 1244 (Admin), at [17].
316 Mr E's goods were liable to forfeiture in their own right; Mr F's were only liable as they were mixed with Mr E's.
317 CEMA 1979, s 88(1)(a).
318 CEMA 1979, s 88(1)(b).
319 CEMA 1979, s 88(1)(c).

forfeiture by the Commissioners looks likely should be familiar with that body of case law.

3.143

Section 89 provides that if any part of the cargo of a ship is thrown overboard or is staved or destroyed to prevent seizure:

- while the ship is in UK waters;[320] or

- where the ship, having been properly summoned to bring to by any vessel in the service of Her Majesty, fails so to do and chase is given, at any time during the chase,[321]

the ship shall be liable to forfeiture.

3.144

For the purposes of this section a ship shall be deemed to have been properly summoned to bring to:

- if the vessel making the summons did so by means of an international signal code or other recognised means and while flying her proper ensign;[322] and

- in the case of a ship which is not a British ship, if at the time when the summons was made the ship was in UK waters.[323]

3.145

Section 90 provides that where a ship has been within the limits of any port in the UK or Isle of Man, or an aircraft has been in the UK or Isle of Man, with cargo on board and a substantial part of that cargo is afterwards found in the UK to be missing, then, if the master of the ship or commander of the aircraft fails to account for it to the satisfaction of the Commissioners, the ship or aircraft shall be liable to forfeiture.

Special provisions for large ships – CEMA 1979, ss 142 and 143

3.146

Notwithstanding any other provision of the Customs and Excise Acts 1979, a ship of 250 or more tons register shall not be liable to forfeiture under or by virtue of any provision of the Customs and Excise Acts 1979, except under s 88 (see 3.141), unless the offence in respect of or in connection with which the forfeiture is claimed:

---

320 CEMA 1979, s 89(1)(a).
321 CEMA 1979, s 89(1)(b).
322 CEMA 1979, s 89(2)(a).
323 CEMA 1979, s 89(2)(b).

- was substantially the object of the voyage during which the offence was committed;[324] or

- was committed while the ship was under chase by a vessel in the service of Her Majesty after failing to bring to when properly summoned to do so by that vessel.[325]

3.147

A ship shall be deemed to have been properly summoned to bring to:

- if the vessel making the summons did so by means of an international signal code or other recognised means and while flying her proper ensign;[326] and

- in the case of a ship which is not a British ship, if at the time when the summons was made the ship was in UK waters.[327]

3.148

All hovercraft (of whatever size) shall be treated as ships of less than 250 tons register.[328]

3.149

The exemption from forfeiture of any ship under this section shall not affect any liability to forfeiture of goods carried in it.[329]

3.150

However, s 143 provides for a nominal penalty where s 142 applies. Where:

- any ship of 250 or more tons register would, without the application of s 142, be liable to forfeiture for, or in connection with, any offence under the Customs and Excise Acts 1979,[330] and

- in the opinion of the Commissioners, a responsible officer of the ship is implicated either by the officer's own act, or by neglect, in that offence.[331]

For the purposes of this section:

- 'responsible officer' means a person who is, or is acting as, the master, a mate, an engineer or the bosun of the ship and, in the case of a ship carrying a passenger certificate, the purser or chief steward;[332]

---

324 CEMA 1979, s 142(1)(a).
325 CEMA 1979, s 142(1)(b).
326 CEMA 1979, s 142(2)(a).
327 CEMA 1979, s 142(2)(b).
328 CEMA 1979, s 142(3) and s 143(2).
329 CEMA 1979, s 142(4).
330 CEMA 1979, s 143(1)(a).
331 CEMA 1979, s 143(1)(b).
332 CEMA 1979, s 143(6)(a).

- without prejudice to any other grounds upon which a responsible officer of any ship may be held to be implicated by neglect, he may be so held if goods not owned to by any member of the crew are discovered in a place under that officer's supervision in which they could not reasonably have been put if he had exercised proper care at the time of the loading of the ship or subsequently.[333]

3.151

The Commissioners may take proceedings in accordance with CEMA 1979, Sch 3, in like manner as they might but for s 142 have taken proceedings for the condemnation of the ship if notice of claim had been given in respect thereof, for the condemnation of the ship in such sum not exceeding £10,000 as the court may see fit.[334]

3.152

The Commissioners may require such sum as they see fit, not exceeding £10,000, to be deposited with them to await the decision of the court, and may detain the ship until that sum has been so deposited.[335]

3.153

No claim shall lie against the Commissioners for damages in respect of the payment of any deposit or the detention of any ship under s 143.[336]

Goods on which excise duty evaded – CEMA 1979, s 170B

3.154

If any person is convicted of being knowingly concerned in the taking of any steps with a view to the fraudulent evasion, whether by himself or another, of any excise duty on any goods[337] those goods shall be liable to forfeiture.[338]

3.155

In *Amber Services Europe Ltd v Director of Border Revenue*,[339] the High Court held that where no criminal proceedings had been brought, an application on complaint for return of goods seized as part of a criminal investigation by the Commissioners would fail. Although there had been no criminal conviction

---

333 CEMA 1979, s 143(6)(b).
334 CEMA 1979, s 143(3).
335 CEMA 1979, s 143(4).
336 CEMA 1979, s 143(5).
337 CEMA 1979, s 170B(1).
338 CEMA 1979, s 170B(2).
339 [2015] EWHC 3665 (Admin).

under s 170B(1), such a conviction was not a pre-requisite to the civil penalty of forfeiture in s 170B(2).[340]

For breach of certain customs or excise conditions – CEMA 1979, s 124

3.156

Where:

- any imported goods have been relieved from customs or excise duty chargeable on their importation or have been charged with duty at a reduced rate;[341] and

- any condition or other obligation required to be complied with in connection with the relief or with the charge of duty at that rate is not complied with,[342]

the goods shall be liable to forfeiture.

3.157

This applies whether or not any undertaking or security has been given for compliance with the condition or obligation or for the payment of the reduced duty payable, and the forfeiture shall not affect any liability of any person who has given any such undertaking or security.[343]

Forfeiture of spirits – CEMA 1979, s 140

3.158

Where, by any provision of, or of any instrument made under, the Customs and Excise Acts 1979, any spirits become liable to forfeiture by reason of some offence committed by a revenue trader, then:

- where that provision specifies the quantity of those spirits but does not specify the spirits so liable, the Commissioners may seize the equivalent of that quantity from any other spirits in the stock of that trader;[344] and

- where that provision specifies the spirits so liable the Commissioners may, if they think fit, seize instead of the spirits so specified an equivalent quantity of any other spirits in the stock of that trader.[345]

---

340 *Amber Services Europe Ltd*, at [26], [28] and [29].
341 CEMA 1979, s 124(1)(a).
342 CEMA 1979, s 124(1)(b).
343 CEMA 1979, s 124(2).
344 CEMA 1979, s 140(1)(a).
345 CEMA 1979, s 140(1)(b).

3.159

For these reasons it is important to ascertain the ownership of the items, which can be complicated if they are in a bonded warehouse, as only the owner of the goods can duly give notice of a claim that those goods are not liable to forfeiture, and thus seek to have them returned.[346]

3.160

Under CEMA 1979, s 140, spirits only become liable to forfeiture if an offence has been committed by a revenue trader. Removal of goods under an approved deferment arrangement would not be an offence. Non-payment is not an offence, so there would be no power to seize the goods removed or an equivalent quantity in the warehouse. Similar considerations apply in relation to import VAT.[347]

---

346 *Everwine Limited v Commissioner for Customs and Excise* [2003] EWCA Civ 953, at [9] and [10].
347 *Forth Wines Ltd v Commissioners of HMRC* [2012] UKFTT 74 (TC), at [35].

4   Compensation Orders

4.01

- The court MUST consider making a compensation order where an offence has caused loss to another.

- Compensation is to be prioritised over the payment of fines, costs, and any other financial orders.

- When making a compensation order, the court MUST have regard to the defendant (D)'s means.

- A compensation order will not be appropriate where there are factual complexities meaning the extent of the loss is not straightforwardly apparent.

- In *Stapylton* the Court of Appeal emphasised the following key principles:[1]

    - the court has no jurisdiction to make an order where there are real issues as to whether the recipient has suffered any, and if so what, loss;

    - there must be evidence of loss;

    - compensation orders are for straightforward cases;

    - a court should not embark on a detailed inquiry as to the extent of any injury, loss, or damage – that is better done through civil proceedings;

    - compensation orders must not be made unless there is a realistic prospect of compliance; and

    - orders should not be made if payment will take a long time, although much will turn on the nature of the offence and the offender.

4.02

Provisions relating to compensation in criminal matters are largely contained within ss 130–133 of the Powers of Criminal Courts (Sentencing) Act (PCC(S) A) 2000, as amended by various later statutes.

4.03

From 3 December 2012, s 63 of the Legal Aid, Sentencing and Punishment of Offenders Act (LASPOA) 2012 inserted s 130(2A) into the PCC(S)A 2000 providing: 'A court MUST consider making a compensation order in any

---

1   [2012] EWCA Crim 728.

case where this section empowers it to do so' (emphasis added). The court is empowered to do so where an offender has caused loss to another resulting from the offence.

4.04

For this reason, the legislation and case law surrounding the making of compensation orders is especially relevant; recent cases have shown that even in what may appear to be a very straightforward area, experienced judges nonetheless may overlook the basics when they order compensation.

4.05

A court imposing a compensation order must have regard to the offender's means 'so far as they appear or are known to the court' (see PCC(S)A 2000, s 130(11)). There is a longstanding principle that an order should not be made in such an amount that the offender will have no prospect of paying within a reasonable period of time,[2] and this principle continues to be applied today.[3] It is important as failure to pay is a criminal (not civil) matter, carrying a penal sanction. What amounts to a 'reasonable period of time' will depend upon the context of the case.

4.06

Thus, the basic position is that in any case where there has been quantifiable loss, there is likely to be an application for compensation. Even if there is not such an application, the court can consider the issue of its own volition. If a court does not make a compensation order it must say why.[4] If there are multiple victims who are to receive compensation, a separate compensation order must be made in relation to each one.[5]

4.07

For an offender over 18, there is now no limit on the amount of compensation that they can be ordered to pay by the magistrates' court.[6] This brings its position into alignment with the Crown Court, which has long had unlimited powers.

4.08

While the court's powers are very widely drawn, the Court of Appeal has stated that compensation orders should only be made in simple, straightforward

---

2   *Webb* (1979) 1 Cr App R (S) 16.
3   *Cooper & Cooper* [2017] EWCA Crim 262.
4   PCC(S)A 2000, s 130(3).
5   *Inwood* (1974) 60 Cr App R 70, at 74.
6   Prior to 2013, the Magistrates' Courts Act (MCA) 1980, s 40(1) meant that the maximum amount of compensation that a magistrates' court could order was £5,000 per charge (see PCC(S)A 2000, s 133 for the position on offences to be taken into consideration (TiCs)). However, Sch 16, para 8(1) to the Crime and Courts Act 2013 amended PCC(S)A 2000, s 131 to remove this limit.

cases.[7] These will usually be those where the facts leading to the entitlement to compensation are either plainly simple, or are not disputed.

Amount

4.09

When considering compensation orders:

- They are ultimately a decision for the court.

- The defendant's means must be taken into account.

- Supporting evidence is not required, but will strengthen an application for compensation. Evidence may need to be heard.

4.10

Compensation shall be the amount the court considers appropriate, taking into account any evidence and representations by the prosecution and defence.[8] A compensation application will be stronger where there is evidence in support, for example an estimate or receipt for the repair where damage has been caused, or proof of financial loss in the case of fraud. 'Loss' may include a sum representing interest.

4.11

In *Schofield*,[9] the Court was concerned with the forerunner legislation to the PCC(S)A 2000 – the Powers of Criminal Courts Act 1973. Section 35(1) of that Act read,

> '… a court by or before which a person is convicted of an offence, in addition to dealing with him in any other way, may, on application or otherwise, make an order (in this Act referred to as "a compensation order") requiring him to pay compensation for any personal injury, loss or damage resulting from that offence, or any other offence which is taken into consideration by the court in determining sentence.'

4.12

The Court held that 'loss' in the statute meant any kind of loss, and where this is financial loss, the court may, in a straightforward case, include a sum by way of interest equivalent to that the victim would be likely to recover if he pursued his claim in the civil courts.

---

7   *White* (1996) 2 Cr App R (S) 58.
8   PCC(S)A 2000, s 130(4).
9   [1978] 1 WLR 979.

4.13

Where the only realistic prospect of recovering money is through a compensation order and the amount is in dispute then a minimum agreed loss can be used to ensure that an order is made. Where a case concerned 20 counts of false accounting by a business adviser,[10] and the method of calculation of the loss caused by the appellant's actions was contested between the parties, the judge had erred in making an order for a sum greater than that proffered by counsel. That sum, of £5,000, was said to represent a compromise between the amount the appellant believed he owed, and what he could realistically afford to pay. The first instance judge had taken an arithmetical approach by deducting the total value of invoices for work undertaken from the total value of monies passing to the appellant from the complainant's businesses; the difference between the two was £13,200.

4.14

The Court of Appeal reduced the sum of the compensation order, in part because they had heard evidence which assisted in more accurately determining the figure owed. They explained their approach:[11]

'We have concluded that the appropriate approach is to take the lowest figure which could have been due and owing by the appellant to Mrs Titley's companies, namely the figure of £12,253.55. We must necessarily, as we have done through these calculations, round up or down as we think fit. Accordingly, in relation to the missing invoice, it seems to us that if a compensation order is to be made, a sum approximating £4,253 can be deducted in relation to that missing invoice; that would leave a round figure of £8,000.

We must of course consider whether it is good practice in circumstances such as this to make a compensation order. We have concluded that where a court is of the opinion that a complete reconciliation as between the parties would present a complex and difficult task but that the calculation of the minimum loss arising is a comparatively simple task, and that it would be in the interests of justice to make a compensation order in a sum representing the minimum loss arising, it should make such an order rather than decline on grounds of complexity.

In the particular circumstances of this case, we share a view, which HHJ Boggis had no doubt reached, that to expect the losing party here to seek recompense in the civil courts, having regard to the amount of money involved and the complexity of the matter, coupled with the appellant's prison sentence, would be wholly unrealistic. The only real

---

10   *James* [2003] EWCA Crim 811.
11   *James*, at [14]–[16].

possibility of compensation being paid would be if a compensation order was made. Since it could be made by comparatively simple calculations, it is our view that it should be made.'

4.15

Even where information is incomplete, the courts do have discretion to make an assessment of the quantum to be awarded. However, if the claim is challenged, the court must hear evidence to determine liability.[12] In *ex p Richards* judicial review was brought of the decision of the justices to award £164 compensation to the victims of thefts from a campsite. The appellant argued that various items had been recovered by the police, and those still missing amounted to a value of less than that claimed in compensation. Considering the provisions of the 1973 Act, the Court of Appeal quashed the compensation order, stating:

'[…] in my judgment the court has no jurisdiction to make a compensation order without receiving any evidence where there are real issues raised as to whether the claimants have suffered any, and if so what, loss. The new subsection seems to contemplate that the court can make assessments and approximations where the evidence is scanty or incomplete. It can then make an order which is "appropriate." But here the applicant was challenging the basis on which any compensation could be paid. He stated that it was his belief that all the goods (apart from a black holdall) had been returned. Thereby he was declining to accept that there was any loss. In these circumstances it seems to me that justice required that the defendant should have a proper opportunity to test the grounds on which the order was to be made against him. In my view it is not enough to say that he could have given evidence himself. In a case such as the present, where there were plain issues as to liability, it was for the prosecution to place evidence before the court.'

4.16

Even with such evidence, there may be disputes as to the amount to which a complainant claims to be entitled. In *White*,[13] the appellant made an insurance claim in respect of a burglary of his home, for £12,651. The insurers paid £8,473 in settlement of the claim, as their liability in respect of certain jewellery was limited to a maximum of £6,000 by the policy. Subsequently police officers searching the appellant's home found items of jewellery for which he had claimed, together with other stolen goods. He was sentenced to a total of 15 months' imprisonment and a compensation order in favour of the insurance company in the amount of £3,500 (the value of the jewellery for which he had falsely claimed) was made. The insurance company had applied

---

12   *Horsham Justices, ex p Richards* (1985) 7 Cr App R (S) 158.
13   See fn 7.

for a compensation order in respect of the full amount that had been paid under the claim.

4.17

The appellant argued that of the total amount that he had claimed, £9,744 related to jewellery, of which £3,609 was suspect, and that there had been a potentially valid claim of £6,135. As the insurers' liability was limited to £6,000 in respect of the jewellery, the only basis for saying that the insurer had suffered a loss was that they were entitled to avoid liability for the claim on the basis of fundamental fraud. No such finding had been made. The Court of Appeal quashed the order, holding that, due to this complexity, no compensation should have been awarded. It would be open to the insurers to claim the amount paid in respect of all the property on the basis that there was a false and fraudulent claim.

4.18

Where calculating the amount of the order had required the court to decide whether to factor in that an appellant who had claimed benefit to which he was not entitled would nonetheless have been entitled to supplementary benefit at a lower rate, on appeal by way of case stated, it was held that the exercise had become too complex:[14]

'There might be circumstances in which it would be proper for a court making a compensation order in respect of unemployment benefit obtained by deception to take account of the fact that the offender would have been entitled to supplementary benefit, but only where there was no issue between the parties as to whether that course should be taken and the amount was not in dispute.'

4.19

When ordering compensation, a judge is not obliged to deduct an amount reflecting that D provided a service of some of value, albeit that the charge he levied for that service was far in excess of what was appropriate.[15]

Means to pay?

4.20

- A compensation order should only be made if it is realistic.

---

14   *Hyde v Emery* (1984) 6 Cr App R (S) 206.
15   *Williams* [2001] 1 Cr App R (S) 140.

- This might mean that it should be postponed until a later date – if, for example, D is also sentenced to immediate imprisonment on the same matter, or is serving for other matters.

- No order should be made on the assumption that a third party will pay the amount (*Inwood*),[16] or that it will be paid by way of a loan if the court is not also satisfied that D will be able to repay that loan (*Carrington*).[17]

4.21

Although there is a presumption in favour of compensation, a compensation order should not be made unless it is 'realistic' in the sense that the court is satisfied that the offender either has the means available, or will have the ability to pay within a reasonable time. Section 130(11) imposes a duty on the court to consider the means of D when deciding whether to make a compensation order and if so the amount. There is no prohibition on making a compensation order that will only take effect at a later date (for example, on release from prison) though the court should consider the likely circumstances of D at that future date, especially if a period of imprisonment is likely to lead to the loss of employment.[18]

4.22

Where a judge is considering making a compensation order s/he is under a duty to raise the matter so that a proper enquiry into means can be made by counsel, and their submissions include information about their client's financial position.[19] Where there is not a sufficient enquiry into D's means, a challenge on appeal is likely to succeed.[20]

4.23

Practitioners are encouraged to use the M100 form produced by the Ministry of Justice,[21] which allows all relevant matters to be set out readily and in an easily-reviewable format. If a client has particularly complex financial circumstances, then time taken to set out those financial affairs in a way that can be easily understood by the sentencing court is likely to make the award of compensation fairer and easier. If D is a company, then company accounts might helpfully be available for a sentencing hearing should the court wish to look at them.

---

16   (1974) 60 Cr App R 70, at 72.
17   [2014] EWCA Crim 325, at [14].
18   *Wing* [2017] EWCA Crim 633, at [18]; *Onopa* [2015] EWCA Crim 1161, at [13]–[16].
19   *Bagga* (1989) 11 Cr App R (S) 497.
20   *Bagga*, at [21].
21   Available at https://assets.publishing.service.gov.uk/government/uploads/system/uploads/attachment_data/file/688361/mc100-eng.pdf.

4.24

A compensation order should not be made against the offender on the assumption
that a third party will pay the compensation on behalf of the offender, especially
where the third parties' means to do so are unclear or conditional on them
securing further funding, eg a mortgage.[22] As the Court of Appeal stated in
Patsalos:[23]

> 'It is well-established that a compensation order should not be used
> where there is a real doubt as to whether the defendant can find the
> compensation: see *R v Inwood* (1974) 60 Cr App R 70. The prospect
> of obtaining the money from a third party by way of gift or loan is not
> necessarily to be disregarded, but the court does have to be satisfied
> that the defendant will be able to pay, and, if he proposes to borrow the
> money, that he will be able to repay the loan: *R v Carrington* [2014] 2 Cr
> App R(S) 41. If there is any doubt on the matter, then further enquiries
> should be made, including, if appropriate, the taking of evidence.'

4.25

A compensation order may be appropriate where an offender has no source of
income, but has assets which have been bought with the proceeds of the theft,[24]
but a compensation order should not be made on the basis that D will raise the
money by selling an asset when there may be difficulty in doing so.[25] There is
no general principle that a compensation order in an amount forcing the sale of
the matrimonial home will be inappropriate.[26]

4.26

When considering the appropriateness and amount of any order, the court will
also need to consider what effect other aspects of the sentence might have on
D's ability to pay compensation. For example, as illustrated in *Woodman,*[27] it
often will not be appropriate to award compensation if also giving immediate
custody such that D is likely to lose their employment. An exception to this
would be if D had a large sum of money in savings etc.

4.27

The court must not make an order based on the judge's 'suspicion' of means
that D might or might not have.[28]

---

22   *Mortimer* [1977] Crim LR 624.
23   [2016] EWCA Crim 768, at [11]–[12].
24   *Workman* (1979) 1 Cr App R (S) 335.
25   *Hackett* (1988) 10 Cr App R (S) 388.
26   *McGuire* (1992) 13 Cr App R (S) 332, at 333.
27   [2016] EWCA Crim 640.
28   *Onopa,* fn 18, at [15].

Time to pay?

4.28

- The magistrates' court will usually consider that a sum should be payable within 12 months of the order being made.

- In more serious cases it might be appropriate to have a much longer period to pay, but regard must be had to what is realistic.

4.29

It is long-established that defendants should not be ordered ordinarily to pay compensation in amounts that would leave them paying off the sum for many years to come. In *Hossain*,[29] the appellants had been committed for sentence having pleaded guilty in the magistrates' court to offences concerning the dishonest claiming of benefits.

4.30

During the course of sentencing the appellants, the judge had said:[30] 'Obviously they owe the money so they have got to find it, by good means or foul. Hopefully good means, but they have to find the money. That is the priority, that is why they are here: for cheating. ... I suppose bailiffs go in, and so on, do they not? I do not know.'[31]

4.31

The Court of Appeal observed; 'This court has also indicated that excessively long periods for payment must be avoided. Two years in a suitable case may be appropriate, or exceptionally three ([*Archbold*] paragraph 5-707).'

4.32

However, the Court then contrasted that established position with the approach of the Court in a case in which compensation orders were upheld which would take eight years and five and a half years respectively to discharge,[32] and acknowledged that there is no set figure which is an acceptable period of time within which a compensation order must be discharged in full.[33] The Court of Appeal has previously approved a figure to be paid, but allowed the appeal

---

29   [2016] EWCA Crim 1099.
30   *Hossain*, at [11].
31   Transcript, p 15B–D.
32   *Molly Ganyo, Prize Ganyo* [2011] EWCA Crim 2491: As observed by the Court, note the highly unusual circumstances of this case – the appellants had fraudulently obtained NHS bursaries for medical training. In the case of MG she had secured a well-paid job as a result of the training that she had undertaken through the bursary. Her husband, PG, had not secured a job as a result of his training, hence the lower amount awarded against him.
33   *Hossain*, fn 29, at [15].

and varied the order to the extent of giving an appellant more time to pay that figure.[34]

4.33

In *Hossain*, the Court concluded that the judge's approach had been seriously flawed, and varied the compensation orders to amounts that would be paid off by the appellants in three years, four years and four years respectively:[35]

'We consider that there were three flaws in the judge's approach. First, she directed herself that the only relevant matter was that the money should be paid back. Second, she took no account at all of the appellants' means. Third, she imposed periods of payment which were utterly unrealistic. In other words, the judge did not have regard, as she was obliged to, to the appellants' ability to pay or to whether these orders were realistic; she simply wanted to make the appellants pay back the full amounts which they had wrongly been paid within a very short space of time.

We consider that this was the wrong approach. There was simply no evidence that the appellants could repay these large amounts over the periods which the judge stipulated, and to make an assumption that they could when she had been told that they were pawns in a bigger fraud organised by others, and when she had been told what the appellants' actual means were, was untenable.'

Collection orders

4.34

The Courts Act 2003 created a fines collection scheme which provides for greater administrative enforcement of fines. This reflected the national problem of a failure by many defendants to pay the compensation, fines or costs that were ordered against them in criminal proceedings.

Attachment of earnings orders/applications for benefit deductions

4.35

Unless it would be impracticable or inappropriate to do so, the court must make an attachment of earnings order (AEO) or application for benefit deductions

---

34   *Campbell* [2015] EWCA Crim 1876.
35   *Bagga*, fn 19, at [16]–[18].

(ABD) whenever compensation is imposed.[36] In other cases, the court may make an AEO or ABD with the offender's consent.[37]

4.36

The court must make a collection order in every case in which a fine or compensation order is imposed unless this would be impracticable or inappropriate.[38] The collection order must state:

- the amount of the sum due, including the amount of any fine, compensation order or other sum;

- whether the court considers the offender to be an existing defaulter;

- whether an AEO or ABD has been made and information about the effect of the order;

- if the court has not made an AEO or ABD, the payment terms;

- if an AEO or ABD has been made, the payment terms that will apply if the AEO or ABD fails ('the reserve terms') must be stated. Often a reserve term of payment in full within 14 days is considered appropriate.

Causation

4.37

- There must be a causal relationship between the conduct of D and the loss suffered by the victim (V).

- That causal relationship must be with the particular D (where there are co-defendants) against whom the compensation order is made.

- If D has been acquitted of an offence which would establish causation, but convicted of an offence the actus reus of which did not cause the loss, no compensation order should be made.

4.38

No compensation order can be made if there is no direct causal relationship between the offending of D and the loss that has been suffered. A paradigm example is the case of *Graves*.[39] The appellant pleaded guilty to false accounting. He was the manager of a public house and was responsible for banking the takings each week. He had left the public house without permission to visit a sick relative and discovered a discrepancy of £3,000 in the takings banked for

---

36   Courts Act 2003, Sch 5, para 7A.
37   Courts Act 2003, Sch 5, para 9.
38   Courts Act 2003, Sch 5, para 12.
39   (1993) 14 Cr App R (S) 790.

that week. He falsified a bank slip to conceal the deficiency. It was accepted that the appellant had not personally benefited from the missing money. As part of his sentence he was ordered to pay £1,500 compensation. The Court of Appeal held that his offending did not cause the loss – rather his offence was a response to a loss caused by another. Therefore, no compensation order was appropriate against him.

4.39

Similarly, if D has handled stolen goods (contrary to Theft Act 1968, s 22) but is not linked to their theft and has not sold them on (or has done so, but bought them back for the purposes of returning them), it is unlikely that he will have benefitted in a way that will make a compensation order appropriate.[40] If D is convicted of possessing an article which causes injury to another, but is not convicted of any offence for which the actus reus is the infliction of that injury, a compensation order in relation to those injuries will not be appropriate.[41]

4.40

Where there are co-defendants charged with different offences, and there has been injury which is the actus reus of an offence of which only one defendant is convicted then it will be inappropriate to order compensation to be paid by both. In *Derby*,[42] the appellant pleaded guilty to affray. His co-defendant pleaded guilty to unlawful wounding contrary to s 20 of the Offences Against the Person Act 1861. The Court of Appeal quashed the compensation order against Derby – his conduct had not been the cause of the injuries suffered by the victim. It was noted that courts are not to apply strict principles of tort and contract when deciding whether a compensation order should be made.[43] In *Woolmer*,[44] the court acknowledged that deciding whether causation is made out in relation to a compensation order will sometimes be difficult.[45]

4.41

A case that fell the other side of the line from *Derby* was *Taylor*,[46] and it was this case that the Court of Appeal in *Woolmer* used to draw its comparison. The Court in *Taylor* cited *Derby*, and concluded thus:[47]

---

40   *Halliwell* (1990–91) 12 Cr App R (S) 692. It is likely to be appropriate where D has sold the stolen property to an innocent purchaser. That innocent purchaser will not have title to the item(s) and will thus have to return the property to its owner, leaving them out of pocket for the amount that they paid for the item in good faith. Compensation to the innocent purchaser for the amount paid can therefore be appropriate.

41   *Wenzel* [2001] EWCA Crim 335, at [5]–[7] – D was acquitted by the jury of an offence under the Offences Against the Person Act 1861, s 20 arising from the same incident.

42   *Derby* (1990–91) 12 Cr App R (S) 502.

43   *Derby*, at 504.

44   [2004] EWCA Crim 2690.

45   *Woolmer*, at [15].

46   (1993) 14 Cr App R (S) 276.

47   *Taylor*, at 280.

'It may well be that, in particular cases, it is appropriate to separate the different phases of the events relied upon by the prosecution in considering what compensation orders should be made. The case of *Derby* is a good example of that. There will be many other cases, however, where the events take place so close to each other in time and are so linked with each other that it would be both artificial and unjust to look narrowly at the physical acts of each defendant relied upon by the prosecution.'

4.42

Courts may well expect assistance from counsel on whether a case falls on the *Derby* side or the *Taylor* side, which will require some thought being given to the exact actus reus elements of the offence of which D has been convicted, and how these did (or did not) directly lead to the loss that V suffered.

4.43

This may be particularly relevant where the Crown has charged a group of defendants with affray, but then individuals within the group with separate offences of causing injury. For example, where the prosecution allowed a count of unlawful wounding against only one defendant to lie on file due to uncertainty as to the identity of who threw the bottle that caused the injuries, compensation will not be appropriate.[48] The courts have thus been clear that the Crown cannot seek to 'paper over cracks' in their case regarding the identity of the person who caused the harm when it comes to the making of a compensation order.

4.44

An even finer line was drawn in *Corbett*,[49] where the Court of Appeal held that the offence need not be the sole cause of the injury, loss or damage, and it is not necessary for the injury to be inflicted intentionally. In that case, a compensation order made on conviction for common assault was upheld where the offender was acquitted of unlawful wounding.

4.45

A compensation order will be appropriate, however, where the loss has been shifted. In *Clarke*,[50] the co-accused approached the appellant with a view to using his account with the Halifax to pay in a stolen cheque. The cheque was not drawn by the appellant, or presented for payment by him, but it was credited to his account. The appellant then periodically withdrew money and paid it to the co-accused. The original loser, from whom the cheque had been stolen, was

---

48 *Deary* (1993) 14 Cr App R (S) 648.
49 *Corbett* (1993) 14 Cr App R (S) 101.
50 [2002] EWCA Crim 2415.

compensated in full by Lloyds TSB to the value of £5,000. Lloyds submitted a statement to the Crown Court setting out this, claiming full restitution in the sum of £5,000. The Court of Appeal held that a compensation order in favour of Lloyds TSB was appropriate.[51]

4.46

Where compensation for fear and distress is sought (see 4.61) the court will apply a 'broad commonsense test' as to whether the fear and distress were sufficiently closely linked to the offence.[52] Although ordinarily the level of compensation sought must be either proved or agreed, that does not apply where the court is making a small award to compensate the victim for injury, fright or distress suffered in the course of the commission of the crime.[53]

Types of compensation

General

4.47

Loss, damage or injury has to result from the offence(s) charged, or formally admitted as offences taken into consideration (TiCs), for a compensation order to be made.[54] Therefore, where a specimen charge is used, the court cannot make a compensation order representing the value of loss stemming from other criminal actions not forming part of that count:[55]

> 'The compensation orders against both appellants had been made on the basis of offences which were represented by specimen charges, but the amount of the orders reflected the whole amounts lost as a result of all the offences, not merely those charged in the indictment. No offences were taken into consideration … It was not open to the court to make a compensation order in respect of loss or damage arising from admitted offences which had not been charged or taken into consideration, on the ground that the offenders had admitted that the offences charged were sample counts representing a substantial number of other offences. It might be desirable to devise a procedure by which, when a defendant was accepting his guilt of a whole series of frauds, a compensation order could properly be made in a sum reflecting the total losses suffered by those who had been defrauded. Where there was no overall count, and no offences were taken into consideration,

---

51   *Clarke*, at [6].
52   *Bond v Chief Constable of Kent* (1983) 76 Cr App R 56, per McCullough J at 59.
53   *Bond v Chief Constable of Kent.*
54   *Crutchley & Tonks* (1994) 15 Cr App R (S) 627.
55   *Crutchley & Tonks*, at 635.

the compensation order could be made only in respect of the offences charged in the indictment.'

4.48

This approach was confirmed in the later case of *Hose*,[56] where three specimen counts of theft were charged. Their value was less than half of the value of the goods that D accepted he had stolen. As in *Crutchley*, however, as the additional value was not represented on the indictment or as TICs, no compensation could be ordered in relation to it.

4.49

The effects of an offence on a victim will often be set out in a Victim Personal Statement (VPS).[57] Prosecutors should be sure to establish whether such a statement has been made prior to any sentencing hearing, and provide it to the court and defence as soon as possible. Compensation can be awarded for loss suffered by a victim who has died before the sentencing hearing – it is not a purely personal right.[58]

Damage to stolen property

4.50

PCC(S)A 2000, s 130(5) allows compensation to be ordered where there is an offence under the Theft Act 1968 or the Fraud Act 2006 in respect of damage caused whilst the property was out of the possession of its lawful owner. By analogy from the Powers of Criminal Courts Act 1973, this applies regardless of how and by whom the damage was caused,[59] provided the property has been recovered.[60] Compensation can also include a sum for travel costs incurred by the owner of a car as a result of their being without the vehicle.[61] It cannot be claimed for any property that has not been recovered, for example contents of a stolen car that are never found.

4.51

Section 35(3) of Powers of Criminal Courts Act 1973 became, to all intents and purposes, s 130(6) and (7) of the 2000 Act, with refinements. Although not expressly linked to s 130(5), the two will often interlink, as is recognised

---

56 (1995) 16 Cr App R (S) 682.
57 The VPS provides victims with an opportunity to explain in their own words how a crime has affected them, whether physically, emotionally, financially or in any other way (Victims Code, Chapter 2, Part A, para 4.12).
58 *Holt v DPP* (1996) 2 Cr App R (S) 314.
59 PCC(S)A 2000, s 130(5)(1).
60 *Ahmad* (1992) 13 Cr App R (S) 212.
61 *Ahmad*, at 213.

by the drafting: the provisions of PCC(S)A 2000, s 130(5) also apply to damage caused to stolen motor vehicles where there is an accident caused by them (s 130(6)(a)).

4.52

Where the theft charge relates to rental property retained after the agreed rental period, but later returned undamaged, compensation for 'loss of use' will not be appropriate as it cannot be easily calculated.[62]

Compensation and motor vehicles

4.53

PCC(S)A 2000, s 130(6) sets out that a compensation order may only be made as a result of an accident arising from the presence of a motor vehicle on a road if:

- the damage is treated by s 130(5) as resulting from an offence under the Theft Act 1968 or the Fraud Act 2006; or

- it is in respect of injury, loss or damage due to an accident arising from the presence of a motor vehicle on the road if the offender was uninsured in respect of that damage, and compensation is not payable by the Motor Insurer's Bureau.

4.54

In *Quigley v Stokes*,[63] D pleaded guilty to taking a conveyance without consent (Theft Act 1968, s 12(1)). He was then involved in a collision with two other cars, causing damage to all three. The Divisional Court held that the Bench were wrong to have concluded under the Powers of Criminal Courts Act 1973 that the damage to the two other cars resulted from the offence to which D had pleaded guilty. The compensation orders in favour of the owners of the two cars with which he had collided were quashed.

4.55

Compensation can include the value of the loss of the whole or part of a driver's 'no claims' bonus as a result of them having to claim on their insurance to have the damage caused by D repaired.[64]

---

62   *Donovan* (1981) 3 Cr App R (S) 192.
63   (1977) 64 Cr App R 198.
64   Implicitly in *Kayani v Barking Magistrates' Court* [2001] EWHC Admin 517, at [5] and [8].

4.56

Compensation is not payable for loss or funeral expenses or bereavement suffered by a person's dependants because of his or her death due to an accident arising from the presence of a motor vehicle on a road.[65] This has led to an examination of when something is attributable to the presence of a motor vehicle on a road, and when a vehicle is on a road. In *Redman v Taylor*,[66] the Divisional Court said, obiter, that a collision in which the intoxicated defendant drove his car into a pillar of a car park entrance was clearly one occurring 'owing to the presence of a motor vehicle on a road' though the vehicle had left the road before impact.[67] Later, in *Mayor v Oxford*,[68] the Court of Appeal held, quashing the compensation order, that regarding the word 'accident' in the 1973 Act:

> 'The word "accident" was to be given its ordinary meaning, and it was not correct to say that because the damage had been caused with foresight it had not been caused by an accident.'

Compensation for death

4.57

Subject to the exception of cases involving death arising from an accident owing to the presence of a motor vehicle on a road, compensation is payable in respect of funeral expenses to any person who incurs them.[69]

4.58

Compensation for bereavement is limited to those who can claim under the provisions of s 1A of the Fatal Accidents Act 1976,[70] that is, the spouse of the deceased, or, in the case of a minor, his parents (or mother in the case of an illegitimate child). The current limit is £12,980.[71]

---

65 PCC(S)A 2000, s 130(1)(b).
66 [1975] Crim LR 348.
67 This approach has more recently been endorsed by the Court of Appeal in *Stapylton* [2012] EWCA Crim 728, at [7].
68 (1980) 2 Cr App R (S) 280.
69 PCC(S)A 2000, s 130(1)(b).
70 Section 1A(3), subject to the power in s 1A(5); 'The Lord Chancellor may by order made by statutory instrument, subject to annulment in pursuance of a resolution of either House of Parliament, amend this section by varying the sum for the time being specified in subsection (3) above.'
71 The current figure substituted by Damages for Bereavement (Variation of Sum) (England and Wales) Order 2013 (SI 2013/510), art 2 (1 April 2013: substitution has effect from 1 April 2013 in relation to causes of action which accrue on or after that date).

Compensation for personal injury

4.59

- Evidence relating to recovery should be provided, including any information about costs for specialist medical equipment or assistance, including ongoing costs such as dentistry.

- Can be sought for fear and distress falling short of recognised psychiatric illness.

4.60

Where compensation for personal injury (physical or psychological) is sought, there should be up-to-date and detailed information provided by the prosecution to the court concerning the extent of the injury, and this must be in the form of admissible evidence.[72] This will usually involve formal medical reports and photographs of the injury at various stages, including ones taken as close in time to the hearing as possible, to give an accurate current picture. As a general rule, the more serious the injury, the more information will be needed by the court including details of the injury itself, treatment, time lost from work and the likely prognosis if recovery is ongoing. Details of expenses such as dentists or opticians should be available.

4.61

A compensation order can be made in respect of fear and distress falling short of actual physical injury, for example where criminal damage to the window of an occupied house at night causes acute fear to the householder, who anticipates a burglary.[73] Conversely, no compensation for a mere witness of an offence would be appropriate unless there was evidence, either express or in some other form, from which a sentencer could properly infer distress to that witness.[74]

4.62

Victims who suffer minor injuries will usually not be eligible to claim under the Criminal Injuries Compensation Scheme as the tariff for claims starts at £1,000.[75] It is therefore of greater importance that appropriate applications for compensation are made during criminal sentencing exercises. A guide to

---

72   *Hobstaff* (1993) 14 Cr App R (S) 605 – prosecution counsel had behaved wholly improperly in opening at the sentencing hearing with the psychological effects on young victims of indecent assaults when no evidence of that had ever been served.

73   *Bond v Chief Constable of Kent* (1983) 76 Cr App R 56. There is no requirement akin to that in *Ireland* [1997] UKHL 34 that the fear must have caused a recognised psychiatric condition.

74   *Vaughan* (1990–91) 12 Cr App R (S) 46.

75   The Ministry of Justice (2012) *The Criminal Injuries Compensation Scheme 2012*, London: Ministry of Justice https://assets.publishing.service.gov.uk/government/uploads/system/uploads/attachment_data/file/243480/9780108512117.pdf, Annex E, p 42 ff.

amounts for specific injuries is found in the Magistrates' Courts Sentencing Guidelines.[76]

Compensation orders and young offenders

4.63

When requiring a child under 18 to pay compensation, the court must make the order against the parents of the young person,[77] unless the parent cannot be found or it would be unreasonable to do so.[78] If made by magistrates such an order can be appealed to the Crown Court,[79] and if made by the Crown Court, to the Court of Appeal.[80]

4.64

PCC(S)A 2000, s 137(8) enables the court to order compensation against a local authority having care of a young offender.

4.65

If considering making an order against a parent or local authority, the court must allow an opportunity for representations from the parent or local authority.[81]

Compensation, serious fraud and deferred prosecution agreements

4.66

In *SFO v Rolls Royce*,[82] when approving a deferred prosecution agreement (DPA) at first instance, the President of the Queen's Bench Division noted that rarely would the facts leading to such an outcome be simple enough for a compensation order to be made, considering the decisions of the Court of Appeal noted at the beginning of this chapter.

---

76 Sentencing Council (2018) *Magistrates' Court Sentencing Guidelines*, London: Sentencing Council https://www.sentencingcouncil.org.uk/wp-content/uploads/MCSG-June-2018-FINAL-3.pdf, pp 430–431.
77 PCC(S)A 2000, s 137(1).
78 PCC(S)A 2000, s 137(1)(i) and (ii).
79 PCC(S)A 2000, s 137(6).
80 PCC(S)A 2000, s 137(7).
81 PCC(S)A 2000, s 137(4).
82 [2017] Lloyd's Rep FC 249, 2017 WL 00219524, at [81]–[84].

Interest

4.67

The Court of Appeal in *Schofield*,[83] held that 'loss' should be given its ordinary meaning, and not be limited to any particular kind of loss. Thus a court may, in the case of financial loss, include a sum by way of interest. That the interest cannot be precisely calculated (and no such attempt should be made) is no bar. In exercising its discretion to include interest in a compensation order the court should bear in mind the amount of the loss, the amount of the interest, the time elapsed since the loss was suffered and the means of the offender.

Effect of appeal

4.68

PCC(S)A 2000, s 132(5) provides that where a compensation order has been made against any person in respect of an offence taken into consideration, the order shall cease to have effect if he successfully appeals against his conviction for the offence(s) which led to the order.[84] The offender may appeal against the order as if it were part of the sentence imposed in respect of the offence(s).[85]

Variation or discharge

4.69

If there is a substantial change in the financial circumstances of a defendant against whom a compensation order has been made, they can apply to the magistrates' court for variation or discharge under PCC(S)A 2000, s 133(1). The magistrates' court alone has jurisdiction relating to enforcement, and thus variation and discharge.

4.70

Compensation shall not be paid until the final date on which an appeal could be made against the order (ignoring leave to appeal out of time).[86] For this reason, the statute provides that where a compensation order that is the subject of an appeal to the Court of Appeal is annulled, the order shall not take effect and, if varied, shall take effect as varied.[87]

---

83 (1978) 67 Cr App R 282.
84 PCC(S)A 2000, s 132(5)(a).
85 PCC(S)A 2000, s 132(5)(b).
86 PCC(S)A 2000, s 132(1).
87 PCC(S)A 2000, s 132(3).

Competing claims

4.71

Where D has insufficient means to pay competing claims, the court can decide on an appropriate figure and apportion it on a pro rata basis. This does not preclude the court from preferring one claim to another. Preference must be given to compensation over fines where there is only sufficient means to pay one or the other.[88]

4.72

In many cases D will be required to pay the victim surcharge.[89] The relevant legislation does not permit the court to order that that surcharge be paid as compensation. By virtue of s 161A(3) of the Criminal Justice Act 2003, where a court dealing with an offender considers that it would be appropriate to make one or more compensation orders, an unlawful profit order and a slavery and trafficking reparation order, but that s/he has insufficient means to pay both the surcharge and appropriate amounts under such orders as it would be appropriate to make, the court MUST reduce the surcharge accordingly, if necessary to nil. It will be expected that if this is done it results from a finding that D had insufficient means to pay both.[90]

4.73

The purposes of confiscation and compensation are very different – confiscation is to deprive D of their ill-gotten gains and is paid to the State.[91] Since the Supreme Court decision in *Waya*,[92] any court making a confiscation order has to ensure the order is proportionate. A compensation order may affect this, as the Court of Appeal has accepted that a confiscation order may be disproportionate if proceeds of crime which have been restored to the loser by way of repayment, either voluntarily or as a result of a compensation order, are nevertheless counted as part of the benefit figure under the Proceeds of Crime Act (POCA) 2002.[93]

4.74

A judge cannot direct that compensation be paid out of the confiscation order monies pursuant to POCA 2002, s 13(6) if D has sufficient means to satisfy both orders.[94]

---

88   PCC(S)A 2000, s 130(12).
89   CJA 2003, ss 161A and 161B.
90   *Hare and Purse* [2016] EWCA Crim 1355, at [18]–[19].
91   *Glatt* [2006] EWCA Crim 605, at [69].
92   [2012] UKSC 51.
93   *Jawad* [2013] EWCA Crim 644, see especially at [27].
94   *Beaumont* [2014] EWCA Crim 1664.

4.75

However, if the only way to satisfy both would require the sale of the family home, due to D and her partner having minimal savings and low income, as in *Beaumont*,[95] then the court may well conclude that 'the value of the family home should not be taken into account when assessing the appellant's means for the purpose of ss 13(5)–(6). If this causes good reason to believe that the appellant will not have sufficient means to satisfy both orders in full then an order should be made so that monies paid under the confiscation order are used to satisfy the compensation order.'[96]

4.76

However, whilst s 13(6) does not permit the court to direct compensation be paid from amounts paid to the state through confiscation unless there are insufficient means to pay both, it is very difficult to see how a confiscation order for the same sum as the separate compensation order could possibly survive the decision on proportionality in *Waya*.[97]

4.77

The decision in *Beaumont*, however, is in opposition to the established line of cases on that point, beginning with *McGuire*.[98] In *Parkinson*,[99] where A was directed to pay the compensation order out of the confiscation order, the Court distinguished *Beaumont* as a decision on its own facts, and relating solely to correcting an order of the Crown Court where no s 13(6) direction had been made. It held that whilst a potential consequential forced sale of the family home is to be taken into account, it is not 'in principle some kind of trump card in resisting the making of a compensation order …'.[100]

4.78

Cases decided under s 72(7) of the Criminal Justice Act 1988 (the precursor to POCA 2002, s 13(5), (6)) provide that in a case where a compensation order pursuant to PCC(S)A 2000, s 130 has been made in addition to a confiscation order, compensation takes priority over confiscation where there are insufficient funds to satisfy both orders.

4.79

The Court of Appeal has made it clear that compensating victims must always take priority.[101] It has applied that principle to cases where no compensation

---

95   [2014] EWCA Crim 1664.
96   *Beaumont*, at [18]–[19].
97   See fn 92.
98   (1992) 13 Cr App R (S) 332.
99   [2015] EWCA Crim 1448.
100 *Parkinson*, at [30]–[31].
101 *Mitchell and Mitchell* [2001] 2 Cr App R (S) 29, at 142.

order was made, but the victim has been compensated through a civil judgment of the High Court which has been enforced,[102] or will be.[103]

4.80

A court should not use a compensation order because confiscation is time-barred: often cases triggering confiscation will be sufficiently complex that compensation is not appropriate in any event.[104]

---

102 *Silvester* [2009] EWCA Crim 2182.
103 *Mitchell and Mitchell*, see fn 101.
104 *Bewick* [2007] EWCA Crim 3297.

5   Restitution Orders[1]

5.01

Section 148 of the Powers of Criminal Courts (Sentencing) Act (PCC(S) A) 2000 provides that a restitution order can be made by the court either on application, or of its own motion,[2] where goods[3] have been stolen, and a defendant (D) is convicted of either:[4]

- any offence with reference to the theft (whether or not the stealing is the central mischief of his offence);[5] or

- any other offence, but only when an offence with reference to the theft is taken into consideration in sentencing.[6]

The Court of Appeal has encouraged sentencing courts to be mindful of this power and to make use of it.[7]

5.02

To qualify as 'stolen goods', the usual definition of theft as found in the Theft Act 1968, s 1(1) applies – that D has dishonestly appropriated property belonging to another with the intention of permanently depriving that other of it.[8] Goods can have been stolen anywhere in the world, and at any time, provided the act amounted to an offence when and where it happened.[9,10] This includes items obtained by blackmail or fraud (within the meaning of the Fraud Act 2006).[11]

5.03

Where this section applies, the court by or before which the offender is convicted may (whether or not deferring sentence in other respects) exercise any of the following powers:

---

1   There was a predecessor to the power under PCC(S)A 2000, s 148 in the Theft Act 1968, s 28 – the authorities from that legislation remain good law for this provision.
2   PCC(S)A 2000, s 149(2) – if the order is to be made under s 148(2)(c) or s 148(4), as confirmed in *Melksham* (1971) 55 Cr App R 400, at 402. No order can be made under s 148(2)(b) without an application – *Thibeault* (1983) 76 Cr App R 201, at 204–205.
3   As defined by PCC(S)A 2000, s 148(10) – 'goods, except in so far as the context otherwise requires, includes money and every other description of property (within the meaning of the Theft Act 1968) except land, and includes things severed from the land by stealing'.
4   There is no power without a conviction – *Mountford* [1972] 1 QB 28, at 31.
5   PCC(S)A 2000, s 148(1)(a).
6   PCC(S)A 2000, s 148(1)(b).
7   *Webbe* [2001] EWCA Crim 1217, at [32].
8   PCC(S)A 2000, s 148(8).
9   Theft Act 1968, s 24(1).
10   PCC(S)A 2000, s 148(9).
11   Theft Act 1968, s 24(4); PCC(S)A 2000, s 148(9).

- order anyone having possession or control of the stolen goods to restore them to any person entitled to recover them from him[12] (if it appears to the court that D has sold the goods to a bona fide purchaser,[13] or has borrowed money with the goods as security from a bona fide lender,[14] the court may order that a sum not exceeding the amount paid by the purchaser or the amount owed under the loan be paid to that person from money found on D on arrest); or

- on the application of a person entitled to recover from D any other goods directly or indirectly representing the stolen goods (as being the proceeds of any disposal or realisation of the whole or part of them or of goods so representing them), the court may order those other goods to be delivered or transferred to the applicant;[15] or

- order that a sum not exceeding the value of the stolen goods shall be paid, out of any money of the person convicted which was taken from him on his apprehension, to any person who, if those goods were in the possession of the person convicted, would be entitled to recover them from him,[16]

where 'the stolen goods' means the goods involved in the offence.

5.04

An order may be made in respect of money owed by the Crown,[17] and s 12(7) of PCC(S)A 2000 provides that D may be made the subject of a restitution order even if s/he is discharged absolutely or conditionally. As observed by the Supreme Court in *Guraj*,[18] although the Proceeds of Crime Act (POCA) 2002, s 15(2) prohibits the court from dealing with various financial/property aspects of sentence until after confiscation proceedings have been concluded, a restitution order under PCC(S)A 2000, s 148, although it may involve payment of money, is not included in the prohibition.[19]

5.05

Where the court has power to make an order both for goods representing the stolen property[20] and a sum representing the value[21] relating to the same goods, the court may make orders under both paragraphs provided that the victim (V) does not thereby recover more than the value of those goods.[22]

---

12 PCC(S)A 2000, s 148(2)(a).
13 PCC(S)A 2000, s 148(4)(a).
14 PCC(S)A 2000, s 148(4)(b).
15 PCC(S)A 2000, s 148(2)(b).
16 PCC(S)A 2000, s 148(2)(c).
17 PCC(S)A 2000, s 148(11).
18 [2016] UKSC 65.
19 *Guraj*, at [11].
20 PCC(S)A 2000, s 148(2)(b).
21 PCC(S)A 2000, s 148(2)(c).
22 PCC(S)A 2000, s 148(3).

5.06

The court shall not exercise these powers unless the relevant facts sufficiently appear from evidence at the trial or the available documents,[23] together with admissions made by or on behalf of any person in connection with any proposed exercise of the powers.[24]

5.07

Under the equivalent subsection in the predecessor power,[25] it was established that evidence upon which a restitution order is based is that which is entitled to be given before sentence – there should be no further evidence received for the application for a restitution order.[26] However, where one D gives evidence and another does not, the court is allowed to take into account the evidence that it has heard from D1 in considering a restitution order against D2.[27]

5.08

Questions of subrogation where a successful claim has been made on insurance are likely to cause complications, as the insurance company then has an interest in any amount recovered by V.[28] If V is to receive money to the value of only some of the assets that were stolen (as others were recovered or insurance paid out) then it will be necessary to have the individual value (or collective value limited to those items outstanding) established through evidence available and admissible at trial if a restitution order is to be made.[29]

5.09

If the magistrates' court is committing D for sentence to the Crown Court, then the power to make a restitution order goes with the case to the Crown Court, and any order made by the justices will be a nullity.[30]

5.10

A restitution order should not be made if there is an issue raised as to ownership of the money in the defendant's possession – the criminal standard of proof applies. Where property might belong to a third party, its ownership should be decided in the civil courts.[31] Likewise where it is not entirely clear which items were stolen and which belonged rightfully to D, no order should be

---

23 As defined in PCC(S)A 2000, s 148(6)(a) and (b): any written statements or admissions made for use, and admissible, as evidence at the trial; and such documents as served on D in pursuance of regulations made under the Crime and Disorder Act 1998, Sch 3, para 1.
24 PCC(S)A 2000, s 148(5).
25 Theft Act 1968, s 28(4).
26 *Church* (1971) 55 Cr App R 65.
27 *Calcutt & Varty* (1985) 7 Cr App R (S) 385, at 392.
28 *Church*, at 71–72.
29 *Church*, at 72.
30 *R v Blackpool Justices, ex p Charlson and Gregory* (1972) 56 Cr App R 823, at 826–827.
31 *Ferguson* (1970) 54 Cr App R 410, at 413–414.

made – the statute prevented third parties from intervening and this could lead to injustice.[32]

Appeal

5.11

Where an order is made against D in respect of an offence taken into consideration in determining his sentence, the order shall cease to have effect if he successfully appeals against his conviction for the offence or all of the offences, of which he was convicted in the proceedings in which the order was made.[33]

5.12

D may appeal against the order as if it were part of the sentence imposed in respect of any offence(s) of which he was convicted.[34]

5.13

Any order made by a magistrates' court shall be suspended until the end of the period for giving notice of appeal against a decision of a magistrates' court,[35] and where notice of appeal is given within that period, until the determination of the appeal.[36] The exception to this is if the order is made under PCC(S) A 2000, s 148(2)(a) or (b) and the court is of the opinion that the title to the goods to be restored, delivered or transferred is not in dispute.

5.14

Any order under PCC(S)A 2000, s 148 shall be treated as an order for the restitution of property within the meaning of s 30 of the Criminal Appeal Act 1968 (which relates to the effect on such orders of appeals).[37] By s 30(2), it has been held that the Court of Appeal can entertain an appeal regarding a restitution order.[38]

---

32 *Calcutt & Varty*, at 390.
33 PCC(S)A 2000, s 149(3)(a).
34 PCC(S)A 2000, s 149(3)(b).
35 PCC(S)A 2000, s 149(4)(a).
36 PCC(S)A 2000, s 149(4)(b).
37 PCC(S)A 2000, s 148(7).
38 *Parker* (1970) 54 Cr App R 339, at 345.

6 Driving Disqualification I

6.01

There are a number of powers under which a court can forbid a defendant from driving a motor vehicle on a public road for a set period of time from the date of sentence.[1] Whichever section is used, the point of a disqualification is to protect the public, punish, and deter others.[2]

6.02

The territorial scope of disqualification is dependent upon mutual recognition, and therefore may alter if England and Wales leave the European Union. However, at the date of writing, s 31 of the Criminal Justice and Courts Act 2015 deals with the position regarding those who are ordinarily resident in the Republic of Ireland, or hold an Irish licence. Section 31 applies s 55 of the Crime (International Co-operation) Act (CICA) 2003. That section provides that when a defendant is convicted of a qualifying English road traffic offence, and a driving disqualification is imposed and that individual resides in Ireland, or is not normally a resident but holds a Republic of Ireland licence, then the English authorities must notify the Irish authorities.

6.03

If someone is a European Community licence-holder, CICA 2003, s 65 covers their situation in so far as their licence must be returned if they leave the jurisdiction. It does not, however, stipulate the effect of being disqualified in England on the lawfulness of driving in another Member State.

6.04

Advocates should also be aware that for the first two years after passing their driving test, new drivers will be disqualified if they get six points on their licence, as opposed to the 12 permitted for more experienced drivers.

6.05

For ease of reference, this chapter contains the provisions in the Powers of the Criminal Courts (Sentencing) Act (PCC(S)A) 2000, which allow a court to disqualify a defendant (D) who has committed any offence, providing there is some nexus between the offence and driving. Chapter 7 deals with the

---

1 Not as part of conditions of bail or at some other stage of proceedings: *R (Toor) v Isleworth Crown Court & DPP* [2011] EWHC 3498 (Admin), at [10]–[12], [15], [18].
2 *Backhouse* [2010] EWCA Crim 1111, at [21].

provisions that are only applicable in cases where the offence itself was a driving offence, and disqualification will be imposed under the Road Traffic Offenders Act (RTOA) 1988.

Powers of Criminal Courts (Sentencing) Act 2000, s 146

6.06

This section creates a power under which a court can disqualify someone from holding or obtaining a driving licence as a result of any offence, for such period as the court thinks fit.

6.07

The enormous breadth of this power has been acknowledged by the appellate courts:[3] it is available to both magistrates' courts and the Crown Court, and is not limited to any particular offence – nor is it required that the offence be connected in any way with the use of a motor vehicle, though it must not be imposed arbitrarily.[4] For example, where D had been convicted of an affray, but had admitted during his evidence that on the night of the offence he had driven a car whilst under the influence of drugs or alcohol, the disqualification was properly imposed.[5] Where, however, an offence has its beginnings in an earlier road rage incident, the Court of Appeal has not always been consistent as to whether disqualification is appropriate – the cases of *Bye*[6] (disqualification upheld) and *Cornell-Gallardo*[7] (disqualification quashed) illustrate this.

6.08

All that appears to distinguish the cases from each other is the time lapse between the initial road rage incident and the criminality that formed the charge (affray and assault occasioning actual bodily harm respectively). Whilst in *Cornell-Gallardo* there was a longer time lapse,[8] it was still not a long period of time, and advocates are likely to be able to use the apparent inconsistency between these cases to mount an argument in either direction.

6.09

A sentencing judge is entitled to make reasonable findings of fact based on inferences from the established and accepted facts to support a disqualification for a non-driving related offence.[9] However, where D had pleaded guilty to one

---

3   *Cliff* [2004] EWCA Crim 3139.
4   *Cliff*, at [14]–[15].
5   *Cliff*, at [15]–[18].
6   [2005] EWCA Crim 1230.
7   [2010] EWCA Crim 3151.
8   *Cornell-Gallardo*, at [3]–[4].
9   *Waring* [2005] EWCA Crim 1080, at [8].

count of disguising criminal property, being a worker at a garage who assisted a criminal gang in perpetrating a fraud relating to stripping down cars that had been stolen, but his only role had been stripping the vehicles, a disqualification was quashed as 'unnecessary and inappropriate'.[10]

6.10

Where there are multiple defendants, and one committed driving offences assisted by the others, the disqualification for those assisting should be for a shorter period than for the offender who committed the driving offences.[11] However, there is nothing improper in principle about disqualifying someone whose role in an offence of theft was as a passenger in one of the vehicles used to commit the theft.[12]

6.11

If D has committed an offence (such as perverting the course of justice) to avoid prosecution for a driving offence, then the court will consider the risk and seriousness of the driving that formed the offence for which D was trying to escape prosecution. Where that underlying offence would not necessarily have resulted in automatic disqualification, or taken D to the 12-point disqualification threshold, and was not serious, a disqualification might even be wrong in principle, as being out of all proportion with the standard of driving.[13] Where the underlying offences would have resulted in a disqualification, a sensible step will be to impose a disqualification under s 146 of the same length as would have been received for the underlying offences.[14]

6.12

Similarly, if as a result of the offence for which D sought to avoid prosecution they would have been disqualified for six months having amassed 12 penalty points, six months will be the appropriate length of driving disqualification.[15] The fact that D(2) assisted in the commission of the offence to avoid D(1)'s prosecution, and would have received penalty points but would not have received a disqualification, will weigh against a disqualification for D(2).[16]

6.13

Whilst the sentencing court should consider the effect that a ban will have on the defendant, its having a serious impact on D's ability to earn a living will not mean that no disqualification should be imposed.[17] However, no disqualification

---

10   *Ashmore* [2006] EWCA Crim 2996, at [12]–[13].
11   *Beaney* [2005] EWCA Crim 1127, at [16].
12   *Gilder* [2011] EWCA Crim 1159, at [10].
13   *Miah* [2008] EWCA Crim 7, at [11]–[12].
14   *Munir* [2008] EWCA Crim 897, at [8]; *Sanchez* [2008] EWCA Crim 2429, at [18].
15   *Henderson and Metcalfe* [2011] EWCA Crim 1152, at [14].
16   *Henderson and Metcalfe*, at [15].
17   *Bye*, at [8].

should be for such a long period of time that D has no encouragement or opportunity to rehabilitate himself on release from custody.[18] Similarly, caring responsibilities involving the use of a car, and other relevant personal mitigation which would suggest particular hardship from disqualification, should be taken into account in the usual way when a judge is considering whether to disqualify.[19]

6.14

The offence must have been committed after 31 December 1997.[20] The court may impose a disqualification under this section instead of, or in addition to, any other way in which they deal with D for the offence,[21] unless D is convicted of an offence which has a sentence fixed by law or is listed below. In those circumstances the court MUST impose a penalty as well as the disqualification:[22]

(a)   Prevention of Crime Act 1953:[23]

  (i)   s 1(2B) – six-month imprisonment mandatory minimum for second offensive weapon conviction; or

  (ii) s 1A(5) – six months' (if D over 18), or four months' (if D between 16 and 18) imprisonment mandatory minimum for threatening with an offensive weapon in a public place.

(b)   Firearms Act 1968:[24]

  (i)   s 51A(2) – five-year mandatory period of imprisonment for offences under s 5(1)(a), (ab), (aba), (ac), (ad), (ae), (af), (c) or (1A)(a) (which refers to s 16) of the 1968 Act, or an offence under any of ss 16, 16A, 17, 18, 19 or 20(1) in respect of a firearm or ammunition specified in any of the subsections of s 5 mentioned earlier in this list.

(c)   Criminal Justice Act 1988:[25]

  (i)   s 139(6B) – six-month imprisonment mandatory minimum for second conviction of having an article with a blade or a point in public;

  (ii) s 139A(5B) – six-month imprisonment mandatory minimum for second conviction of having an article with a blade or a point, or an offensive weapon, on school premises;

  (iii) s 139AA(7) – six-month imprisonment mandatory minimum for second conviction of threatening with article with a blade or a point, or an offensive weapon.

---

18   *Barron* [2012] EWCA Crim 1751, at [9].
19   *Abdulhussain* [2013] EWCA Crim 1212, at [5]–[6].
20   PCC(S)A 2000, s 146(1).
21   PCC(S)A 2000, s 146(1).
22   PCC(S)A 2000, s 146(2).
23   PCC(S)A 2000, s 146(2A)(a).
24   PCC(S)A 2000, s 146(2A)(b).
25   PCC(S)A 2000, s 146(2A)(c).

(d) Powers of Criminal Courts (Sentencing) Act 2000:[26]

   (i) s 110(2) – seven-year mandatory minimum imprisonment for a third Class A drug trafficking offence;

   (ii) s 111(2) – three-year mandatory minimum imprisonment for a third domestic burglary.

(e) Criminal Justice Act 2003:[27]

   (i) s 224A – life sentence for a second listed offence for a dangerous offender;

   (ii) s 225(2) – life sentence for serious offences by dangerous offenders;

   (iii) s 226(2) – detention for life for serious offences committed by dangerous offenders under 18.

(f) Violent Crime Reduction Act 2006:[28]

   (i) s 29(4) – five-year mandatory minimum imprisonment for using someone to mind a weapon (s 28) where the dangerous weapon in respect of which the offence was committed was a firearm mentioned in s 5(1)(a)–(af) or (c) or s 5(1A)(a) of the 1968 Act;[29]

   (ii) s 29(6) – three-year mandatory minimum detention for the same offence as above, but where the offender is under 18.

6.15

A court which makes an order under s 146 disqualifying a person from holding or obtaining a driving licence[30] shall require the production of any such licence (including a Northern Ireland[31] or Community[32] licence) that s/he holds.[33]

Powers of Criminal Courts (Sentencing) Act 2000, s 147

6.16

This section applies where a person is:

(a) convicted before the Crown Court of an offence punishable on indictment with imprisonment of two years or more;[34]

---

26   PCC(S)A 2000, s 146(2A)(d).
27   PCC(S)A 2000, s 146(2A)(e).
28   PCC(S)A 2000, s 146(2A)(f).
29   Violent Crime Reduction Act 2006, s 29(3).
30   Defined in PCC(S)A 2000, s 146(5) as a 'licence to drive a motor vehicle granted under Part III of the Road Traffic Act 1988'.
31   PCC(S)A 2000, s 146(4)(aa).
32   PCC(S)A 2000, s 146(4)(b).
33   PCC(S)A 2000, s 146(4)(a).
34   PCC(S)A 2000, s 147(1)(a).

(b)   committed to the Crown Court for sentence for such an offence;[35]

(c)   convicted by or before any court of common assault or of any other offence involving an assault (including aiding, abetting, counselling or procuring, or inciting the commission of,[36] an offence).[37]

6.17

The Crown Court may impose such period of disqualification from holding or obtaining a licence on D as it thinks fit if:

- In circumstances (a) and (b) above, the Crown Court is satisfied that a motor vehicle was used (by D or by anyone else) for the purpose of committing, or facilitating the commission of, the offence in question.[38]

- In circumstance (c) above, the court is satisfied that the assault was committed by driving a motor vehicle.[39]

6.18

Facilitating the commission of an offence includes taking any steps after it has been committed for the purpose of disposing of any property to which it relates or of avoiding apprehension or detection.[40]

6.19

A court which makes an order under this section disqualifying a person from holding or obtaining a driving licence[41] shall require the production of any such licence (including a Northern Ireland[42] or Community[43] licence) that he/she holds.[44]

6.20

Where the offence could not have been committed but for the driving of the motor vehicle, the use of s 147 is permissible even if the offence itself contains no element that *requires* the driving of a motor vehicle.[45] Even though the offence itself is not a driving-related offence, the judge is not required to ignore the risk caused to other road users by the commission by D of a non-driving

---

35   PCC(S)A 2000, s 147(1)(b).
36   It is unclear whether this would also encompass an offence of assisting and encouraging under the Serious Crime Act 2007 – the statutory successor to the common law offence of incitement.
37   PCC(S)A 2000, s 147(2).
38   PCC(S)A 2000, s 147(3).
39   PCC(S)A 2000, s 147(4).
40   PCC(S)A 2000, s 147(6).
41   Defined in PCC(S)A 2000, s 147(7) by reference to s 146(5) as a 'licence to drive a motor vehicle granted under Part III of the RTA 1988'.
42   PCC(S)A 2000, s 147(5)(aa).
43   PCC(S)A 2000, s 147(5)(b).
44   PCC(S)A 2000, s 147(5)(a).
45   *Ketteridge* [2014] EWCA Crim 1962, at [25].

offence whilst driving (ie indecent exposure).[46] However, there need be no evidence of unsafe driving for a disqualification to be imposed.[47]

6.21

The notion that the car has been 'used' for the purpose of committing the offence has been drawn very widely – using the car to drive to a location where an indecent assault was performed was sufficient in *Roberts*.[48]

6.22

If D receives both a custodial sentence and a period of disqualification from driving under s 147, the disqualification should be for a period equal to or slightly longer than the custodial term, on the basis that the court should not impose a period of disqualification that will inhibit the offender from rehabilitating himself.[49] This is particularly so in cases where the offender is dependent on the ability to drive for his livelihood,[50] and preventing him obtaining new employment will make the punishment disproportionate.[51] To secure this aim, s 147A has been enacted (see 6.30 ff).

6.23

This proposition was clarified in the later case of *Harkins*,[52] where the Court of Appeal noted that a disqualification period should be broadly commensurate with the custodial sentence, but to be effective at all, would need to still be in place after D was released from custody. The sentencing judge was not required to perform minute calculations as to when precisely that would be.[53] Where D is being sentenced for a variety of matters, only some of which give rise to a power under s 147, it is not wrong in principle for the judge to match the period of disqualification to the total sentence, provided that does not cause the disqualification to be disproportionate.[54]

6.24

The sentencing judge must also have regard to the issue of proportionality,[55] and making the disqualification broadly commensurate with the custodial term.[56] Periods of remand need not be taken into account by way of adjustment to the disqualification period if they have been short relative to

---

46   *Ketteridge*, at [26].
47   *Miah* [2001] EWCA Crim 2871, at [7]–[8].
48   [2002] EWCA Crim 2790, at [18]–[19].
49   *Bowling* [2008] EWCA Crim 1148, at [7].
50   *Bowling*, at [7]; *Doick* [2004] EWCA Crim 139.
51   *Kemp* [2010] EWCA Crim 285, at [8].
52   [2011] EWCA Crim 2227.
53   *Harkins*, at [16].
54   *Harkins*, at [17].
55   *Knight* [2012] EWCA Crim 3019, at [13].
56   *Knight*, at [14.]

the overall term imposed, meaning that the length of disqualification would not be disproportionate.[57]

6.25

Where one defendant has driven the car to the location of the planned offence, which is committed with the assistance of three passengers, the Court of Appeal's decision in *Joyce* suggests that only the driver should be disqualified – the disqualifications of the passengers were quashed.[58] However in *Gilder*,[59] the Court of Appeal stated that being a passenger and not a driver was not a bar to disqualification under this section.[60]

6.26

It is permissible to disqualify under s 146 where the car was used in an attempt to avoid apprehension for an offence of conspiracy,[61] though not, on the basis of its predecessor power in the Powers of Criminal Courts Act 1973, s 43(2), where the car was used to facilitate the commission of the conspiracy itself.[62] The only type of conspiracy for which D can be disqualified under s 147(3) is one in which the vehicle was used directly in the formation of the conspiracy itself.[63] To avoid this issue, where there has been a conspiracy offence a sentencing court would be well-advised to disqualify under s 146.

6.27

If a disqualification is imposed under s 147 when there was no power to do so, there will usually have been a power to impose a disqualification under s 146, and the Court of Appeal has indicated its willingness to perform a simple substitution.[64] If the sentencing court could have imposed a disqualification under either section, and does not state which one it has applied, that will not found a successful appeal if either could have been used on the facts.[65]

6.28

Where D is a driver by employment, and certainly if he is an HGV driver, then the advocate would be well-advised to establish if there are any special conditions that will attach to D regaining his HGV licence in the area where he is resident. In *O'Halloran*,[66] the Court was significantly assisted by a letter from

---

57   *Kirk* [2017] EWCA Crim 626, at [41].
58   [2005] EWCA Crim 3067, at [8].
59   [2011] EWCA Crim 1159.
60   *Gilder*, at [10]
61   *Langley* [2014] EWCA Crim 1284, at [24], [26]–[28].
62   *Devine* (1990–91) 12 Cr App R (S) 235, distinguishing the earlier case of *Riley* (1983) 5 Cr App R(S) 335.
63   *Gorry* [2018] EWCA Crim 1867.
64   *McCormack* [2006] EWCA Crim 1247, at [5].
65   *Stanner* [2011] EWCA Crim 1787, at [17].
66   [2003] EWCA Crim 1306.

the local Traffic Commissioner who set out the precise steps (more numerous than to regain a regular licence) that the appellant would have to fulfil to regain his HGV licence,[67] and a letter from a potential employer setting out the effect of the disqualification on his potential employment. As the disqualification in that case had been discretionary, and only imposed for the period for which the appellant would be in custody anyway, the Court of Appeal allowed the appeal against disqualification.

6.29

There is no power under s 147 to order an extended re-test.[68]

Powers of Criminal Courts (Sentencing) Act 2000, s 147A

6.30

This section permits a court to add an extension period to a disqualification imposed under s 146 or s 147. Its rationale is to avoid the offender serving all or part of the period of disqualification while he/she is in custody, and the disqualification thus having no practical effect.

6.31

As stated in *Needham*,[69] and demonstrated in other cases since, the principles regarding RTOA 1988, ss 35A and 35B apply equally to ss 147A and 147B, as the provisions are mirror images.[70] If a court purports in error to extend under the provisions of one Act, when the correct provisions are those in the mirror image in the other Act, then on appeal a straightforward substitution can be made.[71]

6.32

The court must add an extension period to a discretionary disqualification under s 146 or s 147 when it imposes an immediate custodial sentence[72] for the same offence.[73] This provision does not apply where the sentence is one of suspended imprisonment.[74] As these provisions are mandatory, counsel are required to draw them to the attention of the court.[75]

---

67 *O'Halloran*, at [6].
68 *Riley* [2017] EWCA Crim 2035; *Fagan* [2016] EWCA Crim 313, at [5].
69 [2016] EWCA Crim 455.
70 *Johnson* [2017] EWCA Crim 1192, at [16].
71 *Johnson*, at [18].
72 PCC(S)A 2000, s 147A(1)(a).
73 PCC(S)A 2000, s 147A(1)(b).
74 PCC(S)A 2000, s 147A(7)(a).
75 *Martin* [2016] EWCA Crim 15, at [19].

6.33

Any order under s 147A must set out the appropriate extension period, as well as the discretionary disqualification period,[76] which is the length of disqualification that the court would have given under s 146 or s 147 in any event.[77]

6.34

The appropriate extension period is (to the nearest whole day[78]):

- half of the length of:

    – a custodial sentence;[79]

    – a Detention and Training Order;[80]

    – the period imposed under s 236A of the Criminal Justice Act (CJA) 2003 of a special custodial sentence for certain offenders of particular concern;[81]

- two-thirds of the length of:

    – the custodial portion of an extended determinate sentence (under CJA 2003, s 226A where D is over 18,[82] or s 226B if under 18);[83] or

- the tariff period (under PCC(S)A 2000, s 82A(2) or CJA 2003, s 269(2)).[84]

6.35

This section does not apply where the court has made an order that the early release provisions are not to apply to either a mandatory life sentence (under CJA 2003, s 269(4)),[85] or a discretionary life sentence (PCC(S)A 2000, s 82A(4)).[86]

6.36

It does not apply to offences committed before 13 April 2015, and so where an offence was committed before that date, a judge cannot impose an extension period.[87] The alternative way to the same outcome, where cases from before that date are being sentenced, is to impose a longer primary period of disqualification such as to achieve the balance between the disqualification having effect on D's

---

76   PCC(S)A 2000, s 147A(2).
77   PCC(S)A 2000, s 147A(3).
78   PCC(S)A 2000, s 147A(5).
79   PCC(S)A 2000, s 147A(4)(h).
80   PCC(S)A 2000, s 147A(4)(b).
81   PCC(S)A 2000, s 147(4)(fa).
82   PCC(S)A 2000, s 147A(4)(e).
83   PCC(S)A 2000, s 147A(4)(f).
84   PCC(S)A 2000, ss 147A(4)(a) and (g).
85   PCC(S)A 2000, s 147A(7)(b).
86   PCC(S)A 2000, s 147A(7)(c).
87   *Ahmed* [2017] EWCA Crim 303, at [9].

release, but not impairing rehabilitation.[88] Although it has never been challenged before the courts, this seems to create a tension between proportionality and disqualification – if D is for some reason released earlier than anticipated, they may have a longer period of disqualification still to serve than the judge had intended them to experience the practical effect of on their release.

6.37

If it is unclear from the way in which the judge has expressed themselves how the disqualification is structured, then clarification should be sought by counsel so the reasoning is clear.[89]

6.38

An example of s 147A in operation is seen in *Vasey*:[90]

> 'Therefore, in this case the judge clearly having decided a period of 18 months was the appropriate discretionary period of disqualification under s 146, should then have gone on to add an extension period of two months under s 147A(4)(h) being a period equal to half the custodial sentence imposed. The total disqualification should therefore have been 20 months and the disqualification actually imposed (of 18 months) was therefore unlawful.'

6.39

As the Court of Appeal allowed Mr Vasey's appeal against sentence, leading to a suspended custodial term, the questions of extension no longer arose. The Court also reminded sentencing judges that the jurisprudence applying to ss 35A and 35B applied equally to the 'mirror provisions' in ss 147A and 147B.[91]

Powers of Criminal Courts (Sentencing) Act 2000, s 147B

6.40

This section permits a court to add an uplift to a disqualification because the defendant will be serving a custodial sentence for another offence. It is intended to allow a court to have regard to the fact that a defendant is subject to a custodial sentence which would have the consequence of diminishing or removing the effect of any disqualification as a punishment were it to be imposed in the ordinary way (with immediate effect).[92]

---

88   *Ahmed*, at [10] and [12].
89   *Johnson*, at [19]; *Kirk* [2017] EWCA Crim 626, at [38]–[39].
90   [2017] EWCA Crim 434, at [17].
91   *Vasey*, at [17]–[18].
92   *Mascarenas* [2018] EWCA Crim 1467, at [8].

6.41

It applies where a person is disqualified under s 146 or s 147 and either the court will be imposing an immediate custodial sentence for another offence,[93] or the person is already serving a custodial sentence for other matters when they are disqualified.[94]

6.42

In determining the period for which the person is to be disqualified under s 146 or s 147, the court must have such regard as appropriate[95] to the diminished effect of disqualification if the person is in custody.[96]

6.43

Any custodial sentence for the offence for which they are being disqualified under s 146 or s 147 is not to be taken into account at this stage[97] (as it should already have been considered when determining the length of discretionary disqualification).

6.44

Similarly to s 147A, if the sentencing judge wrongly refers to s 147B when s/he should be referring to s 35B of the RTOA 1988, there is no practical effect and substitution is appropriate.[98]

General points

6.45

When considering how to structure a disqualification under s 146 or s 147 in combination with both s 147A and 147B, the judge should be directed to consider the period of operative disqualification that they are seeking to impose after D is released from custody.[99] A broad-brush (as opposed to strictly arithmetical) approach should be taken to considering the appropriate length of disqualification still to be operative on release, and then structuring this so that there is no injustice.[100]

---

93   PCC(S)A 2000, s 147B(1)(a).
94   PCC(S)A 2000, s 147B(1)(b).
95   PCC(S)A 2000, s 147B(2).
96   PCC(S)A 2000, s 147B(3).
97   PCC(S)A 2000, s 147B(4).
98   *Mascarenas*, at [13].
99   *Gregory* [2017] EWCA Crim 2405, at [16]–[17].
100 *Needham*, at [32]–[38].

6.46

Disqualification operates from the date that it is imposed – it cannot be backdated, and neither can multiple periods of disqualification be ordered to run consecutively.[101]

---

101 *Mascarenas*, at [14], citing *Meese* (1973) 57 Cr App R 568.

7 Driving Disqualification II

Road Traffic Offenders Act 1988, s 34

7.01

Section 34 of the Road Traffic Offenders Act (RTOA) 1988 provides for various periods of disqualification in different circumstances. The differing periods are set out below first, before the considerations for advocates representing those faced with such an order are explored.

Disqualification for a minimum of one year (standard provision)

7.02

Under this section, where a person is convicted of an offence involving obligatory disqualification, the court must order disqualification for at least 12 months unless special reasons apply (see 7.19 ff).

Disqualification for such period as the court thinks fit

7.03

Where a person is convicted of an offence involving discretionary disqualification, and has fewer than 12 points[1] or the offence does not involve obligatory endorsement,[2] the court may order him to be disqualified for such period as the court thinks fit.

Disqualification for a minimum of six months

7.04

Where a person convicted of using a vehicle in a dangerous condition[3] has been previously convicted of the same offence within three years before the date of

---

1   RTOA 1988, s 34(2)(a).
2   RTOA 1988, s 34(2)(b).
3   Contrary to the Road Traffic Act (RTA) 1988, s 40A.

the current offence (not the date of conviction), the mandatory disqualification is six months.[4]

Disqualification for a minimum of two years

7.05

There are two circumstances where this applies:

(A)   Any person being disqualified who has received more than one previous disqualification of 56 days or more within three years before the current offence (not the date of conviction) must be disqualified for at least two years.[5]

For these purposes, interim disqualifications under RTOA 1998, s 26 or the Powers of Criminal Courts (Sentencing) Act (PCC(S)A) 2000, s 147, and any disqualification imposed in respect of an offence of stealing a motor vehicle,[6] are to be disregarded,[7] as are any disqualifications which would have been less than 56 days but for an extension period added pursuant to RTOA 1988, s 35A or s 35C,[8] or PCC(S)A 2000, s 147A.[9]

If D has received a mandatory disqualification of a set period, and at the same time has been given points which have taken D to a total of 12 or more, leading to the automatic six-month disqualification being imposed concurrently with the period of mandatory disqualification, that counts as one disqualification for the purposes s 34(4), not two.[10]

(B)   If a person is being sentenced for an offence from the following list (all offences under the Road Traffic Act (RTA) 1988), the mandatory minimum disqualification period is also two years:[11]

- manslaughter;[12]

- s 1 (causing death by dangerous driving);[13]

- s 1A (causing serious injury by dangerous driving);[14]

- s 3ZC (causing death by driving: disqualified drivers);[15]

---

4   RTOA 1988, s 34(4B).
5   RTOA 1988, s 34(4)(b).
6   Contrary to the Theft Act 1968, s 12 or s 25 or RTA 1988, s 178, including an attempt to commit any of those offences.
7   RTOA 1988, s 34(4A).
8   RTOA 1988, s 34(4.
9   RTOA 1988, s 34(4AA)(c).
10   *Learmont v DPP* [1994] RTR 286, at 290–292.
11   RTOA 1988, s 34(4).
12   RTOA 1988, s 34(4)(a)(i).
13   RTOA 1988, s 34(4)(a)(ii).
14   RTOA 1988, s 34(4)(a)(iia).
15   RTOA 1988, s 34(4)(a)(iib).

- s 3ZD (causing serious injury by driving: disqualified drivers);[16]

- s 3A (causing death by careless driving while under the influence of drink or drugs).[17]

Disqualification for a minimum of three years

7.06

If a person is being sentenced for an offence from the following list (all offences under RTA 1988), and has, within the ten years before the date of the current offence,[18] previously committed an offence from the same list, the mandatory minimum disqualification period is three years:[19]

- s 3A (causing death by careless driving when under the influence of drink or drugs);[20]

- s 4(1) (driving or attempting to drive while unfit);[21]

- s 5(1)(a) (driving or attempting to drive with excess alcohol);[22]

- s 5A(1)(a) and (2) (driving or attempting to drive with concentration of specified controlled drug above specified limit);[23]

- s 7(6) (failing to provide a specimen) where that is an offence involving obligatory disqualification;[24]

- s 7A(6) (failing to allow a specimen to be subjected to laboratory test) where that is an offence involving obligatory disqualification.[25]

7.07

The provisions of s 34 apply to convictions for aiding, abetting, counselling or procuring, or inciting[26] the commission of, an offence involving obligatory disqualification as if the offence were an offence involving discretionary disqualification.[27]

---

16 RTOA 1988, s 34(4)(a)(iic).
17 RTOA 1988, s 34(4)(a)(iii).
18 Not the date of conviction – *Beard* [2014] EWCA Crim 2254.
19 RTOA 1988, s 34(3).
20 RTOA 1988, s 34(3)(aa).
21 RTOA 1988, s 34(3)(a).
22 RTOA 1988, s 34(3)(b).
23 RTOA 1988, s 34(3)(ba).
24 RTOA 1988, s 34(3)(c).
25 RTOA 1988, s 34(3)(d).
26 It is unclear whether this would also encompass an offence of assisting and encouraging under the Serious Crime Act 2007 – the statutory successor to the common law offence of incitement.
27 RTOA 1988, s 34(5).

7.08

The contents of s 34 are subject to RTOA 1988, s 48,[28] which provides two exemptions from the requirements to disqualify in s 34:

- On conviction for using a vehicle in a dangerous condition[29] the court must not disqualify D,[30] or order any endorsement or penalty points[31] if D proves that he did not know, and had no reasonable cause to suspect, that the use of the vehicle involved a danger of injury to any person.

- On conviction for breach of requirements as to brakes, steering-gear or tyres,[32] the court must not disqualify D[33] or order any endorsement or penalty points[34] if the defendant proves that he did not know, and had no reasonable cause to suspect, that the offence would be committed.

Considerations of the court when disqualifying

7.09

When imposing a disqualification under s 34, the court should consider the effect of such an order, and its length, upon D in two particular respects:[35]

- it might make it more likely that on release D breaks the law again by driving whilst disqualified; and

- its adverse effect upon D's prospects of effective rehabilitation when released from custody.

7.10

Where D is charged with failing to provide a specimen under RTA 1988, s 7, whether the disqualification is obligatory or mandatory will depend on which section D was trying to avoid the consequences of by refusing to provide.[36] If D was suspected of an offence to which s 7 relates that necessarily involved driving (ie s 3A, s 4 (charged in the 'driving' form), s 5 (charged in the 'driving' form)) then the disqualification is mandatory. If it related to an offence not necessarily involving driving (ie s 4 (charged in the 'being in charge' form) or s 5 (charged in the 'being in charge' form)) then the disqualification is discretionary.[37] The question of which offence was committed goes to the

---

28   RTOA 1988, s 34(6).
29   RTA 1988, s 40A.
30   RTOA 1988, s 48(1)(a).
31   RTOA 1988, s 48(1)(b).
32   RTA 1988, s 41A.
33   RTOA 1988, s 48(2)(a).
34   RTOA 1988, s 48(2)(b).
35   *Russell* [1993] RTR 249.
36   *DPP v Butterworth* [1995] 1 AC 381.
37   *Butterworth*, at 388, 389 and 393.

appropriate penalty and thus must be resolved to the criminal standard – the prosecution must make the court sure that D was driving or attempting to drive before D can be sentenced on that basis.[38] That matter should be the subject of a separate enquiry after any trial, with the justices making a separate decision about it through a Newton hearing to determine which type of disqualification is appropriate.[39]

7.11

Whilst the period of disqualification must not obliterate any prospect of rehabilitation, financial hardship alone will not be a sufficient reason to avoid/ shorten the disqualification – those who are reliant upon their driving licences for their livelihood owe it to themselves and their families to drive with proper respect for other road users; a key component of 'competence' in driving.[40] The guilty plea reduction applies only to punitive aspects of a sentence, and thus does not affect a disqualification period.[41]

7.12

Where there is a driver and a passenger who fall to be disqualified for the same events, it is important that their respective disqualifications mirror their differing roles, with a longer period for the driver.[42]

7.13

Disqualification for life will only be appropriate in extremely rare situations where there is evidence from which the court can infer that D will be a danger to the public indefinitely unless disqualified.[43] Even where D had an alcohol problem, and one previous Road Traffic Act offence, but there was no evidence that she could not or would not address her drinking problem, a shorter disqualification with a requirement to take an extended driving test was the correct ancillary order.[44] In *Rivano*,[45] the Court of Appeal was dealing with an offender at the other end of the spectrum, who, at age 30, had already been disqualified 24 times. Nonetheless, the Court emphasised how exceptional circumstances needed to be to justify a disqualification for life, especially for such a young man.[46]

---

38   *Crampsie v DPP* [1993] RTR 383.
39   *Butterworth*, at 394.
40   *Bannister* (1990–91) 12 Cr App R (S) 314.
41   *Needham* [2016] EWCA Crim 455, at [41].
42   *Gostkowski* [1995] RTR 324.
43   *Hopkins* [2008] EWCA Crim 2971, at [20].
44   *Hopkins*, at [21].
45   (1993) 14 Cr App R (S) 578.
46   *Rivano*, at 581.

7.14

Disqualification for life was upheld in *Lusher*,[47] where D knew that he suffered from epileptic seizures that caused him to black out, including whilst driving, but never reported this to the DVLA, and thus was able to keep his licence. He had a seizure whilst driving to see his dying wife in hospital and fatally injured a pedestrian when he lost control of the car. Disqualification for life was upheld, implicitly because D knew that he was a huge risk behind the wheel, but chose to drive anyway, having never reported his medical issues to the DVLA.[48]

Interaction between disqualification and endorsement

7.15

As recognised by the High Court in *Jones v Chief Constable of West Mercia*,[49] there is a circularity problem between s 34(1) and (2), and s 29(1)(a):[50]

'When, as in the present case, the court is faced with an offence that, in the normal process of the court's exercise of its jurisdiction, would or might attract discretionary disqualification under s 34; but also the offence is an offence that carries penalty points which, when added to the outstanding points, would take the accused over the number of 12; should the court apply the totting up provisions,[51] or should it apply the discretionary disqualification provisions? ... commentary in Current Law Statutes to the Road Traffic Act 1991 [which] asserts that there is an unavoidable circularity between s 29(1)(a) that provides that points in respect of an offence in respect of which an order has been made under s 34 are to be disregarded; and s 34(1) and (2), which assumes that attention is given to the points to be taken into account *before* considering disqualification in respect of such a s 34 offence.'

7.16

The Court consequently approached the case from first principles, and set down the following approach to assist in the avoidance of a double disqualification:[52]

(1)   Should a discretionary disqualification be imposed, considering D's whole record, and remembering that if a longer disqualification is appropriate due to D's number of points, they can disqualify under s 34(2).

---

47   [2016] EWCA Crim 2055.
48   *Lusher*, at [3] and [9].
49   [2001] RTR 8.
50   *Jones*, at [9]–[10].
51   As to totting up provisions see 7.68 ff.
52   *Jones*, at [19].

(2)   If no discretionary disqualification is appropriate, the points are added to the licence and D is disqualified under totting up provisions.

(3)   If a discretionary disqualification is appropriate, the points also imposed for this offence are not taken into account in totting up, so D is not also disqualified under s 35.

(4)   If, in light of D's record, the magistrates think that D should be disqualified for the longer period under the totting up provisions, they achieve that by not disqualifying under s 34.

7.17

It has also been held by the Divisional Court that, under s 44(1), it is not appropriate to order penalty points to be endorsed in relation to an offence if the court ordered the offender to be disqualified in respect of another offence of which he had been convicted on the same occasion.[53] In *Usaceva*,[54] the Court of Appeal confirmed that to impose penalty points where there had also been a disqualification was unlawful, as there was no strong indication in s 44(1) that Parliament had intended to change the position that had existed under the predecessor to RTA 1988,[55] under which it had been held in *Kent* that there could not be endorsement and disqualification.[56]

Appeal

7.18

Any complaint about the length of disqualification imposed by magistrates should be appealed to the Crown Court in the usual way,[57] unless it is so far outside the normal discretionary limits as to enable the court to say that it must have involved an error of law.[58]

Special reasons

7.19

As referred to in s 34(1), a court can choose not to disqualify, or to disqualify for a shorter period than 12 months, if there are 'special reasons' justifying such a course on the basis of circumstances which do not amount in law to a defence, but which display significantly reduced culpability.

---

53   *Martin v DPP* [2000] 2 Cr App R (S) 18.
54   [2015] EWCA Crim 166.
55   *Usaceva*, at [13]–[15].
56   [1983] 1 WLR 794.
57   As provided for by RTOA 1988, s 38(1).
58   *Tucker v DPP* (1992) 13 Cr App R (S) 495.

7.20

In *Whittall v Kirby*,[59] Lord Goddard LCJ set out the test as follows:[60]

> 'A "special reason" within the exception is one which is special to the facts of the particular case, that is, in other words, a mitigating or extenuating circumstance, not amounting in law to a defence to the charge, yet directly connected with the commission of the offence, and one which the court ought properly to take into consideration when imposing punishment.'

7.21

The statute gives little guidance, other than to specify that where a person is convicted of aggravated vehicle taking[61] the fact that they did not drive the vehicle is not a special reason.[62]

7.22

A body of case law has developed on what amounts to 'special reasons', and the proper procedural approach when such an argument is being run.

Procedural notes

7.23

A decision as to whether special reasons exist is a two-stage one:[63]

(1)   Are there any special reasons?

(2)   If so, should the court exercise its discretion not to disqualify D, or to disqualify him for a shorter period than 12 months, considering all the circumstances of the case?

7.24

Special reasons may be found but the court might nonetheless impose a 12-month disqualification. That is properly within its discretion,[64] for example, where D's drink had been spiked, but it must have been apparent to him nonetheless that he was not capable of driving.[65] In these circumstances, however, it would not usually be appropriate to impose a disqualification of

---

59   [1947] KB 194.
60   *Whittall v Kirby*, at 201.
61   Contrary to the Theft Act 1968, s 12A.
62   RTA 1988, s 34(1A).
63   *DPP v O'Connor* (1992) 95 Cr App R 135.
64   *Donahue v DPP* [1993] RTR 156.
65   *Donahue*, at 159–160.

longer than the mandatory minimum.[66] The court cannot decide to impose a period of less than 12 months as a 'halfway house' where it rejects the special reasons but feels sympathy for D.[67]

7.25

The burden of establishing special reasons rests on D,[68] and they must show that they did all that they reasonably could to avoid committing the offence.[69]

7.26

When considering whether special reasons are present, regard should be had to the four criteria in *Wickins*,[70] based upon the articulation of the definition of special reasons as given in *Whittall v Kirby* (see 7.20):[71]

7.27

If one takes the essence of that definition, there are four conditions laid down which have to be satisfied:

(1)   it must be a mitigating or an extenuating circumstance;

(2)   it must not amount in law to a defence to the charge;

(3)   it must be directly connected with the commission of the offence; and

(4)   it is a matter which the court ought properly to take into consideration when imposing punishment.

7.28

If after conviction following a trial where D has given evidence s/he wishes to run special reasons, D may need to be recalled to give further specific evidence about matters pertaining to the special reasons.[72]

Driving a very short distance

7.29

In *DPP v Corcoran*,[73] D had left his car parked on the street outside after arriving late to the theatre. After drinking two lagers, he was moving the car approximately 40 yards to a car park from which it had been agreed a work

---

66   *R v St Albans Crown Court, ex p O'Donovan* [2000] 1 Cr App R (S) 344.
67   *Jarvis v DPP* [2000] 10 WLUK 178, at [21].
68   *Robinson v DPP* [2003] EWHC 2718 (Admin), at [10].
69   *Robinson*, at [16].
70   (1958) 42 Cr App R 236.
71   *Wickins*, at 239–240.
72   *DPP v Kinnersley* (1993) 14 Cr App R (S) 516, at 521.
73   (1990–91) 12 Cr App R (S) 652.

colleague would collect it in the morning. That colleague (who gave evidence) could not be contacted at the time to be told it was elsewhere, and as it was a company car it was needed by the colleague for business purposes the next day. No other cars were in the area. The Court of Appeal held that a reasonable Bench was entitled to find these to be special reasons; however it emphasised that it was not distance alone that allowed a finding of special reasons, but more so that there were no other vehicles on the road, and no danger to other road users.[74]

7.30

Although decided under previous legislation, the considerations laid down in *Chatters v Burke*[75] continue to be cited with approval in such cases:

- distance vehicle driven;
- manner of driving;
- state of the vehicle;
- whether it was the intention of the driver to drive any further;
- prevailing road and traffic conditions;
- any danger by contact with other road users;
- reason for driving at all.

7.31

When considering a case based on the short distance driven, the court must look at the distance D intended to drive, not the distance D in fact drove. If D intended to drive a longer distance but was somehow prevented from doing that, then special reasons will not apply.[76]

Alcohol unwittingly consumed

7.32

In *R v Cambridge Magistrates' Court, ex p Wong*[77] an application for judicial review succeeded where the magistrates had found that, in law, the facts were not capable of amounting to special reasons. D was barely over the limit (within the margin of error whereby, at that time, people would not ordinarily be prosecuted

---

74   *DPP v Corcoran*, at 654.
75   (1986) 8 Cr App R (S) 222.
76   *CPS v Humphries* [2000] 2 Cr App R (S) 1, at 3.
77   [1992] RTR 382.

as stated by a Home Office Circular[78]), and an expert report showed that 1.7mg in 100ml breath would be attributable to two doses of cough medicine.[79]

7.33

Where D's drinks have been spiked by a third party, unless it is entirely clear that the only possible explanation for being over the limit is the alcohol added by spiking (ie D was drinking only soft drinks yet was over the limit), the court is likely to require medical evidence to explain that the additional alcohol over what D had intended to consume was what led to the levels in excess of the legal limit.[80] However, each case turns on its own facts, and a decision will not be susceptible to quashing simply because on D's own evidence, without medical evidence, the magistrates found that she had not felt any effect of the additional alcohol that her drinks had contained as a result of being spiked.[81]

7.34

It will not be possible to show special reasons if D had taken a decision to drink alcohol, in any circumstances, knowing that they would probably drive.[82]

Emergency

7.35

It is well-established law that driving in a genuine emergency can amount to special reasons.[83] For example, where someone is in need of hospital treatment but no ambulance can be sent and nor will a taxi attend due to reasons wholly outside of D's control (large scale disturbance in the area).[84] The emergency needs to be established objectively, not only subjectively.[85]

7.36

'Life and limb' cases are not the only sort of emergencies which can found special reasons, but there is a high hurdle that has to be crossed by the defendant raising this defence, where the burden of proof is on D, to the civil standard of balance of probabilities.[86]

---

78   Number 46/83 – it explained that there was a proper margin of error in readings of breath of 4mg/100ml.
79   *Wong*, at 384–385.
80   *DPP v O'Connor*, at 159.
81   *DPP v Sharma* [2005] EWHC 879 (Admin), at [13].
82   *DPP v Doyle* [1993] RTR 369.
83   *DPP v Upchurch* [1994] RTR 366, at 372.
84   *DPP v Upchurch* at 372.
85   *DPP v Whittle* [1996] RTR 154, at 158.
86   *DPP v Heathcote* [2011] EWHC 2536 (Admin), at [24].

7.37

Where there was a criminal offence that was ongoing, and developing at a rate that D could not ascertain, and although he had called the police he had no way of knowing how soon they would arrive, this was capable of amounting to special reasons.[87] The question for the justices, as when considering an 'emergency' case, is 'what would a sober, reasonable and responsible friend of the defendant, present at the time, but himself a non-driver and thus unable to help, have advised in the circumstances: drive or not drive?'[88] Only if the justices thought that there was a real possibility that that person would have advised D to drive, could they could properly find special reasons.[89]

7.38

If D makes more than one journey as a result of the emergency, then each of the journeys will need to be assessed, and only if all of them amount to emergencies will the special reasons be fulfilled.[90]

7.39

Advocates should be aware of the inter-relation between special reasons and the defences of necessity/duress of circumstances, which would provide a full defence to the conduct charged.[91]

Not driving a vehicle

7.40

Where D had been astride, but using his feet instead of the engine to propel forwards, a Malaguti 50cc bike that he had bought for his four-year-old son, and did not regard as a vehicle due to the material ways in which it was different from a motorbike, nor knew that he required insurance for it, special reasons were upheld by the Divisional Court.[92]

7.41

Regardless of the category of special reasons being advanced, the Divisional Court has noted that magistrates need to be careful not to be taken in by 'hard luck' stories. That said, however, that Court has accepted that, having seen D giving evidence, either as part of the trial or the special reasons hearing, the magistrates will be in the best position to judge D's truthfulness.[93]

---

87   *DPP v Cox* [1996] RTR 123.
88   *DPP v Bristow* [1998] RTR 100, at 107.
89   *DPP v Bristow*, at 109.
90   *DPP v Goddard* [1998] RTR 463.
91   *DPP v Whittle*, at 159; cf case of *Riddell* [2017] EWCA Crim 413.
92   *DPP v Powell* [1993] RTR 266.
93   *DPP v Enston* [1996] RTR 324.

Physiology affecting intoximeter reading

7.42

The case law has been somewhat inconsistent in this area. Whilst a reflux condition leading to D regurgitating alcohol and thus it passing down his oesophagus a number of times and leading to re-absorption was not capable of amounting to a special reason,[94] burping during the intoximeter procedure, causing an artificially inflated reading, can be so capable.[95]

No 'reasonable excuse' in failure to provide cases

7.43

It is open to magistrates to find that there are special reasons where a defence of reasonable excuse to a charge of failing to provide a specimen had failed.[96] D was afraid of contracting HIV and so refused to blow into the intoximeter, and the magistrates found that whilst he genuinely believed that giving a specimen would entail a substantial risk to his health, he did not have a reasonable excuse and convicted him. They allowed the special reasons argument, however. In this situation the court has to be in a position where it accepted the factual basis but found that that basis did not amount to a reasonable excuse.[97]

Appeal

7.44

If D disagrees with the outcome of a special reasons hearing, then the appropriate remedy will usually be by stating a case, not seeking judicial review.[98]

Road Traffic Offenders Act 1988, s 34A – reduced disqualification for attendance on courses

7.45

In prescribed circumstances the court can order the period of disqualification be reduced if by a specified date D has completed an approved course relevant to the offence. D must have been convicted of a relevant drink-drive offence or a specified offence by or before a court,[99] which resulted in an order under

---

94   *Woolfe v DPP* [2006] EWHC 1497 (Admin).
95   *O Sang Ng v DPP* [2007] EWHC 36 (Admin).
96   *DPP v Kinnersley*, at 518–519.
97   *DPP v Daley (No 2)* [1994] RTR 107, at 111.
98   *DPP v O'Connor*, at 136.
99   RTOA 1988, s 34A(1)(a).

RTOA 1988, s 34 (and s 35A if an extension period is used)[100] for disqualification of at least 12 months.[101]

'Relevant drink offence'

7.46

A 'relevant drink offence' means an offence under the following sections of RTA 1988:

- s 3A(1)(a) (causing death by careless driving when unfit to drive through drink or drugs) committed when unfit to drive through drink;[102]

- s 3A(1)(b) (causing death by careless driving with excess alcohol);[103]

- s 3A(1)(c) (failing to provide a specimen) where the specimen is required in connection with drink or consumption of alcohol;[104]

- s 4 (driving or being in charge when under influence of drink or drugs) committed by reason of unfitness through drink;[105]

- s 5(1) (driving or being in charge with excess alcohol);[106]

- s 7(6) (failing to provide a specimen) committed in the course of an investigation into an offence within any of the preceding paragraphs;[107] or

- s 7A(6) (failing to allow a specimen to be subjected to a laboratory test) in the course of an investigation into an offence within any of the preceding paragraphs.[108]

'Specified offence'

7.47

A 'specified offence' means an offence contrary to:

- RTA 1988, s 3 (careless, and inconsiderate, driving);[109]

---

100 RTOA 1988, s 34(1)(b), (5), (6) and (7A) have amendments pending from the Coroners and Justice Act 2009, Sch 21(9), para 90(3)(a)–(d). These would mean that any reduction did not apply to the extension period. However, these have not yet been brought into force and no date has been appointed – *Needham* [2016] EWCA Crim 455, at [44].
101 RTOA 1988, s 34A(1)(b).
102 RTOA 1988, s 34A(2)(a).
103 RTOA 1988, s 34A(2)(b).
104 RTOA 1988, s 34A(2)(c).
105 RTOA 1988, s 34A(2)(d).
106 RTOA 1988, s 34A(2)(e).
107 RTOA 1988, s 34A(2)(f).
108 RTOA 1988, s 34A(2)(g).
109 RTOA 1988, s 34A(3)(a).

- RTA 1988, s 36 (failing to comply with traffic signs);[110]

- Road Traffic Regulation Act (RTRA) 1984, s 17(4) (use of special road contrary to scheme or regulations);[111] or

- RTRA 1984, s 89(1) (exceeding speed limit).[112]

'Reduced period'

7.48

'The reduced period' is the period of disqualification imposed under RTOA 1988, s 34 (disregarding any extension period added pursuant to s 35A as reduced by an order under s 34A).[113]

7.49

Where s 34A applies, the court may make an order that a period of disqualification imposed under s 34 and s 35A shall be reduced if, by the relevant date, the offender satisfactorily completes an approved course[114] specified in the order.[115]

Approved course

7.50

'An approved course' means a course approved by the appropriate national authority for the purposes of s 34A in relation to the description of offence of which the offender is convicted,[116] and 'the relevant date' means such date, at least two months before the last day of the period of disqualification as reduced by the order, as is specified in the order.[117]

7.51

The reduction in length of disqualification by an order under s 34A is a period specified in the order of:

- at least three months;[118] and

- no longer than one quarter of the unreduced period.[119]

---

110 RTOA 1988, s 34A(3)(b).
111 RTOA 1988, s 34A(3)(c).
112 RTOA 1988, s 34A(3)(d).
113 RTOA 1988, s 34A(3A).
114 As approved under RTOA 1988, s 34BA.
115 RTOA 1988, s 34A(5).
116 RTOA 1988, s 34A(6).
117 RTOA 1988, s 34A(6).
118 RTOA 1988, s 34A(7)(a).
119 RTOA 1988, s 34A(7)(b).

7.52

An order cannot be made under s 34A if an offender has been convicted of a specified offence and:

- the offender has committed a specified offence during the three years immediately before commission of this offence, and successfully completed an approved course under either s 34A or 30A after that offence;[120] or

- the specified offence was committed during his probationary period.[121]

7.53

There is no provision in the Act preventing an order being made if D has previously undertaken such a course providing the previous order resulted from a conviction more than three years prior to the current offence.[122] A court should consider affording an opportunity to attend a course to all offenders convicted of a relevant offence for the first time, or of attending a second, but not a third, course where there are good reasons for doing so.[123]

7.54

A court shall not make an order under s 34A unless:

- the court is satisfied that a place on the course specified in the order will be available for the offender;[124]

- the offender appears to the court to be of or over the age of 17[125] (though note 7.52 – a course cannot be taken where the offence was within two years of passing the driving test);

- the court has informed the offender (orally or in writing and in ordinary language) of the effect of the order and of the amount of the fees which he is required to pay for the course and when he must pay them;[126] and

- the offender consents.[127]

7.55

In the Scottish case of *Swift v Macneill*,[128] the High Court of Justiciary held that when imposing a disqualification under the equivalent of s 34, the first instance court should not be influenced in the length of disqualification it imposed by the

---

120 RTOA 1988, s 34A(8)(a).
121 RTOA 1988, s 34A(8)(b).
122 *McDougall v Procurator Fiscal, Perth* [2015] HCJAC 112 – although a Scottish case, the provision is identical.
123 *McDougall v Procurator Fiscal, Perth*, at [4].
124 RTOA 1988, s 34A(9)(a).
125 RTOA 1988, s 34A(9)(b).
126 RTOA 1988, s 34A(9)(c).
127 RTOA 1988, s 34A(9)(d).
128 [2000] 8 WLUK 151.

fact that D has the option to reduce the length of the disqualification through a course. The period of disqualification to be imposed was to be decided by reference to the offence and any statutory principles, with the question of s 34A only arising after the appropriate period has been determined. This is to be contrasted with the English case of *Taylor*,[129] in which an appeal against a period of disqualification was upheld where the Recorder and counsel had not realised that s 34A did not apply to the offence for which D was being sentenced. The Court of Appeal held that the period of disqualification that D would serve, as he was without the option of reducing it through a course, was not the period for which the Recorder had intended him to be disqualified and allowed the appeal.

Road Traffic Offenders Act 1988, s 34B – certificates of completion of courses

7.56

An offender shall be regarded as having completed a course satisfactorily only once certification that he has done so is received by the proper officer[130] of the supervising court before the end of the unreduced period.[131]

'The total reduced period of disqualification'

7.57

This means the period of disqualification imposed under RTOA 1988, s 34 (including any extension period added to that period pursuant to s 35A), as reduced by an order under s 34A.[132]

'The total unreduced period of disqualification'

7.58

This means the period of disqualification imposed under s 34 (including any such extension period), disregarding any reduction by such an order.[133] The

---

129 [2001] EWCA Crim 2746, at [9].
130 As defined in RTOA 1988, s 34C(3): in relation to a magistrates' court in England and Wales, the designated officer for the court, and otherwise, the clerk of the court.
131 RTOA 1988, s 34B(1).
132 RTOA 1988, s 34B(2A).
133 RTOA 1988, s 34B(2A).

certificate is to be given by the course provider and shall be in the form required by the Secretary of State.[134,135]

Issue of certificate

7.59

If the certificate is received before the end of the unreduced period but after the end of the period which would be the reduced period, the reduced period is to be taken to end with the day on which the certificate is so received.[136]

7.60

A course provider must give a certificate to the offender not later than 14 days after the date specified in the order as the latest date for the completion of the course unless the offender:

- fails to make payment of fees for the course;[137]

- fails to attend the course in accordance with the course provider's reasonable instructions;[138] or

- fails to comply with any other reasonable requirement of the course provider.[139]

Refusal to grant certificate

7.61

Where a course provider decides not to give a certificate, it shall give written notice of the decision to the offender as soon as possible, and in any event not later than 14 days after the date specified in the order as the latest date for completion of the course.[140] That notice shall specify the ground for refusal.[141]

7.62

An offender to whom such a notice is given may, within such period as may be prescribed by rules of court, apply to either the supervising court or the relevant local court, for a declaration that the course provider's decision not to

---

134 As defined by RTOA 1988, s 34C(3).
135 RTOA 1988, s 34B(3).
136 RTOA 1988, s 34B(2).
137 RTOA 1988, s 34B(4)(a).
138 RTOA 1988, s 34B(4)(b).
139 RTOA 1988, s 34B(4)(c).
140 RTOA 1988, s 34B(5).
141 RTOA 1988, s 34B(10).

give a certificate was not in line with the reasons why such a refusal may be made under s 34B(4) (see 7.60).[142]

7.63

If the court grants that application, the effect will be as if the certificate had been duly received by the proper officer of the supervising court (see 7.56).

7.64

If 14 days after the date specified in the order as the latest date for completion of the course the course provider has given neither a certificate of completion, nor a notice as to why it will not be giving one, the offender may, within such period as may be prescribed by rules of court, apply to either the supervising court or the relevant local court for a declaration that the course provider is in default.[143]

7.65

If the court grants that application, the disqualification shall be reduced as if the certificate had been duly received by the proper officer of the supervising court (see 7.56).[144]

7.66

Where:

- the proper officer of a court receives a certificate; or

- a court makes a declaration that the refusal to issue a certificate did not fall under s 34B(6); or

- a court makes a declaration that the course provider is in default because neither certificate nor notice has been received,

the proper officer or court must notify the Secretary of State; and the notice must be sent in such manner and to such address, and must contain such particulars, as the Secretary of State may determine.[145]

7.67

Where D makes an application to the court under s 34B, there is a power to suspend the disqualification prior to the application being determined.[146]

---

142 RTOA 1988, s 34B(6).
143 RTOA 1988, s 34B(8).
144 RTOA 1988, s 34B(9).
145 RTOA 1988, s 34B(11).
146 RTOA 1988, s 41A(1).

Road Traffic Offenders Act 1988, s 35

7.68

This is commonly known as the 'totting up' provision – disqualification for a person who has amassed 12 points or more on their licence.

7.69

Where a person is convicted of:[147]

- an offence carrying discretionary disqualification and obligatory endorsement;[148] or

- an offence carrying obligatory disqualification in respect of which no order is made under s 34;[149] and

- the penalty points to be taken into account on that occasion[150] number 12 or more,

the court must order him to be disqualified for not less than the minimum period unless the court is satisfied, having regard to all the circumstances, that there are grounds for mitigating the normal consequences of the conviction and thinks fit to disqualify for a shorter period or not at all.[151]

7.70

The 'minimum period' referred to above is:

- six months if no previous disqualification imposed on the offender is to be taken into account;[152] or

- one year if one, and two years if more than one, such disqualification is to be taken into account.[153]

7.71

A previous disqualification is to be taken into account if it was for a fixed period of 56 days or more and was imposed within the three years immediately

---

147 RTOA 1988, s 35(1)(a).
148 RTOA 1988, s 35(1A)(a).
149 RTOA 1988, s 35(1A)(b).
150 Both this phrase and 'conviction' have been held to refer to the date of sentence – *R v Brentwood Justices, ex p Richardson* [1993] RTR 374, at 378.
151 RTOA 1988, s 35(1)(b).
152 RTOA 1988, s 35(2)(a).
153 RTOA 1988, s 35(2)(b).

preceding the commission of the latest offence[154] in respect of which penalty points are taken into account under RTA 1988, s 29.[155] A previous disqualification is not to be taken into account if that period would have been less than 56 days but for an extension period added pursuant to RTA 1988, s 35A[156] or PCC(S)A 2000, s 147A.[157]

7.72

Where an offender is convicted on the same occasion of more than one offence carrying discretionary disqualification and obligatory endorsement,[158] or an offence carrying obligatory disqualification in respect of which no order is made under s 34,[159] and there are 12 or more penalty points to be taken into account on that occasion:

- not more than one disqualification shall be imposed on him;[160]

- in determining the period of the disqualification the court must take into account all the offences;[161] and

- for the purposes of any appeal any disqualification imposed under s 35(1) shall be treated as an order made on the conviction of each of the offences.[162]

7.73

When a court is considering whether to disqualify someone under s 35(1), no account is to be taken of any of the following circumstances:

- any circumstances that are alleged to make the offence or any of the offences not a serious one;[163]

- hardship, other than exceptional hardship,[164] (see 7.80); or

- any circumstances which, within the three years immediately preceding the conviction, have been taken into account under that subsection

---

154 It has been held that the correct method of counting here is that: 'it should be assumed that the period of three years ended at midnight on the day preceding the date of the offence for which disqualification was being considered, so that the day of the last offence of which the [D] had been convicted fell to be excluded and the period of three years in question ran from 24th July 1990 to 25th July 1987, working backwards from midnight to midnight, taking the whole of each of those days into account' *Keenan v Carmichael* 1991 JC 169, at 172.
155 RTOA 1988, s 35(2).
156 RTOA 1988, s 35(2A)(a).
157 RTOA 1988, s 35(2A)(c).
158 RTOA 1988, s 35(1A)(a).
159 RTOA 1988, s 35(1A)(b).
160 RTOA 1988, s 35(3)(a).
161 RTOA 1988, s 35(3)(b).
162 RTOA 1988, s 35(3)(c).
163 RTOA 1988, s 35(4)(a).
164 RTOA 1988, s 35(4)(b).

in ordering the offender to be disqualified for a shorter period or not ordering him to be disqualified.[165]

7.74

References in this section to disqualification do not include:

- a disqualification imposed under RTOA 1988, s 26 or PCC(S)A 2000, s 147; or

- a disqualification imposed in respect of an offence of:

  - stealing a motor vehicle;

  - an offence under the Theft Act 1968, s 12 or s 25;

  - an offence under RTA 1988, s 178; or

  - an attempt to commit such an offence.[166]

7.75

Section 35 applies to convictions for aiding, abetting, counselling, procuring, or inciting the commission of an offence involving obligatory disqualification as if the offence were an offence involving discretionary disqualification.[167]

7.76

The requirements to disqualify in s 35 are subject to two exemptions in RTOA 1988, s 48,[168] (see 7.08).

7.77

When a court is sentencing in a case where endorsing D's licence with penalty points is obligatory, and that endorsement would take D up to, or over, 12 points, and therefore potentially into a s 35(1) disqualification, the court should proceed in two distinct steps:

(1)   Are there any special reasons under s 44(1) not to endorse D's licence (see 7.19)?

(2)   If not, should the disqualification be shortened or foregone due to special reasons?

---

165 RTOA 1988, s 35(4)(c).
166 RTOA 1988, s 35(5).
167 RTOA 1988, s 35(5A).
168 RTOA 1988, s 35(7).

7.78

The Court has noted that these steps should not be conflated or reversed,[169] and advocates are advised to ensure that when reasons are given in open court for a sentence, as required by s 174 of the Criminal Justice Act (CJA) 2003, it is clear that the court has adopted the correct approach.

7.79

In keeping with the position under the other disqualification powers, disqualification under s 35 is an ancillary order and thus not susceptible to a reduction for a guilty plea; likewise the imposition of points is not susceptible to such a reduction.[170]

Exceptional hardship

7.80

As noted in s 35(4)(b), when a court is deciding whether or not to impose a disqualification, it can have regard to 'exceptional hardship'. A body of case law has elucidated what amounts to such hardship. Exceptional hardship arguments come before the magistrates frequently, and if they are to succeed they will usually need to be focused on the hardship that will be suffered by others who are innocent in D's offending,[171] though this is not an invariable rule – such matters will always depend on fact and degree,[172] and there is no fixed definition.[173]

7.81

In *Marshall v McDougall*,[174] decided under the comparable Scottish provision, the Court held that exceptional hardship would occur where D played such an essential role in his business that it would probably collapse, and five employees would lose their jobs in addition to D and his wife, and customers' heating could not be serviced. This is supported by the Court holding that it was necessary to demonstrate not only that the accused would lose his employment but also that there were other circumstances associated with loss of employment which might involve hardship of a serious kind on the accused's business, his family or his long-term prospects.[175] If D has specific and unusual skills that he uses in

---

169 Considering the identical Scottish legislation: *Robertson (Neil) v McNaughtan* 1993 SLT 1143.
170 *Curtis* [2007] EWCA Crim 2034, at [9].
171 *Cornwall v Coke* [1976] 5 WLUK 89; [1976] Crim LR 519.
172 *Brennan v McKay* 1997 SLT 603, at 604.
173 *Howdle v Davidson* 1994 SCCR 751.
174 1991 SCCR 231.
175 *Brennan v McKay* 1997 SLT 603, at 604.

his job, making him very difficult for the employer to replace, that will also be a relevant factor.[176]

7.82

Dependent family members (ie a single parent to young children with serious long-term illnesses) can establish a case of exceptional hardship, but again, the degree to which it is established will vary with circumstances.[177]

7.83

The sentencing court is permitted to find that, although the usual length of disqualification to be imposed in D's circumstances would cause exceptional hardship, there would be no exceptional hardship from a shorter period of disqualification – the legislation is not 'all or nothing'.[178]

Which power to disqualify under?

7.84

In *Jones v Chief Constable of West Mercia*,[179] an appeal against a decision to disqualify D following his conviction for speeding, the Court determined that the correct approach to be taken by magistrates when they were required to decide between disqualification under RTOA 1988, s 35 by reason of an accumulation of points and discretionary disqualification under s 34 was as follows:

(1)   consideration should be given to the imposition of discretionary disqualification under s 34(2), such consideration taking into account the whole record of the accused;

(2)   in the event of disqualification under s 34(2), points for the offence should not be taken into account under the totting up provision; and

(3)   if the decision was not to disqualify the accused under s 34(2), points should be added to his licence and action taken as necessary under s 35.

7.85

It is respectfully suggested that step 3 should be broken down into parts (a) and (b) in light of other decided cases detailed above:

(a)   points should be added to D's licence if no special reasons not to do so are found; and

---

176 *Findlay v Walkingshaw* 1998 SCCR 181.
177 Compare the Scottish cases of *Colgan v MacDonald* 1999 SCCR 901 (single mother to severely disabled children – exceptional hardship) with that of *Ewan v Orr* 1993 SCCR 101 (D lived with and supported members of his mother's family – no exceptional hardship).
178 *McLaughlin v Docherty* 1991 SCCR 227.
179 [2001] RTR 8.

(b)   if that takes D over 12 points, then s 35 will be utilised.

And then followed with a step 4:

(4)   the court will impose a disqualification under s 35, subject to any successful arguments on exceptional hardship.

7.86

Where D has succeeded in an exceptional hardship submission, the court is not bound to allow D their costs – by not disqualifying for those reasons the court is showing mercy, as opposed to making a decision on the merits regarding the offence.[180]

7.87

If an argument of exceptional hardship is allowed under s 35, the court should not then move to considering a discretionary disqualification afresh.[181]

Appeal

7.88

Appeal lies to the Crown Court against a disqualification under s 35, as under s 34.[182] In the usual way, a disqualification or endorsement of points can be increased on appeal to the Crown Court, providing D has been warned at the beginning of the hearing that this is a possibility, and providing that if the tribunal has any questions of fact, there should be evidence called so that they can satisfy themselves as to the relevant material facts.[183]

Road Traffic Offenders Act 1988, ss 35A and 35B

7.89

The rationale of these provisions is the same as that behind PCC(S)A 2000, s 147A and s 147B (see 6.30 and 6.40). These provisions came into force on 13 April 2015, having been inserted into RTOA 1988 by the Coroners and Justice Act 2009 (but not brought into force) and then amended and brought into force by the Criminal Justice and Courts Act 2015. They do not apply to offences committed before 13 April 2015.[184] They mirror the provisions of ss 147A and 147B of the PCC(S)A 2000 (see 6.30 and 6.40), meaning that case

---

180 *R (Pluckrose) v Snaresbrook Crown Court* [2010] RTR 12, at [17]–[18].
181 Based on the Scottish case on the equivalent provisions – *Hamand v Procurator Fiscal, Glasgow* [2016] SAC (Crim) 15.
182 RTOA 1988, s 38(1).
183 *R (Tottman) v DPP* [2004] EWHC 258 (Admin), at [31]–[32].
184 *Needham* [2016] EWCA Crim 455, at [13]–[15].

law on the 2000 provisions can also be applied to the interpretation of these provisions, and vice versa.[185] Their respective roles and inter-relation has caused some confusion.[186]

7.90

Although each is set out in more detail below, the practitioner's first port of call should be the checklist created by the Court of Appeal in *Needham*,[187] which subsequent courts have endorsed as a blueprint for determining whether s 35A and s 35B apply in any case.[188]

7.91

If these are not correctly applied, then on any appeal to the Court of Appeal they can only be rectified if the substantive part of the sentence is reduced, so that s 11(3) of the Criminal Appeal Act 1968 is not breached by dealing with the offender more harshly than s/he was in the lower court.[189] Sometimes appropriate adjustments can be made by restricting the overall period of disqualification:[190]

- **Step 1** – Does the court intend to impose a 'discretionary' disqualification under s 34 or s 35 for any offence?

  YES – go to step 2.

- **Step 2** – Does the court intend to impose a custodial term for that same offence?

  YES – s 35A applies and the court must impose an extension period (see s 35A(4)(h) for that same offence and consider step 3).

  NO – s 35A does not apply at all – go on to consider s 35B and step 4.

- **Step 3** – does the court intend to impose a custodial term for another offence (which is longer or consecutive) or is the defendant already serving a custodial sentence?

  YES – then consider what increase ('uplift') in the period of 'discretionary disqualification' is required to comply with s 35B(2) and (3). In accordance with s 35B(4) ignore any custodial term imposed for an offence involving disqualification under s 35A.

  Discretionary period + extension period + uplift = total period of disqualification

  NO – no need to consider s 35B at all.

---

185 *Needham*, at [5].
186 *Needham*, at [3].
187 *Needham*, at [31].
188 *Wickens* [2016] EWCA Crim 2077, at [14].
189 *Aldhain* [2018] EWCA Crim 1359, at [22].
190 *Wilding* [2016] EWCA Crim 1802, at [39].

Discretionary period + extension period = total period of disqualification

- **Step 4** – does the court intend to impose a custodial term for another offence or is the defendant already serving a custodial sentence?

  YES – then consider what increase ('uplift') in the period of 'discretionary disqualification' is required to comply with s 35B(2) and (3).

Discretionary period + uplift = total period of disqualification.

7.92

A very clearly-articulated example by a different constitution of the Court of Appeal applying *Needham* can be seen in Lewis J's judgment in *Barratt*:[191]

'The starting point is that a discretionary period of disqualification will be imposed under s 34 of the 1988 Act. That would be for 18 months. As s 35A provides in respect of the driving offence for which a sentence of four months' imprisonment was imposed, an extension period of two months – one half of the custodial sentence – is to be imposed. Further, as custodial sentences were imposed for other offences, s 35B applies and the court needs to consider the fact that the effect of disqualification would be diminished as a result of the fact that part of the period of the disqualification would be spent in custody. The period of disqualification should have been further increased, therefore, by 10 months to reflect that. That would give rise to a total period of disqualification of 30 months. That is comprised of the 18 months from the date of conviction that would normally have been imposed under s 34, plus two months imposed under s 35A and a further discretionary uplift of 10 months, having regard to s 35B. The period of disqualification imposed under s 35B is 10 months not 16 to take into account the fact that the Appellant spent 6 months on remand in custody. That period would not count towards the period of 18 months disqualification under s 34 as that runs only from the date of conviction. A period of 10 months disqualification under s 35B will ensure that the period of disqualification remaining on release from custody will be 18 months, that is 6 months from the disqualification period imposed under s 34, 2 months under s 35A and 10 months under s 35B.'

7.93

The Court of Appeal has since emphasised that sentencing judges should specifically state in open court the discretionary, extended and uplift periods referable to each count on the indictment to which they relate.[192] Counsel

---

191 [2017] EWCA Crim 1631, at [30].
192 *Watson* [2016] EWCA Crim 2119, at [19].

should not be afraid to ask judges to specify the periods in this manner if they do not initially do so in sentencing remarks.

Section 35A – extension of disqualification where custodial sentence also imposed

7.94

This section permits a court to add an extension period to a disqualification imposed under s 34 or s 35. Its rationale is to avoid the offender serving all or part of the period of disqualification while he or she is in custody, and the disqualification thus having no practical effect.

7.95

As stated in *Needham*, and demonstrated in other cases since, the principles regarding ss 35A and 35B apply equally to PCC(S)A 2000, s 147A and s 147B, as the provisions are mirror images.[193] If a court purports to extend under the provisions of one Act, when the correct provisions are those in the mirror image in the other Act, then a straightforward substitution can be made.[194]

7.96

The provisions are mandatory where the court imposes an immediate custodial sentence[195] and a driving disqualification under s 146 or s 147 for the same offence.[196] They do not apply where the sentence is suspended imprisonment.[197] As these provisions are mandatory, counsel are required to draw them to the attention of the court.[198]

7.97

Any order under s 147A must set out the appropriate extension period, as well as the discretionary disqualification period,[199] which is the length of disqualification that the court would have given under s 146 or s 147 in any event.[200]

7.98

The appropriate extension period is (to the nearest whole day[201]):

---

193 *Johnson* [2017] EWCA Crim 1192, at [16].
194 *Johnson*, at [18].
195 RTOA 1988, s 35A(1)(a).
196 RTOA 1988, s 35A(1)(b).
197 RTOA 1988, s 35A(7)(a).
198 *Martin* [2016] EWCA Crim 15, at [19].
199 RTOA 1988, s 35A(2).
200 RTOA 1988, s 35A(3).
201 RTOA 1988, s 35A(5).

- half of the length of:

  - a custodial sentence;[202]

  - a Detention and Training Order;[203]

  - the period imposed under CJA 1993, s 236A of a special custodial sentence for certain offenders of particular concern;[204]

- two-thirds of the length of:

  - the custodial portion of an extended determinate sentence (under CJA 2003, s 226A where D is over 18[205], or s 226B if under 18[206]);

- the tariff period (under PCC(S)A 2000, s 82A(2) or CJA 2003, s 269(2)).[207]

7.99

This section does not apply where the court has made an order that the early release provisions are not to apply to either a mandatory life sentence (under CJA 2003, s 269(4),[208] or a discretionary life sentence (PCC(S)A 2000, s 82A(4)).[209]

7.100

It does not apply to offences committed before 13 April 2015, and so where an offence was committed before that date, a judge cannot impose an extension period.[210] The alternative way to the same outcome, where cases from before that date are being sentenced, is to impose a longer primary period of disqualification such as to achieve the balance between the disqualification having effect on D's release, but not impairing rehabilitation.[211] If it is unclear from the way in which the judge has expressed her/himself how the disqualification is structured, then clarification should be sought by counsel so the reasoning is clear.[212]

7.101

When a sentencing court is trying to take fair account of a period spent on remand when calculating the driving disqualification, that adjustment needs to be done by using the general discretion in s 35B as the period under s 35A must

---

202 RTOA 1988, s 35A(4)(h).
203 RTOA 1988, s 35A(4)(b).
204 RTOA 1988, s 35(4)(fa).
205 RTOA 1988, s 35A(4)(e).
206 RTOA 1988, s 35A(4)(f).
207 RTOA 1988, s 35A(4)(a); PCC(S)A 2000, s147A(4)(g).
208 RTOA 1988, s 35A(7)(b).
209 RTOA 1988, s 35A(7)(c).
210 *Ahmed* [2017] EWCA Crim 303, at [9].
211 *Ahmed*, at [10] and [12].
212 *Johnson*, at [19]; *Kirk* [2017] EWCA Crim 626, at [38]–[39].

be half of the custodial term, and cannot be adjusted.[213] However, in *Oliver*,[214] the Court of Appeal suggested that there did not need to be arithmetical exactness when calculating the extension period where D had been on remand, and rounding down from seven and a half months to six months for ease of calculation would be acceptable.[215]

7.102

Where D is disqualified for life and given a custodial sentence, technically the provisions of s 35A apply, but the Court of Appeal has taken the view that 'the requisite extension period is incorporated by implication when a period of disqualification for life is imposed, and that therefore no correction is required'.[216]

7.103

Where D appeals against sentence successfully, leading to a reduction in the custodial term, the extension period will need to be adjusted accordingly.[217] It will need to be removed altogether if D's appeal leads to their sentence becoming non-custodial (or suspended custodial) when it had previously been immediate custodial.[218]

Section 35B – effect of custodial sentence in other cases

7.104

This section permits a court to add an uplift to a disqualification because the defendant will be serving a custodial sentence for another offence. It is intended to allow a court to have regard to the fact that a defendant is subject to a custodial sentence which would have the consequence of diminishing or removing the effect of any disqualification as a punishment were it to be imposed in the ordinary way (with immediate effect).[219]

7.105

It applies where a person is disqualified under s 34 or s 35 and either the court will be imposing an immediate custodial sentence for another offence,[220] or the person is already serving a custodial sentence for other matters when they are disqualified.[221]

---

213 *Abbassi* [2017] EWCA Crim 779, at [11].
214 [2016] EWCA Crim 2017.
215 *Oliver*, at [15]–[16].
216 *Lusher* [2016] EWCA Crim 2055, at [15].
217 *Bravender* [2018] EWCA Crim 723, at [30]–[31].
218 *Hristov* [2017] EWCA Crim 1736, at [12].
219 *Mascarenas* [2018] EWCA Crim 1467, at [8].
220 RTOA 1988, s 35B(1)(a).
221 RTOA 1988, s 35B(1)(b).

7.106

In determining the period for which the person is to be disqualified under s 34 or s 35, the court must have such regard as appropriate[222] to the diminished effect of disqualification if the person is in custody.[223]

7.107

Section 35B provides significant latitude to a sentencing judge, as it does not apply a simple mathematical exercise as s 34A does.[224]

7.108

Any custodial sentence for the offence for which they are being disqualified under s 34 or s 35 is not to be taken into account at this stage[225] (as it should already have been considered when determining the length of discretionary disqualification).

7.109

Similarly to PCC(S)A 2000, s 147A, if the sentencing judge wrongly refers to s 147B when s/he should be referring to RTOA 1988, s 35B, there is no practical effect and substitution is appropriate.[226]

7.110

Section 35B mirrors the provisions in PCC(S)A 2000, s 147B – it is the like provision in relation to disqualifications under s 34.[227] Therefore, should a judge state that s/he is applying s 35B to a s 34 disqualification, when s/he should have made a disqualification under s 146 or s 147 and applied s 147B to it (or vice versa) there will be no practical effect of the error, as the judge's intended result is clear.[228]

Road Traffic Offenders Act 1988, s 36 – disqualification until test is passed

7.111

Section 36 of RTOA 1988 sets out the circumstances in which D can be disqualified until they have passed an appropriate driving test.

---

222 RTOA 1988, s 35B(2).
223 RTOA 1988, s 35B(3).
224 *Lee* [2018] EWCA Crim 715, at [10].
225 RTOA 1988, s 35B(4).
226 *Mascarenas*, at [13].
227 *Mascarenas*, at [8].
228 *Mascarenas*, at [13].

7.112

It provides that where D has been disqualified under s 34 having been convicted of the following offences, they MUST be disqualified until they (re)-pass the 'appropriate driving test':[229,230]

- manslaughter by the driver of a motor vehicle;[231]

- an offence under RTA 1988, s 1 (causing death by dangerous driving) or s 2 (dangerous driving);[232]

- a person disqualified under RTOA 1988, s 34 or s 35 in such circumstances or for such period as the Secretary of State may by order prescribe;[233]

- causing death by careless driving when under the influence of drink and drugs (contrary to RTA 1988, s 3A);[234]

- other persons convicted of such offences involving obligatory endorsement as may be so prescribed.[235]

7.113

Where D is convicted of any other offence involving obligatory endorsement, the court MAY order him to be disqualified until he passes the appropriate driving test (whether or not he has previously passed any test).[236]

7.114

When deciding whether to exercise this power, the court must have regard to the safety of road users.[237] This means that where someone is disqualified under PCC(S)A 2000, s 146, which can apply to any offence (see 6.07) they nonetheless cannot be ordered to re-take their test unless the offence carries penalty points.[238] This was demonstrated in *Patel*,[239] which concerned the then-equivalent power to s 146 – the Powers of Criminal Courts Act 1973, s 44.[240]

7.115

Where D has been convicted of a serious offence (such as causing death by careless driving), the court should give thorough consideration to whether an

---

229 As defined in RTOA 1988, s 36(5), see 7.116.
230 RTOA 1988, s 36(1).
231 RTOA 1988, s 36(2)(a).
232 RTOA 1988, s 36(2)(b).
233 RTOA 1988, s 36(3)(a).
234 Driving Licences (Disqualification Until Test Passed) (Prescribed Offence) Order 2001 (SI 2001/4051).
235 RTOA 1988, s 36(3)(b).
236 RTOA 1988, s 36(4).
237 RTOA 1988, s 36(6).
238 As illustrated in *Large* [2011] EWCA Crim 2970, at [8], [10]–[11], where D had been convicted of GBH after ramming another car and seriously injuring a passenger.
239 (1995) 16 Cr App R (S) 756.
240 *Patel*, at 760.

extended re-test is appropriate, and not simply impose it automatically, if D has an otherwise good driving record.[241]

7.116

- 'Appropriate driving test' means:

  - an extended driving test, where a person is convicted of an offence involving obligatory disqualification or is disqualified under RTOA 1988, s 35;[242]

  - a test of competence to drive, other than an extended driving test, in any other case;[243]

- 'extended driving test' means a test of competence to drive prescribed for the purposes of this section;[244]

- 'test of competence to drive' means a test prescribed by virtue of RTA 1988, s 89(3).[245]

7.117

The Court of Appeal has emphasised that sentencing judges should attend to which sort of test is to be required dependent upon the offence of which D has been convicted.[246]

7.118

A disqualification under this section shall be deemed to have expired for the classes of vehicles for which evidence of passing the required test can be produced,[247] on production to the Secretary of State of evidence, as may be prescribed by regulations under RTA 1988, s 105, that the person disqualified has passed the required test since the order was made.[248]

7.119

Where a person's driving record is endorsed with particulars of a disqualification under this section, it shall also be endorsed with the particulars of any test of competence to drive that he has passed since the order of disqualification was made.[249]

---

241 *Hall* [2010] EWCA Crim 2135, at [8]–[12].
242 RTOA 1988, s 36(5)(a).
243 RTOA 1988, s 36(5)(b).
244 RTOA 1988, s 36(5).
245 RTOA 1988, s 36(5).
246 *Watson* [2013] EWCA Crim 2316, at [7].
247 RTOA 1988, s 36(9).
248 RTOA 1988, s 36(8).
249 RTOA 1988, s 36(10A).

7.120

For the purposes of an order under this section, a person shall be treated as having passed a test of competence to drive other than an extended driving test if he passes a corresponding test conducted under the law of Northern Ireland, the Isle of Man, any of the Channel Islands, another EEA State, Gibraltar or a designated country or territory,[250] or for the purposes of obtaining a British Forces licence (as defined by RTA 1988, s 88(8)).[251] 'Designated country or territory' means a country or territory designated by order under RTA 1988, s 108(2) but a test conducted under the law of such a country or territory shall not be regarded as a corresponding test unless a person passing such a test would be entitled to an exchangeable licence as defined in s 108(1) of that Act.[252]

7.121

The contents of s 36 are subject to the two exemptions in RTOA 1988, s 48 [253] (see 7.08).

7.122

If D has previously been ordered to take an extended re-test and has not done so by the time he is sentenced for new offences, the previous order still stands, and no further order for an extended re-test should be made;[254] in fact, the court has no power to do so due to RTOA 1988, s 36(7)(b).[255] Even if a previous period of disqualification has been served, the order to take an extended re-test does not cease to have effect until that re-test is taken. For clarity a DVLA printout might be needed to ascertain whether any such test was taken.[256]

7.123

There is no principle that it is inappropriate to disqualify passengers who are accomplices in a planned cash machine raid of which dangerous driving is an integral part – although their culpability will usually be less than that of the driver, it is not so low as to never require disqualification until an extended re-test.[257]

---

250 RTOA 1988, s 36(11)(a).
251 RTOA 1988, s 36(11)(b).
252 RTOA 1988, s 36(11A).
253 RTOA 1988, s 36(12).
254 *Abdullahi* [2010] EWCA Crim 1886, at [5].
255 *Anderson* [2012] EWCA Crim 3060, at [12].
256 *John* [2016] EWCA Crim 2284, at [21].
257 *Beech* [2016] EWCA Crim 1746, at [24]–[26].

7.124

Technically, even if disqualifying for life, the court should make an order that D is not to drive again until they have taken an extended re-test, even though this seems to be unnecessary.[258]

7.125

Where the imposition of a re-test is discretionary, the Court of Appeal has acknowledged that, for example, where there was 'momentary distraction with no previous history of motoring offences' if there had been a full acceptance of guilt then the protection afforded by requiring a re-test might not be necessary.[259]

7.126

In *Broad*,[260] the Court of Appeal held that despite the operation of s 11(3) of the Criminal Appeal Act 1968 (no sentence can be increased on appeal), it was permissible to require an extended driving test to be passed under s 36(2)(b) where the sentencing judge had omitted to do so, even if no other aspect of the sentence was reduced on appeal.[261] This is inconsistent with other decisions of the Court, which have adopted the view that to impose a requirement for a re-test where this has been overlooked below is not permissible under the 1968 Act.[262]

7.127

Where a person is given a conditional discharge but ordered to be disqualified until passing an appropriate driving test, the disqualification lasts until that test is passed, even if that is long after the period of the conditional discharge has expired.[263]

Road Traffic Offenders Act 1988, s 37 – effect of disqualification

7.128

Where the holder of a licence is disqualified by an order of a court, the licence shall be treated as being revoked with effect from the beginning of the period of disqualification.[264]

---

258 *Lusher*, at [16].
259 *Frewin* [2016] EWCA Crim 1737, at [30].
260 [2007] EWCA Crim 2146.
261 *Broad*, at [38].
262 *Lauder* [1998] 10 WLUK 452.
263 *Re Hamill* [2001] EWHC 762 (Admin).
264 RTOA 1988, s 37(1).

7.129

Where the disqualification is for fewer than 56 days (disregarding any extension period under RTOA 1988, s 35A[265] or PCC(S)A 2000, s 147A[266])[267] in respect of an offence involving obligatory endorsement,[268] or the order is under RTOA 1988, s 26,[269] the licence simply has effect again at the end of the period of disqualification (including any extension period), and D can obtain one by writing to the DVLA. The licence has, in effect, been 'dormant' for that period – it has not ceased to exist, and D has technically 'held a licence' in that period of time.[270]

7.130

Where D appeals against the disqualification and it is suspended under s 39, the period of disqualification shall be treated as beginning on the day on which the disqualification ceases to be suspended.[271]

7.131

A person disqualified under RTOA 1988, s 36 is (unless he is also disqualified under some other provision) entitled to obtain and hold a provisional licence and to drive a motor vehicle in accordance with the conditions subject to which the provisional licence is granted.[272] Similarly, a person who holds a Community licence which authorises them to drive vehicles of a particular class, but who is disqualified under s 36, is (unless the person is also disqualified under some other provision) entitled to drive a motor vehicle of that class in accordance with the same conditions as if the person were authorised to drive a motor vehicle of that class by a provisional licence.[273]

Road Traffic Offenders Act 1988, s 39 – suspension of disqualification

7.132

Any court which makes an order disqualifying a person may, if it thinks fit, suspend the disqualification pending an appeal against the order.[274] Disqualification is not suspended automatically on notice of an appeal being given. This means that if D drives having put in a notice of appeal, but having

---

265 RTOA 1988, s 37(1B)(a).
266 RTOA 1988, s 37(1B)(c).
267 This amendment was brought into effect on 16 July 2018.
268 RTOA 1988, s 37(1A)(a).
269 RTOA 1988, s 37(1A)(b).
270 *R v Crawley Borough Council, ex p Crabb* [1996] RTR 201.
271 RTOA 1988, s 37(2).
272 RTOA 1988, s 37(3).
273 RTOA 1988, s 37(4).
274 RTOA 1988, s 39(1). This power is also conferred on the appellate courts by virtue of RTOA 1988, s 40.

not been granted a suspension, he will be guilty of driving whilst disqualified in that period, as he is validly disqualified, even if the appeal is eventually successful.[275]

7.133

Similarly, if a person is convicted in absence and without his knowledge, any disqualification imposed in his absence is valid unless and until he serves a notice under s 14 of the Magistrates' Courts Act 1980 which states that proceedings will be invalid where the accused did not know of them.[276]

7.134

Where a court exercises that power, it must send notice of the suspension to the Secretary of State[277] in the form required by the Secretary of State.[278]

Road Traffic Offenders Act 1988, s 26 – interim disqualification

7.135

This section provides for interim disqualification for up to six months whilst D is awaiting sentence.[279] There is no power to disqualify prior to conviction – if the court thought that D should not be driving in that period then it would have to be made a condition of their bail not to drive.

7.136

Where a magistrates' court:

- commits an offender to the Crown Court under PCC(S)A 2000, s 6 or any enactment mentioned in s 6(4) of that Act;[280] or

- remits an offender to another magistrates' court under PCC(S)A 2000, s 10,[281] to be dealt with for an offence involving obligatory or discretionary disqualification,

it may order him to be disqualified until he has been dealt with in respect of the offence.

---

275 *R v Thames Magistrates' Court, ex p Levy* [1997] 6 WLUK 266.
276 *DPP v Singh* [1999] RTR 424.
277 RTOA 1988, s 39(3).
278 RTOA 1988, s 39(4).
279 RTOA 1988, s 26(4).
280 RTOA 1988, s 26(1)(a).
281 RTOA 1988, s 26(1)(b).

7.137

Where a court:

- defers passing sentence on D under PCC(S)A 2000, s 1 for an offence involving obligatory or discretionary disqualification;[282] or

- adjourns after convicting an offender of such an offence but before dealing with him for the offence,[283]

it may order D to be disqualified until he has been dealt with for the offence.

7.138

Where a court orders a person to be disqualified under this section, no court shall make a further order under this section for the same offence or any offence in respect of which an order could have been made at the same time the order was made.[284]

7.139

Where a court makes an order under this section it must:

- require D to produce to the court any licence he holds; and

- retain the licence until it deals with him or send it to the proper officer of the court (the designated officer in the magistrates' court[285] or the clerk in any other court[286]) which is to deal with him.

7.140

It is an offence for the licence-holder not to produce, post or cause the licence to be delivered,[287] unless:

- D satisfies the court that he has applied for a new licence and has not received it;[288] or

- D surrenders to the court a current receipt for his licence showing it has been surrendered on account of a fixed penalty notice, as provided for under RTOA 1988, s 56, and produces the licence to the court immediately on its return.[289]

---

282 RTOA 1988, s 26(2)(a).
283 RTOA 1988, s 26(2)(b).
284 RTOA 1988, s 26(6).
285 RTOA 1988, s 26(7A)(a).
286 RTOA 1988, s 26(7A)(b).
287 RTOA 1988, s 26(8).
288 RTOA 1988, s 26(9)(a).
289 RTOA 1988, s 26(9)(b).

7.141

Where a court imposes an interim disqualification, RTOA 1988, ss 44(1) (if D convicted of an offence carrying obligatory endorsement, the particulars of disqualification must be endorsed on his licence); 47(2) (if D disqualified for more than 56 days, licence must be sent to Secretary of State), 91ZA(7) (applying those provisions to NI licence-holders) and 91A(5) (applying those provisions to Community licence-holders) shall not apply to the order, but:

- the court must send notice of the order to the Secretary of State,[290] in the prescribed form;[291] and

- if the court which deals with the offender determines not to order him to be disqualified under RTOA 1988, s 34 or s 35, it must send notice of the determination to the Secretary of State.[292]

7.142

Further to the above a notice sent by a court to the Secretary of State must be sent in such manner and to such address and contain such particulars as the Secretary of State may determine.

7.143

Where on any occasion a court deals with an offender:

- for an offence in respect of which an interim disqualification was imposed;[293] or

- for two or more offences in respect of any of which interim disqualification was imposed;

any period of disqualification imposed under RTOA 1988, s 34 or 35 shall be treated as reduced by any period during which he was disqualified by reason only of an order made under s 26 in respect of any of those offences.[294]

7.144

As characterised by the Court in *Mascarenas*, an interim disqualification has the same effect on disqualification as remand does on a prison sentence,[295] meaning the time counts towards any period of disqualification imposed on sentence.

---

290 RTOA 1988, s 26(10)(a).
291 RTOA 1988, s 26(11).
292 RTOA 1988, s 26(10)(b).
293 RTOA 1988, s 26(12)(a).
294 RTOA 1988, s 26(12)(b).
295 *Mascarenas*, at [18]

7.145

Any reference in RTOA 1988, or any other Act (including any Act passed after it) to the length of disqualification shall, unless the context otherwise requires, be construed as a reference to its length before any reduction under this section,[296] to reflect any interim disqualification period.

7.146

Where D is remanded in custody an interim disqualification is likely to be inappropriate, as it runs counter to the intention of Parliament that disqualification should be served whilst the offender is at liberty, and makes for additional complications when sentencing.[297] However, if D has had an interim disqualification during a lengthy period of remand, the Court of Appeal has acknowledged that it would be unfair for D to then have to serve the entirety of the period of disqualification on release.[298] Ultimately the Court endorsed the approach taken in *Harkins*[299] to seeking commensurability between the custodial term and the disqualification, and advocated a broad-brush approach.[300]

7.147

The maximum interim disqualification is six months in England and Wales (not to be confused with RTOA 1988, s 26(5), which applies only to Scotland).[301]

Road Traffic Offenders Act 1988, s 42 – removal of disqualification

7.148

A person subject to disqualification may apply to the court which made the order to remove the disqualification,[302] but they cannot seek the removal of a requirement to take a mandatory extended re-test under RTOA 1988, s 36(1) (see 7.112).[303]

7.149

This cannot be done sooner than the following periods from the order being imposed,[304] or, if there is an extension period under s 35A[305] or

---

296 RTOA 1988, s 26(13).
297 *Needham*, at [33].
298 *Needham*, at [35].
299 [2011] EWCA Crim 2227.
300 *Needham*, at [37]–[38].
301 *Mascarenas*, at [15].
302 RTOA 1988, s 42(1).
303 RTOA 1988, s 42(6).
304 RTOA 1988, s 42(3A)(a).
305 RTOA 1988, s 42(3B)(a).

PCC(S)A 2000, s 147A,[306] the date of disqualification plus the amount of the extension period:[307]

- two years, if the disqualification is for less than four years (disregarding any extension period);[308]

- half of the disqualification period (disregarding any extension period), if the disqualification (disregarding any extension period) is more than four but fewer than 10 years; or

- five years in any other case.

Any time during which the disqualification was suspended does not count towards these periods.[309]

7.150

On such an application the court may either remove the disqualification as from a date specified in the order or refuse the application.[310]

7.151

In exercising this discretion the court will have regard to:

- D's character and their conduct subsequent to the order;[311]

- the nature of the offence;[312] and

- any other circumstances of the case.[313]

7.152

If the application is refused, no further application can be made within three months after the date of the refusal.[314]

7.153

If the court orders a disqualification to be removed, the court:

- must send notice of the order to the Secretary of State,[315] in the prescribed form;[316]

---

306 RTOA 1988, s 42(3B)(c).
307 RTOA 1988, s 42(3A)(b).
308 RTOA 1988, s 42(3)(a).
309 RTOA 1988, s 42(3).
310 RTOA 1988, s 42(2).
311 RTOA 1988, s 42(2)(a).
312 RTOA 1988, s 42(2)(b).
313 RTOA 1988, s 42(2)(c).
314 RTOA 1988, s 42(4).
315 RTOA 1988, s 42(5)(a).
316 RTOA 1988, s 42(5B).

- may in any case order the applicant to pay the whole or any part of the costs of the application.[317]

7.154

If the disqualification was imposed in respect of an offence carrying obligatory endorsement, the Secretary of State must, on receiving notice of an order removing the disqualification, make any necessary adjustments to the endorsements on the person's driving record to reflect the order.[318]

7.155

The existence of this provision should not be used by judges to justify imposing a longer term of disqualification than is appropriate on the facts of the case.[319]

---

317 RTOA 1988, s 42(5)(b).
318 RTOA 1988, s 42(5AA).
319 *R (Corner) v Southend Crown Court* [2005] EWHC 2334 (Admin).

8 Company Directors Disqualification Act 1986

8.01

The Company Directors Disqualification Act (CDDA) 1986 provides the power to disqualify a person from acting as the director of a company. Depending on the circumstances, it is sometimes mandatory, sometimes discretionary.[1] In other circumstances, the Secretary of State for Business, Energy and Industrial Strategy (formerly the Department for Trade and Industry) might agree to accept a disqualification undertaking from a person who would otherwise face proceedings that would almost certainly end in their disqualification by court order.[2]

8.02

This chapter seeks to extract the most important principles relating to company directors' disqualifications. As these orders operate in both the criminal and civil courts, and it is possible to foresee contested orders in the criminal courts leading to a hearing, this chapter makes reference to both criminal and civil precedent. As will be seen, the courts themselves refer to precedents across the jurisdictions.

8.03

Where a disqualification order is made against a person already subject to such an order or to an undertaking, the periods specified in those orders and/or undertakings shall run concurrently.[3]

8.04

A disqualification order may be made on grounds which are or include matters other than criminal convictions, notwithstanding that the person in respect of whom it is to be made may be criminally liable in respect of those matters.[4]

8.05

There are many cases on the appropriate lengths of disqualifications in certain circumstances. These remain relevant as there are no sentencing guidelines to

---

1   CDDA 1986, s 1.
2   CDDA 1986, s 2.
3   CDDA 1986, s 1(3).
4   CDDA 1986, s 1(4).

assist the court in deciding what length of disqualification to impose. Although the most important cases are covered here, those appearing in a case where such an order is likely to be made are encouraged to consult the case law as well.

Disqualification undertakings

8.06

In the circumstances specified in CDDA 1986, ss 5A, 7, 8, 8ZC and 8ZE the Secretary of State may accept a disqualification undertaking by any person undertaking that, for a period specified, the person:

- will not be a director of a company, act as receiver of a company's property or in any way, whether directly or indirectly, be concerned or take part in the promotion, formation or management of a company unless (in each case) s/he has the leave of a court;[5] and

- will not act as an insolvency practitioner.[6]

8.07

The maximum period which may be specified in a disqualification undertaking is 15 years.[7] The minimum period which may be specified in a disqualification undertaking under s 7 or s 8ZC is two years.[8] By implication this suggests that there is no minimum period for an undertaking under s 5A, s 8 or s 8ZE.

8.08

Where a disqualification undertaking is accepted from a person who is already subject to such an undertaking or to a disqualification order, the periods specified in those undertakings and/or orders shall run concurrently.[9]

8.09

In determining whether to accept a disqualification undertaking by any person, the Secretary of State may take account of matters other than criminal convictions, notwithstanding that the person may be criminally liable in respect of those matters.[10]

---

5   CDDA 1986, s 1A(1)(a).
6   CDDA 1986, s 1A(1)(b).
7   CDDA 1986, s 1A(2).
8   CDDA 1986, s 1A(2).
9   CDDA 1986, s 1A(3).
10   CDDA 1986, s 1A(4).

8.10

When accepting an undertaking, the Secretary of State has the power to require a statement of grounds of unfitness, though they have the freedom to implement the undertaking without a statement if it is expedient and in the public interest to do so.[11] In most cases the public interest would justify requiring such a statement as it would be of use in any subsequent application for variation or discharge under CDDA 1986, s 8A, and if D sought leave to act for a particular company.[12] The practice of requiring an admission of misconduct was approved in *Secretary of State for Trade and Industry v Bairstow.*[13]

8.11

If the defendant (D) later seeks to be released from an undertaking, it is the case law on release from civil undertakings generally that is of assistance;[14] there needs to be 'special circumstances' and 'good cause' with the court's discretion being exercised 'only in a situation where circumstances have subsequently arisen, which by reason of their type or gravity, were not circumstances which were intended to be covered or ought to have been foreseen at the time the undertaking was given.'[15] In *Jonkler*, D had been unrepresented when she offered the undertaking on the basis of an omission to sufficiently supervise the company. New evidence persuaded the Secretary of State no longer to view the undertaking as in the public interest.[16] The Court was keen to observe, however, that this discretion should be used sparingly.[17]

8.12

Although the Secretary of State can accept an undertaking without any oversight from the court, the Secretary of State cannot grant leave under s 17 of the Act to allow D to act as a director notwithstanding an undertaking.[18] Such applications must always be made to the court, which will take into account the seriousness of the misconduct versus D's need to be able to act as a director to earn a living.[19] The application should have a hearing fixed, and D's attendance is necessary.[20]

---

11 *Re Blackspur Group Plc (No 3)* [2001] 5 WLUK 570 (upheld in the Court of Appeal – see below).
12 *Re Blackspur Group Plc (No 3)* [2001] EWCA Civ 1595.
13 [2004] EWHC 1730 (Ch).
14 *Secretary of State for Trade and Industry v Jonkler* [2006] EWHC 135 (Ch).
15 *Secretary of State for Trade and Industry v Jonkler*, at [40].
16 *Secretary of State for Trade and Industry v Jonkler*, at [41]–[42].
17 *Secretary of State for Trade and Industry v Jonkler*, at [43].
18 *In the matter of Morija Plc* [2007] EWHC 3055 (Ch), at [32].
19 *In the matter of Morija Plc*, at [34]–[35].
20 *Buckley v Secretary of State for Business, Energy and Industrial Strategy* [2017] CSOH 105 (a Scottish case under mirror provisions to the English and Welsh).

8.13

Where leave is granted, there will need to be a careful examination of the companies for which D wishes to act as a director, their circumstances, and whether there are additional directors to D to be involved.[21] The imposition of the standard conditions which are set out in every undertaking as applying, if leave is given to act as a director, are necessary for the protection of the public. But certain additional conditions might also be needed depending on the specific circumstances of the company. It may be appropriate to grant leave to D to act as director of certain sorts of companies, but not others, depending on the nature of the conduct that had led to the undertaking in the first place.[22]

8.14

The Secretary of State can accept a disqualification undertaking after the expiry of the two-year period to bring proceedings for a disqualification order even if proceedings had not been commenced in time. CDDA 1986, s 7(2A) does not preclude acceptance of an undertaking if an order has not been applied for in time and is wide enough to include applying for leave of the court to apply for an order out of time if necessary. The two-year period is not an absolute bar: the Act specifically provides for relief with the leave of the court.[23] If D seeks to argue that an undertaking was procured from him by duress, because the Secretary of State knew they were out of time to bring proceedings, then the burden is on D to show that, to the usual standard of the balance of probabilities.[24]

8.15

The position regarding costs on an undertaking is set out in the Practice Direction: Directors Disqualification Proceedings.[25]

8.16

It may be that the Secretary of State will be willing to accept an undertaking in place of instituting criminal proceedings, if it is a first offence and not the most serious, hence the brief overview of applicable law here.

8.17

The main difference between an undertaking and a disqualification order is that breaching an undertaking is a civil contempt of court, with a maximum penalty of two years' imprisonment. Breaching a disqualification order is a criminal offence punishable by a maximum of five years' imprisonment (see 8.75).[26]

---

21 *Harris v Secretary of State for Business, Innovation and Skills* [2013] EWHC 2514 (Ch), [53]–[54], [56], [59].
22 *Harris v Secretary of State for Business, Innovation and Skills*, at [89], [96].
23 *Gardiner v Secretary of State for Business, Enterprise and Regulatory Reform* [2009] BCC 742, at [50].
24 *Gardiner v Secretary of State for Business, Enterprise and Regulatory Reform*, at [89].
25 [2015] BCC 224, at part 7.
26 An offence contrary to CDDA 1986, s 17.

8.18

From the view of a defendant, if the Secretary of State is willing to accept an undertaking, D benefits from the fact that there is no public register on which the undertaking could appear. However, from the court's point of view, if proceedings have been instituted and an undertaking is being offered as a compromise, if D is to be prohibited from acting as a director, the public is entitled to know as early as reasonably practicable the grounds on which s/he has been found unfit.[27]

Disqualification orders

8.19

CDDA 1986 sets out the various offences and findings which can lead to a person being disqualified as a company director. It is not the role of this book to go through each individual offence or way of imposing such an order. Instead, this chapter deals with the over-arching principles that a court will need to take into account when it is imposing such an order in criminal proceedings under ss 2, 4 and 5.

Disqualification on conviction for an indictable offence – s 2

8.20

Section 2(1) provides the court with a power to make a disqualification order against a person where s/he is convicted of any indictable offence[28] before any court in connection with the promotion, formation, management, liquidation or striking off of a company,[29] with the receivership of a company's property or with his/her being an administrative receiver of a company.

8.21

For these purposes, 'the court' is:

- any court having jurisdiction to wind up the company in relation to which the offence was committed;[30] or

- in relation to an overseas company not falling within the winding up jurisdiction, the High Court;[31] or

---

27   *Secretary of State for Trade and Industry v Carr* [2005] EWHC 1723 (Ch), [2006] BCC 295, at [49].
28   As defined in the Interpretation Act 1978, Sch 1.
29   Including an overseas company – CDDA 1986, s 2(1A).
30   CDDA 1986, s 2(2)(a).
31   CDDA 1986, s 2(2)(aa).

- the court by or before which the person is convicted of the offence;[32] or

- in the case of a summary conviction, any other magistrates' court in the same local justice area.[33]

8.22

The maximum period of disqualification under this section is:

- where the disqualification order is made by a court of summary jurisdiction, five years;[34] and

- in any other case, 15 years.[35]

Disqualification for fraud etc, in winding up – s 4

8.23

If D has been convicted of an offence under s 993 of the Companies Act 2006 before a criminal court, there is an additional power to disqualify at the court's disposal.

8.24

The court[36] may make a disqualification order against a person if, in the course of the winding up of a company, it appears that s/he:

- has been guilty of an offence for which s/he is liable (whether s/he has been convicted or not) under s 993 of the Companies Act 2006 (fraudulent trading);[37] or

- has otherwise been guilty, while an officer[38] or liquidator of the company, receiver of the company's property, or administrative receiver of the company, of any fraud in relation to the company or of any breach of his/her duty as such officer, liquidator, receiver or administrative receiver.[39]

8.25

The maximum period of disqualification under this section is 15 years.[40]

---

32 CDDA 1986, s 2(2)(b).
33 CDDA 1986, s 2(2)(c).
34 CDDA 1986, s 2(3)(a).
35 CDDA 1986, s 2(3)(b).
36 CDDA 1986, s 4(2) – meaning any court having jurisdiction to wind up any of the companies in relation to which the offence or other default has been or is alleged to have been committed.
37 CDDA 1986, s 4(1)(a).
38 CDDA 1986, s 4(2) – 'officer' includes a shadow director.
39 CDDA 1986, s 4(1)(b).
40 CDDA 1986, s 4(3).

Disqualification on summary conviction for specific offences – s 5

8.26

The court has the power to disqualify a person for up to five years pursuant to s 5.[41] The legislation is opaquely drafted, but in short, if D is convicted (summarily) of an offence of the type set out in s 5(1) AND D has (including that conviction) three convictions for such offences (whether on indictment or summarily) within the past five years then the magistrates' court has the power to disqualify.

8.27

It requires a person to have been convicted (either on indictment or summarily) in consequence of a contravention of, or failure to comply with, any provision of the companies legislation[42] requiring a return, account or other document to be filed with, delivered or sent, or notice of any matter to be given, to the registrar of companies (whether the contravention or failure is on the person's own part or on the part of any company[43]).[44]

8.28

In those circumstances, the court by which s/he is convicted (or any other magistrates' court acting in the same local justice area) may make a disqualification order against him/her[45] if:

- during the five years ending with the date of the conviction;

- D has had made against him/her, or has been convicted of, in total not less than three default orders and offences contrary to the companies legislation requiring a return, account or other document to be filed with, delivered or sent, or notice of any matter to be given, to the Registrar of Companies (whether the contravention or failure is on D's own part or on the part of any company); and,

- those offences may include the offence for which s/he is currently being sentenced, and any other offence of which s/he is convicted on the same occasion.

---

41   CDDA 1986, s 5(5).
42   This is defined by CDDA 1986, s 5(4A) as the Companies Acts and Parts 1 to 7 of the Insolvency Act 1986 (company insolvency and winding up).
43   This includes an overseas company – CDDA 1986, s 5(4B).
44   CDDA 1986, s 5(1).
45   CDDA 1986, s 5(2).

Offences for which disqualification may be imposed

8.29

The purpose of a company director's disqualification is to protect the public from the actions of those not competent to act as directors – it is not purely aimed at punishing D.[46]

8.30

Where A pleaded guilty to an offence contrary to s 2 and s 14 of the Insurance Companies Act 1982 and was committed for sentence the Court of Appeal held that the offence of which A was convicted was one directed at the whole purpose for which the company was in existence, as opposed to any particular aspect of its affairs, and that accordingly CDDA 1986, s 2(1) applied.[47] Carrying on an insurance business through a limited company was a function of management and if that function is performed unlawfully in any way which makes a person guilty of an indictable offence it can properly be said that that is in connection with the management of the company.[48]

8.31

Counsel for the appellant did not seek to argue that s 2(1) could only apply to offences under the companies' legislation and the Court accepted that the precise scope of the subsection may at some date fall to be considered. However, the Court of Appeal in *Georgiou* applied by analogy two recent decisions on the similar powers under the Companies Acts 1948 (s 188(1)) and 1985 (s 295).

8.32

In those cases (*Corbin* and *Austen*) there is assistance regarding the scope of conduct that will bring an offence under the section. *Corbin* held that s 2(1) (of the predecessor legislation – Companies Act 1948) applied to offences of obtaining property by deception where D operated a business of dealing in yachts. Through various deceptions they obtained money and boats. The Court of Appeal held that the only relevant words are, 'Where a person is convicted on indictment of any offence in connection with the ... management of a company ...'. This does not restrict itself to the management of a company's affairs internally; external dealing with third parties is also covered.[49] There is no reason in the language of the statute for differentiating between internal and external affairs.[50]

---

46 *Re Jaymar Management Ltd* [1990] BCC 303, at 307.
47 *Georgiou* (1988) 87 Cr App R 207.
48 *Georgiou*, at 211, applying *Corbin* and *Austen* (see citations at notes 49 and 50).
49 *Corbin* (1984) 6 Cr App R (S) 17, at 20.
50 *Austen* (1985) 7 Cr App R (S) 214, at 216, in which D pleaded guilty to counts relating to use of fraudulent hire-purchase agreements.

8.33

Similarly, in accordance with the legislature's intent, the section should cover activity in relation to the birth, life and death of a company including the offending transactions entered into by the appellant.[51]

8.34

As the wording of CDDA 1986, s 2 requires a 'connection with the management of a company' there has to be some relevant factual connection with the management of the company, but the test is no stricter than that.[52]

8.35

It must be properly demonstrated by the Crown, however, that there is a factual connection between the offences committed and the management of a company. A conviction will not demonstrate that in and of itself.[53]

8.36

Where there is no evidence of dishonesty, and the charge was of causing or allowing loans to be made to the detriment of the company's creditors, but the relevant knowledge that D needed was available to him on looking at the accounts, that was a failure amounting to serious incompetence for a corporate financier and director.[54] A failure to appreciate what would have been obvious if he had read the accounts amounted to gross incompetence justifying disqualification.

8.37

Where D has been convicted of offences which are strict liability, and incurred by virtue of holding the position of director, as opposed to requiring any misconduct on the part of D, an order under CDDA 1986, s 2 is likely to be inappropriate.[55] This applied even where there had been fraud counts on the indictment, but pleas to regulatory consumer protection offences had been accepted, leading to not guilty pleas being entered to the fraud counts.[56] In these circumstances the sentencing judge, if imposing an order under s 2, would need to clearly identify the conduct which made D unfit to be a director of a company in their sentencing remarks,[57] especially if this required a departure from an accepted basis of plea.[58]

---

51 *Austen*, at 216.
52 *Goodman* (1993) 14 Cr App R (S) 147, at 150.
53 *Bond* [2015] EWCA Crim 634, at [16]–[21].
54 *Re Continental Assurance Co of London Plc (in liquidation)* [1996] BCC 888.
55 *Chandler* [2015] EWCA Crim 1825.
56 *Chandler*, at [11].
57 *Chandler*, at [11].
58 *Chandler*, at [12].

Procedure

8.38

Imposing a director's disqualification does not stop a person from carrying on most commercial activities in their own name, but prevents them from using the medium of a limited company – these proceedings do not involve determination of a criminal charge, and Article 6 of the European Convention on Human Rights thus does not apply.[59] These proceedings are determining civil rights and obligations.[60]

8.39

Whilst no explicit application by the Crown is required for an order under s 2 to be made, the sentencing judge should always invite submissions to ensure that it is appropriate to make such an order at all, and if so, its length.[61] There should be opportunities for the defence to make submissions on any disqualification order in open court. A failure to do so will not render the order a nullity, but it can give rise to a ground of appeal.[62]

8.40

CDDA 1986, s 16, setting out procedural time limits for an application for a disqualification order to the civil courts, does not apply in proceedings under s 2 or s 5.[63]

Circumstances affecting court's decision whether to disqualify

8.41

The court retains jurisdiction to disqualify under CDDA 1986, s 6 regardless of the nationality and present residence of a director. Likewise the conduct complained of need not have occurred within the jurisdiction.[64] However, the court has a discretion not to order service out of the jurisdiction and should not do so where it is not satisfied that there is a good arguable case that the conditions in s 6 have been satisfied.[65]

---

59   *R v Secretary of State for Trade and Industry, ex p McCormick* [1998] BCC 379, at 387; *DC v United Kingdom* [2000] BCC 710.
60   *Wilson v United Kingdom* (1998) 26 EHRR CD195.
61   *Ravjani* [2012] EWCA Crim 2519, at [108]–[109].
62   *Randhawa* [2012] EWCA Crim 1, at [42].
63   *Secretary of State for Trade and Industry v Langridge* [1991] BCC 148, at 162.
64   *Re Seagull Manufacturing Co Ltd (No 2)* [1994] Ch 91.
65   *Re Seagull Manufacturing Co Ltd (No 2)*, at 105.

8.42

A disqualification was not appropriate where a man, guilty of managing a company as an undischarged bankrupt, had subsequently been discharged and had carried on business successfully.[66] Section 2 gave the court a completely unfettered discretion to make a disqualification order against a person convicted of an indictable offence committed in connection with the promotion, formation, management or liquidation of a company, or the receivership or management of the company's property. This includes offences where there is no element of dishonesty, and where a conviction may follow without any evidence of dishonesty or fraudulent misconduct.[67] Parliament had decided not to give any guidance to the sentencing court as to the way in which it ought to exercise its powers. The power to disqualify a director under CDDA 1986, s 6, exercised by the judges of the Chancery Division, required an express finding that the person concerned was guilty of conduct which made him unfit to be concerned in the management of a company, but the criminal courts were concerned with a different situation.[68]

8.43

Where there are multiple companies and all have directors all of whom are from the same family, it might be appropriate for D to remain as a director to one or more of the companies, providing that additionally a nominated solicitor be appointed to, and remain on, the boards as a director who was independent of the family – these are conditions that the court could properly impose.[69]

8.44

In *Sivyer*,[70] the Court of Appeal removed the disqualification orders:

> 'not because we are persuaded that the learned judge was wrong to assume jurisdiction but for these reasons, which we state shortly. First, the long and respectable history of the company itself. Secondly, the impact that their being unable to operate the company would be likely to have on employees who we infer are good and respectable people. Thirdly, the hardship that it threw upon the son who was forced to defer his own plans and see to his parents' affairs.'[71]

---

66   *Young* (1990–91) 12 Cr App R (S) 262.
67   *Young*, at 265.
68   *Young*, at 266–267.
69   *Secretary of State for Trade and Industry v Palfreman* [1995] BCC 193, at 196 (under the Scottish equivalent legislation).
70   (1987) 9 Cr App R (S) 428.
71   *Sivyer*, at 435–436.

8.45

Where a director has effectively lent their company to a fraudster for malign purposes, disqualification will still be appropriate, but for a shorter period than had D been the brains behind the operation.[72]

Scope of disqualification

8.46

There is no jurisdiction to limit a disqualification order made under CDDA 1986, s 2 to public companies – such an order has to apply to all companies.[73]

8.47

In *Creggy*,[74] D consented to being disqualified, providing that it did not extend to his directorship of his private companies through which he managed his assets.[75] However, he then appealed against the imposition of the disqualification. The Court of Appeal upheld the order, though shortened it, stating:

> 'first, that any period of disqualification, however short, will have the same consequences in relation to the management of the appellant's private companies. Secondly, if the consequence of the disqualification order is that the appellant has to manage his primary assets personally, without the benefit of limited liability, that is one of the purposes of the disqualification order. Thirdly, we remind ourselves that there is the power to apply for leave if there be fresh reason for doing so.'[76]

Period of disqualification

8.48

Where D has been incompetent (even 'in a very marked degree') the disqualification should be for a shorter period than if he has been dishonest.[77] The Court of Appeal in *Re Sevenoaks Retailers*[78] set out a broad hierarchy of the seriousness of different sorts of offending, and the periods of disqualification which would properly reflect these.

---

72 *More* [2007] EWCA Crim 2832, at [14].
73 *Ward* [2001] EWCA Crim 1648, at [30].
74 [2008] EWCA Crim 394.
75 *Creggy*, at [8].
76 *Creggy*, at [17].
77 *Re Sevenoaks Stationers (Retail)* [1991] Ch 164, at 184.
78 *Re Sevenoaks Stationers (Retail)*, at 184.

8.49

The guidance given by establishing the three brackets of length of disqualification in *Sevenoaks* was adopted by the Court of Appeal in a criminal context in *Millard*,[79] *Cadman*,[80] and *Chandler*.[81] The highest bracket was likely to be reserved for situations where D had been disqualified before, there was a large total deficiency, and the fraudulent conduct had lasted for many years.[82] The guidance in *Millard* was endorsed in *Steel*,[83] where the Court also reminded advocates that, although all cases are fact-specific, there remains a need to direct a sentencing judge to relevant authorities assisting them.[84]

8.50

Where D1 and D2 had paid themselves too high a salary/consulting fees, and should have realised some months before that the business was in trouble, a short period of disqualification (two years) was appropriate, as was giving leave for D2 to be engaged as a general manager in his subsequent employment.[85] However he would not prospectively be given leave to act as director; an application for that would have to be made to the court when such circumstances arose as required him so to act.[86]

8.51

Factors such as youth, lack of experience and qualifications and a plea of guilty will often lead to a shorter period of disqualification,[87] as will a subordinate role in the company and the fact that professional advice was taken; though D will not be permitted to hide behind professional advisers.[88]

8.52

Similarly, where D had been involved in a relatively minor capacity at the end of the scheme, having been persuaded to participate in the fraudulent enterprise as a director, for which role he was quite unsuited by reason of his inexperience, a short period of disqualification would suffice.[89] This was on the basis that:

> 'the rationale behind disqualification from being a company director was to protect the public from the activities of persons, who whether

---

79   (1994) 15 Cr App R (S) 445.
80   [2012] EWCA Crim 611.
81   [2015] EWCA Crim 1825.
82   *Chandler*, at 448.
83   [2014] EWCA Crim 787, at [9]
84   *Steel*, at [14].
85   *Re Cargo Agency Ltd* [1992] BCC 388, at 392.
86   *Re Cargo Agency Ltd*, at 393.
87   *Re Carecraft Construction Co Ltd* [1993] BCC 336, at 347.
88   *Official Receiver v Ireland* [2002] BCC 428, at 439.
89   *Edwards* [1998] 2 Cr App R (S) 213.

for reasons of dishonesty, naivete or incompetence, used or abused their role and status as a company director to the detriment of the public.'[90]

8.53

An order made under CDDA 1986, s 1(1) commences on the date that the order is made – thus, the clock counting the time period for which D is to be disqualified begins ticking on that day. However, r 9 of the Insolvent Companies (Disqualification of Unfit Directors) Proceedings Rules 1987[91] then takes effect unless the court specifically disapplies it. This suspends the operation of the order for 21 days – ie D will not be committing an offence providing s/he has ceased to act as a director within 21 days of the order.[92] These provisions are not inconsistent – indeed, they might be seen as highly sensible, where D is a director when the order is made and thus needs to resign their directorship and deal with such necessary formalities as follow. Providing s/he has done that within 21 days, no breach offence will be committed.

8.54

In calculating the period of disqualification, there should be no arithmetical comparison with the period of imprisonment that would be appropriate.[93] Where there are multiple defendants who bear differing levels of culpability, the burden of a director's disqualification should be borne in mind in examining any questions of disparity of sentence.[94]

8.55

Where disqualification has been imposed by the civil court, and has begun to run already, and then a further period is imposed after conviction by a criminal court (which has to run consecutively), the court must be mindful of the overall period of disqualification that this will create.[95]

8.56

Where the offence was acting as a director whilst subject to an undertaking, any order imposed should extend past the end of that undertaking.[96]

---

90   *Edwards*, at 215–216.
91   SI 1987/2023.
92   *Secretary of State for Trade and Industry v Edwards* [1997] BCC 222, at 223.
93   *Evans* [2000] BCC 901.
94   *Myatt* [2004] EWCA Crim 206, at [16].
95   *Nevitt* [2007] EWCA Crim 1210, at [17]–[19].
96   *Randhawa* [2008] EWCA Crim 2599, at [27].

Leave to act as director

8.57

CDDA 1986, s 17 makes provision for applications by those on whom directors' disqualification orders are imposed to seek leave to act in a prohibited capacity in relation to specific companies on specific facts.

8.58

Where D is:

- a person subject to a disqualification order made under s 2 by a court other than a court having jurisdiction to wind up companies;[97] or

- a person subject to a disqualification order made under s 5,[98]

any application for leave shall be made to any court which, when the order was made, had jurisdiction to wind up the company (or, if there is more than one such company, any of the companies) to which the offence (or any of the offences) in question related.

8.59

When considering an application under s 17, the court has to be satisfied that there is a need to make the order granting leave to act, and that if that order is made, the public will remain adequately protected.[99] This is likely to be achieved by additional safeguards restricting particular activities, or requiring additional checks and balances, within the company.[100] For these purposes, the public includes all relevant interest groups such as employees, customers, and so on.[101] The High Court (Chancery Division) has expressed the high hurdle that D has to cross to secure leave as being a 'heavy presumption against granting permission' which D will have to displace.[102]

8.60

Section 17 gives the court an unfettered discretion, which should not be limited so as to exclude consideration of an applicant's personal non-business purpose.[103] Due to this unfettered discretion, the appellate court will rarely intervene, but should try to ensure overall fairness and expediency, and wherever possible questions of disqualification and leave to act should always be listed before the same judge.[104]

---

97   CDDA 1986, s 17(2)(a).
98   CDDA 1986, s 17(2)(b).
99   *Re Gibson Davies Chemists Ltd* [1995] BCC 11, at [14]–[15].
100 *Re Gibson Davies Chemists Ltd*, at [16].
101 *Re Tech Textiles* [1998] 1 BCLC 259.
102 *Official Receiver v Stern* [2001] BCC 305, at 365.
103 *Shuttleworth v Secretary of State for Trade and Industry* [2000] BCC 204.
104 *Secretary of State for Trade and Industry v Collins & Ors* [2000] BCC 998, at 1010, 1015.

8.61

Where there can be appropriate arrangements made for D to secure the outcome that he wants from the business of the company with which he seeks leave to be involved, but with the safety net of the necessary involvement of other directors and legal teams, that is likely to be the outcome favoured. In *In the matter of Portland Place (Historic House) Ltd*,[105] D, who had been convicted of a serious fraud, wished to be able to deal with a very valuable property, the freehold of which he owned, vested in a company of his. The Court gave limited permission only for D to be able to instruct the company on how to deal with the property as against a bank in accordance with the deed of trust.[106] Morgan J concluded with the following observations:[107]

> 'D says that he wishes to negotiate with the Bank. I do not see why the directors of the Company cannot carry out any appropriate negotiations. If anything, the Bank might pay more attention to points made by the directors than they would pay to points made by Mr Davenport, given that he is a convicted fraudster.
>
> Accordingly, I am not persuaded that the right thing to do in this case, taking account of the interests of the Company, of the public, and even of Mr Davenport himself, is to allow Mr Davenport to conduct the litigation and negotiations on behalf of the Company. I consider there is a real advantage in leaving the litigation and negotiation to be conducted by the Company through its directors, who will consider whether the deed of trust is effective and, if so, they will be obliged to act in accordance with the directions of Mr Davenport, which I will permit him to give. That result gives Mr Davenport all of the benefits of the arrangements he created in 2005 when he vested the title in the Company and caused the Company to enter into the deed of trust. The only difference is that Mr Davenport was in 2005 a director of the Company, and now he cannot be a director of the Company. But that does not change the substance of the matter. Conversely, the involvement of directors of this company conducting the litigation and any negotiation, even in a case where they are acting on the directions of Mr Davenport, will, or at least might, provide a worthwhile control on Mr Davenport's conduct.'

8.62

In *Re Liberty Holdings Unlimited*,[108] the Court endorsed a six-stage test when considering a s 17 application:[109]

---

105 [2012] EWHC 4199 (Ch).
106 *Portland Place (Historic House) Ltd*, at [22].
107 *Portland Place (Historic House) Ltd*, at [23]–[24].
108 [2017] BCC 298 (Ch D).
109 *Liberty Holdings Unlimited*, at [19] and [26].

(1) There is no threshold requirement but the court must take into account and consider the 'need' or 'legitimate interests' of the applicant and the relevant company as part of all the circumstances of the case.

(2) The 'legitimate interests' of the applicant and the company may go beyond mere commercial interests.

(3) Such 'legitimate interests' as are established have to be weighed with the other factors (particularly, the question of public protection) pointing for and against the grant of permission.

(4) The strength of the 'legitimate interests' which are required in any one case to tip the scales in favour of the grant of permission will depend on all the circumstances: there is no one standard or strength of 'interest' or 'need' the presence of which will automatically justify the grant (or the absence of which will automatically justify the refusal) of permission.

(5) In many cases, the absence of a strong 'need' for permission will result in permission being refused. As a general rule, it will be a rare case where permission will be given in the absence of some need of the company for the services of the applicant in a prohibited capacity.

(6) Equally, however, a strong case of need will not necessarily be sufficient to justify the grant of permission and may be outweighed by other factors, notably the protection of the public and the maintenance of disqualification as an effective general deterrent.

8.63

In a helpful judgment, Mr Registrar Baister continued:

'[28] It seems to me that any court faced with an application of this kind (which is, I accept, unusual and fact specific) must be careful to distinguish between the purposes and effects of the criminal law and civil law provisions ... The purpose of the criminal proceedings was necessarily punitive; the purposes of the disqualification order were primarily public protection ... As far as the criminal proceedings are concerned, the punitive purpose has already been achieved: D has been convicted and sentenced; he has served his time and paid compensation. The civil consequences of the disqualification order are different in nature and should not be used as further punishment, in effect an extension of the criminal sanctions exposed.

[29] Whilst the Secretary of State may be free to adopt what [counsel] calls "a blanket policy of opposing an application for permission simply because the disqualification arose as a result of s 2 of the Act" it follows from the foregoing paragraph that the court may not. It must exercise its discretion having regard to all the relevant factors and circumstances while disregarding factors

and circumstances which do not properly fall to be taken into account. It must conduct the balancing exercise referred to in the authorities. It must look at each application on its merits, even if the Secretary of State decides not to do so. It must exercise the unfettered discretion it has been given in a judicial manner …

[31] The court must also have regard to the deterrent function of disqualification. I am satisfied that giving limited permission to act and subject to conditions in exceptional circumstances is unlikely to detract from that function in this case. Similarly, I am convinced by the evidence that Mr Owen has learned his lesson and that there is unlikely to be a recurrence of the offences that resulted in his conviction, not least because LHU and Copperidge are engaged in wholly different businesses …

[33] I conclude, however, by emphasising that this is, in my view, an exceptional case and by stating that as a general rule I accept the principle enunciated by Ms Parke in the final paragraph of her skeleton argument that an applicant who seeks permission following conviction of an indictable offence indeed faces "an extremely steep uphill struggle in persuading the court to exercise its discretion to permit him to act in the management of … companies".'

Interaction between civil and criminal disqualification

8.64

Where there are contemporaneous criminal and civil proceedings, both can run alongside each other. There is no requirement for civil proceedings to be stayed simply because there are criminal proceedings. Where D wanted the proceedings stayed as he argued that filing his evidence in the civil proceedings would prejudice his case in the criminal trial, it was for D to satisfy the Court that they would be, or were at real risk of being, materially prejudiced in the preparation of their defence to criminal charges if they were to file evidence in disqualification proceedings before commencement of the criminal trial.[110] If they could show material prejudice, it would be oppressive and unfair to insist on the evidence being filed at that stage, though a stay would not be justified.[111]

8.65

In *Carr*, although the trial of the disqualification proceedings was not likely to occur before conclusion of the criminal trial, the defendants argued the requirement to serve written evidence in the disqualification proceedings

---

110 *Secretary of State for Trade and Industry v Carr* [2005] EWHC 1723 (Ch), [2006] BCC 295, at 302–303.
111 *Carr*, at 306.

would jeopardise their proper preparation of a defence to the criminal charges. They also claimed that it was impractical to prepare for both proceedings at the same time because of the nature and volume of the evidence which each set of proceedings required. The Court held that a stay on case management grounds was not appropriate.[112]

8.66

There is no abuse of the court's process in bringing disqualification proceedings in the Companies Court where D had already been disqualified by the criminal court after conviction for an indictable offence. The power to make an order under s 2 stemmed from D's conviction, whilst the power to make an order under s 6 derived from D's unfit conduct.[113] A disqualification order made in criminal proceedings was penal in nature whereas an order made in the Companies Court had the primary aim of protecting the public.[114] For this reason, it is also not an abuse of process to stay civil disqualification proceedings to await the outcome of a criminal trial, and then restore them on conclusion of that trial.[115]

8.67

Where there had been an expectation that an order under s 2 would be sought on sentencing at the conclusion of the criminal proceedings, but for whatever reason that application was not made to the criminal court, and thus the issue not adjudicated upon, it would not be an abuse to bring civil disqualification proceedings at a later date.[116]

8.68

The position is different, understandably, where at the conclusion of a criminal trial an application for such an order under s 2 was made but was refused, and there were no earlier proceedings in the civil court which had been stayed whilst the criminal proceedings took their course. In those circumstances, it will be an abuse for any applicant, be that the Secretary of State, creditors, or anyone else, to seek to obtain a s 2 order from the civil courts,[117] because:

'even if different applicants might be permitted to place before the court different evidence going to the circumstances, consequences or gravity of the offences for which the defendant has been convicted, all the claims are still ultimately founded on that conviction and whether it shows a need to protect the public from his activities as a director.'[118]

---

112 *Carr*, at 305.
113 *Re Cedarwood Productions Ltd* [2001] EWCA Civ 1083, at [13].
114 *Cedarwood Productions Ltd*, at [16].
115 *Secretary of State for Trade and Industry v Newstead* [2001] 2 BCLC 48, at [18].
116 *Re Denis Hilton Ltd* [2002] 1 BCLC 302.
117 *Secretary of State for Business, Innovation and Skills v Weston* [2014] EWHC 2933 (Ch).
118 *Weston*, at [51].

8.69

In his judgment, HHJ Cooke concluded:[119]

'Standing back, this claim is no more than an attempt by the Secretary of State to obtain a different decision from this court than was given on identical issues by the criminal court, which had the issues placed before it and made a positive decision to refuse an order. It is in my view unfair that the defendants should be thus exposed to the same claim on two occasions. The unfairness is not relieved by the argument that the claim is being pursued by a different entity; firstly I am not persuaded that in fact there is a complete separation between the two applicants, because it appears that the Insolvency Service was in liaison with the prosecutor when he made his application for HHJ Rundell to consider disqualification, so that even if as Mr. Morgan submits, there are criticisms that can be made of that application, it would appear the Secretary of State was content at the time to allow the matter to be pursued in the criminal court rather than at that stage bringing it to the civil court and to some extent at least participated in the application made. Secondly there is the general point that where the basis of the claim and the relief sought is essentially identical it is just as much unfair to the defendant to have to face it twice at the hands of two applicants as it would be if there were only one.'

8.70

This could not be said to be unduly restrictive on the Secretary of State, because s/he can preserve the possibility of his/her own application if dissatisfied with the outcome of a criminal trial, by either:[120]

- initiating and staying s 6 proceedings pending the outcome of the criminal case; or

- in an appropriate case, making a subsequent application under (for example) s 4 rather than s 2, on a basis sufficiently different from the facts of any conviction.

8.71

This position was endorsed by Stephen Jourdan QC, sitting as a Deputy High Court Judge, who noted that a court may have more information on a CDDA 1986, s 6 application than on such an application under s 2. Where there was additional evidence available in a s 6 application, it might be appropriate to make an application for a s 6 order even where a s 2 order has already been made.[121]

---

119 *Weston*, at [52].
120 *Weston*, at [55].
121 *Secretary of State for Business, Innovation and Skills v Rahman* [2017] EWHC 2468 (Ch), at [47]–[48].

Interaction between directors' disqualification and other orders

8.72

It will not normally be appropriate to impose a director's disqualification under s 2 where the defendant has been given a conditional discharge, because an order for disqualification under s 2 has been characterised by the Court as 'unquestionably punishment'.[122] It would therefore be quite inappropriate for a punishment of this kind to be linked with a conditional discharge when the sentencing court thought that a punishment was inexpedient.

8.73

Where there are to be confiscation proceedings concerned with the financial benefit that D gained from a company with which s/he was involved in breach of a director's disqualification order or undertaking, the approach to calculating benefit will be the same as in any other sort of case where D has benefitted from illegal conduct.[123] This includes the approach to when the corporate veil can be pierced.[124] The approach of the Court in *May*[125] in determining benefit was applicable whatever the facts of the misconduct.

Appeals

8.74

An appeal against an order made under s 2 lies to the Court of Appeal in the usual way of an appeal against sentence. As with any other appeal against sentence, the question for the Court of Appeal will be whether the sentence was wrong in principle, or the length of it was manifestly excessive.[126]

Breach

8.75

If a person acts in contravention of a disqualification order s/he is liable:

- on conviction on indictment, to imprisonment for not more than two years or a fine, or both;[127] and

---

122   *Young* (1990–91) 12 Cr App R (S) 262, at 267.
123   *Seager and Blatch* [2009] EWCA Crim 1303, at [68]–[69].
124   *Seager and Blatch* at [68]–[69].
125   [2008] 1 AC 1053.
126   *Clayton* [2017] EWCA Crim 49, at [24].
127   CDDA 1986, s 13(a).

- on summary conviction, to imprisonment for not more than six months or a fine not exceeding the statutory maximum, or both.[128]

8.76

By analogy with the offence of acting as a director whilst an undischarged bankrupt, it seems that this is an offence of strict liability, meaning that D's awareness that he was disqualified will not be relevant.[129] It is also not an offence of dishonesty.[130]

8.77

A custodial sentence will usually be imposed for breach of a director's disqualification, as the orders are to protect the public, but where D is to be sentenced on the basis of recklessness instead of dishonesty, a short term will be appropriate.[131]

8.78

If D runs a number of companies then there is nothing wrong in principle with consecutive sentences to reflect the running of each company whilst disqualified, having considered the number of companies and the way in which they were run.[132] Where there had been several consecutive companies then longer sentences for the later offences were justified, as they were aggravated by the offences of running the earlier companies.[133]

---

128 CDDA 1986, s 13(b).
129 *Brockley* [1994] BCC 131.
130 *Cowley-Hurlock* [2014] EWCA Crim 1702, at [19].
131 *Atterbury* [1996] 2 Cr App R (S) 151, at 152.
132 *Cowley-Hurlock*, at [22].
133 *Cowley-Hurlock*, at [23].

9 Sexual Harm Prevention Orders (on conviction)

'But although the SOPO may appear to be of comparatively less importance, each of its prohibitions creates for the defendant a new and personal criminal offence carrying up to five years' imprisonment for breach. It is likely to remain with the defendant for many years after the end of the principal sentence imposed, whether custodial or otherwise. The terms of the order are likely to have to be considered and applied by probation officers, policemen, defendants and courts for many years to come.' Hughes LJ in *Smith* [2011] EWCA Crim 1772, at [3]

9.01

The Anti-social Behaviour, Crime and Policing Act 2014, Sch 5, para 2 added s 103A to the Sexual Offences Act (SOA) 2003. Section 103A(1) brought in Sexual Harm Prevention Orders (SHPOs) from 8 March 2015.

9.02

For some years prior to this, there had been mechanisms for securing a similar effect – the restriction of certain behaviours by those convicted of sexual offences. From 1 May 2004 until 8 March 2015, the relevant order was a Sexual Offence Prevention Order (SOPO), which was drafted in similar terms, and found in SOA 2003, s 103(2)–(4). The minimum term of a SOPO was five years,[1] with no maximum period; they could be indefinite.[2] Therefore, the courts may be called upon to deal with breaches of SOPOs for many years yet.

9.03

Prior to SOPOs (and repealed by the SOA 2003) the Sexual Offences Act 1997 had given the courts power to make a restraining order. This power no longer exists since the repeal of the SOA 1997,[3] but the courts may still be called upon to deal with breaches of such orders.

---

1 SOA 2003, s 107(1).
2 SOA 2003, s 103C(2)(b).
3 *Monument* [2005] EWCA Crim 30.

9.04

There is also assistance to be gained from case law on SOPOs as the orders are similar in many ways. The principles therefore remain sound in relation to SHPOs.

The basic principle

9.05

• Always discretionary.

• No risk of 'serious sexual harm' needed – any level of 'sexual harm' sufficient.

9.06

These orders were intended to provide additional protection in cases where a person has been found to have done the actus reus of a sexual offence (whether admitted or proven).

9.07

It is worth noting that SHPOs are ALWAYS discretionary.[4] In other words, there are no circumstances in which it is mandatory for a court to impose an SHPO. This means that advocates should not be afraid to challenge the making or terms of these orders in appropriate situations. It is clear from the case law that they are applied for by the CPS, and made by some judges, as a matter of simple routine as if they are the automatic consequences of a sexual offence. This should not be so.

The legislation

9.08

SOA 2003 gives the court the power to make SHPOs in two situations:

(1) when the Crown applies to the court for an SHPO because the court is dealing with an offender for an offence (s 103A); and

(2) when the police apply to a court as they are concerned about the behaviour of someone with previous convictions (see Chapter 21 for detail on this second situation).

---

4   SOA 2003, s 103A(1).

9.09

Section 103A(1) allows a court the discretion to make an order. Section 103A(2) provides for the first circumstance in which this can happen. It requires that the conditions in s 103A(2)(a) and (b) are fulfilled:

(a)　that the offence for which the defendant is being dealt with is contained in SOA 2004, Sch 3 or Sch 5. This covers cases in any of the following three situations:

- the offender is being dealt with by the court for an offence listed in SOA 2003, Sch 3 or Sch 5;[5]

- there is a finding that the offender is not guilty of a Sch 3 or 5 offence by reason of insanity;[6] or

- that the offender is under a disability and has done the act charged in respect of an offence found in Sch 3 or Sch 5;[7]

　　AND

(b)　that the court is satisfied that it is *necessary* to make an SHPO *for the purpose of* either:[8]

- protecting the public or any particular member of the public from sexual harm from the defendant; or

- protecting children or vulnerable adults generally, or any particular children or vulnerable adults, from sexual harm from the defendant outside the UK.

For the second circumstance, see Chapter 21.

9.10

'Sexual harm' means physical or psychological harm caused:[9]

- by the person committing one or more offences listed in Sch 3; or

- (in the context of harm outside the UK) by the person doing, outside the UK, anything which would constitute an offence listed in Sch 3 if done in any part of the UK.

9.11

Before a court can consider imposing an SHPO, both conditions must be fulfilled. Even where they are fulfilled, the court 'may' make an SHPO – it is

---

5　SOA 2003, s 103A(2)(a)(i).
6　SOA 2003, s 103A(2)(a)(ii).
7　SOA 2003, s 103A(2)(a)(iii).
8　SOA 2003, s 103A(2)(a)(i) or (ii).
9　SOA 2003, s 103B(1).

not mandatory.[10] Therefore, a court should always have its attention directed to whether it is necessary for one to be made at all – they should not be made as a matter of routine where they do not fulfil any purpose that is not fulfilled by the sentence itself, or the notification requirements (see 9.18 and 9.61).

9.12

Schedules 3 and 5 are lengthy, and anyone who is dealing with an offence which has any sexual element is advised to check them to see if the offence they are dealing with is listed. The Schedules include offences under old legislation which has now been repealed, but under which it is not uncommon for historical offences to be prosecuted, a number of which are continuing to come through the courts.

9.13

Although the guidance in *Smith*[11] remains generally sound,[12] it has been updated, as it was a judgment under the SOPO regime (which could only be used to protect against 'serious' sexual harm). Thus, in *NC*, the Court of Appeal updated the guidance to:[13]

'(i)   is the making of an order necessary to protect the public from sexual harm through the commission of scheduled offences?

(ii)   if some order is necessary, are the terms imposed nevertheless oppressive? and

(iii) overall, are the terms proportionate?'

Procedure

9.14

The Court of Appeal has expressed its frustration on many occasions with the prosecution's failure properly to serve draft SHPOs on the defence in advance of the hearing at which they will be considered, and in electronic form so that the fruit of discussions between counsel can be reflected in amendments without delay.[14] It has also made clear that judges should not simply 'rubber-stamp' these orders, but properly consider whether their content is appropriate and whether they are necessary.[15]

---

10   SOA 2003, s 103A(1).
11   [2011] EWCA Crim 1772.
12   *Parsons* [2017] EWCA Crim 2163, at [30].
13   [2016] EWCA Crim 1448, at [9].
14   *Smith* [2011] EWCA Crim 1772, at [26].
15   *Lewis* [2016] EWCA Crim 1020, at [7]–[9].

9.15

The Criminal Procedure Rules (CrimPR) require service at least two working days in advance.[16] Both prosecution and defence advocates are encouraged to be alert to situations where an SHPO is likely to be sought, and ensure that a draft is available, preferably uploaded to the digital case system (DCS) and with the defence explicitly notified of its presence. Defence advocates should not be afraid to ask for a matter to be adjourned or put down the list if they have an order 'sprung on them' at court, or if there are difficulties in taking instructions from their client due to mental health problems.[17]

9.16

Judges should support advocates in ensuring that proper time is given to ensuring that the order is workable by going through it in open court, even if there is a busy list.[18] To protect their client's best interests defence counsel will need to explain fully the ramifications of each term to the client, and consider themselves whether the order is proportionate in light of their client's personal and professional situation.

9.17

This is consistent with CrimPR, r 31.2(1), which sets out very clearly that:

'The court must not make a behaviour order unless the person to whom it is directed has had an opportunity—

(a)   to consider—

(i)   what order is proposed and why, and

(ii)   the evidence in support; and

(b)   to make representations at a hearing (whether or not that person in fact attends)'.

Is the order necessary?

9.18

The Court in *NC* (see 9.13) reiterated the three aspects which must be addressed when considering making an SHPO, derived from the judgment of Rose LJ in *Collard*.[19]

---

16   CrimPR, r 31.3(5)(a).
17   *Connor* [2019] EWCA Crim 234, at [5].
18   *Connor* [2019] EWCA Crim 234, at [32].
19   [2004] EWCA Crim 1664.

9.19

An SHPO should not be used to impose terms that duplicate those to which D will be subject under other regimes: namely notification,[20] disqualification from working with children, or terms of a licence.[21]

9.20

In only the most unusual cases will an SHPO be appropriate where D receives an indefinite sentence.[22] Equally, the availability of an SHPO, and the protection it offers, will not mean that an indefinite sentence will not be appropriate for serious contact sex offenders.[23] Its terms may, however, be able to place such restrictions on an offender that they do not need to be subject also to the dangerousness provisions of the Criminal Justice Act 2003 for the public to be properly protected, especially in cases of a non-contact offences.[24] This interplay is not dealt with at all in the statutes.

9.21

An SHPO should not be imposed simply as a matter of routine,[25] and consideration should be given in each case to whether it is necessary. If there is a factual matrix suggesting that the sexual offence was a true 'moment of madness' by someone of otherwise good character, in circumstances highly unlikely to ever be repeated, then it may be appropriate not to make an order.[26] Likewise, where the victim was an adult aged 25, a condition preventing contact with those under 18 was not justified.[27]

9.22

A court must also take care if the prosecution, in support of the making of the order, seek to rely on acquittals relating to previous alleged sexual offences – such should only be accepted as support where the court has been able to hear the full facts of the offences that led to acquittals, and only then use them in support of making an order after careful consideration.[28]

9.23

Where an offender suffers from learning or other mental disabilities such that they would not be able to understand the SOPO (or SHPO) and therefore be at constant risk of breach, it would seem appropriate that the same considerations

---

20   Under SOA 2003, s 82.
21   *Smith*, at [9].
22   *L* [2010] EWCA Crim 2046.
23   *N* [2010] EWCA Crim 1624, at [18].
24   *Terrell* [2007] EWCA Crim 3079.
25   *R & C* [2010] EWCA Crim 907, at [11].
26   *Ryan P* [2018] EWCA Crim 1076.
27   *Hughes* [2018] EWCA Crim 495, at [16] – and on the facts the Court held that no order at all was appropriate.
28   *Hughes*, at [15].

would apply as to the making of anti-social behaviour orders (ASBOs): that it is not proper to make an order where the offender is incapable of understanding it by reason of mental illness, but that the fact that an offender will, as a result of mental illness, be more likely to breach the order is not in itself a reason not to make such an order.[29]

9.24

In *MB*,[30] the appellant had been found unfit to plead under s 4 of the Criminal Procedure (Insanity) Act 1964, but was found to have committed the act of voyeurism. In addition to a two-year supervision order, the judge imposed a SOPO for five years. This was quashed, the Court of Appeal holding that there was no evidence before the judge that enabled him to conclude that the appellant was a risk from which the public needed to be protected – rather, psychiatrists concluded that he had no exaggerated sexual urges,[31] and that his offending came from a lack of understanding or insight resulting from his learning disabilities and being on the autistic spectrum. The necessity as required by the Act was therefore not made out.

9.25

However, in *Pashley*,[32] where a 23-year-old appellant had the broad functioning of a nine-year-old, and was unfit to plead, a SOPO, albeit in amended form, was upheld. The Court of Appeal accepted that the terms as drafted would not easily be understood, let alone by someone with the functioning equivalent to a nine-year-old. It consequently upheld the order, but made additions and re-wordings to aid understanding, and stated that it could be expected that those supervising the appellant assist him in understanding what was required of him.[33]

9.26

Assessing risk is the metier of the Probation Service. Where a pre-sentence report (PSR) has been produced that does not suggest that an SHPO is necessary, there should be extreme caution before one is imposed as a result of the freestanding assessment of the judge, or on a prosecution application that is not supported by evidence of risk from a probation officer.[34]

29   *R (Cooke) v DPP* [2008] EWHC 2703 (Admin), at [20], applied in *Fairweather v Commissioner of Police of the Metropolis* [2008] EWHC 3073.
30   [2012] EWCA Crim 770.
31   *MB*, at [73]–[75].
32   *Pashley* [2015] EWCA Crim 1540.
33   *Pashley*, at [13]–[20].
34   *MSS* [2018] EWCA Crim 266, as quoted in *Hughes*, at [10], commented on at [11]–[12].

Length of order

9.27

- Minimum duration of an SHPO is 5 years.[35]

- Maximum duration is indefinite.[36]

9.28

It has been recognised by the Court of Appeal that an SHPO's length should be commensurate with the notification period.[37] The notification period is determined by the type and length of sentence given, as set out under SOA 2003, s 82. Section 82 does not differentiate between sentences of immediate imprisonment and sentences of suspended imprisonment for the purposes of the length of the notification period.[38]

9.29

The Court has repeatedly warned judges against making SHPOs 'until further order'.[39] The oppressive effect of an order 'until further order' is such that it will rarely be compatible with a defendant's fundamental rights. In the recent case of *Coggins*,[40] the Court upheld an indefinite order having amended some of its terms, on the basis that, given D's previous serious offending, there was no way of knowing when he would stop being a danger. If that situation did arise, he could return to court to apply for a variation of the SHPO. It was not disproportionate having regard to the modifications to it made by the court.

9.30

Section 103C(3) allows different terms to be made for different fixed periods, or in the context of an indefinite order, some terms to be for a fixed period and others to be indefinite.

---

35   SOA 2003, s 103C(2)(a).
36   SOA 2003, s 103C(2)(b).
37   *JB* [2017] EWCA Crim 568; also *Moxham* [2016] EWCA Crim 182, at [14].
38   This is consistent with the fact that seriousness of the offence determines the length of the custodial sentence, and the decision to suspend is entirely a matter of judicial discretion.
39   *McLellan & Bingley* [2017] EWCA Crim 1464, at [25](iii).
40   [2019] 3 WLUK 77.

Terms of order

9.31

The only prohibitions that may be included in an SHPO are those necessary for the purpose of:[41]

- protecting the public or any particular members of the public from sexual harm from the defendant; or

- protecting children or vulnerable adults generally, or any particular children or vulnerable adults, from sexual harm from the defendant outside the UK.

Computing and internet

9.32

The Court of Appeal in *Roskams*[42] made clear that a prohibition on computer possession without notifying the police was likely to be inappropriate in the current day and age as so many people owned computer equipment, including smart phones. They quashed that paragraph. This is consistent with the earlier judgment in *Smith*, in which Hughes LJ (as he then was) stated that it would be hard to imagine a case in which a ban on the use of computer equipment could be justified.[43]

9.33

In *Connor*,[44] the Court of Appeal was deeply concerned by the lack of thought that had been given to the terms of the SOPO (as it was made in 2015) imposed:[45]

> '17. In *Smith*, Hughes LJ as he then was, made it clear that orders must be tailored to the circumstances of each case but there are some principles of broad application including that a blanket prohibition on computer use or internet access is not permissible. As was pointed out by this court in *R v Parsons* [2017] EWCA Crim 2163 the internet is a far greater feature of everyday life now than it was in 2012 and we have no doubt that this was true when the appellant's case was before the Crown Court. The failure to take into account the principles in *Smith* was an error which we must correct, as Mr Heptonstall who did not appear below, readily accepted. We are grateful to him for the helpful written

---

41   SOA 2003, s 103C(4).
42   [2018] EWCA Crim 1653, [2018] 6 WLUK 553
43   *Smith*, at [20](i).
44   [2019] EWCA Crim 234.
45   *Connor*, at [17]–[19].

submissions he provided at very short notice which were then developed orally.

18. The assertion by counsel for both sides at the time it was made that it was proportionate and workable was made without proper thought. Whilst the judge accepted their submissions we note that he said "one can always make an application for variation". No doubt it was upon that statement that the appellant later relied in his application to vary. The GMP [Greater Manchester Police] and the sex offender manager both agreed that the order was not workable.

19. As drafted, paragraph one of the order would probably have the effect of preventing the appellant from using the internet at all for any purposes since it permits use only of a desktop computer provided by his employer. Even were he to obtain employment it does not follow that he would be provided with a desktop computer. The prohibition is obviously oppressive and disproportionate.'

Contact

9.34

Concerning a non-contact requirement, the Court stated that there was no rule that a contact offence was required before a non-contact restriction could be imposed, but that there had to be an identifiable risk of contact offences occurring and the court had to consider whether there was such a risk so as to justify the imposition of such a paragraph.[46] In the instant case there was not and that paragraph was quashed.[47]

9.35

Care must be taken to ensure that the terms of the order do not effectively prevent a defendant from contacting their own children.[48] It is not enough for the Crown to assert that the prohibition is necessary on the 'safety first' principle in case the defendant might graduate to contact offences of that nature in the future. That does not make a prohibition on contact or requirement of supervised contact a necessary requirement for the protection of the public.[49]

---

46 *Roskams*, at [9]–[12].
47 *Roskams*, at [13].
48 *NC*, at [17].
49 *Lewis*, at [10].

Age

9.36

The legislation for these purposes defines a 'child' as being a person under the age of 18. However, the Court of Appeal has accepted in both *Smith*,[50] and more recently in *Parsons*,[51] that a lower age (16) is more appropriately incorporated into the conditions unless there is a specific risk of the commission of offences in SOA 2003 which relate to victims over the age of 16 (offences committed under SOA 2003, ss 16–19 against those in respect of whom the defendant stands in a position of trust, as defined in s 21, together with family offences under ss 25 and 26):[52]

> 'If the risk is genuinely of these latter offences, prohibitions on contact with children under 18 may be justified. Otherwise, if contact with children needs to be restricted, it should relate to those under 16, not under 18.'

Gender

9.37

Where D's offending has shown a predilection exclusively for children of one gender, an order that restricts unsupervised contact with children of both genders will be unnecessary as it is not supported by evidence.[53]

Risk management monitoring software

9.38

When dealing with a term which required the installation of risk management software by the police onto any device capable of accessing the internet that was owned by the subject of an SHPO, the Court observed the impracticality of such a term for busy police forces. The likely consequence being that, because a resource-stretched force could not easily attend at the subject's home to install the software, there would be a period of time where use of the device was effectively prohibited under the SHPO as it did not have such software installed.[54]

---

50   [2011] EWCA Crim 1772.
51   [2017] EWCA Crim 2163.
52   *Smith* at [21].
53   *Franklin* [2018] EWCA Crim 1080; *Littlewood* [2018] EWCA Crim 1614.
54   *Parsons*, at [18].

9.39

The Court instead preferred the following:[55]

> 'The trigger should be notification by the offender to the Police of his acquisition of a computer or device capable of accessing the internet; the Police cannot be expected to know otherwise. The device should have the capacity to retain and display the history of internet use and the offender should be prohibited from deleting such history. The device should be made available immediately on request for inspection by a Police officer (or employee) and the offender should be required to allow any such person to install risk management software *if* they so choose. The offender should further be prohibited from interfering with or bypassing the normal running of any such software. For our part, this is a workable and proportionate solution to the questions raised by risk management monitoring software.'

Cloud storage

9.40

The Court of Appeal in *Parsons* acknowledged that cloud storage is 'practically ubiquitous', being pre-installed on almost all devices now on the market. Thus, a blanket prohibition was 'too blunt': unnecessary and capable of trapping an unwary user. The Court noted that the vice such a term in an SHPO sought to guard against was:[56]

> 'the deliberate installation of a remote storage facility, specifically installed by an offender without notice to the police and which would not be apparent from the device he is using – and not intrinsic to the operation of any such device.'

Encryption software

9.41

A term which prohibited any use of encryption software was noted by the Court in *Parsons* as requiring consideration against 'the reality of devices available to consumers for everyday legitimate use'.[57] The Court concluded:[58]

---

55   *Parsons*, at [19].
56   *Parsons*, at [25].
57   *Parsons*, at [27].
58   *Parsons*, at [28].

'a prohibition here must be fashioned in such a manner as neither to be a blunt instrument nor a trap for the unwary (simply using the default setting of a device in everyday legitimate use). A suitable prohibition must instead be targeted – and aimed at the installation of encryption or wiping software on any device other than that which is intrinsic to its operation.'

Foreign travel prohibition

9.42

Prohibitions on foreign travel are permitted by SOA 2003, s 103D. They cannot be for more than five years,[59] but can be extended an unlimited number of times, providing each extension given is not longer than five years.[60] The subject of the SHPO will be required to surrender their passport to police,[61] this to be returned as soon as practicable after the prohibition expires.[62]

9.43

The main purpose behind the provisions is to prevent what is known as sex tourism, ie travel to countries with the purpose of engaging in conduct there that would amount to a sexual offence in this jurisdiction. Such an order, of course, must be proportionate to the risk involved.[63]

9.44

In *Burrows,* D had lived in the Philippines for 30 years. He had a wife and property there, and regarded it as home. There was no evidence that he travelled to the Philippines, or any other particular country, including those named in the order, with the intention of committing such offences or to increase his opportunity so to do.[64] Consequently there was no proper basis for an order in such wide terms. Given his personal ties there, the Court of Appeal considered that an order prohibiting the appellant from travelling to (and, of course, therefore living in) the Philippines would amount to a disproportionate response to the risk to children that he posed.[65]

---

59   SOA 2003, s 103D(1).
60   SOA 2003, s 103D(3).
61   SOA 2003, s 103D(4).
62   SOA 2003, s 103D(5).
63   *Burrows* [2015] EWCA Crim 2046, at [25].
64   *Burrows,* at [26].
65   *Burrows,* at [27].

No duplication of notification requirements

9.45

Any defendant convicted of a sexual offence will become subject to the notification requirements as set out in SOA 2003, s 80, for the period of time that corresponds with their sentence length as set out in SOA 2003, s 82.

9.46

Under SOA 2003, s 103G(1) as amended, where an SHPO is made in respect of a defendant who has committed the actus reus of a SOA 2003, Sch 3 offence, the defendant automatically remains subject to the notification requirements while the order has effect (see 9.82 ff).

9.47

The key thrust of precedent has been that an SHPO should not be used to duplicate notification requirements:[66]

> 'It is not necessary to have a specific term in the order which simply reflects the terms of the [Safeguarding Vulnerable Groups Act 2006] legislation itself. It is only if there is a real risk that he may undertake some activity outside the terms of the order that such a term may be justified.'

9.48

Similarly, in *Sokolowski*,[67] the Court of Appeal noted that:

> 'a person subject to an SHPO is automatically subject to notification requirements under section 103G(1). An SHPO must operate in tandem with the statutory notification scheme. It must not therefore conflict with the notification requirements; and it is not normally a legitimate use of an SHPO to use it simply to extend the notification requirements prescribed by law.'

Clarity of order

9.49

The terms of an SHPO must be sufficiently clear on their face for the defendant, those ordinarily in contact with him, and those responsible for enforcement, to understand exactly what he can and cannot do without real difficulty, or

---

66 *Lewis* [2016] EWCA Crim 1020, at [15] drawing on *Smith*, at [25].
67 [2017] EWCA Crim 1903, at [5](iv).

legal advice. Real risk of unintentional breach must be avoided,[68] particularly considering the consequences of breach (see 9.71).

Concurrent orders

9.50

Concurrent orders are not permissible: where an order is made regarding someone who is already subject to an SHPO, the earlier order will cease to have effect.[69]

9.51

Where the offender is subject to a SOPO, and subsequently receives an SHPO, the SOPO ceases to have effect unless the court orders otherwise.[70]

Variation/renewal/discharge

9.52

Under SOA 2003, s 103E, applications for variation, renewal or discharge can be made by the following people:[71]

(a)   the defendant;

(b)   the chief officer of police for the area in which the defendant resides;

(c)   a chief officer of police who believes that the defendant is in, or is intending to come to, that officer's police area;

(d)   where the order was made on an application by a chief officer of police under s 103A(4), that officer.

9.53

On the application the court, after hearing the person making the application and (if they wish to be heard) the other persons listed in 9.52, may make any order, varying, renewing or discharging the SHPO, that the court considers appropriate.[72]

9.54

Section 103E(5) limits the circumstances in which an application can be made:

---

68   See *Hemsley* [2010] EWCA Crim 225.
69   SOA 2003, s 103C(6).
70   Anti-social Behaviour, Crime and Policing Act 2014, s 136ZB.
71   SOA 2003, s 103E(2).
72   SOA 2003, s 103E(4).

'An order may be renewed, or varied so as to impose additional prohibitions on the defendant, only if it is necessary to do so for the purpose of:

(a)   protecting the public or any particular members of the public from sexual harm from the defendant, or

(b)   protecting children or vulnerable adults generally, or any particular children or vulnerable adults, from sexual harm from the defendant outside the United Kingdom.

Any renewed or varied order may contain only such prohibitions as are necessary for this purpose.'

Variation of terms

9.55

Where there is an application to vary the terms of an SHPO under SOA 2003, s 108, the appropriate procedure must be adopted – evidence served in advance in line with the CrimPR, and the hearing of an appropriately formal and structured nature to preserve procedural fairness.[73] Where a judge had varied an SHPO of his own motion after the Crown offered no evidence in proceedings for breach of the SHPO, as it was not expressed in sufficiently clear terms for a breach to be proven to the criminal standard,[74] these safeguards had not been applied. In fact, large quantities of highly prejudicial, and sometimes misleading, material had been placed before the court in inadmissible forms.[75] Variations flowing from procedural failure fall to be quashed.[76]

9.56

Where an SHPO has been made for less than the five-year period permitted by the statute, it will be unlawful. As an appellant cannot be dealt with more severely on appeal than s/he was by the first instance court, an SHPO that is unlawful for being too short must be quashed – it cannot be substituted by a longer, lawful SHPO once the period for alteration under the slip rule (56 days)[77] has elapsed.[78]

---

73   *Aldridge* [2012] EWCA Crim 1456.
74   *Aldridge*, at [17].
75   *Aldridge*, at [18]–[22].
76   *Aldridge*, at [28].
77   Powers of Criminal Courts (Sentencing) Act 2000, s 155.
78   *Eaton* [2012] EWCA Crim 1456, at [35]–[36], [39].

9.57

In *Thompson*, the Court of Appeal recognised that SHPOs could be added to a sentence on appeal if the custodial period was reduced, but that this would require the sentence as a whole to then be re-assessed for overall severity.[79] This carries a recognition that these orders do have a punitive effect, and their existence impacts on the severity of a sentence.

9.58

Where there is to be an application to vary an order, the CrimPR prescribes the procedural steps that must be taken.[80]

9.59

If unforeseen difficulties arise with an order once it is in operation, the defence should write to the CPS setting out these difficulties and why they arise. This might enable the matter to be dealt with administratively by agreement, and if not will at least have narrowed the live issues.[81] The court will be looking for a change of circumstances such that the original order's terms are no longer necessary to secure the requisite protection, or that that protection can be achieved by the terms in their proposed varied form.[82]

9.60

It is permissible to seek a variation where information which materially influenced the terms of the SHPO became known to the police belatedly,[83] even though they could have discovered it earlier.[84] The Court of Appeal rejected the submissions on behalf of the appellant that there was no change of circumstances as required by the Act, and that there is a general principle of change being required before a protective order can be varied. The Court concluded that this submission went 'far too far':[85]

> 'In this case it is in our judgment clear that, even if there was fault on the part of the Police Force in not learning as much as they did do by April, and if that should have been learned in January, then that would be a perfectly proper basis – indeed a compelling basis – for the application for the variation as it was sought here. The order proceeds from a protective duty and after-gained knowledge does justify an application of this kind.'

---

79 [2018] EWCA Crim 639, at [23].
80 CrimPR, r 31.5.
81 *Hoath and Standage* [2011] EWCA Crim 274, [2011] 1 WLR 1656, at [9].
82 *Hoath* at [11].
83 *Cheyne* [2019] EWCA Crim 182.
84 *Cheyne*, at [16]–[18].
85 *Cheyne*, at [18].

9.61

Any challenge in principle to the terms of an SHPO should be made by way of appeal and not by an application to vary under s 108.[86] In *Hoath and Standage* itself the Court rejected an appeal against a refusal to vary on the grounds that it was in substance an appeal out of time against the scope of the original order.

9.62

Where amendments are made to a SOPO or an SHPO, in order for them to be valid, they must be signed by, or on behalf of, the chief constable.[87] Where this has not occurred, the validity of the application for amendment itself is vitiated, despite its being a technical error.[88]

Discharge of SHPO

9.63

This can be applied for by any of those persons listed in SOA 2003, s 103E(2) (see 9.52), after five years of the SHPO have elapsed.

9.64

SOA 2003, s 103E(7) stipulates:

> 'The court must not discharge an order before the end of 5 years beginning with the day on which the order was made, without the consent of the defendant and—
>
> (a)   where the application is made by a chief officer of police, that chief officer, or
>
> (b)   in any other case, the chief officer of police for the area in which the defendant resides.'

9.65

However, by s 103E(8), the above does not apply to an order containing a prohibition on foreign travel and no other prohibitions, as, in any event, such a prohibition cannot be in force for more than five years.[89]

---

86   *Hoath and Standage* [2011] EWCA Crim 274.
87   *Hamer* [2017] EWCA Crim 192.
88   *L* [2017] EWCA Crim 1439, at [26].
89   SOA 2003, s 103D(1).

9.66

Evidence to support a proposition that the original order should not have been made should not be adduced,[90] and the question on an application to discharge will be whether there has been a change of circumstances. Otherwise, the application amounts to no more than an appeal,[91] applying *Hope and Standage*.[92]

Interim SHPOs

9.67

These are provided for under SOA 2003, s 103F. An interim SHPO can only be made where there is an application for an SHPO ('the main application') under s 103A(4) which has not yet been determined.[93] An application for an interim SHPO may be made as part of the main application,[94] or in a freestanding application to the court seized of the main application.[95]

9.68

It is a discretionary order to be made on the basis of what is 'just'.[96] It lasts only for a fixed period specified in the order,[97] and ceases on determination of the main application.[98]

9.69

An application to vary, renew or discharge an interim SHPO can be made by the applicant or the defendant.[99] Appeal against the imposition of an interim SHPO lies to the Crown Court.[100]

9.70

On an application for an interim SHPO by a chief officer of police, the court may, if it considers it just to do so, make an interim notification order (either in addition to or instead of an interim SHPO).[101]

---

90 *Sadler v Worcester Magistrates' Court* [2014] EWHC 1715 (Admin).
91 *Sadler v Worcester Magistrates' Court,* at [16]–[19].
92 See fn 84[GP – check when para numbering finalised and changes accepted].
93 SOA 2003, s 103F(1).
94 SOA 2003, s 103F(2)(a).
95 SOA 2003, s 103F(2)(b).
96 SOA 2003, s 103F(3).
97 SOA 2003, s 103F(4)(a).
98 SOA 2003, s 103F(4)(b).
99 SOA 2003, s 103F(5).
100 SOA 2003, s 103H(2).
101 SOA 2003, s 103G(7).

Breach of SHPO/interim SHPO

9.71

This is a separate offence in its own right under SOA 2003, s 103I:

'A person commits an offence if, without reasonable excuse, he does anything that he is prohibited from doing by:

(a) a sexual harm prevention order,

(b) an interim sexual harm prevention order,

(c) a sexual offences prevention order,

(d) an interim sexual offences prevention order, or

(e) a foreign travel order.'[102]

9.72

The offence is triable either way and is punishable:[103]

- on summary conviction – six months' imprisonment or a fine not exceeding the statutory maximum;

- on indictment – imprisonment not exceeding five years.

9.73

Any court dealing with this offence should be referred to the Sentencing Guidelines on Breach of Protective Orders applicable from 1 October 2018.[104] A court cannot impose a conditional discharge as the penalty for any offence under s 103I.[105]

9.74

Where an SHPO is breached by the commission of a new sexual offence (such as the downloading of further images of children), the court must take care not to double count. Further convictions soon after the first are likely to involve the breach of an SHPO, the breach of a community or suspended sentence order (leading to resentencing), and will be a 'potent aggravating feature' by virtue of those things. Therefore, careful regard must be had to totality as a result of these 'different consequences [which] are all conceptually different, but ... may arise from the same factual consideration'.[106]

---

102 SOA 2003, s 103I(1)(a)–(e).
103 SOA 2003, s 103I(1)(a) and (b).
104 Sentencing Council (2018) *Breach Offences: Definitive Guideline*, London: Sentencing Council https:// www.sentencingcouncil.org.uk/wp-content/uploads/BreachOffencesDefinitiveGuideline_WEB.pdf.
105 SOA 2003, s 103I(4).
106 *Richardson* [2017] EWCA Crim 886, at [8]–[9].

9.75

When sentencing for new offences, and a resultant breach of an SHPO, the court should be reminded of the principle of totality and directed to the relevant Sentencing Guideline.[107]

9.76

When there has been a sentencing exercise for breach of an SHPO, the most appropriate course is likely to be to leave the existing SHPO in place, unaltered.[108] At the conclusion of its term, it is open to the Crown to apply for an extension, which should be considered by a judge in the course of a proper application, on the basis of the position at that future time.[109]

9.77

The fact that a term that is breached is later varied or removed is not mitigation for the purposes of a breach whilst the term is in force.[110] Similarly, that a breach does not involve conduct that would be otherwise criminal were it not prohibited by the order is not mitigation: 'the significant feature of the offence is the breaching of a court order. The precise nature of the image is not so important as the fact that the appellant knowingly breached the order of the court.'[111] Where there are repeated, deliberate breaches of an order that are varied in nature, but can be seen to be part of a pattern in a wider pattern of past, current or future (albeit of course pre-sentencing) offending, consecutive sentences are likely to be appropriate.[112]

9.78

On proceedings for breach, it is not for the court to decide that a valid order should not have been made, though breadth and lack of clarity in its terms might mean that a tribunal finds that D's conduct was not in breach of it, for example, if the lack of clarity provided a reasonable excuse for a breach.[113]

9.79

Where the breach of the SHPO is also itself a criminal offence, a judge will be justified, considering totality, in considering the breach of the SHPO as an aggravating factor and giving no separate penalty on the count that charges it.[114]

---

107 *Burrow* [2018] EWCA Crim 866, at [16].
108 *Richardson* [2017] EWCA Crim 886, at [21].
109 SOA 2003, s 103E(5).
110 *Beeden* [2013] EWCA Crim 63, at [12].
111 *Joy* [2017] EWCA Crim 2004, at [8].
112 *Defalco* [2015] EWCA Crim 1759, at [16].
113 Analysis by analogy from the ASBO case of *DPP v T* [2006] EWHC 728 (Admin).
114 *Craddock* [2017] EWCA Crim 992, at [8]–[9].

9.80

As Leveson J (as he then was) observed in *Fenton*:[115]

> "If the breach does not involve any real or obvious risk to that section
> of the public whom it is intended should be protected by the order, a
> community penalty which further assists the offender to live within the
> terms of the order may well be appropriate, although repeated breaches
> will necessarily involve a custodial sentence, if only to demonstrate that
> orders of the court are not to be ignored and cannot be broken with
> impunity. Any breach which does create a real or obvious risk to those
> whom the order is intended to protect must inevitably be treated more
> seriously, and multiple or repeated breaches may well justify sentences
> that might otherwise have been considered far higher than any specific
> criminal offence or misconduct would have attracted. That, after all, is
> the statutory purpose behind the legislation in the first place.'

9.81

There is no power to make an SHPO for a breach of a SOPO, as breach is not
an offence within SOA 2003, Sch 3 or Sch 5.

Interaction with notification requirements

9.82

Any offender who is found to have committed the actus reus of an offence in
SOA 2003, Sch 3 through any of the following ways:

- conviction;

- found not guilty by reason of insanity;

- found to have done the act whilst under a disability; or

- caution,

will be subject to notification requirements as set out in SOA 2003, s 80 for the
period of time stipulated in SOA 2003, s 83. Any such person is referred to as
a 'relevant offender'.

9.83

Where an SHPO is made in respect of a defendant who was a relevant
offender immediately before the making of the order, and the defendant would
otherwise cease to be subject to the notification requirements of SOA 2003,

---

115 [2006] EWCA Crim 2156, at [25].

Part 2 while the order (including any renewals) has effect, they remain subject to the notification requirements.[116]

9.84

Where an SHPO is made in respect of a defendant who was not a relevant offender immediately before the making of the order, the order causes the defendant to become subject to the notification requirements from the making of the order until the order ceases to have effect, the relevant date for notification purposes being the date of service of the order.[117]

Appeals

9.85

Where there is an appeal against an SHPO made on conviction for an offence,[118] or on a finding of not guilty by reason of insanity,[119] or having done the act whilst under a disability[120] under SOA 2003, Sch 3 or 5, it should be made to the court to which an appeal against sentence (after conviction) would lie.[121]

9.86

Where minor but necessary adjustments are required, an application should be made to the Crown Court to vary the order (not an amendment under the 'slip rule'), but in circumstances where a defendant has not appealed to the Court of Appeal, it has been made clear that the Court of Appeal would not expect the Crown Court to make other than minor adjustments to the terms of the order.[122]

Jurisdiction

9.87

The youth court is empowered to decide an application for an SHPO or interim SHPO where the offender is under 18.[123] However, the youth court can also decide an application for an SHPO in relation to a person over 18 if rules of court have so provided. This covers situations where;

---

116 SOA 2003, s 103G(1)(a) and (b).
117 SOA 2003, s 103G(2)(a) and (b).
118 SOA 2003, s 103H(1)(a).
119 SOA 2003, s 103H(1)(b).
120 *Aldridge* [2012] EWCA Crim 1456, at [6]–[12].
121 SOA 2003, s 103H(1)(a).
122 *Hoath,* at [10].
123 SOA 2003, s 103A(8).

- an application to the youth court has been made, or is to be made, under SOA 2003, s 103 against a person aged under 18, and the youth court thinks that it would be in the interests of justice for the applications to be heard together;[124] or

- in relation to a person attaining the age of 18 after proceedings against that person by virtue of SOA 2003, ss 103A, 103E, 103F or 103G(6) or (7) have begun, rules of court prescribe circumstances in which the proceedings may or must remain in the youth court, or make provision for the transfer of the proceedings from the youth court to a magistrates' court that is not a youth court (including provision applying SOA 2003, s 103F with modifications).[125]

---

124 SOA 2003, s 103K(1)(a)(i) and (ii).
125 SOA 2003, s 103K(1)(b)(i) and (ii), s 103G(3).

10 Serious Crime Prevention Orders (on conviction)

10.01

The Serious Crime Act (SCA) 2007 provides for the making of a serious crime prevention order (SCPO).

10.02

There are two methods by which an SCPO can be made:

- on application to the High Court (SCA 2007, s 1),[1] if that Court:

  - is satisfied that a person has been involved in serious crime (whether in England and Wales or elsewhere);[2] and

  - has reasonable grounds to believe that the order would protect the public by preventing, restricting or disrupting involvement by the person in serious crime in England and Wales;[3] or

- following conviction for a 'serious crime' in the Crown Court,[4] if that court has reasonable grounds to believe that the order would protect the public by preventing, restricting or disrupting involvement by the person in serious crime in England and Wales.[5]

10.03

No more is said in this chapter about SCPOs made on application to the High Court – these are covered in Chapter 24.

10.04

An SCPO can only be made in addition to sentencing the defendant (D) for the offence,[6] though it can still be made on a defendant given a conditional discharge.[7] It is unclear whether an SCPO can be made alongside an absolute discharge following conviction, though it would seem that it can be, as ss 12 and 14 of the Powers of Criminal Courts (Sentencing) Act (PCC(S)A) 2000

---

1   See Chapter 24.
2   SCA 2007, s 1(1)(a).
3   SCA 2007, s 1(1)(b).
4   SCA 2007, s 19.
5   SCA 2007, s 19(2).
6   SCA 2007, s 19(2), (7)(a).
7   SCA 2007, s 19(7)(b).

(discharging the offender absolutely or conditionally shall be deemed not to be a conviction for any purpose other than the purposes of the proceedings in which the order is made) are effectively disapplied by SCA 2007, s 36(5).

Pre-requisite 1 – conviction for a 'serious offence'

10.05

Where D has been convicted of a 'serious offence' in England and Wales, either by or before the Crown Court,[8] or has been committed to the Crown Court having been convicted (on plea or after trial) before the magistrates,[9] the Crown Court may make an SCPO.[10]

10.06

For these purposes, a 'serious offence' is an offence that:

- is specified, or falls within a description specified, in Part 1 of Sch 1 to the SCA 2007;[11,12] or

- is one which, in the particular circumstances of the case, the court considers to be sufficiently serious to be treated for the purposes of the application or matter as if it were so specified.[13]

10.07

SCA 2007, Sch 1, as amended, sets out an extensive list of offences under 18 paragraph headings:

- drug trafficking;

- slavery;

- people trafficking (amended by the Protection of Freedoms Act 2010, Sch 9, para 142);

- firearms offences;

- prostitution and child sex;

- armed robbery etc;

- money laundering;

- fraud;

---

8   SCA 2007, s 19(1)(b).
9   SCA 2007, s 19(1)(a).
10 SCA 2007, s 19(8).
11 Which may be amended by the Secretary of State by order – SCA 2007, s 4(4).
12 SCA 2007, s 2(2)(a).
13 SCA 2007, s 2(2)(b), as demonstrated in *Brown* [2016] EWCA Crim 1437, at [16].

- offences in relation to public revenue (amended by the Taxation (International and Other Provisions) Act 2010, Sch 7, para 101(2));

- bribery (amended by the Bribery Act 2010, Sch 1, para 14);

- counterfeiting;

- blackmail;

- computer misuse;

- intellectual property;

- environment (as amended by Sch 22 to the Marine and Coastal Access Act 2009, Part 5, B);

- organised crime;

- offences relating to financial sanctions under EU, UN and counter-terrorism legislation;[14]

- attempting or conspiring to commit an offence specified or described in Sch 1, Part 1 (except common law conspiracy to defraud[15]);[16]

- encouraging or assisting (contrary to SCA 2007) where the offence (or one of the offences) which the person in question intends or believes would be committed is an offence specified or described in Sch 1, Part 1 (except common law conspiracy to defraud[17]);[18]

- aiding, abetting, counselling or procuring the commission of an offence specified or described in Sch 1, Part 1 (except common law conspiracy to defraud[19]).[20]

10.08

This list is also applicable to any conduct before the passing of the 2007 Act, as if the offences described in Part 1 included any corresponding offences under the law in force at the time of the conduct.[21]

10.09

SCA 2007, s 4 also supplements this definition. A court can only decide that D has committed a serious offence if:

- he has been convicted of the offence;[22] and

---

14   SCA 2007, Sch 1, Part 1, para 13B.
15   SCA 2007, Sch 1, Part 1, para 14(4).
16   SCA 2007, Sch 1, Part 1, para 14(1).
17   SCA 2007, Sch 1, Part 1, para 14(4).
18   SCA 2007, Sch 1, Part 1, para 14(2).
19   SCA 2007, Sch 1, Part 1, para 14(4).
20   SCA 2007, Sch 1, Part 1, para 14(3).
21   SCA 2007, Sch 1, Part 1, para 15(1).
22   SCA 2007, s 4(1)(a)(i).

- the conviction has not been quashed on appeal nor has the person been pardoned for the offence.[23]

10.10

Unless these circumstances are fulfilled, the court is expressly prohibited from deciding that D has committed the offence.[24]

10.11

Where D has been convicted of facilitating the commission of a serious offence by another person,[25] or of conducting himself in a way that is likely to facilitate the commission by himself or another person of a serious offence (whether or not such an offence is committed), the court must ignore any act that the respondent can show to be reasonable in the circumstances;[26,27] and subject to that, his intentions, or any other aspect of his mental state, at the time.[28,29]

10.12

SCPOs are not restricted to violent or sexual crimes: it might be appropriate to make an SCPO against a defendant who had committed fraud offences, as a sole offender, over a period of years.[30]

Pre-requisite 2 – making the order would prevent/restrict/disrupt 'involvement in serious crime'

10.13

An SCPO can only be made if the court has reasonable grounds to believe that the order would protect the public by preventing, restricting or disrupting involvement by the person in serious crime in England and Wales.[31]

10.14

'Involvement in serious crime in England and Wales' is any one or more of the following:

- the commission of a serious offence in England and Wales;[32]

---

23 SCA 2007, s 4(1)(a)(ii).
24 SCA 2007, s 4(1)(b).
25 SCA 2007, s 4(2).
26 SCA 2007, s 4(2)(a).
27 SCA 2007, s 4(3)(a).
28 SCA 2007, s 4(2)(b).
29 SCA 2007, s 4(3)(b).
30 *Batchelor* [2010] EWCA Crim 1025.
31 SCA 2007, s 19(2).
32 SCA 2007, s 2(3)(a).

- conduct which facilitates the commission by another person of a serious offence in England and Wales;[33]

- conduct which is likely to facilitate the commission, by the person whose conduct it is or another person, of a serious offence in England and Wales (whether or not such an offence is committed).[34]

10.15

This requirement necessitates the court to direct its mind to future risk, which must be real or significant, not a bare possibility.[35] Whilst a judge is entitled to depart from probation's risk assessment, to do so may lead the Court of Appeal to quash the SCPO for want of proportionality where the PSR states that D is at low risk of reconviction and poses a low risk of harm to the public.[36]

SCPOs against legal persons

10.16

SCPOs can also be made against legal persons – corporate bodies, partnerships and unincorporated associations.

SCPOs against bodies corporate – SCA 2007, s 30

10.17

The fact that an order is being, or has been made, against a body corporate does not prevent an order also being made against one of its officers or employees or any other person associated with it, provided the court is satisfied that they personally qualify under SCA 2007, s 1 or s 19.[37]

10.18

Care will be needed by all advocates to ensure that the appropriate company is named in the application and order. Prosecution advocates must be cautious against confusing a holding company with a subsidiary or associated company which is actually responsible for the acts which it is sought to prohibit, restrict or disrupt.

---

33   SCA 2007, s 2(3)(b).
34   SCA 2007, s 2(3)(c).
35   *McGrath* [2017] EWCA Crim 1945, at [10].
36   *Mangham* [2012] EWCA Crim 973, at [24].
37   SCA 2007, s 30(3).

SCPOs against partnerships – SCA 2007, s 31 (excluding limited liability partnerships)

10.19

An order can be obtained against a partnership and must be made in the name of the partnership (but not in the name of any of the individual partners).[38] However, this does not prevent orders also being obtained against individual partners,[39] senior officers, employees or other persons associated with the partnership.[40] A senior officer of a partnership means anyone who has the control or management of the business carried on by the partnership at the principal place where it is carried on.[41]

10.20

An SCPO remains valid against a partnership despite changes of partners providing at least one of the remaining partners was in the partnership at the time the order was made.[42]

10.21

Proof of involvement of a partnership in serious crime in England and Wales or elsewhere is satisfied by showing that the partnership or any of the partners is involved.[43]

SCPOs against unincorporated associations – SCA 2007, s 32

10.22

These provisions precisely mirror the provisions of s 31 on partnerships as detailed above.

Procedure

10.23

Proceedings before the Crown Court concerning SCPOs are civil proceedings,[44] meaning that the civil standard of proof is to be applied according to the

---

38   SCA 2007, s 31(1).
39   SCA 2007, s 31(10)(a).
40   SCA 2007, s 31(10)(b).
41   SCA 2007, s 31(11).
42   SCA 2007, s 31(2).
43   SCA 2007, s 31(3).
44   SCA 2007, s 36(1).

legislation.[45] However, case law is clear that the correct standard is in fact that of beyond reasonable doubt.[46]

10.24

It also means that the court is not restricted to considering evidence that would have been admissible in the criminal proceedings in which the person concerned was convicted.[47] The court may adjourn any proceedings in relation to an SCPO even after sentencing D.[48]

10.25

However, when the Crown Court is exercising its jurisdiction in England and Wales under this Part of the Act, it is a criminal court for the purposes of Part 7 of the Courts Act 2003, and is thus required to follow the Criminal Procedure Rules and practice directions.[49]

Content of orders

10.26

Section 19 of the SCA 2007 provides that an SCPO may contain such prohibitions, restrictions or requirements;[50] and such other terms;[51] as the court considers appropriate for the purpose of protecting the public by preventing, restricting or disrupting involvement by the person concerned in serious crime in England and Wales, subject to the safeguards contained in ss 6 to 15.[52]

10.27

SCA 2007, s 5 provides examples of the types of provisions that may be made by SCPOs, but does not limit them.[53]

---

45   SCA 2007, s 36(2).
46   *Orford and Barnes* [2012] EWCA Crim 2549, at [15].
47   SCA 2007, s 36(3)(a).
48   SCA 2007, s 36(3)(b).
49   SCA 2007, s 36(4).
50   SCA 2007, s 19(5)(a).
51   SCA 2007, s 19(5)(b).
52   SCA 2007, s 19(6).
53   SCA 2007, s 5(1).

Individuals

10.28

Examples of prohibitions, restrictions or requirements that may be imposed on individuals (including partners in a partnership) by SCPOs include those in relation to:[54]

- an individual's financial, property or business dealings or holdings;[55]

- an individual's working arrangements;[56]

- the means by which an individual communicates or associates with others, or the persons with whom he communicates or associates;[57]

- the premises to which an individual has access;[58]

- the use of any premises or item by an individual;[59]

- an individual's travel (whether within the UK, between the UK and other places or otherwise);[60]

- an individual's private dwelling (including, for example, where an individual may reside).[61]

Companies

10.29

Possible provisions for an SCPO against a body corporate, partnership or unincorporated associations include prohibitions, restrictions or requirements in relation to:

- financial, property or business dealings or holdings of such persons;[62]

- the types of agreements to which such persons may be a party;[63]

- the provision of goods or services by such persons;[64]

- the premises to which such persons have access;[65]

---

54   SCA 2007, s 5.
55   SCA 2007, s 5(3)(a).
56   SCA 2007, s 5(3)(b).
57   SCA 2007, s 5(3)(c).
58   SCA 2007, s 5(3)(d).
59   SCA 2007, s 5(3)(e).
60   SCA 2007, s 5(3)(f).
61   SCA 2007, s 5(6).
62   SCA 2007, s 5(4)(a).
63   SCA 2007, s 5(4)(b).
64   SCA 2007, s 5(4)(c).
65   SCA 2007, s 5(4)(d).

- the use of any premises or item by such persons;[66]

- the employment of staff by such persons.[67]

Any person

10.30

Possible provisions for an SCPO against any person include:

- a requirement on a person to answer questions, or provide information, specified or described in an SCPO:

    - at a time, within a period or at a frequency;[68]

    - at a place;[69]

    - in a form and manner;[70] and

    - to a law enforcement officer or description of law enforcement officer;[71,72]

    notified to the person by a law enforcement officer specified or described in the order;

- a requirement on a person to produce documents[73] specified or described in an SCPO:

    - at a time, within a period or at a frequency;[74]

    - at a place;[75]

    - in a manner;[76] and

    - to a law enforcement officer as defined;[77]

    notified to the person by a law enforcement officer specified or described in the order.

---

66 SCA 2007, s 5(4)(e).
67 SCA 2007, s 5(4)(f).
68 SCA 2007, s 5(5)(a)(i).
69 SCA 2007, s 5(5)(a)(ii).
70 SCA 2007, s 5(5)(a)(iii).
71 *Per* SCA 2007, s 5(7): (a) a constable; (b) a National Crime Agency officer who is for the time being designated under s 9 or 10 of the Crime and Courts Act 2013; (c) an officer of HM Revenue & Customs; or (d) a member of the Serious Fraud Office.
72 SCA 2007, s 5(5)(a)(iv).
73 Defined in SCA 2007, s 5(7) as anything in which information of any description is recorded (whether or not in legible form), which is expanded in s 5(8) to include in the case of a document which contains information recorded otherwise than in legible form, a reference to the production of a copy of the information in legible form.
74 SCA 2007, s 5(5)(b)(i).
75 SCA 2007, s 5(5)(b)(ii).
76 SCA 2007, s 5(5)(b)(iii).
77 SCA 2007, s 5(5)(b)(iv).

Financial reporting orders

10.31

Section 50 of the Serious Crime Act 2015 repealed financial reporting orders (FRO), consolidating these within SCPOs for simplification. Financial reporting requirements can now be imposed through the terms of an SCPO. Section 86(7) provides that existing FROs will remain active until they expire and the existing offence of breaching an FRO remains.

10.32

Whilst orders should not be unduly oppressive, they need to be effective, and should not be 'watered down' such that there is the possibility of D circumventing them to commit further serious crime.[78] Orders should take account of modern day living in respect of electronic devices which are supplied encrypted, for example, but it is proper to require that D does not take deliberate steps himself to encrypt items so as to obscure activities from the police.[79]

10.33

In *Hancox*,[80] the Court of Appeal held that the principles expounded by the Court in *Mee*,[81] a case concerning Travel Restriction Orders,[82] applied equally to the making of SCPOs.[83] Due to their contents, SCPOs will almost inevitably engage Article 8 of the European Convention on Human Rights,[84] and are not to be seen as a punishment, or additional or alternative form of sentence.[85]

10.34

The regime of SCPOs has been deliberately intended to add to the licence regime, not to be obsolete where D will be released on licence from a determinate sentence.[86]

10.35

Specific contents of each SCPO will depend on the facts of the offence – even for one type of case (eg drugs cases) the same terms will not be appropriate for every case.[87]

---

78   *McGrath* [2017] EWCA Crim 1945, at [14]–[15].
79   *McGrath*, at [19]–[21].
80   [2010] EWCA Crim 102.
81   [2004] EWCA Crim 629.
82   See Chapter 12.
83   *Hancox*, at [10].
84   *Hancox*, at [10].
85   *Hancox*, at [12].
86   *Hall* [2014] EWCA Crim 2046, at [32].
87   *Seale* [2014] EWCA Crim 650, at [20].

Safeguards

General

10.36

SCPOs can only be imposed on defendants who are over 18,[88] on the application of the Director of Public Prosecutions (DPP)[89] or the Director of the Serious Fraud Office (SFO).[90]

10.37

The Crown Court must, on an application by a person, give that person an opportunity to make representations in proceedings before it which arise by virtue of conviction in the Crown Court, or variation/replacement of orders on conviction or breach, if it considers that the making or variation of the SCPO concerned (or a decision not to vary it) would be likely to have a significant adverse effect on that person.[91]

10.38

Section 10 sets out stringent notice requirements which require that, to be bound by an SCPO, D must have been represented when it was made,[92] or a notice setting out the terms of the order has been served on him.[93]

10.39

Such a notice may be served by delivering it to him in person;[94] or sending it by recorded delivery to him at his last-known address (whether residential or otherwise).[95]

10.40

A body corporate can be served by a notice setting out the terms of the order being delivered to an officer of the body in person,[96] or sent by recorded delivery to the body at its last known address.[97] A partnership is served if the notice is given in person to one of the partners or a senior officer of the partnership [98]

---

88 SCA 2007, s 6.
89 SCA 2007, s 8(a)(i).
90 SCA 2007, s 8(a)(iii).
91 SCA 2007, s 9(4).
92 SCA 2007, s 10(1)(a).
93 SCA 2007, s 10(1)(b).
94 SCA 2007, s 10(2)(a).
95 SCA 2007, s 10(2)(b).
96 SCA 2007, s 30(1)(a)(i).
97 SCA 2007, s 30(1)(a)(ii).
98 SCA 2007, s 31(4)(a)(i).

or sent by recorded delivery to any of the partners or a senior officer of the partnership at the principal office of the partnership in the UK.[99]

10.41

In this legislation, body corporate includes a limited liability partnership.[100]

10.42

To deliver a notice to D or an organisation in person, a constable or a person authorised for the purpose by the relevant applicant authority[101] may (if necessary by force) enter any premises where he has reasonable grounds for believing D to be;[102] and search those premises for D,[103] an officer of a body corporate against whom an order is sought,[104] or a partner or senior officer of the partnership.[105]

Information

10.43

An SCPO may not require D to provide information orally, whether or not in response to questions.[106]

10.44

It is also not permitted to require D to:

- answer any privileged question,[107]

  – defined as one which D would be entitled to refuse to answer on grounds of legal professional privilege in High Court proceedings.[108]

- provide any privileged information,[109]

  – defined as that which D would be entitled to refuse to provide on grounds of legal professional privilege in High Court proceedings.[110]

---

99 SCA 2007, s 31(4)(a)(ii).
100 SCA 2007, s 30(4).
101 As defined in s 10(4)(a)(i) – the DPP, where s/he applied for the order; and s 10(4)(a)(iii) – Director of the SFO, where s/he applied for the order.
102 SCA 2007, s 10(3)(a).
103 SCA 2007, s 10(3)(b).
104 SCA 2007, s 30(1)(b).
105 SCA 2007, s 31(4)(b).
106 SCA 2007, s 11.
107 SCA 2007, s 12(1)(a).
108 SCA 2007, s 12(2).
109 SCA 2007, s 12(1)(b).
110 SCA 2007, s 12(3).

- produce any privileged document,[111]

  – defined as one which D would be entitled to refuse to produce on grounds of legal professional privilege in High Court proceedings;[112]

- answer any question if the disclosure concerned is prohibited under another enactment;[113]

- provide any information if the disclosure concerned is prohibited under another enactment;[114]

- produce any document if the disclosure concerned is prohibited under another enactment;[115]

- produce any excluded material as defined by s 11 of the Police and Criminal Evidence Act 1984;[116]

- disclose any information or produce any document in respect of which he owes an obligation of confidence by virtue of carrying on a banking business unless:[117]

  – the person to whom the obligation of confidence is owed consents to the disclosure or production;[118] or

  – the SCPO contains a requirement to disclose:

    (a) information, or produce documents, of this kind;[119] or

    (b) specified information which is of this kind or to produce specified documents which are of this kind.[120]

10.45

This does not prevent an SCPO from requiring a lawyer to provide the name and address of their client.[121]

10.46

A statement made by D in response to a requirement imposed by an SCPO may not be used in evidence against him in any criminal proceedings unless:[122]

---

111 SCA 2007, s 12(1)(c).
112 SCA 2007, s 12(4).
113 SCA 2007, s 14(1)(a).
114 SCA 2007, s 14(1)(b.
115 SCA 2007, s 14(1)(c).
116 SCA 2007, s 13(1)(a).
117 SCA 2007, s 13(2).
118 SCA 2007, s 13(3).
119 SCA 2007, s 13(4)(a).
120 SCA 2007, s 13(4)(b).
121 SCA 2007, s 12(5).
122 SCA 2007, s 15(1).

- the criminal proceedings relate to an offence under SCA 2007, s 25;[123] or
- the criminal proceedings relate to another offence;[124] and
  - the person who made the statement gives evidence in the criminal proceedings;[125]
  - in the course of that evidence, the person makes a statement which is inconsistent with the statement made in response to the requirement imposed by the order;[126] and
  - in the criminal proceedings evidence relating to the statement made in response to the requirement imposed by the order is adduced, or a question about it is asked, by the person or on his behalf.[127]

Duration

10.47

An SCPO must specify its start and end dates[128] and cannot be in force for more than five years.[129] It need not commence on the date it is made, and indeed it is likely to be of far more utility if it is specified 'to commence on the date of D's release from custody'.[130]

10.48

An SCPO can specify different times for the coming into force, or ceasing to be in force, of different provisions of the order.[131] If it does so, it must specify when each provision is to come into force and cease to be in force;[132] and overall must not be in force for more than five years from the first provision coming into force.[133]

10.49

There is one exception to this, which is when an SCPO is extended pending the outcome of criminal proceedings,[134] because D, already under an SCPO,

---

123 SCA 2007, s 15(2).
124 SCA 2007, s 15(3)(a).
125 SCA 2007, s 15(3)(b).
126 SCA 2007, s 15(3)(c).
127 SCA 2007, s 15(3)(d).
128 SCA 2007, s 16(1).
129 SCA 2007, s 16(2).
130 *Deeds* [2013] EWCA Crim 1624, at [5] and [10].
131 SCA 2007, s 16(3).
132 SCA 2007, s 16(4)(a).
133 SCA 2007, s 16(4)(b).
134 SCA 2007, s 16(7) referring to s 22E.

is charged with a serious offence,[135] or an offence of failing to comply with the SCPO.[136]

10.50

In those circumstances, the relevant applicant authority may make an application to the Crown Court[137] which may vary the SCPO so that it continues to be in force until:[138]

- following the person's conviction of the offence mentioned in SCA 2007, s 22E(1):[139]

  - the order is varied under s 20 or s 21, or under s 22B or s 22C, by reference to the offence;[140]

  - a new SCPO is made under s 19 or s 21, or under s 22A or s 22C, by reference to the offence;[141] or

  - the court deals with the person for the offence without varying the order or making a new one;[142]

- the person is acquitted of the offence;[143]

- the charge is withdrawn;[144]

- proceedings in respect of the charge are discontinued;[145] or

- an order is made for the charge to lie on the file.[146]

10.51

An order may be made only if the SCPO is still in force,[147] and the court has reasonable grounds for believing that the order would protect the public by preventing, restricting or disrupting involvement by the person in serious crime.[148]

---

135 SCA 2007, s 22E(1)(a).
136 SCA 2007, s 22E(1)(b).
137 SCA 2007, s 22E(2).
138 SCA 2007, s 22E(3).
139 SCA 2007, s 22E(4)(a).
140 SCA 2007, s 22E(4)(a)(i).
141 SCA 2007, s 22E(4)(a)(ii).
142 SCA 2007, s 22E(4)(a)(iii).
143 SCA 2007, s 22E(4)(b).
144 SCA 2007, s 22E(4)(c).
145 SCA 2007, s 22E(4)(d)(i).
146 SCA 2007, s 22E(4)(d)(ii).
147 SCA 2007, s 22E(5)(a).
148 SCA 2007, s 22E(5)(b).

10.52

The fact that an order, or any provision of an order, ceases to be in force does not prevent the court from making a new order to the same or similar effect,[149] and a new order may be made in anticipation of an earlier order or provision ceasing to be in force.[150]

Concurrent orders

10.53

If D is already the subject of an SCPO, the court must discharge that existing order.[151]

Variation of SCPOs

10.54

D is only bound by a variation in an SCPO if the notice requirements of SCA 2007, s 10 in relation to the making of an order have been fulfilled (see 10.38 ff).[152]

10.55

A variation of an SCPO may be made in spite of anything in ss 12 and 14 of the PCC(S)A 2000.[153]

10.56

The Crown Court has no power to vary an SCPO unless D is brought back for breach or convicted of a new offence (see 10.62 ff). Any application for variation must be made to the High Court.

Variation by application to High Court

10.57

SCA 2007, s 17(1) provides that the High Court may, on an application under this section, vary an SCPO in England and Wales if it has reasonable grounds to believe that the terms of the order as varied would protect the public by

---

149 SCA 2007, s 16(5).
150 SCA 2007, s 16(6).
151 SCA 2007, s 19(2A).
152 SCA 2007, s 10(1)(a) and (b).
153 SCA 2007, s 36(6).

preventing, restricting or disrupting involvement, by the person who is the subject of the order, in serious crime in England and Wales.

10.58

An application for the variation of an SCPO may be made by the relevant applicant authority;[154] the defendant subject to the order;[155] or any other person.[156]

10.59

The court must not entertain an application by D unless it considers that there has been a change of circumstances affecting the order.[157]

10.60

The court must not entertain an application by any other person unless it considers that:

- the person is significantly adversely affected by the order;[158] and

  - the person has, on an application under SCA 2007, s 9, been given an opportunity to make representations;[159] or has made an application otherwise than under s 9[160] in earlier proceedings in relation to the order and there has been a change of circumstances affecting the order;[161,162] OR

  - the person has not made an application of any kind in earlier proceedings in relation to the order,[163] and it was reasonable in all the circumstances for them not to have done so;[164] and

- the application is not for the purpose of making the order more onerous on the person who is the subject of it.[165]

10.61

A variation on an application by the relevant applicant authority may include an extension of the period during which the order, or any provision of it, is in force (subject to the original limits imposed by SCA 2007, s 16(2) and (4)(b)).[166]

---

154 SCA 2007, s 17(3)(a) – which will be the DPP or the Director of the SFO where there has been a conviction.
155 SCA 2007, s 17(3)(b)(i).
156 SCA 2007, s 17(3)(b)(ii).
157 SCA 2007, s 17(4).
158 SCA 2007, s 17(5)(a).
159 SCA 2007, s 17(6)(a)(i).
160 SCA 2007, s 17(6)(a)(ii).
161 SCA 2007, s 17(6)(b).
162 SCA 2007, s 17(6).
163 SCA 2007, s 17(7)(a).
164 SCA 2007, s 17(7)(b).
165 SCA 2007, s 17(5)(c).
166 SCA 2007, s 17(8).

Variation on further conviction by Crown Court

10.62

Furthermore, where the Crown Court sentences a defendant who is already subject to an SCPO for a new offence, it has powers to vary the existing SCPO under SCA 2007, s 20.

10.63

Where D, who is already subject to an SCPO,[167] has been convicted of a 'serious offence' in England and Wales, either by or before the Crown Court,[168] or has been committed to the Crown Court having been so before the magistrates,[169] the court may vary the SCPO in addition to dealing with D in any other way;[170] by way of sentence[171] or a conditional discharge.[172]

10.64

It may vary the order if the relevant applicant authority has made an application for it to be varied,[173] and if the court has reasonable grounds to believe that the terms of the order as varied would protect the public by preventing, restricting or disrupting involvement by the person in serious crime in England and Wales.[174]

10.65

A variation may include an extension of the period during which the order, or any provision of it, is in force (subject to the original limits imposed on the order by SCA 2007, s 16(2) and (4)(b)).[175]

Variation on breach proceedings

10.66

Where D has been convicted of breaching an SCPO, either by or before the Crown Court,[176] or has been committed to the Crown Court having been convicted before the magistrates,[177] the Crown Court may vary or replace the

---

167 SCA 2007, s 20(2)(a).
168 SCA 2007, s 20(1)(b).
169 SCA 2007, s 20(1)(a).
170 SCA 2007, s 20(2)(b).
171 SCA 2007, s 20(6)(a).
172 SCA 2007, s 20(6)(b).
173 SCA 2007, s 20(5).
174 SCA 2007, s 20(2).
175 SCA 2007, s 20(7).
176 SCA 2007, s 21(1)(b).
177 SCA 2007, s 21(1)(a).

SCPO in addition to dealing with D in any other way;[178] by way of sentence[179] or a conditional discharge.[180]

10.67

It may vary or replace the order if the relevant applicant authority has made an application for it to be varied,[181] and if the court has reasonable grounds to believe that the terms of the order as varied, or the new order, would protect the public by preventing, restricting or disrupting involvement by the person in serious crime in England and Wales.[182]

10.68

Replacing an SCPO amounts to discharging the old order and making a new order.[183]

10.69

A variation may include an extension of the period during which the order, or any provision of it, is in force (subject to the original limits imposed on the order by SCA 2007, s 16(2) and (4)(b)).[184]

Discharge of SCPOs

10.70

On application by the relevant applicant authority,[185] the defendant subject to the order,[186] or any other person,[187] the High Court may discharge an SCPO.[188]

10.71

The court must not entertain an application by D unless it considers that there has been a change of circumstances affecting the order.[189]

---

178 SCA 2007, s 21(2)(b).
179 SCA 2007, s 21(6)(a).
180 SCA 2007, s 21(6)(b).
181 SCA 2007, s 21(5).
182 SCA 2007, s 21(2).
183 SCA 2007, s 21(8).
184 SCA 2007, s 21(7).
185 SCA 2007, s 18(2)(a).
186 SCA 2007, s 18(2)(b)(i).
187 SCA 2007, s 18(2)(b)(ii).
188 SCA 2007, s 18(1).
189 SCA 2007, s 18(3).

10.72

The court must not entertain an application by any other person unless it considers that:[190]

- the person is significantly adversely affected by the order;[191] and

    - the person has, on an application under SCA 2007, s 9, been given an opportunity to make representations;[192] or has made an application otherwise than under s 9[193] in earlier proceedings in relation to the order and there has been a change of circumstances affecting the order;[194,195] OR

    - the person has not made an application of any kind in earlier proceedings in relation to the order,[196] and it was reasonable in all the circumstances for them not to have done so.[197]

Appeal from the Crown Court

10.73

By virtue of SCA 2007, s 9(5), a court which is considering an appeal in relation to an SCPO must, on an application by a person, give that person an opportunity to make representations in the proceedings if they had that opportunity in the proceedings being appealed.

10.74

An appeal against a decision of the Crown Court in relation to an SCPO may be made to the Court of Appeal (Criminal Division)[198] by the D subject to the order;[199] or the relevant applicant authority.[200]

10.75

This statutory route of appeal operates instead of any power for D to appeal against a decision of the Crown Court in relation to an SCPO by virtue of s 9 or s 10 of the Criminal Appeal Act 1968.[201]

---

190 SCA 2007, s 18(4).
191 SCA 2007, s 18(4)(a).
192 SCA 2007, s 18(5)(a)(i).
193 SCA 2007, s 18(5)(a)(ii).
194 SCA 2007, s 18(5)(b).
195 SCA 2007, s 18(5).
196 SCA 2007, s 17(7)(a).
197 SCA 2007, s 17(7)(b).
198 SCA 2007, s 24(5).
199 SCA 2007, s 24(1)(a).
200 SCA 2007, s 24(1)(b).
201 SCA 2007, s 24(11).

10.76

An appeal may be made to the Court of Appeal (Criminal Division)[202] in relation to a decision of the Crown Court to make an SCPO;[203] or to vary, or not to vary, an SCPO,[204] by any person who was given an opportunity to make representations in the proceedings concerned by virtue of SCA 2007, s 9(4).

10.77

Both types of appeal require the leave of the Court of Appeal,[205] unless the judge who made the decision certifies that the decision is fit for appeal.[206]

10.78

An appeal against a decision of the Court of Appeal on either type of appeal may be made to the Supreme Court by any person who was a party to the proceedings before the Court of Appeal.[207] Leave is required, to be granted by the Court of Appeal or the Supreme Court,[208] only if it is certified by the Court of Appeal that a point of law of general public importance is involved in the decision;[209] and it appears to the Court of Appeal or (as the case may be) the Supreme Court that the point is one which ought to be considered by the Supreme Court.[210]

10.79

Section 33(3) of the Criminal Appeal Act 1968 (limitation on appeal from Criminal Division of the Court of Appeal: England and Wales) does not prevent an appeal to the Supreme Court.[211]

10.80

In *Silk*, the Court of Appeal set out its powers on an appeal from an SCPO imposed by the Crown Court:[212]

'Our powers on an appeal under section 24(1) are prescribed by the Serious Crime Act. Under paragraph 4(1) every appeal will be limited to a review of the decision of the Crown Court and under paragraph 4(2) the Court of Appeal would allow an appeal where the decision of the Crown Court was wrong or unjust. The Court

---

202 SCA 2007, s 24(5).
203 SCA 2007, s 24(2)(a).
204 SCA 2007, s 24(2)(b).
205 SCA 2007, s 24(3).
206 SCA 2007, s 24(4).
207 SCA 2007, s 24(6).
208 SCA 2007, s 24(7).
209 SCA 2007, s 24(8)(a).
210 SCA 2007, s 24(8)(b).
211 SCA 2007, s 24(12).
212 [2010] EWCA Crim 3140, at [6].

of Appeal under paragraph 5 has all the powers of the Crown Court. Paragraph 5(2)(b) allows this court to affirm, set aside or vary any order or judgment made or given by the Crown Court if we are satisfied that paragraph 4(2) applies.'

10.81

These powers are derived from the Serious Crime Act 2007 (Appeals under Section 24) Order 2008.[213]

10.82

In *Silk*, despite appropriate submissions having been made by counsel to the judge, and the judge having properly considered those matters,[214] the Court held that one paragraph of the order was framed too widely, and was consequently capable of being unjust or leading to unintended breaches of the order by the appellant.[215] This was capable of remedy by the addition of a single word, to narrow the class of buildings about which D had to notify the police of his having access.

Breach

10.83

Failing to comply with an SCPO without reasonable excuse is an offence by virtue of SCA 2007, s 25(1).

10.84

A person who commits an offence under s 25 is liable:

- on summary conviction, to imprisonment for a term not exceeding 12 months, or to a fine not exceeding the statutory maximum, or to both;[216]

- on conviction on indictment, to imprisonment for a term not exceeding five years, or to a fine, or to both.[217]

10.85

In proceedings for an offence under SCA 2007, s 25, a copy of the original order or any variation of it, certified as such by the proper officer of the court which made it, is admissible as evidence of its having been made and of its

---

213   SI 2008/1863.
214   *Silk*, at [8].
215   *Silk*, at [9].
216   SCA 2007, s 25(2)(a).
217   SCA 2007, s 25(2)(b).

contents to the same extent that oral evidence of those things is admissible in those proceedings.[218]

Breach by body corporate

10.86

If a breach committed by a body corporate is proved to have been committed with the consent or connivance of an officer of the body corporate;[219] or a person who was purporting to act in any such capacity;[220] that person (as well as the body corporate) is guilty of the offence and liable to be proceeded against and punished accordingly.

Breach by partnership

10.87

If a breach is committed by a partnership, proceedings must be brought in the name of the partnership (and not in that of any of the partners).[221]

10.88

For the purposes of such proceedings, rules of court relating to the service of documents have effect as if the partnership were a body corporate;[222] and s 33 of the Criminal Justice Act 1925[223] and Sch 3 to the Magistrates' Courts Act 1980 apply as they apply to a body corporate.[224]

10.89

If a breach committed by a partnership is proved to have been committed with the consent or connivance of a partner or a senior officer, or person purporting to be such,[225] of the partnership, the partner (as well as the partnership) is guilty of the offence and liable to be proceeded against and punished accordingly,[226] even where the breach proceedings are brought in the name of the partnership.[227]

---

218 SCA 2007, s 25(4).
219 SCA 2007, s 30(2)(a).
220 SCA 2007, s 30(2)(b).
221 SCA 2007, s 31(5).
222 SCA 2007, s 31(6)(a).
223 SCA 2007, s 31(6)(b)(i).
224 SCA 2007, s 31(6)(b)(ii).
225 SCA 2007, s 31(9)(a).
226 SCA 2007, s 31(8).
227 SCA 2007, s 31(9)(b).

10.90

A fine imposed on the partnership on its conviction for breach is to be paid out of the partnership assets.[228]

---

228 SCA 2007, s 31(7).

11 Restraining Orders (on conviction)

11.01

A court sentencing or otherwise dealing with a defendant (D) convicted of an offence may (as well as sentencing him or dealing with him in any other way) make a restraining order under s 5 of the Protection from Harassment Act (PHA) 1997.[1]

11.02

When making such an order, the judge should regard the power to impose a sentence by way of punishment, and the protection which an order under s 5 provides for the victim (V), as complementary, rather than in opposition to one another.[2] The imposition of an order should be viewed as protective, and thus an application for judicial review to quash a term in a s 5 order that prevented D from going within 50 yards of the block of flats at which both he and V were tenants did not meet the threshold for being quashed, where the judge imposing it had heard all the evidence.[3] It should instead be the subject of an application to the Crown Court (which had imposed it on appeal from the magistrates' court against both conviction and sentence) for variation.[4]

Pre-requisites for making such an order

11.03

Conviction for any offence will suffice, since an amendment in 2009 flowing from the Domestic Violence, Crime and Victims Act 2004 removed the restriction that restraining orders could only be made after convictions for offences under PHA 1997, s 2 or s 4.

11.04

There is no necessity requirement as there is for an order under s 5A (see Chapter 20).[5]

---

1   PHA 1997, s 5(1).
2   *Miah* [2000] 3 WLUK 593, at [21].
3   *R v Southwark Crown Court, ex p Howard* [2000] 4 WLUK 345 (DC), at [22].
4   *Ex p Howard*, at [23].
5   *James* [2013] EWCA Crim 655, at [11].

11.05

In *Debnath*,[6] the Court of Appeal set out five principles for courts imposing restraining orders:[7]

- The purpose of a restraining order is to prohibit particular conduct with a view to protecting the victim(s) of the offence and preventing further offences under PHA 1997, s 2 or s 4.[8]

- A restraining order must be drafted in clear and precise terms so there is no doubt as to what the defendant is prohibited from doing.

- Orders should be framed in practical terms (for example it may be preferable to frame a restriction order by reference to specific roads or a specific address). A radius restriction will not necessarily invalidate an order. If necessary a map should be prepared.[9]

- In considering the terms and extent of a restraining order the court should have regard to considerations of proportionality.[10]

- The power of the court to vary or discharge the order in question by a further order under s 5(4) is an important safeguard to defendants. The Court of Appeal Criminal Division is unlikely to interfere with the terms of a restraining order if an application to the court which imposed the restraining order to vary or discharge it was, in the circumstances, the appropriate course.

Whether to make an order

11.06

The Court of Appeal has noted that where there is a history of exaggerated and false allegations, there is a real risk that a restraining order, far from mending affairs for the future, will give an opportunity for further such complaints to be made, meaning anxious consideration should be given to whether to make such an order.[11] In such circumstances, the making of an order would be wrong in principle.[12]

---

6   [2005] EWCA Crim 3472.
7   *Debnath*, at [20].
8   This case pre-dating the amendment that allowed a restraining order to be made when D was convicted of any offence.
9   *R v Robert Beck* [2003] EWCA Crim 2198, [2003] 7 WLUK 755, Mance LJ, at [9].
10 *Beck*, at [13].
11 *James*, at [13].
12 *James*, at [14].

11.07

Where at trial, on all important matters, conflicts in evidence had been resolved in favour of D, and no comparable order could be made against the complainant (C) to maintain some balance, it was unfair to single out D for a restraining order when on the verdict of the jury most of the trouble was attributable to false accusations and significant provocation by C.[13]

Content of the order

11.08

The order may prohibit D from doing anything described in the order,[14] for the purpose of protecting the victim(s) of the offence, or any other person mentioned in the order, from conduct which:

- amounts to harassment;[15] or

- will cause a fear of violence.[16]

11.09

The terms must be readily understandable.[17] If they are not, this should be the subject of an application to vary the order, not only raised when a breach is alleged.[18] Words should be taken to bear their ordinary meaning, not a specially narrow or strained meaning.[19] The terms must also be precise, and go above and beyond phrasing that its subject must refrain from unlawful behaviour.[20] If there is a particular lack of clarity, then this will go towards establishing a defence of reasonable excuse against an allegation of breach.[21]

11.10

Terms' compliance with the European Convention on Human Rights (ECHR) should be scrutinised, but sometimes, on the facts of particular cases, even orders with draconian conditions, such as 'not publishing any information about X and Y, whether true or not' will be proportionate and justified.[22]

---

13 *James*, at [12].
14 PHA 1997, s 5(2).
15 PHA 1997, s 5(2)(a).
16 PHA 1997, s 5(2)(b).
17 *Evans* [2004] EWCA Crim 3102, at [10].
18 *Evans*, at [10].
19 *Evans*, at [18].
20 *Searle* [2013] EWCA Crim 1845, at [11] and [14].
21 *Evans*, at [21].
22 *Debnath*, at [24] and [26].

11.11

Whilst a judge may take the view that a victim's wish to continue a relationship with the defendant is unwise, it is not for the judge to make an order to prevent that when it is the expressed wish of the victim[23] – there is no 'jurisdiction to prevent an adult from deciding who she wants to live with'.[24] It is also not appropriate to impose a restraining order with the intention of protecting a third party (not named in the order) who would have to mediate the contact between the two parties (ie the Probation Service).[25]

11.12

In *Nilsson and Williams*,[26] the Court of Appeal noted that in small, close-knit communities where the parties lived close together and all had children attending the village school, a restraining order might serve to exacerbate instead of calm a situation of continuing animosity between families.[27] But by the time of the later hearing of an appeal in relation to PHA 1997, s 5A orders imposed on three people acquitted of their role in the joint enterprise assault in the same proceedings,[28] the court indicated that, with hindsight, the decision in *Nilsson* had been overly ambitious.[29] This was in light of further reported intimidation of the victim set out in victim personal statements which was so severe that he had had to leave his home for an undisclosed location.[30] These cases serve to illustrate the care that a court must take in balancing the possibility that a restraining order will prevent parties from moving past a short-term disagreement, versus providing protection where bad feeling will continue to be manifested over a much longer period.

Victims

11.13

The victim(s) will need to be specifically identified within the order – a class of persons (such as 'all staff at the Probation Hostel') is not a permissible form of order.[31] It can also not protect a number of people who together do not form a 'close-knit group' – employees, for example, will not be sufficient.[32] The Court of Appeal has, more recently, however, not fundamentally excluded the possibility

---

23 *Brown* [2012] EWCA Crim 1152, at [11]–[12].
24 *Herrington* [2017] EWCA Crim 889, at [7].
25 *Herrington*, at [10].
26 [2012] EWCA Crim 2421.
27 *Nilsson and Williams*, at [30]–[31].
28 *McDermott* [2013] EWCA Crim 607.
29 *McDermott*, at [14].
30 *McDermott*, at [9].
31 *Mann* [2000] 2 WLUK 760, at [8] and [10]–[11].
32 *DPP v Dziurznski* [2002] EWHC 1380, at [32].

of using a restraining order to protect a limited company or employees where proper evidence was put forward by the Crown in a considered application.[33]

11.14

The order should not simply name all members of a family living at one address where there were individuals in the family who had not been involved in the incident leading to the conviction.[34]

11.15

The victim need not consent to the imposition of the order, and even if they have expressly stated that they do not wish a restraining order to be imposed, the judge has the power to make such an order.[35] However, as noted above at 11.11, judges should not place their judgement about the desirability of a relationship above that of the victim. Ideally, they will hear from the party that has intimated that they do not want the order to more carefully examine the motivations for that assertion, especially considering the complex internal dynamics often present in relationships involving domestic violence.

Locations

11.16

The order needs to be framed in practical terms, meaning that references to road names or easily-identifiable locations are to be preferred in the drafting to a distance ('not to go within 2km of X's house').[36] Reference to a distance, however, will not invalidate the order.[37] Nevertheless, unclear terms will – such as by reference to the 'town centre' of a place as it is not possible to establish exactly where this is held to be.[38] Naming a village and 'the surrounding areas' is also insufficient.[39] Describing the area D was prohibited from being in as 'Bournemouth as defined by the Borough of Bournemouth boundaries' was praised by the Court of Appeal as being 'entirely reasonable and entirely easy to understand and enforce' – where D had committed a number of offences in different parts of the Borough.[40]

---

33 *Buxton* [2010] EWCA Crim 2923, at [25]–[26].
34 *Stanton* [2010] EWCA Crim 797, at [13]–[15].
35 *Selvatharai* [2011] EWCA Crim 2503, at [18]–[20].
36 *Beck*, at [9].
37 *Beck*, at [9].
38 *Humphries* [2005] EWCA Crim 3469, at [17].
39 *Cornish* [2016] EWCA Crim 1450, at [19].
40 *Johns* [2005] EWCA Crim 2086, at [9]–[10].

11.17

A five-mile exclusion zone from the home of an individual, however, is likely to be too broad to be proportionate.[41]

11.18

Where there is a simple typographical error relating to an address, but it is clear which address is meant, and D knows that, that will not invalidate the order.[42]

11.19

Imposing a clause that prevents D from visiting a house of which he is the joint owner, with the motivation that it will cause him to sell the property and move elsewhere, will be susceptible to quashing on the grounds of fairness – it both punishes the (innocent) co-owner, and adds to the penalty imposed upon D by way of the sentence.[43]

11.20

Where the imposition of a term of a restraining order requires D to be re-housed in another area by the local authority on her release from prison, and prevents her from visiting her mother's house, it may nonetheless be proportionate where D has demonstrated in her previous conduct that if she sees the victim, she is unable to resist harassing her.[44] Where this deliberate behaviour by D had caused V to have to move out of the area where V had lived almost all of her life, but wished to move back, the only possibility was of a wide-ranging order.[45] There was no practical and operable alternative to excluding D from the whole area to give V the protection to which she was entitled.[46]

Other conditions

11.21

No complaint can be made of a term requiring D not to be drunk in a public place, especially if the offence occurred whilst under the influence of alcohol – the Court of Appeal noted that the argument 'I have a right to be drunk in a public place' was an 'unattractive' one.[47]

---

41 *Brotherwood* [2013] EWCA Crim 752, at [10] and [12].
42 *Beck* [2003] EWCA Crim 2198, at [8].
43 *Lewis* [2003] EWCA Crim 395, at [12].
44 *Richardson* [2013] EWCA Crim 1905, at [35].
45 *Richardson*, at [40].
46 *Richardson*, at [45]–[47].
47 *Wiggins* [2011] EWCA Crim 1792, at [32].

11.22

There is no provision to require D to report changes of address to the police.[48]

Duration of the order

11.23

The order may have effect for a specified period or until further order.[49]

11.24

Whilst a restraining order 'until further order' is a significant order, the 'strong protection' that it provides may mean that a stalking victim and her family can be properly protected from a benign albeit persistent stalker. The context was that, on appeal, the Court of Appeal held that the proper determinate sentence was of a length that meant neither condition under s 226A(2) and (3) of the Criminal Justice Act (CJA) 2003 applied and therefore the question of dangerousness, answered in the positive in the lower court, did not apply.[50] The restraining order offered sufficient protection.

11.25

An indefinite restraining order is not permanent, as the subject can apply for it to be varied (see 11.37 ff), and the success of that application will depend on the conduct of D and how much of a risk he is assessed to pose in the future.[51] It will not necessarily be inappropriate simply because in protecting the mother, it will effectively prevent contact between a child and its father.[52]

11.26

It has been argued that an indefinite order, requiring D to move out of his home, would breach Article 8 of the ECHR (though that was not in application in domestic law at the date of the Court of Appeal's judgment).[53] However, where D's conduct was making life intolerable for a neighbour in her own home, despite warnings and a caution, the court had to balance the respective interest in their homes between a guilty offender and an innocent individual whose life was being spoiled.[54] Weight would also be given to the fact that D had agreed to the making of the order in those terms, though that would not be decisive.[55]

---

48 *Beck*, at [2].
49 PHA 1997, s 5(3).
50 *Holehouse* [2018] EWCA Crim 1596, at [35] and [36].
51 *Cerovic* [2001] EWCA Crim 2868, at [54].
52 *Cerovic*, at [53]–[56].
53 *Beck*, at [13].
54 *Beck*, at [13].
55 *Beck*, at [13].

11.27

Where D was given an indeterminate sentence for public protection under CJA 2003, now no longer possible since the Legal Aid, Sentencing and Punishment of Offenders Act 2012, that did not automatically make a restraining order otiose where the tariff was for a shorter period than the contemplated restraining order would be, and the order should have been made.[56]

Interaction between a s 5 order and other orders

11.28

In persistent domestic violence contexts, it is not unusual for one course of conduct to generate concurrent proceedings in the criminal, family and civil courts. In *Lomas v Parle*,[57] the Court of Appeal offered guidance supplementing that in *Hale v Tanner*.[58] Where there are multiple proceedings, courts, which are not sharing the same objective or ranges of disposals, must reflect any sentence or penalty imposed by an earlier court when imposing a new one.[59] The court should be fully informed about other orders that D is under, and outcomes of other breach proceedings in other jurisdictions – ideally by way of a transcript.[60] Within the constraints of the maximum 24-month sentence for harassment in breach of a protective injunction (under s 42 of the Family Law Act 1996), judges should try to guard against manifest discrepancy with sentences for offences under PHA 1997, ss 3, 4 or 5 (though the more serious the offences the less achievable relating the respective sentences to one another will be).[61] This has since been confirmed in *H v O (Contempt of Court: Sentencing)*.[62]

11.29

There should not be a situation where a D is subject to multiple restraining orders in the same terms, relating to the same victim(s). If this occurs, an application should be made to the court to discharge one or the other.[63]

11.30

One solution to such difficulties is for the wording of a restraining order to be such as 'D is prohibited from contacting X, or her children, A, B and C, save for any contact through his lawyers to the children or as permitted by the County Court'.[64] That permits the family or county court order to be accommodated

---

56 *Davison* [2008] EWCA Crim 1004, at [15] and [23].
57 [2003] EWCA Civ 1804, at [47]–[52].
58 [2000] 1 WLR 2377, at [24]–[35].
59 *Lomas*, at [47]–[48].
60 *Lomas*, at [48].
61 *Lomas*, at [50].
62 [2004] EWCA Civ 1691.
63 *Beck*, at [23].
64 *H* [2011] EWCA Crim 1826, at [18].

within the terms of the s 5 order. A restraining order should not prevent contact with children outright – 'the issue of contact is not capable of being adjudicated upon as a by-product of criminal proceedings in a criminal court on scant information and solely as a protective device to benefit the mother'.[65] It must set out clearly what methods of organising contact with children are acceptable in precise terms.[66]

11.31

Where a restraining order is in place, a Sexual Harm Prevention Order (SHPO) may not be necessary to protect the victim in a situation of one-off offending triggered by a concatenation of mental health factors of D.[67]

Procedure

11.32

Part 50 of the Criminal Procedure Rules (CrimPR) applies to an application for a restraining order under PHA 1997, s 5.[68] If the requirements of Part 50 are to be varied by the court in its discretion under CrimPR, r 50.9, proper consideration must be given to the variation sought and the reasons for it.[69] In proceedings under this section both the prosecution and the defence may lead, as further evidence, any evidence that would be admissible in proceedings for an injunction under PHA 1997, s 3,[70] which provides that a course of conduct amounting to harassment can also found a civil claim for damages, without time limit.[71] However, there is no obligation to lead any evidence.[72]

11.33

If it is apparent from the Crown's opening that there will be an order sought, then that has been adjudged by the Court of Appeal to be sufficient to alert defence counsel that representations should be made on the matter, or an adjournment sought if needed. Defence counsel should thus be alive to such suggestions in openings for sentence.[73]

11.34

The views of the victim should be ascertained through a witness statement taken by police – especially as any order is, at the very least, likely to make any

---

65 *C* [2014] EWCA Crim 343, at [11].
66 *Kaddu* [2015] EWCA Crim 2531, at [14], [21], [22].
67 *Allan* [2012] EWCA Crim 2085, at [18].
68 *Stanton* [2010] EWCA Crim 797, at [11] and [13].
69 *Stanton*, at [13].
70 PHA 1997, s 5(3A).
71 PHA 1997, s 5(6), applying the provisions of the Limitation Act 1980, s 11(1A).
72 *Selvatharai* [2011] EWCA Crim 2503, at [16] and [19].
73 *Cornish* [2016] EWCA Crim 1450, at [17].

continuing personal relationship untenable.[74] If V's views have not been sought, then an adjournment should be permitted for the Crown Prosecution Service (CPS), through an officer, to do so. Without this information, an order should not be made.[75]

11.35

Where a restraining order is applied for, it should be upon instructions (V's views having been sought, as above). The basis for seeking the order should be clear. It should not be made of the judge's own motion with prosecution counsel's acquiescence, with no opportunity for the defendant to make submissions, and if that is the case, it is liable to be quashed.[76] Similarly, where there is a proper application concerning a mother, the judge should not automatically impose one covering a child of D and the mother as well.[77]

11.36

A failure by the sentencing court to record the making of a restraining order, where the judge's sentencing remarks make it clear that one was made, do not invalidate the order providing the court had jurisdiction to make it.[78]

Variation and discharge

11.37

The prosecutor, the defendant or any other person mentioned in the order may apply to the court which made the order for it to be varied or discharged by a further order.[79] This includes an application to extend it where there are grounds to think that the protection for the victim is still needed when the order is about to expire.[80] The only court that can exercise the power under PHA 1997, s 5(4) to vary or discharge is the court that made the order, and any purported extension by another court will be unlawful.[81]

11.38

Any person mentioned in the order is entitled to be heard on the hearing of an application for variation or discharge.[82] This means that the prosecution should seek the view of the victim, through a witness statement, and the defendant would be well-advised to have material supporting their application for the variation, especially if it relates to circumstances such as a new job, or other

---

74 *Picken* [2006] EWCA Crim 2194, at [17].
75 *Picken*, at [17].
76 *Zakacura* [2013] EWCA Crim 2595, at [17].
77 *G* [2015] EWCA Crim 1506, at [12]–[14].
78 *Curtis* [2012] EWCA Crim 2295, at [13]–[14].
79 PHA 1997, s 5(4).
80 *DPP v Hall* [2005] EWHC 2612 (Admin).
81 *Kealey* [2008] EWCA Crim 1531, at [8]–[9].
82 PHA 1997, s 5(4A).

legitimate reason for needing to enter an area from which they are excluded.[83] If there are problems concerning contact, and an order is made by the family court which is incompatible with the s 5 order, then the Court of Appeal has described it as 'inconceivable' that the criminal court would not allow variation to permit whatever action the family court endorsed.[84]

11.39

Where there is a successful application for variation, the Court of Appeal has noted that it is highly desirable to draw up a new order in the amended terms so that there can be no confusion as to the terms of the order that are operative at any particular point in time.[85]

11.40

If an application to vary or discharge is refused by the magistrates' court, there is no jurisdiction to appeal that refusal to the Crown Court, as PHA 1997 is silent and the variation is not a 'sentence' under the Magistrates' Courts Act 1980, s 108.[86] Therefore the only method of challenging a refusal to vary or discharge is judicial review or appeal by way of case stated.

11.41

It has also not been resolved whether an application to vary or discharge is a sentence for the purposes of s 9 of the Criminal Appeal Act 1968 – when the issue arose the Court of Appeal circumvented it by treating the application to vary as an appeal against the original order.[87]

Offence of breach

11.42

If without reasonable excuse the defendant does anything which s/he is prohibited from doing by an order under PHA 1997, s 5, s/he is guilty of an offence.[88] This offence is triable either way, and carries sentences of:

- on conviction on indictment, imprisonment for a term not exceeding five years, or a fine, or both;[89] or

- on summary conviction, imprisonment for a term not exceeding six months, or a fine not exceeding the statutory maximum, or both.[90]

---

83 *Bradfield* [2006] EWCA Crim 2917, at [15]–[16].
84 *B* [2016] EWCA Crim 309, at [8].
85 *Liddle* [2001] EWCA Crim 2512, at [6].
86 *R (Lee) v Leeds Crown Court* [2006] EWHC 2550 (Admin).
87 *Bradfield*, at [8].
88 PHA 1997, s 5(5).
89 PHA 1997, s 5(6)(a).
90 PHA 1997, s 5(6)(b).

11.43

The offence is one of strict liability.[91] Whilst the prosecution must prove that a valid restraining order was in place, it can do this through producing a copy of the order, or through adducing other admissible evidence, such as an admission in interview by D that there was an order in force at the time.[92]

11.44

The identity of the specific restraining order that is being breached is a material averment. Therefore, if D is subject to multiple such orders both counsel should be alert to which it is that D is alleged to have breached, and ensure that that is reflected clearly in the particulars.[93]

11.45

A court dealing with a person for an offence under this section may vary or discharge the order in question by a further order.[94]

11.46

Where D has a background of non-compliance, this will aggravate the sentence imposed for a breach.[95] Any court sentencing for breach must adhere to the Sentencing Council Definitive Guidelines on Breach of a Protective Order.

Defence of reasonable excuse

11.47

This must be raised by the defendant.[96] The burden of disproving reasonable excuse is on the Crown once D has raised it.

Appeal

11.48

There is no specific mention in PHA 1997, s 5 of the right to, and route of, an appeal. Therefore it is to be assumed that it can be appealed as part of the sentence to the court to which an appeal against sentence would lie.

---

91 *Barber v CPS* [2004] EWHC 2605 (Admin), at [15].
92 *Barber v CPS*, at [15].
93 *Beck*, at [29].
94 PHA 1997, s 5A(2) applying s 5(7).
95 *Young (Justin James)* [2013] 11 WLUK 304.
96 *Evans*, at [24]–[25].

12 Travel Restriction Orders

12.01

The power to make a travel restriction order (TRO) is contained in s 33 of the Criminal Justice and Police Act (CJPA) 2001.

12.02

Such an order prohibits an offender from leaving the UK for a period of time that is not less than two years,[1] starting with the date of his/her release from custody.[2]

Requirements before a TRO can be imposed

12.03

An order may be made following a conviction by any court for a 'drug trafficking offence' committed after 1 April 2002,[3] where the sentence is a term of imprisonment of four years or more.[4]

12.04

The definition of 'drug trafficking offence' for the purpose of TROs is provided in CJPA 2001, s 34. It is significantly narrower than the definition of the same expression in the Drug Trafficking Act 1994 (s 1). The offences which permit the imposition of a TRO are:

- **Misuse of Drugs Act 1971**

    - an offence under s 4(2) or (3) (production and supply of controlled drugs);

    - an offence under s 20 (assisting in or inducing commission outside UK of an offence punishable under a corresponding law);

    - any such other offence under that Act as may be designated by order made by the Secretary of State.

---

1   CJPA 2001, s 33(3)(b).
2   CJPA 2001, s 33(3)(a).
3   CJPA 2001, s 33(1)(a) – notably possession with intent to supply (PWITS) Class A is not such an offence, as the judge overlooked in *Whittle* [2007] EWCA Crim 539, meaning the order had to be quashed for want of jurisdiction (at [9]). The situation arose again, much to the Court of Appeal's displeasure, in *Boland* [2012] EWCA Crim 1953. This is inconsistent with the fact that actual supply is an offence to which TROs apply.
4   CJPA 2001, s 33(1)(b) and (c).

- **Customs and Excise Management Act 1979**

  - s 50(2) or (3) (improper importation);

  - s 68(2) (exportation); or

  - s 170 (fraudulent evasion),

in connection with a prohibition or restriction on importation or exportation having effect by virtue of s 3 of the Misuse of Drugs Act 1971.

12.05

Notably, it does not include either possession with intent to supply (PWITS) or 'money laundering' offences.

12.06

It does, however, include the commission of any of the listed offences as a secondary party – aiding, abetting, counselling or procuring.[5] Similarly a conspiracy,[6] attempt[7] or incitement under common law or s 19 of the Misuse of Drugs Act 1971[8] will suffice. CJPA 2001, s 34(1)(c) also gives the Secretary of State the power to designate any other offence to fall within these provisions, providing this is done by statutory instrument and with the resolution of both houses of Parliament.[9]

12.07

Any court sentencing in those circumstances MUST consider making such an order,[10] and must give reasons if it does not make such order.[11] Where a court decides to make a TRO it must make such an order as it 'thinks suitable in all the circumstances', which are expressly stated to include 'any other conviction for post-commencement drug trafficking offences in respect of which the court is also passing sentence'.[12]

12.08

The sentence of four years or more required by CJPA 2001, s 33(1)(c) applies to the sentence for the trafficking offence itself only, and not to other related, but non-drug trafficking, offences for which the defendant is sentenced at the same time to a consecutive term.[13]

---

5   CJPA 2001, s 34(1).
6   CJPA 2001, s 34(1)(f).
7   CJPA 2001, s 34(1)(e).
8   CJPA 2001, s 34(1)(g).
9   CJPA 2001, s 34(2).
10   CJPA 2001, s 33(2)(a).
11   CJPA 2001, s 33(2)(c).
12   CJPA 2001, s 33(2)(b) .
13   *Alexander* [2011] EWCA Crim 89, at [29], [32]–[34].

12.09

Prosecutors must ensure that if an offence may attract a TRO they are ready to assist the court by drawing the court's attention to the power to make a TRO, and should identify the facts of the index offence that will affect the length of any such order.

12.10

In *Mee*,[14] the first case in which TROs came before the Court of Appeal, the Court considered the regime, and emphasised the discretionary nature of such orders:[15]

'The discretion, as it will be seen from what we have said, is conferred in broad terms … Notwithstanding its broad ambit general principles govern the exercise of the discretion. It must be exercised for the purpose for which it was granted and proportionally. As to its purpose, it is plain that it is not intended to be a substitute for the appropriate period of imprisonment to which the circumstances of the offence give rise. Its purpose, and undoubtedly a very important public interest is served by this legislative provision, is to prevent or reduce the risk of reoffending after the defendant's release from prison.'

Length of TRO

12.11

An order cannot be for less than two years, but there is no maximum period prescribed in legislation.[16] It runs from the date of release from custody, not the date of sentence.[17]

12.12

In *Mee*,[18] the Court noted that the effects of an order must be weighed against the things of which the specific offender would be deprived, and every case would turn on its own facts:[19]

'It is unrealistic, if not impossible, to set out the broad range of facts which are likely to arise in individual cases. Suffice it to say, that the starting point should be a careful consideration of the circumstances

---

14 [2004] EWCA Crim 629.
15 *Mee*, at [8].
16 CJPA 2001, s 33(3)(b).
17 CJPA 2001, s 33(3)(a), emphasised in *Campbell* [2004] EWCA Crim 2333, at [11].
18 [2004] EWCA Crim 629.
19 *Mee*, at [11]–[12].

of the offence and of the offender with a view to making a realistic assessment of the risk which arises from the facts of the case.

Assuming that a risk has been identified, and a need for an order arises, the principles of proportionality and fairness require a balanced approach to the length of the restriction to be imposed. A restriction on a person's freedom to travel is, as has been pointed out in the skeleton argument presented for this appellant, a restriction on a significant aspect of modern life. It is not to be taken away from a person for a number of years unless there are grounds for doing so. It cannot be for less than two years. It could in many cases affect his right to live and work abroad, to visit his family and so forth. That is a matter to which the court will wish to have regard. But having said that, we must emphasise that the weight to be given to such factors, when they are present to be taken into account, is to a significant degree, affected by s 35, which provides for the revocation and suspension of a travel restriction order. In our judgment the legislature must have contemplated that an order of this sort could affect an individual so as to prejudice his future employment and his personal life. Such prejudice must be regarded as being the contemplated and necessary consequence of the imposition of an order for which the statute provides a specific regime of relief.'

The appellant had imported 1.955 kg of pure cocaine from Jamaica. It had a street value of just under £150,000. At first instance a TRO for 15 years was imposed, running from his release from a seven-year custodial sentence. This was reduced to five years on appeal. As the Court observed,[20]

'Having regard to the impact of the restrictions, the length of an order should be measured to the defendant. Some factors can be enumerated by way of example; his age, his previous convictions, the risk of reoffending, which can be assessed generally, and of course, as we have mentioned, family contacts, employment considerations and so forth. The length should be that which is required to protect the public in the light of the assessment of the degree of risk which is presented by the facts. But, as we have said, it should be tailored to the defendant to such a degree as the court feels able when balanced against the risk. It is to be noted that the drug trade is truly international. It is no doubt for that reason that the provisions of this Act, and in particular s 33, do not of themselves contemplate a travel restriction order which is linked to only certain parts of the world where the drug trade flourishes with its greatest potency.'

---

20 *Mee*, at [14].

12.13

When there is support in the facts of the offence that the offending will be a one-off occurrence, a TRO might not be appropriate. In *Fuller*,[21] D was a 25-year-old woman of good character who pleaded guilty to importing 570g of cocaine. A five-year TRO was imposed, running after a custodial sentence of four years. Quashing the TRO in its entirety, the Court of Appeal noted the facts of the offence, as well as the appellant's personal circumstances, especially that her young son would be severely affected by a prohibition on his mother travelling:[22]

'We have noted that the appellant is young, of good character, and is responsible for a 3 year old child who has had meningitis and who still suffers from the effects of that condition. The appellant's part in this offence was quite clearly, in our judgment, one-off; it involved her carrying the Class A drug from Jamaica to the United Kingdom. Although she clearly had had some contact with somebody who suborned her into bringing the drugs to this country and who paid her the money, she was not in any network (in any true sense of the word); nor had she any contacts with the drug trade such as to attract the condign punishment reserved for people who regularly traffic in drugs. Her motive (as so often with these "mules") was because she was in substantial debt totalling £5,000. Further, the facts reveal that she was born in Jamaica, although she is a British national. Her parents live about half the year in Jamaica, but the plans are that they will spend more time in Jamaica. The appellant is estranged from her husband at the present time. He lives in Jamaica. However, despite that estrangement, he still remains the child's father. Furthermore, the rest of the appellant's family live in Jamaica.

We have examined with care the appellant's past travel pattern. There was evidence before the judge that she had made previous visits to Jamaica in 2000 and twice in 2003. Each journey was proved to have an innocent explanation, namely a death in the family and the appellant's marriage to the husband we have mentioned. [...] we do not consider that, when the appellant has served her sentence, there is any risk indicated in any of the reports on her, or by reason of the facts of the case, that she will further offend.'

12.14

Where the defendant is a mere courier and of previous good character a TRO is unlikely to be appropriate.[23] Similarly, where there was evidence that the

---

21 [2005] EWCA Crim 1029.
22 *Fuller*, at [5]–[7].
23 *Azeem* [2007] EWCA Crim 1614.

offence was a one-off motivated by a need for money in order to visit his ill mother, and the defendant's family were living in Nigeria and dependent upon him, an appeal against the imposition of a TRO was allowed.[24] However, where an offence was motivated by ongoing financial hardship, even if there is family abroad, a TRO for the shortest possible period is appropriate.[25]

12.15

If there is nothing to indicate high risk other than the facts of the index offence, then the Court of Appeal has implied that judges should err on the side of a shorter order.[26] High frequency of travel between the UK and a country where there is known to be an active drugs' trade is likely to support the making of such an order, even where this would prevent family contact.[27] Where an appellant was committing the offence whilst travelling with children whose existence she prays in aid, and the children are of secondary school age, the court is likely to be less sympathetic.[28]

12.16

Where the combination of the appellant's age and the length of the ban under a TRO would, in reality, amount to a lifetime ban on foreign travel, careful scrutiny and application of the guidance in *Mee* will be required. If this is not carried out, the order is likely to be quashed, as in *Moss*:[29] M was 56, and a 25-year TRO, to begin on his release from a 17-year sentence of imprisonment was imposed after he pleaded guilty to importing 113kg of cocaine. This was reduced to 15 years on appeal. However, there are circumstances where even a lengthy TRO, with its accompanying personal hardships to the appellant, will be appropriate:[30]

> 'It is undoubtedly a long order, but the applicant has played a major part in an extremely large importation of Class A drugs. It was not a one-off transaction. He was not a man of unblemished record. He is plainly acquainted with major players in the international drug scene. He has close links with a country which is a major exporter of drugs to the United Kingdom. Whether his relationship with the mother of his children survives the lengthy custodial term only time will tell. If it does, then the Travel Restriction Order is very likely to impinge upon his family and his relationship to its members. He can, however, if the circumstances are appropriate, apply for it to be lifted partially or completely. However, given the seriousness of this case, the impact

---

24 *Onung* [2006] EWCA Crim 2813.
25 *Parsons* [2006] EWCA Crim 464.
26 *Ali (Farman)* [2008] EWCA Crim 1855, at [56].
27 *Cruikshank* [2012] EWCA Crim 1519, at [8]–[9].
28 *Watson* [2013] EWCA Crim 182, at [12].
29 *Moss* [2006] EWCA Crim 1580, at [15].
30 *Pettitt (Karl)* [2008] EWCA Crim 1094, at [20].

of the Travel Restriction Order upon his family life is not something that leads us to the conclusion that its length was in any way excessive.'

12.17

Where a defendant will be elderly on release from prison, there is less likely to be justification for a TRO, such as in *Brooks*, where the appellant would be 75 on his release.[31]

12.18

Appropriate differentiation in the length of TROs imposed should be made between co-defendants on the basis of their respective roles in any offending.[32]

12.19

Ideally, a pre-sentence report will be available which covers the matter of a TRO, and its effects:[33] similarly, counsel should make detailed submissions on such an order having had regard to the factors in *Mee* with which the judge will want assistance.

12.20

The Court of Appeal has articulated on more than one occasion that a TRO is not to be used solely as a deterrent measure – it is a preventative one, following a term of imprisonment which will itself, for many defendants of good character, serve the purpose of deterrence.[34]

Procedure

12.21

Judges have been encouraged to adopt a rigorous procedure when considering making an order, including warning counsel they are considering doing so, and then giving counsel time to take instructions from the defendant about any issues that might be specifically affected by the imposition of such an order.[35] They should also give clear reasons for the period of the order that they have selected, and set out why, on the facts of the index offence, such a period is the appropriate one.[36] They must take care to start from the position of considering whether an order is necessary (as required by CJPA 2001, s 33(2)), not an

---

31 [2014] EWCA Crim 562, at [53]–[54].
32 *Sacco* [2006] EWCA Crim 1391, at [9] and [15].
33 *Hesketh* [2006] EWCA Crim 1031, at [7].
34 *Brown (Claudette)* [2010] EWCA Crim 2454, at [9]; *Graham (Lesley)* [2011] EWCA Crim 1905, at [9].
35 *Mee*, at [15].
36 *Mee*, at [25].

assumption that it is necessary.[37] Where a judge is not applying the correct test, counsel can expect criticism from the Court of Appeal if they do not intervene.[38]

12.22

The Court of Appeal has indicated that not only should first instance judges turn their minds to the factors set out in *Mee*, but that they must give sufficiently detailed reasons to demonstrate both that they have turned their minds to relevant matters, and how those matters have directly impacted on the length of TRO imposed, taking into account both the facts of the case, and evidence (or the lack thereof) about the personal circumstances of the defendant:[39]

> 'In our judgment the imposition of the order imposing a travel restriction and the term to which it is to run requires a sharp focus on the facts of the case, and an assessment of the risk of reoffending of the particular defendant, after her discharge from prison, in this case having served a very long sentence. That is to be balanced against the adverse consequence of the order upon the defendant and her family life. The judge did not here undertake such an analysis. He found that she was a courier, but he did not make any finding of the risk of reoffending particularly after release from such a sentence. He did not suggest any reason for thinking that she would, or even could, again be selected as a courier. Furthermore, there was no detailed evidence-based assessment of the impact upon her family life of being unable to visit her husband in Jamaica. For these reasons we think the travel restriction order must be quashed.'

12.23

Unless the reasons for the imposition of a TRO are clear from the facts, reasons should be given, despite there being no requirement in the statute.[40] There is, however, a requirement in the statute at s 33(2)(c) to give reasons if an order is NOT imposed.

12.24

Where the defendant has not received a sentence of imprisonment of four years or more for a drug trafficking offence for any reason, including that the sentence was much reduced to take account of his having serious physical disabilities, the court should consider a Serious Crime Prevention Order instead (see Chapter 10).[41]

---

37 *Powell (Karlton)* [2014] EWCA Crim 1606, at [5].
38 *Powell (Karlton)*, at [6].
39 *Williams (Kelly)* [2009] EWCA Crim 2165, at [7].
40 *Ferguson* [2010] EWCA Crim 2860, at [20].
41 *Hall (Daniel)* [2013] EWCA Crim 82, at [21].

Effect of a TRO

12.25

Under a TRO the offender may be directed to surrender their UK passport to the court, which will then send the passport to the Secretary of State.[42] Where the Secretary of State holds the passport pursuant to such a direction, s/he may retain it for the period for which the prohibition contained within the order is in force (but not if it is suspended).[43] The Secretary of State shall return the passport only on application by the offender if it remains valid AND either the prohibition has ceased to apply, or is suspended.[44]

Revocation

12.26

CJPA 2001, s 35 provides for the court which made a TRO to revoke or suspend it under certain circumstances.

12.27

The subject of the TRO can apply for it to be revoked at any time:[45]

- after the end of the 'minimum period';[46] and

- not within three months of making any previous application for the revocation of the prohibition.[47]

12.28

CJPA 2001, s 35(7) defines the 'minimum period' as:

- **TRO for four years or less** – two years beginning at the time when the period of the prohibition began;

- **TRO for more than four years but less than ten years** – four years beginning at that time; and

- **in any other case** – five years beginning at that time.

12.29

In response to such an application, the court can revoke the prohibition imposed by the order with effect from such date as the court may determine.

---

42 CJPA 2001, s 33(4).
43 CJPA 2001, s 33(5)(a).
44 CJPA 2001, s 33(5)(b).
45 CJPA 2001, s 35(1)(a).
46 CJPA 2001, s 35(1)(a)(i), as defined in s 35(7).
47 CJPA 2001, s 35(1)(a)(ii).

12.30

A court is required to consider all the circumstances when deciding whether to revoke a TRO, and direct its attention to three specific matters:[48]

- D's character;

- D's conduct since the making of the order; and

- the offences of which D was convicted on the occasion on which the order was made.

12.31

This power has not specifically attracted any decisions of the appellate Court, save that it has often been mentioned in passing by courts highlighting that where an appellant's personal circumstances are expected to, but may not, change in the future, there is the possibility for revocation or suspension, and consequently a judge making the order at first instance need not consider every possible permutation of possible future circumstances.[49]

Suspension

12.32

It is also open to the subject of a TRO to apply to the court that made the order at any time after it was made, for a suspension of the prohibition imposed by the order for such period as the court may determine.[50]

12.33

A suspension shall not be granted at all unless the court is satisfied that there are exceptional circumstances, in that person's case, that justify the suspension of that prohibition for that period on compassionate grounds.[51]

12.34

When determining an application for suspension of a TRO, CJPA 2001, s 35(4) requires that a court shall also have regard to:

- D's character;

- D's conduct since the making of the order;

- the offences of which D was convicted on the occasion on which the order was made; and

---

48 CJPA 2001, s 35(2)(a)–(c).
49 *Shaw* [2011] EWCA Crim 98, at [49].
50 CJPA 2001, s 35(1)(b).
51 CJPA 2001, s 35(3).

- any other circumstances of the case that the court considers relevant.

12.35

CJPA 2001, s 35(5) states that where the prohibition imposed on any person by a TRO is suspended, it is the duty of that person:

- to be in the UK when the suspension ends; and

- if the order contains a direction under s 33(4), to surrender, before the end of the suspension period, any passport returned or issued to him/her by the Secretary of State as a result of the suspension.

12.36

Any passport that is required to be surrendered under s 35(5)(b) shall be surrendered to the Secretary of State as the Secretary of State may direct at the time when s/he returns or issues it.

12.37

The effect of a suspension, unsurprisingly, is that when the order resumes, it runs for the amount of time remaining on the order at the time it was suspended – the end date is postponed by the period of the suspension.[52]

Breach

12.38

There are three ways in which a TRO can be breached, and this is reflected in the three separate offences of breach contained in CJPA 2001, s 36:

(1) **Section 36(1)** – A person who leaves the UK when prohibited from doing so by a TRO commits a criminal offence.[53]

The offence is triable either way and is punishable by:

- on summary conviction – six months imprisonment, or a fine not exceeding the statutory maximum;

- on indictment – imprisonment not exceeding five years.

(2) **Section 36(2)** – A person who is not in the UK at the end of a period during which a prohibition imposed on him by a TRO has been suspended commits an offence.[54]

The offence is triable either way and is punishable by:

---

52 CJPA 2001, s 35(6).
53 CJPA 2001, s 36(1).
54 CJPA 2001, s 36(2).

- on summary conviction – six months imprisonment, or a fine not exceeding the statutory maximum;

- on indictment – imprisonment not exceeding five years.

(3) **Section 36(3)** – A person who fails to comply with:[55]

- a direction contained in a TRO to deliver up a passport to a court, or to cause such a passport to be delivered up; or

- any duty imposed on him to surrender a passport to the Secretary of State,

shall be guilty of an offence.

The offence is a summary-only offence, and carries a maximum sentence of six months' imprisonment and/or a fine not exceeding level 5 on the standard scale.

Interaction between TROs and prescribed removal powers

12.39

This is addressed in CJPA 2001, s 37: a TRO shall not prevent the exercise of any prescribed removal power on the subject of the order.[56]

12.40

If a prescribed removal power is exercised over the subject of a TRO, the TRO shall remain in force,[57] except in so far as either the Secretary of State by order otherwise provides;[58] or if the TRO is suspended or revoked under CJPA 2001, s 35.[59]

12.41

No person shall be guilty of an offence under CJPA 2001, s 36 in respect of any act or omission required of him by an obligation imposed in the exercise of a prescribed removal power.[60] Practitioners are therefore advised to pay particular attention to the matter of a TRO where their client is a foreign national likely to be deported upon their release from custody – although s 37 will provide a defence to a departure from the country effected by the State, the utility of imposing a TRO on such an offender is difficult to discern.

---

55 CJPA 2001, s 36(3).
56 CJPA 2001, s 37(1).
57 CJPA 2001, s 37(2).
58 CJPA 2001, s 37(2)(a).
59 CJPA 2001, s 37(2)(b).
60 CJPA 2001, s 37(3).

Travel prohibitions as part of compliance orders – Proceeds of Crime Act 2002

12.42

A similar order is available to a court that is making a confiscation order, under s 13A of the Proceeds of Crime Act (POCA) 2002.

12.43

That section provides that the court 'may make such order as it believes is appropriate for the purpose of ensuring that the confiscation order is effective' (a 'compliance order').[61]

12.44

In considering whether to make a compliance order, the court must, in particular, consider whether any restriction or prohibition on the defendant's travel outside the UK ought to be imposed for the purpose mentioned in POCA 2002, s 13A(2).[62]

12.45

The court may discharge or vary a compliance order on an application made by the prosecutor, or any person affected by the order.[63]

12.46

When considering the length of a travel restriction as part of a compliance order, the court should follow the same considerations as when imposing a TRO under CJPA 2001.[64] It will be rare that an indefinite prohibition on travel will be appropriate.[65] Although the Court of Appeal found reference to *Mee* and other 2001 Act authorities of assistance,[66] they made clear that the threshold for the POCA 2002, s 13A order was what was 'appropriate', not what was 'necessary', in-keeping with the wording of the 2002 Act, and that this distinction stemmed from the differing purposes of the orders. Whilst a TRO was to prevent re-offending, the Court said, a travel prohibition as part of a confiscation compliance order was to ensure compliance with the confiscation order.[67]

---

61 POCA 2002, s 13A(2).
62 POCA 2002, s 13A(4).
63 POCA 2002, s 13A(5)(a) and (b).
64 *Pritchard* [2017] EWCA Crim 1267.
65 *Pritchard*, at [35].
66 *Pritchard*, at [22].
67 *Pritchard*, at [24].

13 Football Banning Orders (on conviction)

13.01

These orders, in very basic terms, prohibit the defendant (D) from attending regulated football matches. A sentencing court MUST make a football banning order (FBO) under s 14A of the Football Spectators Act (FSA) 1989 if an offender has been convicted of a 'relevant offence' (condition 1), and the court is satisfied that there are reasonable grounds to believe that making a banning order would help to prevent violence or disorder at or in connection with any regulated football matches (condition 2).

13.02

The legislation is by no means straightforward.[1] The situation was described by the late David Thomas QC thus; 'Banning orders under the heavily amended and virtually incomprehensible Football Spectators Act 1989 are probably the most difficult orders for a sentencing court to make.'[2] As will be seen below, the Court of Appeal has been vocal in criticising those advocates who have not assisted judges properly, and those judges who have not followed the procedure set out by the legislation of identifying and explaining the factual elements that fulfil conditions 1 and 2. FBOs are not intended to be punitive, though they inevitably will have that effect[3] – they are intended as a preventive measure to allow peaceful spectators to enjoy matches with their families, and to allow other members of the public in the vicinity to go about their lives without the interruption of football-related violence.[4] The Court has held that they are not penalties within the meaning of Article 7 of the European Convention on Human Rights (ECHR).[5]

13.03

However, defence advocates should be aware of the words of Hughes LJ (then-VP) in *Boggild*:[6]

---

1   *Doyle* [2012] EWCA Crim 995, at [1].
2   (2004) Crim LR 394–395 (May).
3   *Doyle*, at [6c].
4   *Doyle*, at [3]; *Boggild* [2011] EWCA Crim 1928, at [15].
5   *Gough v Chief Constable of Derbyshire Constabulary* [2001] EWHC 554 (Admin) – in the further appeal to the Court of Appeal the party who had raised the Article 7 point did not renew their appeal and so this was not further argued.
6   [2011] EWCA Crim 1928, at [20].

'it is palpably not the scheme of the Act to make a football banning order the inevitable consequence of a football related conviction. By contrast, what the Act does is to pose a test for the judge to address and require an order only if that test is met ... There has thus been ample opportunity, both at the outset and subsequently, so to frame the Act as to make a football banning order a mandatory consequence of a football related conviction. That opportunity has plainly deliberately not been taken.'

Condition 1 – 'relevant offence'

13.04

'Relevant offence' is defined in FSA 1989, s 14(8). There are two ways in which an offence may be a 'relevant offence':

- it is as an offence to which Sch 1 to the 1989 Act applies.

- para 1(r) contains a list of offences which CAN be relevant offences if the court makes a declaration of relevance in respect of them.

13.05

At para 1(r) there is also the wider definition to be applied if the offence under consideration is not intrinsically a football-related offence and thus listed in the other sub-paragraphs of Sch 1, para 1:

'any offence involving the use or threat of violence by the accused towards another person —

(i)   which does not fall within paragraph (d) or (m) above,

(ii)   which was committed during a period relevant to a football match to which this Schedule applies, and

(iii) as respects which the court makes a declaration that the offence related to that match, or to that match *and* any other football match which took place during that period.'

13.06

Schedule 1 contains a long list of offences, all of which are capable of fulfilling the relevant offence condition, if a declaration of relevance is made in respect of them (see 13.08):

- any offence under s 2(1); s 5(7); s 14J(1), or s 21C(2) of FSA 1989;[7]

---

7   FSA 1989, Sch 1, para 1(a).

- any offence under s 2 or s 2A of the Sporting Events (Control of Alcohol etc) Act 1985 committed by the accused at any football match to which Sch 1 applies or while entering or trying to enter the ground;[8]

- any offence under s 5 of the Public Order Act (POA) 1986, or any provision of Part III of that Act committed during a period relevant to a football match to which Sch 1 applies at any premises while the accused was at, or was entering or leaving or trying to enter or leave, the premises;[9] or any such offence committed while the accused was on a journey to or from a football match to which Sch 1 applies, if a declaration of relevance is made;[10]

- any offence involving the use or threat of violence by the accused towards another person,[11] or towards property,[12] or the use, carrying, or possession of an offensive weapon or firearm[13] committed during a period relevant to a football match to which Sch 1 applies at any premises while the accused was at, or was entering or leaving or trying to enter or leave the premises;

- any offence under s 12 of the Licensing Act 1872 of being found drunk on a highway or in another public place committed while the accused was on a journey to or from a football match to which Sch 1 applies, if a declaration of relevance is made;[14]

- any offence under s 91(1) of the Criminal Justice Act (CJA) 1967 committed on a highway or in another public place while the accused was on a journey to or from a football match to which Sch 1 applies, if a declaration of relevance is made;[15]

- any offence under s 1 of the Sporting Events (Control of Alcohol etc) Act 1985 committed while the accused was on a journey to or from a football match to which Sch 1 applies, if a declaration of relevance is made;[16]

- any offence under s 4 or s 5 of the Road Traffic Act 1988 committed while the accused was on a journey to or from a football match to which Sch 1 applies, if a declaration of relevance is made;[17]

---

8   A 'regulated football match' being 'an association football match (whether in [the United Kingdom] or elsewhere) which is a prescribed match or a match of a prescribed description' according to s 14(2) – see 13.41.
9   FSA 1989, Sch 1, para 1(c).
10 FSA 1989, Sch 1, para 1(k).
11 FSA 1989, Sch 1, para 1(d).
12 FSA 1989, Sch 1, para 1(e).
13 FSA 1989, Sch 1, para 1(f).
14 FSA 1989, Sch 1, para 1(g).
15 FSA 1989, Sch 1, para 1(h).
16 FSA 1989, Sch 1, para 1(j).
17 FSA 1989, Sch 1, para 1(l).

- any offence involving the use or threat of violence by the accused towards another person,[18] or towards property,[19] or the use, carrying, or possession of an offensive weapon or firearm[20] committed while one or each of them was on a journey to or from a football match to which Sch 1 applies, if a declaration of relevance is made;

- any offence under the Football (Offences) Act 1991;[21]

- any offence:

  - under POA 1986, s 5 or any provision of Part III of that Act;

  - involving the use or threat of violence (includes POA 1986, s 4) by the accused towards another person;[22] towards property,[23] or the use, carrying or possession of an offensive weapon or a firearm;[24]

  - which does not fall within paras (c) or (k),[25] (d) or (m),[26] (e) or (n),[27] and (f) or (o)[28] of Sch 1, para 1;

  - which was committed during a period relevant to a football match to which Sch 1 applies; and

  - as respects which the court makes a declaration that the offence related to that match, or to that match and any other football match which took place during that period.

- any offence under s 166 of the Criminal Justice and Public Order Act 1994 which relates to tickets for a football match;[29]

- any attempt, conspiracy or incitement to commit an offence listed above;[30] and

- any aiding and abetting, counselling or procuring the commission of such an offence.[31]

13.07

For the purposes of paras 1(g)–(o) of Sch 1, para 3 defines 'journey to or from', clarifying that a person may be regarded as having been on a journey to or from

---

18   FSA 1989, Sch 1, para 1(m).
19   FSA 1989, Sch 1, para 1(n).
20   FSA 1989, Sch 1, para 1(o).
21   FSA 1989, Sch 1, para 1(p).
22   FSA 1989, Sch 1, para 1(r).
23   FSA 1989, Sch 1, para 1(s).
24   FSA 1989, Sch 1, para 1(t).
25   FSA 1989, Sch 1, para 1(q).
26   FSA 1989, Sch 1, para 1(r).
27   FSA 1989, Sch 1, para 1(s).
28   FSA 1989, Sch 1, para 1(t).
29   FSA 1989, Sch 1, para 1(u).
30   FSA 1989, Sch 1, para 2(a).
31   FSA 1989, Sch 1, para 2(b).

a football match to which Sch 1 applies whether or not he attended or intended to attend the match.[32] A journey includes breaks (including overnight breaks).[33]

Declarations of relevance

13.08

The court can make a declaration that, for the purposes of FSA 1989, Sch 1, an offence related to football matches, or that it related to one or more particular football matches,[34] if the two conditions found at s 23 of the Act are met. These are:

- The prosecutor gave notice to the defendant, at least five days before the first day of the trial, that it was proposed to show that the offence related to football matches, to a particular football match or to particular football matches (as the case may be);[35]

- If five days' notice has not been given, a court may make a declaration of relevance if D consents to waive the giving of full notice or the court is satisfied that the interests of justice do not require more notice to be given.[36]

13.09

Ideally, the CPS will have agreed with the police that a notice will be served on the defendant at the time of charge, and provision made for proving service so as to satisfy the court, most likely by a copy notice.

13.10

The court may conduct a voire dire to determine the question of relevance, and both prosecutors and defence advocates should be prepared for such. Witnesses are likely to be police officers, but CCTV evidence may be the most persuasive, and will allow the prosecution to minimise the need to call police witnesses at the voire dire. If the offence has occurred some way away from the match in time or place, the prosecutor may wish to consider what evidence can be used in support of the events being related to football. This may include items such as a match ticket, programme, fanzine, season ticket, train tickets, football-related paraphernalia (ie pin badges, 'calling cards', tattoos showing team/group allegiances), or a photograph of the person wearing team colours. Similarly, where there is no evidence of such, a defence advocate will wish to rely on this to strengthen their argument that the events are not football-related.

---

32   FSA 1989, Sch 1, para 3(a).
33   FSA 1989, Sch 1, para 3(b).
34   FSA 1989, s 23(5).
35   FSA 1989, s 23(1).
36   FSA 1989, s 23(2).

13.11

There can be no hard and fast rules about when conduct will be 'related' to a football match:[37]

> 'The Act offers no definition of when this condition will be met. It is (no doubt deliberately) left to the judgment of the judge on the particular facts before him. It would be wrong to attempt to define when the condition will be met. The facts which may occur will vary too much. It is not difficult to say that a pitched battle between opposing fans as they walk away from the ground is "related", or that a defendant who, when on his own twenty miles away from the ground on his journey home meets a rival for a woman's affections and hits him, is *not* committing an offence related to football matches. But in between there will be infinite gradations of conduct, and they must be left to the judge in each case … We offer only the observation that it will not by itself be enough, to make an offence "related to football matches" that it would not have occurred "but for" the fact that D was en route to or from a match. If that by itself were enough, then every offence of the listed kind which was committed on a journey to or from a match would automatically qualify and the additional test of relation to football matches would be unnecessary and meaningless.'

13.12

In *Irving*,[38] it was contended that no relevant offence had taken place. The appellants were supporters of West Ham, and lived in Dagenham. There was a match between Dagenham and Millwall that was played at Dagenham's home ground, and the appellants shouted and gesticulated at a group of Millwall supporters being corralled by police after the game. The Court of Appeal noted that:[39]

> 'In relation to whether this was a "relevant offence" within the legislation, we do not think that the fact that the appellants had not attended the game and were not supporters of either team necessarily means that this was not an offence related to football matches. If a group of supporters from one football club decided to ambush supporters from another football club who were on their way to or from a match involving a third football club, that might well be sufficient to amount to a relevant offence.'

---

37 *Doyle*, at [14].
38 [2013] EWCA Crim 1932.
39 *Irving*, at [12].

13.13

The appellants having pleaded guilty to POA 1986, s 4 offences,[40] it was necessary that there be a declaration of relevance, as required under paras 1(m) or (r) of Sch 1. However, in a sentencing exercise with which the Court of Appeal were wholly unimpressed:[41]

> '[The Judge] stated his view, in our judgment reached in unsatisfactory circumstances, that the appellants had attended the underground station for the purpose of causing trouble with Millwall supporters. However, he made no declaration of relevance in the terms envisaged by the statute. Such a declaration appears to be necessary if the provisions of either of the paragraphs (m) or (r) of Schedule 1 of the Act are to apply. If they do not apply, then the offence is not a relevant offence within section 14A(1) and the banning order should not have been made. Having stated that he had no doubt that the appellants had attended for the purpose of causing trouble with Millwall supporters, the judge appears to have proceeded to stage 2 of the necessary exercise by saying:
>
> "I have no doubt that making the banning order that is sought by the Crown in this case would help to prevent violence in connection with regulated football matches".
>
> The threshold for this second condition is not a high or exacting one, but the judge did not give any explanation at all as to why he considered the second limb was satisfied.'

13.14

Concluding that the FBOs were to be quashed, the Court described the proceedings in the lower court as 'fatally flawed'.[42]

13.15

Those representing defendants in respect of whom the Crown are likely to apply for an FBO might want to consider how arguable it is that their conduct was NOT linked to football. In many cases the immediate cause of the disorder is the over-consumption of alcohol, and thus questions of conduct some distance from the match come under scrutiny as inebriated fans make their way home. The Court of Appeal has taken varying, fact-specific, views on whether conduct some time and distance away from a ground is 'related to football'.

---

40   It was held in *O'Keefe* [2003] EWCA Crim 2629 that any offence under the auspices of POA 1986, s 4(1)(a) can be a relevant offence. They fall into eight categories and might be committed either by words or by actions. The offences might be committed with any one of four different types of intent or likely consequences as set out in the latter part of the subsection. Each of these categories of offence carried with it a substantial risk that violence would ensue, and thus could be relevant offences.

41   *Irving*, at [18]–[19].

42   *Irving*, at [23].

13.16

In *Parkes*,[43] D had pleaded guilty to a POA 1986, s 4 offence. He was a Wolves supporter, and had travelled to Birmingham anticipating attending a match between his team and Birmingham City. Due to weather conditions, it was cancelled, but another locally-based team, West Bromwich Albion, did play against Peterborough United. The Court of Appeal sought to identify whether 'the spark which caused the violence in this case [could] be said to be something wholly unrelated to football'.[44]

13.17

Dismissing the appeal, the Court found that 'the fact that the Wolves supporters were not involved in the match which West Bromwich Albion had earlier played is a point of little substance when the whole picture is considered'.[45] The Court concluded that: 'it is sophistry to suggest that it was anything other than the enmity which existed between the two sets of fans. The spark was football.'[46]

13.18

Conversely, in *Arbery*,[47] the Court of Appeal quashed FBOs in light of an earlier quashing by the Court of the FBOs imposed on other appellants involved in the very same disturbance.[48] It was held that a large-scale fight on the Caledonian Road in North London between Northampton Town and Charlton Athletic supporters occurred not due to football, but due to the coincidental presence in the same place of a large number of drunken football fans, whereby violence was sparked, on the evidence of a police officer, due to a racist comment, not a comment related in any way to football.[49] Thus the Recorder had erroneously made a declaration of relevance.[50] A further two sets of conjoined appeals were brought by others sentenced at the same time, and all were allowed.[51]

13.19

Similarly in *Smith*,[52] the appellant had not actually made it to the football match – somewhere en route his group of supporters had been turned back by police. As they returned home on a train there was significant disorder, with supporters smashing a window on the train, standing on seats and behaving in a generally disorderly manner.[53] To try to contain the violence within the train, the police

---

43   [2010] EWCA Crim 2803.
44   *Parkes*, at [19].
45   *Parkes*, at [21].
46   *Parkes*, at [22].
47   [2008] EWCA Crim 702.
48   *Arbery*, at [12], referring to the case of *Mabee* [2007] EWCA Crim 3230.
49   *Arbery*, at [5].
50   *Mabee*, at [4].
51   *Goedhart* [2008] EWCA Crim 2968 (a three-paragraph judgment) and *Mabee* [2007] EWCA Crim 3230 were the other two cases.
52   [2003] EWCA Crim 2480.
53   *Smith*, at [2].

ordered that the doors be locked, and no passengers were permitted to alight. The appellant was threatening towards a police officer on the train, but his case was that that occurred only because the police would not let him off the train, and was nothing to do with the clear wider context of football. The order was quashed by the Court of Appeal, though they were keen to emphasise that this was a decision on the facts, and not an establishment of principle.[54]

13.20

In *Elliott*,[55] the Court noted that there were stronger grounds for making the order than there had been on the facts in *Smith*. Elliott and other Wolves supporters became involved in violence after a rude comment was directed to a female companion of another Wolves' fan. Although this comment happened to come from supporters of another football team, it was held that, on the facts, there was not sufficient nexus between football and the disorder, and thus the declaration of relevance had been improperly made, leading to the quashing of the FBOs:[56]

'In the present case, however, the spark was unconnected with football, and although those participating in the violence were Wolverhampton supporters, the incident had nothing else to do with the football match. Therefore, there was no evidence on the basis of which the judge, properly applying the requirements of the Act, could have made the declaration he did.'

13.21

The later case of *Powner* arose out of the same episode of disorder, and thus the FBOs in that case were also quashed.[57]

13.22

However, the Court in *Elliott* did identify the important aspect that events need not be between rival sets of supporters:[58]

'It is important to emphasise that Parliament has required that the violence in question, that is to say, here the offences of affray and violent disorder, must relate to the match. Parliament has not made it a sufficient condition of the imposition of a football banning order that those involved in the offence, those who commit the offence are supporters of a particular team. Parliament has not made it a precondition either that, if there is violence, it should be between opposing supporters of

---

54 *Smith*, at [7].
55 [2007] EWCA Crim 1002.
56 *Elliott*, at [22].
57 [2007] EWCA Crim 1569.
58 *Elliott*, at [13].

teams involved in a football match. What is required is that the offence relates to the match.'

13.23

In *DPP v Beaumont*,[59] the DPP appealed by way of case stated after the Crown Court allowed an appeal against the imposition of FBOs by the magistrates' court. The respondents had been part of a group that had behaved rowdily on, and caused significant damage to, a train on the way back from a match.[60] The Crown Court held that an offence could not be related to a football match unless it took place within the period specified in FSA 1989, s 1(8) and therefore could not be related if it took place more than one hour after the end of the match. There was no evidence that the offences were committed within that time and, indeed, they were probably committed later. It therefore held that the POA 1986, s 5 offences were not related to football matches and that there was no power to make an FBO.[61] The High Court held that this had been a misdirection, and no time restrictions operated on when behaviour could properly be said to be linked to a football match in the required sense.

13.24

If the court does not expressly make a declaration of relevance, but it is clear from the proceedings and other sentencing remarks that the necessary factors were properly considered, then the technical absence of a clear and stated declaration will not invalidate the making of a declaration of relevance and the consequent FBO.[62]

Relevant offences outside of England and Wales

13.25

FSA 1989, s 22 provides that Her Majesty the Queen may, by Order in Council, specify 'corresponding offences' under the law of any country outside England and Wales which appear to correspond to any offence to which Sch 1 applies.[63] This allows an FBO to be imposed where D has convictions abroad for football-related violence.

13.26

The order may specify what form of document should be used by any particular country to give details of:

---

59   [2008] EWHC 523 (Admin).
60   *Beaumont*, at [3].
61   *Beaumont*, at [9].
62   *Beaumont*, at [24].
63   FSA 1989, s 22(1).

- the conviction of D in that country of a corresponding offence;[64]

- the nature and circumstances of the offence;[65] and

- whether or not the conviction is the subject of proceedings in that country.[66]

13.27

Such a document shall be:

- admissible in any relevant proceedings as evidence of the facts stated in it;[67] and

- taken as such a document,

unless the contrary is proved.[68] Thus the prosecution can rely on it as evidence of behaviour in other countries that amounted to a 'relevant offence' unless D can prove that the document is not accurate (on the balance of probabilities).

13.28

The facts stated in such a document shall, on production of the document and proof that the person before the court is the same person to whose conviction the document refers, be taken to be proved unless the contrary is proved.[69]

13.29

Where an information is laid before a magistrates' court that a person has been convicted of a corresponding offence in a country outside England and Wales, the magistrates may issue:

(a) a summons requiring that person to appear before a magistrates' court to answer to the information;[70] or

(b) a warrant to arrest that person and bring him before a magistrates' court,[71] provided that the information is in writing and substantiated on oath.[72]

13.30

Where a person is consequently before a magistrates' court, the court, if satisfied that:

64　FSA 1989, s 22(9)(a).
65　FSA 1989, s 22(9)(b).
66　FSA 1989, s 22(9)(c).
67　FSA 1989, s 22(10)(a).
68　FSA 1989, s 22(10)(b).
69　FSA 1989, s 22(11).
70　FSA 1989, s 22(2)(a).
71　FSA 1989, s 22(2)(b).
72　FSA 1989, s 22(3).

(a)   he is ordinarily resident in England and Wales;[73] and

(b)   has been convicted in the country outside England and Wales of the corresponding offence,[74] may make an FBO in relation to him.

13.31

The exception to this power is if it appears that the conviction is the subject of court proceedings equivalent to an appeal against conviction in that country.[75]

13.32

The court can bail, but not remand, someone with whom they are dealing under this section,[76] and the usual powers for adjourning apply as to a summary trial.[77] The provisions for appeal are the same as for FBOs made on the basis of offences committed in England and Wales.[78]

13.33

Unfortunately there is no case law on the operation of FSA 1989, s 22 – whether this is because such orders are very rarely sought, or are simply not appealed, it is impossible to say.

'Relevant period'

13.34

Paragraph 4(2) of FSA 1989, Sch 1 sets out the 'relevant periods' for regulated football matches:

- in the case of a match which takes place on the day on which it is advertised to take place, the period:

    – beginning 24 hours before whichever is the earlier of the start of the match and the time at which it was advertised to start; and

    – ending 24 hours after it ends;

- in the case of a match which does not take place on the day on which it was advertised to take place, the period:

    – beginning 24 hours before the time at which it was advertised to start on that day; and

    – ending 24 hours after that time.

---

73   FSA 1989, s 22(4)(a).
74   FSA 1989, s 22(4)(b).
75   FSA 1989, s 22(4).
76   FSA 1989, s 22(6).
77   FSA 1989, s 22(6).
78   FSA 1989, s 22(7).

Condition 2 – 'reasonable grounds to believe that making an FBO would help to prevent violence or disorder at or in connection with any regulated football matches'

13.35

It should be noted here that the FBO can only be imposed if it would stop violence or disorder at or in connection with any *regulated* football match, not any football match of any type.

13.36

In considering whether an order would have this effect, a court may consider any evidence from either prosecution or defence,[79] and this need not be evidence that would have been admissible at any trial for the index offence.[80]

13.37

Even where D is a person of effective good character, and there is one fairly brief incident of football-related violence, if their behaviour in offending was sufficient to warrant a custodial sentence (albeit suspended) the judge is entitled to draw the conclusion that condition 2 has been fulfilled.[81] Similarly, where D is of good character but played a very visible role in the incident, and there is material before the court to show that he has been in association with others known to be 'risk supporters', an FBO will be justified.[82] There is no requirement under FSA 1989, s 14A for either repetition or propensity.[83]

13.38

The Court of Appeal has, however, sought to emphasise that there will be situations where it is not appropriate to impose an FBO:[84]

'In our view, the judge was fully entitled to take into account the deterrent nature of orders such as this and the fact that this particular fixture was a well-known flash-point. That is not to say that in every case of a football-related offence of this type a banning order must be imposed. All depends on the facts of the incident, the precise behaviour of the offender in context, and his character in the past.'

---

79   FSA 1989, s 14A(3A).
80   FSA 1989, s 14A(3B).
81   *Morgan* [2012] EWCA Crim 1390, at [22].
82   *Allen* [2011] EWCA Crim 3076, at [7].
83   *Hughes* [2005] EWCA Crim 2537, at [13].
84   *Curtis* [2009] EWCA Crim 1225, at [13].

'Violence and disorder'

13.39

'Violence' means violence against persons or property and includes threatening violence and doing anything which endangers the life of any person.[85]

13.40

Disorder includes:[86]

- stirring up hatred against a group of persons defined by reference to colour, race, nationality (including citizenship) or ethnic or national origins, or against an individual as a member of such a group;[87]

- using threatening, abusive or insulting words or behaviour or disorderly behaviour;[88]

- displaying any writing or other thing which is threatening, abusive or insulting.[89]

13.41

The terms 'violence' and 'disorder' are not limited to violence or disorder in connection with football.[90]

'Regulated football matches'

13.42

FSA 1989, s 14(2) states that a regulated football match is 'an association football match (whether in the United Kingdom or elsewhere) which is a prescribed match or a match of a prescribed description.'

13.43

The definition of an association football match for the purposes of the FSA 1989 is set out in the Football Spectators (Prescription) Order 2004,[91] as follows:

---

85   FSA 1989, s 14C(1).
86   FSA 1989, s 14C(2).
87   FSA 1989, s 14C(2)(a).
88   FSA 1989, s 14C(2)(b).
89   FSA 1989, s 14C(2)(c).
90   FSA 1989, s 14C(3).
91   SI 2004/2409, as amended by the Football Spectators (Prescription) (Amendment) Order 2006 (SI 2006/761), the Football Spectators (Prescription) (Amendment) Order 2010 (SI 2010/584) and the Football Spectators (Prescription) (Amendment) Order 2013 (SI 2013/1709).

Within England and Wales

13.44

Article 3(2) and (3) define an association football match within England and Wales:

'(2)   A regulated match is an association football match in which one or both of the participating teams represents—

(a)   a club which is for the time being a member (whether a full or associate member) of the Football League, the Football Association Premier League, the Football Conference, the Welsh Premier League or the Scottish Professional Football League;

(b)   a club whose home ground is situated outside England and Wales; or

(c)   a country or territory.

(3)   A regulated football match is an association football match played in the Football Association Cup (other than in a preliminary or qualifying round).'

Outside England and Wales

13.45

Article 4 sets out the criteria for an association football match outside of England and Wales:

'(2)   A regulated match is an association football match involving—

(a)   a national team appointed by the Football Association to represent England or appointed by the Football Association of Wales to represent Wales;

(b)   a team representing a club which is for the time being a member (whether a full or associate member) of the Football League, the Football Association Premier League, the Football Conference, the Welsh Premier League or the Scottish Professional Football League;

(c)   a team representing any country or territory whose football association is for the time being a member of FIFA, where—

(i)   the match is part of a competition or tournament organised by, or under the authority of, FIFA or UEFA, and

(ii)   the competition or tournament is one in which a

    team referred to in sub-paragraph (a) above is eligible to participate or has participated; or

(d) a team representing a club which is for the time being a member (whether a full or associate member) of, or affiliated to, a national football association which is a member of FIFA, where—

  (i) the match is part of a competition or tournament organised by, or under the authority of, FIFA or UEFA, and

  (ii) the competition or tournament is one in which a club referred to in sub-paragraph (b) above is eligible to participate or has participated.'

Procedure

13.46

When the application is made under FSA 1989, s 14A, the Criminal Procedure Rules (CrimPR), r 31 require that notice should be given to the defendant of the intention to apply for an FBO. Although CrimPR, r 31.3 states that the application must be on the requisite form, no form has been specified in the rules. Whatever form the application takes, this must be signed by the prosecutor.

13.47

Where a person is convicted of a 'relevant offence', the court must make an FBO in addition to any sentence for the offence, if it is satisfied that there are reasonable grounds to believe that it would help to prevent violence or disorder at or in connection with any regulated football matches.[92] If the court is not so satisfied, it must state its reasons in open court.[93]

13.48

An FBO can be made where the defendant is sentenced to an absolute or conditional discharge.[94] This is because the Act explicitly provides so despite the contents of ss 12 and 14 of the Powers of Criminal Courts (Sentencing) Act (PCC(S)A) 2000. The general position established by PCC(S)A 2000, s 14(1) is that an offence for which an absolute or conditional discharge is given (as permitted in PCC(S)A 2000, s 12(1)) is not to be recorded as a conviction; hence orders available only on conviction would not be expected to be available. In *Clarke*, the appellant contended that as he had been conditionally

---

92 FSA 1989, s 14A(1).
93 FSA 1989, s 14A(2).
94 FSA 1989, s 14A(4) and (5).

discharged for money laundering, there could be no confiscation proceedings. The Court highlighted the FSA 1989 as an example where creating legislation explicitly permitted an ancillary order to be made against an absolutely or conditionally discharged defendant.[95]

13.49

A court may wish to hear further evidence as part of a sentencing hearing at which it is considering an FBO, particularly from football intelligence officers (FIOs).[96] If this is to be done it need not take the form of a Newton hearing if there is nothing to be gained from that, because there is, in reality little real distance between what the defendant is saying about his behaviour on occasions other than the index offence, and what an FIO is saying.[97]

13.50

A court may not make an FBO limited to certain teams – for example, in *Commissioner for the Police of the Metropolis v Thorpe*,[98] magistrates purported to make an FBO (on a complaint under FSA 1989, s 14B, see Chapter 22) that prevented T's attendance only at games involving any of three named teams. This was held to be in error, as the legislation requires that an FBO prevents its subject from attending 'any regulated football matches'.[99]

13.51

The court has the power to adjourn consideration of an FBO, even after sentence has been passed,[100] and failure to attend on a later occasion allows the court to issue a warrant for arrest, or further adjourn.[101] In the usual way, the court may not issue a warrant if D fails to surrender unless it is satisfied that he has had adequate notice of the time and place of the adjourned proceedings.[102] If the court adjourns under these provisions then it is open to the court to remand the offender.[103] Alternatively, if given bail, the court has a discretion to require the offender to:

- not leave England and Wales before his next appearance before the court;[104] and

---

95 *Clarke* [2009] EWCA Crim 1074, at [54]-[55]
96 *Hughes*, at [6] and [8]
97 *Hughes*, at [14]
98 [2015] EWHC 3339 (Admin).
99 FSA 1989, s 14(4)(a).
100 FSA 1989, s 14A(4)(4A).
101 FSA 1989, s 14A(4)(4B).
102 FSA 1989, s 14A(4)(4C).
103 FSA 1989, s 14A(4)(4BA).
104 FSA 1989, s 14A(4)(4BB)(a).

- surrender his passport to a police constable, if within the control period of a regulated football match outside of the UK, or an external tournament containing such matches.[105]

13.52

FSA 1989, s 18(1) provides that where a court makes an FBO, the court (if a magistrates' court) or the appropriate officer (if the Crown Court) shall:

- give a copy of it to the person to whom it relates;[106]

- send a copy of it to the enforcing authority and to any prescribed person (as soon as reasonably practicable);[107]

- (as soon as reasonably practicable) send a copy of it addressed to the officer responsible for the police station at which the person subject to the order is to report initially;[108] and

- in a case where the person subject to the order is in custody, send a copy of it to the person in whose custody he is detained, as soon as reasonably practicable.[109]

Requirements of an FBO

13.53

When a court makes an FBO, it must explain the effects of it in ordinary language to D who will be subject to it.[110]

13.54

There are three requirements which it is mandatory for any FBO to contain.

D must:

(1)   s 14E(2) – report initially to the police station specified in the FBO within five days beginning on the day of the order being made;[111] and

(2)   s 14E(2A) – give notification within seven days[112] of the events mentioned in sub-s (2B) to the enforcing authority; and

---

105 FSA 1989, s 14A(4)(4BB)(b).
106 FSA 1989, s 18(1)(a).
107 FSA 1989, s 18(1)(b).
108 FSA 1989, s 18(1)(c).
109 FSA 1989, s 18(1)(d).
110 FSA 1989, s 14E(1).
111 Unless s/he is in custody, in which case the requirements are suspended until their release from custody (s 14E(5)). If s/he is released from custody more than five days before the order expires (s 14E(6)(a)), and could not report initially due to being in custody (s 14E(6)(b)), s/he is deemed to have been required to report within five days beginning with the date of his/her release.
112 FSA 1989, s 14E(2C).

(3)   s14E(3) – surrender his passport prior to regulated football matches outside the UK.

13.55

The events listed in s 14E(2B) are as follows:

(a)   change of any of D's names;

(b)   the first use by them after the making of the order of a name for themselves that was not disclosed by them at the time of the making of the order;

(c)   a change of their home address;

(d)   their acquisition of a temporary address;

(e)   a change of their temporary address or their ceasing to have one;

(f)   D becoming aware of the loss of their passport;

(g)   receipt by D of a new passport;

(h)   an appeal made by D in relation to the order;

(i)   an application made by D under s 14H(2) for termination of the order;

(j)   an appeal made by D under s 23(3) against the making of a declaration of relevance in respect of an offence of which they have been convicted.

13.56

In addition to notification of any of those matters being given within seven days, the subject of the order must:

- in the case of a change of a name or address or the acquisition of a temporary address, specify the new name or address;

- in the case of a first use of a previously undisclosed name, specify that name; and

- in the case of a receipt of a new passport, give details of that passport.

13.57

If a defence advocate is on notice, or suspects, an application for an FBO they should ensure that they have details of any foreign trips for non-football related purposes falling around the time of foreign matches that D plans to take, especially if they are already booked (see 13.77).

'Control periods'

13.58

FSA 1989, s 14(5) defines 'control period' for the purposes of this legislation. The term applies to regulated matches being played outside of the UK, and means the period:

(a)   beginning five days before the day of the match;[113] and

(b)   ending when the match is finished or cancelled.[114]

13.59

In relation to an external tournament, 'control period' means any period described in an order made by the Secretary of State:

(a)   beginning five days before the day of the first football match outside the UK which is included in the tournament;[115] and

(b)   ending when the last football match outside the UK which is included in the tournament is finished or cancelled,[116]

but, for the purposes of para (a), any football match included in the qualifying or pre-qualifying stages of the tournament is to be left out of account.[117]

13.60

References to football matches are to football matches played or intended to be played.[118]

13.61

FSA 1989, s 22A(2) provides that the Secretary of State may, if he considers it necessary or expedient for effective enforcement, by order provide for a control period to have effect in relation to any, or any description of, regulated football match or external tournament for up to ten days, as specified in the order.

---

113   FSA 1989, s 14(5)(a).
114   FSA 1989, s 14(5)(b).
115   FSA 1989, s 14(6)(a).
116   FSA 1989, s 14(6)(b).
117   FSA 1989, s 14(6).
118   FSA 1989, s 14(7).

Reporting

13.62

FSA 1989, s 19 provides for the enforcing authority, and the officer responsible for the police station to which the subject of an FBO initially reports, to set any requirements necessary or expedient to give effect to the FBO at regulated matches outside the UK.[119]

13.63

If, in connection with any regulated football match outside the UK, the enforcing authority decides that requiring any person subject to an FBO to report is necessary or expedient to reduce the likelihood of violence or disorder at or in connection with the match, the authority must give him/her a notice in writing.[120]

13.64

That notice must require that person to:

- report at a police station specified in the notice at the time, or between the times, specified in the notice;[121]

- surrender his/her passport at a specified police station at the time, or between the times, specified in the notice.[122]

13.65

The notice may:

- require him/her to comply with any additional requirements of the order in the manner specified in the notice;[123] and

- specify additional requirements,[124] which may have been determined by criteria selected by the enforcing authority.[125]

13.66

A notice under this section has limited ambit – it may only require the subject of the FBO to:

---

119 FSA 1989, s 19(1) and (2).
120 FSA 1989, s 19(2A).
121 FSA 1989, s 19(2B)(a).
122 FSA 1989, s 19(2B)(b).
123 FSA 1989, s 19(2B).
124 FSA 1989, s 19(2C).
125 FSA 1989, s 19(2D).

- report in the control period in relation to a regulated football match outside the UK or an external tournament;[126]

- surrender his/her passport in the control period in relation to a regulated football match outside the UK or an external tournament which includes such matches.[127] Where this is required, the passport must be returned to him/her as soon as reasonably practicable after the end of that control period.[128]

13.67

Such a notice must require him/her to notify the enforcing authority, within the time period specified in the notice, of each address at which s/he intends to stay, or has stayed, for one night or more in a period which is the control period in relation to a regulated football match.[129]

13.68

A person who, without reasonable excuse, fails to comply with any requirement imposed on him/her under FSA 1989, s 19(2) shall be guilty of an offence,[130] and liable on summary conviction to a fine not exceeding level 2 on the standard scale.[131]

Exemptions from reporting

13.69

There are some circumstances in which subjects of FBOs who would ordinarily be required to report can apply to be exempt from such a requirement for a particular game[132] or period of time.[133] These are set out in FSA 1989, s 20.

13.70

The enforcing authority may grant exemptions under this section in all cases.[134] The officer responsible for a police station shall not grant an exemption without referring the question of exemption to the enforcing authority, unless

---

126 FSA 1989, s 19(2E)(a).
127 FSA 1989, s 19(2E)(b).
128 FSA 1989, s 19(2F).
129 FSA 1989, s 19(2E)(c).
130 FSA 1989, s 19(6).
131 FSA 1989, s 19(7).
132 FSA 1989, s 20(1)(a).
133 FSA 1989, s 20(1)(b).
134 FSA 1989, s 20(2).

he considers that it is not reasonably practicable to do so,[135] or the application is made during the control period of the match which the application concerns.[136]

13.71

The exemption to all or any requirements shall be granted if the applicant shows to the authority's satisfaction that:

- there are special circumstances which justify his/her being so exempted;[137] and

- because of those circumstances, s/he would not attend the match or matches if s/he were so exempted.[138]

13.72

When taking this decision, the exempting authority shall have regard to any guidance issued by the Secretary of State under FSA 1989, s 21.[139]

13.73

Where an exemption is granted the FBO is to have effect subject to the exemption and, accordingly, no requirement is to be imposed under FSA 1989, s 19 which is inconsistent with the exemption.[140]

13.74

If the application is refused, the applicant can appeal to a magistrates' court, providing s/he has given the enforcing authority notice in writing of his/her intention to do so.[141] On any appeal the court may make such order as it thinks fit,[142] and may order the appellant to pay all or any part of the costs of an appeal.[143]

13.75

It is an offence if, in an application for an exemption, the subject of the FBO:

- makes a statement which s/he knows to be false or misleading in a material particular or recklessly makes a statement which is false or misleading in a material particular;[144] or

---

135 FSA 1989, s 20(3).
136 FSA 1989, s 20(2).
137 FSA 1989, s 20(4)(a).
138 FSA 1989, s 20(4)(b).
139 FSA 1989, s 20(5).
140 FSA 1989, s 20(6).
141 FSA 1989, s 20(7).
142 FSA 1989, s 20(8).
143 FSA 1989, s 20(9).
144 FSA 1989, s 20(10)(a).

- produces, furnishes, signs or otherwise makes use of a document which s/he knows to be false or misleading in a material particular or recklessly produces, furnishes, signs or otherwise makes use of a document which is false or misleading in a material particular.[145]

13.76

This offence is summary only, and carries punishment of a fine not exceeding level 3 on the standard scale.[146]

13.77

The Court in *Gough* considered the possibility of exemption in a case where the FBO had been made on complaint under FSA 1989, s 14B (see Chapter 22). The Court held that whilst the statutory test for a restriction on travel, enforced by the required surrender of their passports, was (under FSA 1989, s 19B(1)) that the enforcing authority should have determined it to be 'necessary or expedient for giving effect to the banning order', the enforcing authority is required to consider the individual circumstances of each case, and in each case to be satisfied that such a restriction is no more than is necessary to accomplish the objective of the banning order in the individual case. It therefore concluded that if an individual subject to an FBO on complaint, and whose travel outside this jurisdiction had been restricted pursuant to FSA 1989, s 19, could demonstrate that, on a balance of probabilities, his or her reason for going abroad was other than attendance at a prescribed match, that would constitute 'special circumstances' warranting exemption from the restriction.[147] As an order under s 14A is made where there has been a conviction, as opposed to on complaint as under s 14B, it cannot be said confidently that this would apply equally to s 14A.

Additional requirements – s 14G

13.78

FSA 1989, s 14G(1) provides that: 'A banning order may, if the court making the order thinks fit, impose additional requirements on the person subject to the order in relation to any regulated football matches.'

13.79

As observed in *Doyle*:[148]

---

145 FSA 1989, s 20(10)(b).
146 FSA 1989, s 20(11).
147 *Gough*, as summarised by Hildyard J in *JSC Mezhdunarodniy Promyshlenniy Bank, State Corporation 'Deposit Insurance Agency' v Sergei Viktorovich Pugachev* [2015] EWHC 1586 (Ch).
148 *Doyle*, at [5].

'These additional requirements are the *only* part of an FBO which is in the control of the court. Given the extent of the controls provided by the standard terms of an FBO, careful consideration ought to be given to whether any additional requirements sought are indeed required.'

13.80

In *Irving*,[149] the Court of Appeal noted that care must be taken regarding additional requirements, and that they should not simply be added as a matter of course without full submissions, due to their draconian nature:[150]

'Moreover, it incorporates a number of additional requirements which are available to the judge, if he thinks fit, under section 14G of the Act. Some of these additional requirements imposed draconian geographical conditions which appear to lose sight of the fact that these appellants live in the Dagenham area, and one of them imposes a reporting condition requiring attendance every Saturday afternoon at 2 pm at Dagenham police station. Even had some form of football banning order properly been made, these additional requirements seem disproportionate. They do not appear to have been the subject of any consideration at all by the court below and are nowhere reflected in the transcript. We suspect that the judge, having been asked to make a football banning order and having come to the conclusion which he expressed without going through the proper procedure of having an evidential hearing, simply rubber-stamped a draft banning order without considering its terms. This is perhaps a further indication that this whole aspect of the proceedings below was not conducted in a satisfactory manner.'

13.81

Care must be taken that the reality of an additional condition is not to require the defendant to, for example, move out of his home address for the day if a particular team comes to play at his local stadium.[151]

Photographs

13.82

Under POA 1986, s 35, a court making an FBO can make an order requiring a police officer to take, or have another take, a photograph of the subject,[152] and require the subject to go to a specified police station not later than seven clear

---

149 [2013] EWCA Crim 1932.
150 *Irving*, at [22].
151 As in *Doyle*, at [22].
152 POA 1986, s 35(1)(a).

days after the day on which the order is made, and at a specified time of day or between specified times of day, in order to have his photograph taken.[153]

13.83

An application may only be made to the court under this section by or on behalf of the prosecutor of the offence leading to the banning order.[154] If the subject of the FBO fails to comply with an order under this section a constable may arrest him without warrant so that his photograph can be taken.[155]

Length of FBOs – s 14F

13.84

If D receives an immediate custodial sentence, an FBO must be for at least six, but no more than ten, years.[156]

13.85

If no immediate imprisonment is ordered, the FBO must be for at least three, and no more than five, years.[157] This also applies where the defendant receives an absolute or conditional discharge.[158]

13.86

The length of the FBO will need to be balanced against the length of the sentencing disposal used – in *Dore*,[159] the Court of Appeal allowed an appeal against sentence, but in light of reducing the term of imprisonment, extended the length of the FBO from five to six years.[160] With respect, because D had received an immediate custodial sentence at first instance, the FBO should have been for no shorter period than six years in any event, and so, although not portrayed as such by the Court, this was in fact a necessary correction to an error fallen into by the Crown Court judge.

13.87

Counsel should always engage with the process of making an FBO, and not simply leave the judge to fall into error. In *Wiggins*,[161] the Court of Appeal described as 'an unsatisfactory state of affairs' a sentencing hearing in which

---

153 POA 1986, s 35(1)(b).
154 POA 1986, s 35(3).
155 POA 1986, s 35(4).
156 FSA 1989, s 14F(3).
157 FSA 1989, s 14F(4).
158 *Davies* [2009] EWCA Crim 2968.
159 [2017] EWCA Crim 837.
160 *Dore*, at [13].
161 [2014] EWCA Crim 1433.

no submissions at all were made to the Circuit Judge by counsel about FBOs, whereupon the judge made them for the maximum duration.[162] This criticism became somewhat ironic when the Court of Appeal allowed the appeal against the duration of the FBOs (reducing them from ten years to six) without carrying out any enquiry or discussion of the reasons for doing so.[163]

Application to terminate or vary an FBO

13.88

This is governed by FSA 1989, s 14H. If an FBO has had effect for at least two-thirds of its duration, the person subject to the order may apply to the court which made it (or, if made by magistrates, to any other magistrates' court in the same local justice area)[164] to terminate it.[165] The court can either terminate the FBO as from a specified date, or refuse the application.[166]

13.89

When it is deciding the application, the court must have regard to:[167]

- the person's character;

- his/her conduct since the banning order was made;

- the nature of the offence or conduct which led to it; and

- any other circumstances which appear to it to be relevant.

13.90

If the application is refused, no further application in respect of the order may be made within the period of six months beginning with the day of the refusal.[168] Regardless of the outcome, the court may order the applicant to pay all or any part of the costs of an application under this section.[169]

13.91

FSA 1989, s 18(2) provides that where a court terminates an FBO, the court (magistrates' court) or the appropriate officer (Crown Court) shall:

(a)   give a copy of the terminating order to the person to whom it relates;

---

162 *Wiggins*, at [34].
163 *Wiggins*, at [35].
164 FSA 1989, s 14H(6).
165 FSA 1989, s 14H(1).
166 FSA 1989, s 14H(2).
167 FSA 1989, s 14H(3).
168 FSA 1989, s 14H(4).
169 FSA 1989, s 14H(5.)

(b)   send a copy of it to the enforcing authority and to any prescribed person, as soon as reasonably practicable; and

(c)   if the subject is in custody, send a copy of the terminating order to the person in whose custody s/he is detained, as soon as reasonably practicable.

Appeal

13.92

Any notice of appeal must be served within 21 days of the FBO being made or refused.[170]

Against refusal to make an FBO, by the Crown

13.93

If the court refuses to make an FBO, an appeal lies to the Crown Court or Court of Appeal under FSA 1989, s 14A(5A). An appeal to the Court of Appeal can only be lodged if that Court gives permission, or the judge grants a certificate that their decision is fit for appeal.[171] Unusually, this appeal lies to the Civil Division of the Court of Appeal, and not the Criminal Division.[172]

13.94

A judge might not view both Conditions 1 and 2, as set out above, as met if s/he has addressed the risk of further football-related violence through, for example, a prohibited activity requirement on a suspended sentence or community order which, whilst different to an FBO in structure and effect,[173] is sufficiently specific to address the risk of further incidents.[174]

Against a declaration of relevance, by the defence

13.95

A person convicted of an offence as respects which the court makes a declaration of relevance may appeal against the making of the declaration of relevance as if the declaration were included in any sentence passed on him for the offence,[175] and an FBO made upon a person's conviction of a relevant offence shall be

---

170   CrimPR, r 63.1(c)(i) (prosecutors) and r 63.1(d)(iv) (subject of the banning order).
171   FSA 1989, s14A(5B).
172   *Boggild* [2011] EWCA Crim 1928, at [5]–[6].
173   Notably the penalty on breach.
174   *Boggild*, at [23]–[24].
175   FSA 1989, s 23(3).

quashed if the making of a declaration of relevance as respects that offence is reversed on appeal.[176]

Breach

13.96

There are four ways in which a person subject to an FBO might breach it:[177]

- failing to comply with a requirement under the FBO;[178]

- failing to report to the specified police station at the specified times;[179]

- failing to surrender his/her passport to the specified police station at the specified time;[180] or

- failing to comply with any additional requirements specified and notified to the subject of the FBO in writing by the enforcing authority relating to any regulated football match.[181]

13.97

Breach in any of these ways is a summary-only offence, and the maximum penalty is imprisonment for a term not exceeding six months, or a fine not exceeding level 5 on the standard scale, or both.[182]

Engaging Article 8 rights

13.98

Because an FBO can prevent its subject from undertaking any foreign travel whilst international regulated matches are being played, it is capable of engaging Article 8 ECHR rights.[183] However, there is no case law where it has actually done so.

13.99

In *Thorpe*, Edis J stated:[184]

---

176 FSA 1989, s 23(4).
177 FSA 1989, s 14J(1).
178 FSA 1989, s 14J(1)(a).
179 FSA 1989, s 14J(1)(b) citing s 19(2B)(a).
180 FSA 1989, s 14J(1)(b) citing s 19(2B)(b).
181 FSA 1989, s 14J(1)(b) citing s 19(2C).
182 FSA 1989, s 14J(2).
183 *Gough v Chief Constable of Derbyshire Constabulary* [2002] EWCA Civ 351, at [99] – on the specific facts of the case it did not engage Article 8.
184 *Thorpe*, at [19]–[20].

'There is therefore no human right protected by the ECHR to attend football matches as a paying spectator. This does not diminish the importance of football and other entertainments in society, but to involve human rights in this sphere would, in my judgment, undermine the importance to be attached to those rights in areas where they are genuinely engaged. In any event, the rights, if they are engaged, are not unqualified.'

Youths

13.100

There is a potential conflict between the duty to remit young offenders to the youth court for sentence (under PCC(S)A 2000, s 8(2)(b)) and the requirement for the court that convicts an offender (or to whom the defendant is committed for sentence) to deal with an application for a post-conviction FBO.[185] This risks youths convicted of football-related violence and disorder being remitted to their home youth courts for sentencing, having had a first appearance or trial at the court local to where the disorder happened and they were charged. This would lead to applications for FBOs being rejected due to the definition of 'the court' in FSA 1989, s 14A(6).

13.101

A youth should normally be charged and bailed to their 'home' court, even when the offence charged is committed away from their home town/city. After conviction, it will be necessary for the prosecutor to make representations, citing the exception in PCC(S)A 2000, s 8(2), stating that it would be undesirable to remit the case to the 'home' court, as it would deprive the prosecution of the ability to apply for a banning order.

13.102

For this reason, in cases of large-scale disorder it is good practice to charge each defendant separately: youths to the 'home' court and adults to the 'away' court.

---

185 FSA 1989, s 14A(6)(a) and (b).

14 Destruction and Disqualification – Dangerous Dogs Act 1991

14.01

The Dangerous Dogs Act (DDA) 1991 gives a sentencing court a number of powers to deal with dogs whose behaviour has led to a person's conviction under certain sections of the Act. These orders are also available without a conviction – see Chapter 19.

Qualifying offences

14.02

A person (D) convicted of an offence under the following sections has committed a 'qualifying offence':

(1)   Section 1(2) – Acts or omissions in relation to dogs bred for fighting

An offence under s 1(2), which bans the following acts in relation to dogs of a type bred for fighting, or having such characteristics as that type (pit bull terriers,[1] Japanese tosas,[2] and any other type of dog designated by an order of the Secretary of State[3]):

- breeding, or breeding from;[4]

- selling, exchanging, offering, advertising or exposing for sale or exchange;[5]

- making or offering to make a gift or advertising or exposing as a gift;[6]

- allowing, as owner or person currently in charge, to be in a public place without being muzzled and kept on a lead;[7] or

- abandoning if the owner, or allowing to stray if currently in charge.[8]

---

1   DDA 1991, s 1(1)(a).
2   DDA 1991, s 1(1)(b).
3   DDA 1991, s 1(1)(c).
4   DDA 1991, s 1(2)(a).
5   DDA 1991, s 1(2)(b).
6   DDA 1991, s 1(2)(c).
7   DDA 1991, s 1(2)(d).
8   DDA 1991, s 1(2)(e).

(2) Section 2 – Omissions in relation to other specially dangerous dogs

The Secretary of State may make an order relating to any type of dog not specified in s 1 of the 1991 Act that presents a serious danger to the public, making the following acts, in relation to dogs of those types, offences:[9]

- allowing, as owner or person currently in charge, to be in a public place without being muzzled and kept on a lead; or

- abandoning (if the owner), or allowing to stray (if currently in charge),

subject to any exceptions stated in the order.[10]

(3) Section 3 – Failing to keep a dog under proper control

An offence under s 3(1), which is that the owner[11] or person currently in charge[12] has allowed a dog to become dangerously out of control, in circumstances not covered by the 'householder defence'.[13] There need not be any injury caused – if there is, that is an aggravating factor.[14]

Destruction

14.03

Where the offence of which the defendant (D) is convicted falls under headings (2) or (3) above, the court is empowered by DDA 1991, s 4 to order the destruction of the dog. Where the offence is contrary to s 1, or the aggravated form of s 3(1) (involving injury), the court MUST make the order unless s 4(1A) applies. Section 4(1A) allows the court to make a contingent destruction order instead if the dog is not a danger to public safety (see 14.12)).[15]

14.04

If the court is satisfied that the dog would not constitute a danger to public safety it does not have to make such an order, even where s 4(1)(a) purports to make it mandatory.[16] This apparent inconsistency seems to arise from the 1997 insertion of s 4(1A) without any amendment to s 4(1)(a). When deciding whether the dog is a danger to public safety, the court must consider the temperament of the dog and its past behaviour,[17] and whether the owner of the dog, or the person

---

9   DDA 1991, s 2(1).
10 DDA 1991, s 2(2).
11 DDA 1991, s 3(1)(a).
12 DDA 1991, s 3(1)(b).
13 DDA 1991, s 3(1A).
14 If caused to a human or an assistance dog.
15 DDA 1991, s 4(1)(a).
16 DDA 1991, s 4(1A)(a).
17 DDA 1991, s 4(1B)(a)(i).

currently in charge of it, is a fit and proper person to be in charge of the dog.[18] Where a court finds that someone is not a fit and proper person to be looking after a dog it should state why it came to this finding, and balance all of the information that it has in concluding so.[19] Failing properly to consider this is likely to lead to the quashing of an order as wrong in principle.[20]

14.05

It seems likely, from *R v Trafford Magistrates' Court, ex p Riley*,[21] though *obiter*, that the person 'in charge of the dog' must be so with the full consent, be it express or implied, of the owner, to prevent the malicious release of the dog by someone without the owner's consent leading to a destruction order. The court may also take into account any other relevant considerations.[22] Where a dog had escaped from a run on private property and attacked another dog and its owner in the street, it was not appropriate to speculate how the dog came to be loose, and as there was no evidence that the dog had been out of control on a previous occasion, and there had been no repetition since, it was not appropriate to make a discretionary destruction order.[23]

14.06

When deciding whether to make a discretionary destruction order under DDA 1991, s 4(1)(a), a judge can only take account of proper evidence. Neither a petition from neighbours, nor the opinion of a dog breeder without veterinary qualifications who later visited the dog in kennels to check on its welfare, and was not present at the incident, amounted to such evidence.[24] Similarly a court should not consider whether, in circumstances other than the ones in which the dog was kept, it would be aggressive – consideration had to be of the dog as it was, in its present conditions.[25]

14.07

If suitable new and experienced homes have been found for dogs which have been made subject to destruction orders, because another dog (which has been destroyed) owned by the same person was involved in a DDA 1991, s 3(1) offence in conditions which can lead to a finding that the other dogs are not a danger to the public, then it is likely to be appropriate to quash a destruction order.[26] However, a destruction order should not be quashed where it is the dog

---

18 DDA 1991, s 4(1B)(a)(ii).
19 *Singh* [2013] EWCA Crim 2416, at [21]–[26].
20 *Singh*, at [23].
21 [1995] 3 WLUK 235.
22 DDA 1991, s 4(1B)(b).
23 *Gordon v Reith* 1997 SLT 62 (a Scottish case under the almost identical provisions). Though note that mandatory destruction should have applied. However, it could not as the notice of penalty served stated only that discretionary destruction was available.
24 *Holland* [2002] EWCA Crim 1585, at [6]–[7].
25 *Donnelly* [2007] EWCA Crim 2548, at [15].
26 *Webb* [2009] EWCA Crim 538, at [7]–[13].

itself that was the subject of the offence, and the possibility of re-homing it is hypothetical, as opposed to the subject of firm offers from suitably-experienced individuals with suitable accommodation.[27]

14.08

When making a destruction order, the court may appoint a person to destroy the dog and require the person with custody of the dog to deliver it up for that purpose.[28] To fail to do so is a summary-only offence under DDA 1991, s 4(8)(b), with a maximum punishment of a fine not exceeding level 5 on the standard scale.

14.09

On making a destruction order the court may also order the offender to pay the reasonable expenses (as determined by the court) of both keeping the dog pending destruction, and destruction.[29] That money shall be enforced as if it were imposed by way of a fine on conviction.[30]

14.10

A destruction order is not a penalty.[31] Where an order is required to be made as a result of the conviction (eg for a DDA 1991, s 1 or s 3(1)(b) offence), but the offender was not the owner, it is a breach of natural justice for the owner not to be notified of the hearing at which the court will be compelled to make that order, and allowed to make representations. An order made without notice to the owner is susceptible to judicial review.[32]

14.11

A destruction order is mandatory only in relation to the dog that caused the injury in the aggravated DDA 1991, s 3(1) offence (subject in any event to the caveats in 14.04). In relation to other dogs of the same owner, a destruction order is discretionary (see 14.12 ff).[33]

Suspended/contingent destruction orders

14.12

The court should ordinarily consider, before ordering immediate destruction, whether to exercise the power under DDA 1991, s 4A; failure to do so may

---

27 *Jobe* [2010] EWCA Crim 2503, at [6]–[8].
28 DDA 1991, s 4(4)(a).
29 DDA 1991, s 4(4)(b).
30 DDA 1991, s 4(5).
31 *Normand v Freeman* 1992 SLT 598 – a Scottish case decided under the almost identical provisions.
32 *R v Trafford Magistrates' Court, ex p Riley* [1995] 3 WLUK 235.
33 *Davies* [2010] EWCA Crim 1923, at [14].

render the immediate order liable to being quashed.[34] Section 4A allows for a contingent destruction order, sometimes called a 'suspended destruction order'.

14.13

A contingent destruction order allows that where:

- D is convicted under DDA 1991, s 1, or of an aggravated offence under s 3(1);[35]

- destruction is not ordered;[36] and

- (if offence under s 1) the dog is subject to the prohibition in s 1(3),[37]

the court shall order that, unless the dog is exempted from that prohibition within two months[38] (which can be extended)[39], it shall be destroyed.

14.14

However, as set out in *Kelleher v DPP*, the legislation is not well-drafted:[40]

'It is clear that s 4A(4) applies both to aggravated and non-aggravated offences. The power to make a destruction order applies in both cases. The distinction, which is made clear by s 4(1A), read with s 4A(4), is that in the case of an aggravated offence there must be a destruction order unless the dog would not constitute a danger to public safety, and in the case of a discretionary order the court has to decide whether it is appropriate, in all the circumstances, having regard to the facts, to make a destruction order ... The test, which, as it seems to me, should be applied in either case, essentially relates to whether the dog is a danger to the public. If it is, whichever way round, as it were, the burden lies for showing it, then the destruction order is appropriate.'

Non-aggravated s 3 offence

14.15

Where the conviction was under DDA 1991, s 3(1) (but not aggravated),[41] and the court decides that the dog is a danger to public safety, the court may order that, unless the dog is kept under proper control, the dog shall be

---

34 *Hill* [2010] EWCA Crim 2999.
35 DDA 1991, s 4A(1)(a).
36 DDA 1991, s 4A(1)(b).
37 DDA 1991, s 4A(1)(c).
38 DDA 1991, s 4A(3).
39 DDA 1991, s 4A(2).
40 *Kelleher v DPP* [2012] EWHC 2978 (Admin), at [11]–[12].
41 As has been noted in *Archbold* and by the Court in *Kelleher v DPP* in a case stated, DDA 1991, s 4A(1) is regrettably lacking in sense due to poor drafting – contingent destruction orders are not available where the offence was under s 3(1) and injury was caused.

destroyed.[42] A suspended order of destruction under that provision may specify the measures to be taken by the owner for keeping the dog under control whether by muzzling, keeping it on a lead, or excluding it from a specified place or otherwise.[43] It can also require that a male dog be castrated if to do so would make it less dangerous.[44]

14.16

The court will not make a destruction order unless, on the available material, it takes the view that a destruction order is necessary.[45] Where the court has wrongly proceeded on the basis that, where a non-aggravated offence has occurred (another dog, but not an assistance dog, had been bitten), the onus lay on the applicant to establish that the dogs were not a danger to public safety for the consideration of a contingent destruction order, the order was quashed.[46]

14.17

Therefore, it is for the prosecution to prove that the dog is a danger to public safety and, if this is done, a contingent destruction order can be made.

Aggravated s 3 offence

14.18

The Court in *Kelleher v DPP* stated that the burden is on the defendant to show that the dog is not a danger to public safety, and if this can be shown, then a contingent destruction order can be made.[47] If the defendant cannot show this, then an immediate destruction order is technically mandatory. In line with well-established principles, it is to be assumed that this burden is borne on the balance of probabilities.[48]

14.19

It is unclear, however, how the Court's decision in *Kelleher* sits with the literal reading of s 4(1A), that even a 'mandatory' destruction order is not required where it can be proved that the dog is not a danger to public safety. This is consistent with the Court's guidance in *Flack* (see 14.23). The problem in consistency of interpretation of this statute displays the mischiefs of unclear drafting starkly.

---

42 DDA 1991, s 4A(4).
43 DDA 1991, s 4A(5)(a).
44 DDA 1991, s 4A(5)(b) – though strangely the court cannot make the same order regarding the spaying of a female dog, even if it is thought that that would reduce the level of danger posed by her – *Kelleher v DPP*, at [10].
45 *Kelleher v DPP*, at [11].
46 *Kelleher v DPP*, at [23]–[24].
47 *Kelleher v DPP*, at [11].
48 *Attorney General's Reference No. 1 of 2004* [2004] EWCA Crim 1025, following *Woolmington v DPP* [1935] AC 462.

Section 1 offence

14.20

If a contingent destruction order is made on conviction for a DDA 1991, s 1 offence, with a condition that the dog be granted a certificate of exemption from the Department for Environment, Food & Rural Affairs, all the court is concerned with under s 4(1A)(a) is the characteristics of the dog – is it a danger to public safety? There can be no consideration of the circumstances in which the dog will be kept, and there is no power for the court to impose conditions.[49]

14.21

If the police believe that the exemption has ceased to exist or apply, they cannot summarily destroy the dog in question – they must apply to the court for a destruction order, otherwise the destruction would be unlawful.[50] A contingent destruction order ceases to have effect once the dog becomes exempted within the specified requisite period.

14.22

When considering whether a dog is a danger to public safety, the consideration is not restricted to those occasions when the dog is in public – it can be a danger to public safety within the home of the owner. As a matter of policy, 'public safety' has to be wide enough to embrace the safety of the public in private spaces.[51]

Procedure

14.23

The process a court should go through when considering whether to impose an immediate or contingent destruction order in a DDA 1991, s 3(1) case is set out helpfully in para 11 of the judgement in *Flack*.[52]

- The court is empowered under s 4(1) to order the destruction of the dog.

- Nothing in that provision shall require the court to order destruction if the court is satisfied that the dog would not constitute a danger to public safety: s 4(1)(a).

- The court should ordinarily consider, before ordering immediate destruction, whether to exercise the power under s 4A(4) to order that,

---

49 *R (Sandhu) v Isleworth Crown Court* [2012] EWHC 1658 (Admin), at [25]–[27].
50 *R (Ali) v Chief Constable of Merseyside* [2014] EWHC 4772 (Admin), at [25].
51 *Blake v CPS* [2017] 1 WLUK 494.
52 [2008] EWCA Crim 204.

unless the owner of the dog keeps it under proper control, the dog shall be destroyed ('a suspended order of destruction').

- A suspended order of destruction under that provision may specify the measures to be taken by the owner for keeping the dog under control whether by muzzling, keeping it on a lead, or excluding it from a specified place or otherwise: see s 4A(5).

- A court should not order destruction if satisfied that the imposition of such a measure would mean the dog would not constitute a danger to public safety.

- In deciding what order to make, the court must consider all the relevant circumstances which include the dog's history of aggressive behaviour and the owner's history of controlling the dog concerned.

14.24

Whether the offence is aggravated or non-aggravated, relevant factors in whether the order should be immediate or suspended will be the previous character of the dog, any assessments done by animal behaviourists of that animal, and the character of the owner.[53] Proper consideration may require an adjournment to allow a suitably qualified animal behaviourist, or a veterinary surgeon, to prepare a report on the dog's temperament.[54]

14.25

The principles enunciated in *Flack*, above, have also been extended to deciding the fate of dogs after a conviction under DDA 1991, s 1(3), where the dogs in question were not the ones that had carried out the attack.[55]

14.26

When considering a destruction order made after an offence (aggravated or not) under DDA 1991, s 3(1), it may be possible to say that the dog will not be a danger if properly trained, and to make a contingent destruction order that it remain at the police (or other) kennels where it has been held, and rehomed to a suitable home within a period of time. If that rehoming cannot be undertaken within the period of time set by the court (susceptible to extension on application, if so ordered), then the destruction order takes effect.[56]

14.27

Where there is conflicting evidence about the behaviour of a dog, the court is entitled to conclude which side's evidence it prefers, and providing that is

---

53 *Flack*, at [12].
54 *Harry* [2010] EWCA Crim 673, at [12]–[13].
55 *Babella* [2010] EWCA Crim 1950, at [4] and [23].
56 *Devon* [2011] EWCA Crim 1073, at [13].

a conclusion that it is entitled to reach on the facts, the order will not be susceptible to appeal.[57]

14.28

Where a dog subject to a destruction order has been destroyed prematurely (ie before the period for an appeal has expired) it is not appropriate for a court to decide whether the destruction order was properly made. Any such decision would be an improper use of the Court's jurisdiction as it would be deciding an academic question, likely so that the aggrieved owner could then seek civil recourse against the police for destroying the dog, if the order was quashed.[58] An owner in those circumstances would simply have to take civil action against the police with no ruling on the correctness of a destruction order.

14.29

Providing a contingent destruction order has been considered, and an order for immediate destruction is not irrational, unreasonable, or made following the court acting unlawfully, immediate destruction of a dog that has bitten multiple people, and whose owner had not made sufficient attempts to obtain a muzzle or additional training for it, and where no behavioural report was available despite ample time to obtain one, will not be susceptible to judicial review.[59]

14.30

Where the consideration of whether to make an immediate or contingent destruction order is the only live matter for a hearing, the Divisional Court has, perplexingly, ruled that there is no need to refer to relevant statutory provisions or the leading authority of *Flack*.[60]

Disqualification

14.31

Regardless of the section under which D is convicted, the court may order that the offender be disqualified, for such period as it thinks fit, from having custody of a dog.[61]

14.32

The purpose of disqualification is both punitive and preventive.[62] In principle, no disqualification should be unnecessarily long when impeding the pursuit

---

57 *Brough v St Helens MBC* [2013] EWHC 4747 (Admin).
58 *Bernard* [2010] EWCA Crim 2083, at [4].
59 *R (Hooker) v Ipswich Crown Court* [2013] EWHC 2899 (Admin).
60 *R (Killeen) v Birmingham Crown Court* [2018] EWHC 174 (Admin).
61 DDA 1991, s 4(1)(b).
62 *Holland* [2002] EWCA Crim 1585, at [9].

of otherwise lawful activities such as dog ownership.[63] Where the incident concerned a neighbour's visiting grandchildren, the Court of Appeal endorsed the approach taken by the first instance judge to balance the sensitivities of the bitten victim with the restriction on the freedom of D. Although a disqualification order prevents the defendant from keeping any dog, not just a dangerous one, the judge was entitled to conclude that the risk of emotional harm to the child through fear was a continuing one.[64]

14.33

There is no power to disqualify a person from keeping more than a certain number of dogs, or to make an order that dogs can be kept but only on conditions, such as being castrated. Either the defendant is permitted to keep as many dogs as s/he wishes, or he is not permitted to keep any.[65]

14.34

Disqualification for life is a serious order for a court to make; however, it will sometimes be appropriate. An example is the case of *Fitzgerald*,[66] where a lifetime disqualification was properly made against a defendant with a serious history of offending, a longstanding alcohol problem and having made no attempts at all to socialise the dog, instead training it actively to bite those who approached the defendant.

Forfeiture of dogs

14.35

No order can be made for forfeiture of dogs under the 1991 Act – such an order would have to be made under the Powers of the Criminal Courts (Sentencing) Act 2000, s 143.[67] When deciding whether to order destruction, forfeiture or disqualification, the court should take into account the willingness of the offender to cooperate with requirements to minimise risk, such as a comprehensive written undertaking to the court as to how he will care for a dog he is permitted to keep.[68]

---

63 *Donnelly* [2007] EWCA Crim 2548, at [12].
64 *Donnelly*, at [11]–[12].
65 *Haynes* [2003] EWCA Crim 3247, at [12].
66 [2017] EWCA Crim 514, at [19].
67 *Haynes*, at [9].
68 *Haynes*, at [14]–[16].

Variation

14.36

Any person subject to a disqualification order may, once it has been in force for a year, apply to any magistrates' court in the same local justice area as that which made it, for it to be terminated.[69]

14.37

When deciding whether to allow the application, the court can have regard to the applicant's character, his/her conduct since the disqualification, and any other circumstances of the case.[70] Regardless of the outcome, they can order the applicant to pay all or part of the costs of the application.[71] If the application is refused, no further application can be made within a year.[72]

Offence of breach

14.38

Any person who has custody of a dog in contravention of a disqualification order under DDA 1991, s 4(1)(b) is guilty of a summary-only offence, with a maximum punishment of a fine not exceeding level 5 on the standard scale.[73]

Appeal

14.39

If an order for destruction is made against an offender who is not the owner, the owner may appeal to the Crown Court.[74] The destruction shall not occur until the time for giving notice of appeal against the conviction or order has ended.[75] If any appeal is instituted within that time, the dog shall not be destroyed until the appeal has been determined or withdrawn.[76]

---

69 DDA 1991, s 4(6).
70 DDA 1991, s 4(7)(a).
71 DDA 1991, s 4(7)(b).
72 DDA 1991, s 4(7).
73 DDA 1991, s 4(8)(a).
74 DDA 1991, s 4(2).
75 DDA 1991, s 4(3)(a).
76 DDA 1991, s 4(3)(b).

15 Costs Orders Against the Accused (prosecution costs)

15.01

Where:

- the defendant (D) is convicted of an offence before the magistrates' court[1] or the Crown Court;[2]

- D has an appeal against conviction or sentence dismissed by the Crown Court;[3]

- an appeal or application for leave to appeal to the Court of Appeal is dismissed;[4]

- an application for leave to appeal to the Supreme Court is dismissed;[5]

- an appeal or application for leave to appeal a ruling at a preparatory hearing, as provided for by s 9(11) of the Criminal Justice Act 1987[6] or s 35(1) of the Criminal Procedure and Investigations Act 1996[7] is dismissed; or

- the Court of Appeal reverses or varies a ruling on an appeal by the Crown against a terminating ruling under the Criminal Justice Act 2003,[8]

the court has discretion to make D pay the whole or part of the prosecution's costs to the prosecutor as it considers just and reasonable, under s 18 of the Prosecution of Offences Act (POA) 1985. Where the appeal was to the Court of Appeal or Supreme Court, costs ordered to be paid may include the reasonable cost of any transcript of proceedings made in accordance with rules of court as required under s 32 of the Criminal Appeals Act 1968.

15.02

It does not matter whether the accused is the appellant or respondent, as illustrated by the inclusion of appeals from terminating rulings and rulings at preparatory hearings.[9]

---

1 POA 1985, s 18(1)(a).
2 POA 1985, s 18(1)(c).
3 POA 1985, s 18(1)(b).
4 POA 1985, s 18(2)(a).
5 POA 1985, s 18(2)(b).
6 POA 1985, s 18(2)(c).
7 POA 1985, s 18(2)(d).
8 POA 1985, s 18(2A).
9 *A Ltd* [2016] 12 WLUK 280, at [6]–[8].

15.03

The references to an appeal or application for leave have been held to include applications for an extension of time to bring an appeal.[10]

15.04

The amount to be paid by the accused in pursuance of an order under this section shall be specified in the order.[11]

15.05

Where D is convicted before a magistrates' court and the court orders payment of any sum not exceeding £5[12] as a fine, penalty, forfeiture or compensation[13] the court shall not order D to pay any costs unless in the particular circumstances of the case it considers it right to do so.

15.06

Where a D under 18 is convicted before a magistrates' court, the amount of any costs ordered to be paid shall not exceed the amount of any fine imposed on him.[14]

15.07

This legislation is supplemented by the Criminal Practice Direction 2015,[15] Part 3 of the Practice Direction (CA Crim Div): Costs in Criminal Proceedings,[16] and Part 45 of the Criminal Procedure Rules.

15.08

Section 28A of the Senior Courts Act 1981 provides that the Divisional Court has the power to award costs *inter partes* on an appeal by way of case stated and on an application for any prerogative orders whether from or in respect of a decision of a magistrates' court or the Crown Court. Such orders are at the discretion of the court. Where the Court allows a prosecution appeal by way of case stated, it is unjust to make an order for costs against the respondent who was neither present nor represented at the hearing and who had not been asked whether they would consent to the appeal being allowed in her absence.[17]

---

10   *Kirk* [2015] EWCA Crim 1764, at [17]–[23].
11   POA 1985, s 18(3).
12   POA 1985, s 18(4)(b).
13   POA 1985, s 18(4)(a).
14   POA 1985, s 18(5).
15   [2015] EWCA Crim 1567.
16   [2015] EWCA Crim 1568.
17   *Canterbury City Council v Cook* [1992] 10 WLUK 162.

Procedure

15.09

There is no requirement that a claim for costs by the prosecution be made orally to the court, and no prohibition on its being notified to D in the same document as the statement of facts required under s 12(1)(b) of the Magistrates' Courts Act 1980. That document allows D to plead guilty by post and not attend court, although it nonetheless did not form part of the statement.[18] Where such a claim for costs was contained in the statement of facts, the legal advisor is obliged to draw it to the court's attention and it is the court's duty then to adjudicate upon it.[19]

15.10

The prosecution should serve on the defence, as early as possible, full details of its costs to allow the defence a proper opportunity to consider them and make representations on them. If D wishes to dispute any of the costs schedule, they should give proper notice of the objections. In exceptional cases a full hearing might be necessary for resolution, as there is no provision for the taxation of the prosecution's costs in a criminal case.[20]

15.11

There is no requirement that a costs order is made by the same constitution as the court which convicted D or heard the plea.[21]

General principles

15.12

The Court of Appeal has given the following guidance:[22]

(1)   an order for costs should never exceed the sum which, having regard to D's means and any other financial order imposed, s/he is able to pay and which it is reasonable to order him/her to pay;[23]

(2)   an order for costs should never exceed the sum which the prosecutor actually and reasonably incurred;

(3)   the purpose of the order is to compensate the prosecutor. Where the conduct of the defence has put the prosecutor to avoidable expense, the

---

18   *R v Coventry Justices, ex p DPP* [1991] 1 WLR 1153, at 1159–1160.
19   *R v Coventry Justices, ex p DPP*, at 1159.
20   *Associated Octel Ltd* [1997] 1 Cr App R (S) 435, at 441–442.
21   *Liverpool Magistrates' Court, ex p Abiaka* [1999] 3 WLUK 87.
22   *Northallerton Magistrates' Court, ex p Dove* [2000] 1 Cr App R (S) 136, at 137.
23   Confirming *R v Nottingham Justices, ex p Fohmann* (1987) 84 Cr App R 316, at 319.

offender may be ordered to pay some or all of that sum to the prosecutor but the offender must not be punished for exercising the right to defend themselves;

(4) the costs ordered to be paid should not be grossly disproportionate to any fine imposed for the offence. This principle was affirmed in *BPS Advertising Limited v London Borough of Barnet*,[24] in which the Court held that, while there is no question of an arithmetical relationship, the question of costs should be viewed in the context of the maximum penalty considered by Parliament to be appropriate for the seriousness of the offence;

(5) if the total of the proposed fine and the costs sought by the prosecutor exceeds the sum which the offender could reasonably be ordered to pay, the costs order should be reduced rather than the fine;

(6) it is for the offender to provide details of his or her financial position so as to enable the court to assess what he or she can reasonably afford to pay. If the offender fails to do so, the court is entitled to draw reasonable inferences as to means from all the circumstances of the case;

(7) if the court proposes to make any financial order against the offender, it must give him or her fair opportunity to adduce any relevant financial information and to make appropriate submissions.

15.13

An order for costs is to compensate the prosecutor, not to punish D.[25]

Matters for which costs can be sought

15.14

Where the prosecutor is the CPS, prosecution costs exclude the costs of the investigation, which are met by the police. In non-CPS cases where the costs of the investigation are incurred by the prosecutor a costs award may cover the costs of investigation (which will not have been done by the police) as well as prosecution. However, the order should exclude any costs incurred by the police, which must be met by the police.[26] The corollary of this is that where the prosecutor is not the CPS and the investigation has not been done by the police the investigation costs are also recoverable.

15.15

Investigation costs include:

---

24 [2006] EWHC 3335 (Admin).
25 *Kesteven* [2012] EWCA Crim 2029, at [8].
26 Para 3.7 of the Practice Direction (CA (Crim Div): Costs in Criminal Proceedings.

- obtaining sufficient evidence either at the initial stage or later at the request of the prosecuting body;

- re-interviewing witnesses;

- seeking medical or expert evidence as part of the investigation (where a witness is required to attend court, the cost of the attendance falls on the prosecuting body).

15.16

Where D had been prosecuted under the Ancient Monuments and Archaeological Areas Act 1975, it was held not proper to award costs to cover the investigation by English Heritage – an order for payment of costs is limited to the costs of the prosecution itself and did not extend to the costs of the investigation, especially when that was done by a different body.[27] That decision, however, has since been held to be per incuriam due to the Court misunderstanding a change in the law.[28] Costs of prosecuting might include the costs of carrying out pre-charge investigations into a suspect where a prosecution results and the defendant is convicted.[29] That the prosecution eventually modified its case was not a reason for denying or reducing costs which had been incurred.[30]

15.17

The whole of the prosecution's costs in investigating an offence includes time taken in investigation by salaried employees, which could be calculated by apportionment of the salaries.[31] However, it has been said that care must be taken not to overload the costs by reference to the investigation to maintain proportionality.[32] For example, an officer of the council who did the investigation in an advertising case was being paid as an officer for carrying out his duties in the normal way. He would have received payment whatever he had been doing at the relevant time[33] and, when looking at proportionality, that is a relevant consideration to be taken into account when deciding the appropriate amount.

15.18

In *B&Q plc*,[34] the Court of Appeal set out some principles applicable to aborted trials, and where there are mixed verdicts in the trial that does conclude:[35]

---

27 *Seymour* (1987) 9 Cr App R (S) 395, at 401.
28 *Associated Octel Ltd*, at 440.
29 *Associated Octel Ltd*, at 441.
30 *Associated Octel Ltd*, at 441.
31 *Federation Against Copyright Theft v North West Aerials* [2006] 2 Costs LR 361.
32 *BPS Advertising Ltd v London Borough of Barnet* [2006] EWHC 3335 (Admin), at [14].
33 *BPS Advertising Ltd v London Borough of Barnet*, at [14].
34 [2005] EWCA Crim 2297.
35 *B&Q plc*, at [56].

- Due to the differing nature of the statutory provisions relating to costs in criminal proceedings and the way in which costs are borne by different departments of the Executive in matters such as health and safety prosecutions, the judge should approach costs by making orders under the different provisions rather than adopting a global approach.

- Where there are aborted trials before one which concludes, the costs in relation to the aborted trials should be considered when those trials fail and the proceedings are adjourned. The Court held that the appellants should have received a sum by way of credit that properly reflected the costs incurred by them in relation to the aborted trials and should not have been required to pay the prosecution costs of those trials, as they were caused by the prosecution's failure to ensure that equipment to play CCTV evidence was operating correctly.

- Some allowance must be made for acquittal on the direction of the judge and by the jury on some counts. Little by way of the overall costs related to the acquittals on the direction of the judge; all the evidence on count 7 was relevant to count 8; the evidence on the other counts on which there was an acquittal took about two days.

15.19

Even where the trial and the charges are much more straightforward, the Court of Appeal has confirmed that acquittals must be taken into account.[36]

15.20

Costs properly incurred after charge, as opposed to in the initial investigation, such as expert reports, can form part of a costs figure. In *Balshaw v CPS*,[37] the police incurred costs in obtaining an expert report from KPMG. The Court refused the application, holding that whilst an order to pay costs to a prosecutor for which the prosecutor is not liable is neither just nor reasonable, provided that the order does not lead to a windfall for the prosecutor or to a disguised fine or penalty, there is no reason why it would not be just and reasonable to make an order to the prosecutor in respect of sums which the court is satisfied are part of those costs of investigation which the prosecutor will itself satisfy.[38]

15.21

There is no principle that an order cannot be made where the costs are to compensate a third party, or that the CPS may only recover costs that it itself has directly incurred: the statute does not prevent the recovery by a prosecutor of fees which it will pay to another body which has itself incurred liability to

---

36   *Splain* [2010] EWCA Crim 49, at [14]–[15].
37   [2009] EWCA Crim 470.
38   *Balshaw*, at [12].

pay those fees. The only test is that it is just and reasonable for the prosecutor to meet those fees.[39]

15.22

If there has had to be an investigation into a prosecution witness whose credibility comes to be doubted, the costs of that investigation can properly be included in an order against D.[40] Whether carrying out that investigation earlier would have truncated proceedings was a speculative question.[41]

Whether to make an order

15.23

A costs order was quashed by the Court of Appeal where a judge made the order in the expectation that it would be enforced as a civil debt, knowing that D's means were limited to his net sickness benefit, but under the impression that his means to pay would be judged in due course by the Department for Work and Pensions, as the prosecution had suggested, meaning that it would be many years before the costs order was met.[42] In reality, a costs order is enforced as if it had been adjudged to be paid on conviction in the magistrates' court (see s 41 of the Administration of Justice Act 1970). The only evidence of means before the learned Recorder was the appellant's sickness benefit which, after deduction of the ongoing repayment of the housing benefit unlawfully obtained, amounted to only about £260 per month.

15.24

There is no necessary correlation between sentence and an order for costs.[43] However, in *Rakib*,[44] D had spent a long period on remand due to other charges of which he was acquitted after a trial on an indictment severed from the one on which he was convicted and faced a costs order. The Court of Appeal held that it was incumbent upon the judge, when assessing whether a costs order was just and reasonable to take into account the time spent on remand, over and above his eventual community order, because during that period he was unable to earn. The sentencing judge having not appeared to have taken that into account when making the costs order, the order was quashed.

---

39   *Balshaw*, at [13].
40   *Huhne* [2014] EWCA Crim 2541, at [25]–[26].
41   *Huhne*, at [27].
42   *Nuthoo* [2010] EWCA Crim 2383, at [12].
43   *Rakib* [2011] EWCA Crim 870, at [45].
44   *Rakib*, at [45].

15.25

If a defendant wishes to challenge the detail in the breakdown of the prosecution's application for costs, then he must do so at first instance, not raise that complaint only on appeal.[45]

Amount

15.26

Where the defence does not accept that the figures given by the prosecution are reasonable, it is possible for the costs to be assessed by a proper officer of the Crown Court to resolve the issue.[46] However, the matter must be adjourned for that to be done, as when an order is made, it must specify the amount, as required by POA 1985, s 18(3). If the order simply says 'prosecution costs to be taxed if not agreed', it is invalid.[47]

15.27

If the prosecution chooses to instruct specialist counsel in a case that does not demand it, that is their privilege, but there is no reason why the unsuccessful appellant should have to reimburse the respondents for the fees that the respondents chose to agree.[48] The Divisional Court regarded the legal aid scale fees payable to solicitors and counsel as a useful marker as to the fees that it would be reasonable to expect an unsuccessful appellant to pay.[49]

15.28

Where there is an unsuccessful appeal to the Crown Court, the court has jurisdiction to increase the amount of costs awarded.[50] The prosecutor should give notice if they are going to seek a variation in the costs awarded by the magistrates and the Crown Court should consider carefully before varying the costs aspect of a sentence on an unsuccessful appeal.[51] The exception is where the reason for a variation is obvious; for example where the offence was against animal welfare and the animals are being cared for at the cost of the state, it is only sensible to realise that those costs will increase with time, and thus be greater by the end of an appeal than they were on conviction.[52]

---

45 *Splain*, at [9].
46 *CPC (UK) Ltd* [1994] 7 WLUK 208.
47 *Ford-Sagers* [2006] EWCA Crim 2255, at [16]–[17].
48 *Griffiths v Pembrokeshire County Council* [2000] Env LR 622, at 629.
49 *Griffiths v Pembrokeshire County Council*, at 629.
50 *Hamilton-Johnson v RSPCA* [2000] 2 Cr App R (S) 390, at 395.
51 *Hamilton-Johnson*, at 396–397.
52 *Hamilton-Johnson*, at 396.

15.29

However, if the Crown are asked to set out a detailed schedule of their costs for appeal, and that document contains a subsequent correction as to quantum (on a different basis and without any particularity) it could not be used to displace the figure which the Crown were seeking to claim at first instance.[53] The Court of Appeal did not go so far as to say that such a figure could never be used, however.

15.30

Any order for costs must reflect D's means: if the amount of costs has been greatly increased by counsel taking myriad technical points that the court views as unnecessary, D is not to be punished for that in having to bear greater costs that were caused by the trial or appeal taking much longer, and requiring the calling of more witnesses, than was necessary.[54]

15.31

If D is a company and does not furnish the court with information as to its resources then its ability to pay cannot be considered.[55] Fines and costs should not be aggregated for the purposes of deciding the correct sentencing category of a company.[56]

15.32

If quantification of costs is agreed, it is not necessary for the judge to investigate whether costs in that sum had been actually or reasonably incurred.

15.33

In principle there is no issue with a judge using the CPS scale of costs table,[57] despite it not having been updated since 2009, to establish a reasonable figure for the prosecution costs of a certain type of hearing.[58] The Court of Appeal reached this conclusion having received evidence about the way in which the scale was calculated.[59] However, the Court did accept that sometimes in particular cases those figures would not represent a fair amount,[60] and advocates will need to be alive to this possibility if they have an unusual case. No legitimate complaint can be made of the fact that the scale of costs identify an average

---

53   *Azam* [2010] EWCA Crim 512, at [18].
54   *Jones v Guildford Crown Court* [2004] EWHC 2393 (Admin), at [12].
55   *Bodycote HIP* [2010] EWCA Crim 802, at [29]; *Merlin Attractions Operations Ltd* [2012] EWCA Crim 2670, at [57].
56   *Bodycote HIP*, at [28]–[30], endorsed in *Merlin Attractions Operations Ltd*, at [51].
57   https://www.cps.gov.uk/legal-guidance/costs-annex-1.
58   *Dickinson* [2010] EWCA Crim 2143, at [11]–[12].
59   *Dickinson*, at [12]–[13].
60   *Dickinson*, at [13].

figure for proceedings of that type, as opposed to the specific costs incurred in the particular trial with which the court is concerned.[61]

15.34

Where a prosecution was brought by a local authority, the judge need not use the CPS scale of costs for their calculations.[62]

Ability to pay

15.35

No order for costs should be made on the assumption that a third party will pay the sum.[63] Neither should an order be made on the basis of income from a discretionary trust, where D has only a hope that the discretion will be exercised in favour of him as opposed to other beneficiaries.[64]

15.36

Where D is able to pay the whole amount of prosecution costs, there is no reason in principle for the court not to make that order.[65]

15.37

If the judge is told that D has no means to pay but is planning to reject that submission, then the judge should hear evidence as to D's ability to pay and make a reasoned decision on the issue.[66] However, where D chooses not to put financial evidence before the court, and neither does his counsel seek an adjournment, the court is entitled to proceed on the basis of knowledge it has gleaned through other sources such as a pre-sentence report.[67]

15.38

If further detail comes to light after the sentencing hearing that means that D cannot now pay the costs order because the sole possible source contemplated is no longer possible (eg where the judge had made the order on the basis that further borrowing against a house would be possible) the order may be quashed if the judge would not have made the order had he had that knowledge at sentencing.[68]

---

61   *Ozoemena* [2014] EWCA Crim 961, at [9].
62   *Rahal* [2017] EWCA Crim 1779, at [14].
63   *R v Barnet Magistrates' Court, ex p Cantor* [1999] 1 WLR 334, at 342.
64   *Ex p Cantor*, at 341.
65   *F Howe and Son (Engineers) Ltd* [1999] 2 Cr App R (S) 37, at 44.
66   *Tian* [2011] EWCA Crim 3221, at [7]–[8].
67   *Burger* [2013] EWCA Crim 2601, at [22].
68   *Young* [2010] EWCA Crim 1276, at [6]–[8].

15.39

If D has an interest in a property, but the costs order forces D to sell the family home, it is unlikely to be just or reasonable.[69] This was especially so when its state of repair meant that no mortgage would be available to a buyer, and D had three resident children aged between 18 and 21, all in full time education, one of whom had Asperger's syndrome.[70]

15.40

Where D has an interest in a house which means that he may become able to pay costs at some time in the future, it is not improper to make an order for costs, but there should not be a collection order made, meaning that the order will simply be enforceable in the civil jurisdiction.[71]

15.41

There is no prohibition on a costs order being made on the expectation that it could be met from capital.[72]

15.42

If D is sentenced to immediate custody, then it will usually be the case that they will not have employment to return to on release.[73] Therefore, unless there is evidence of significant capital it will not be appropriate to make an order, and particularly not one that requires payments to commence whilst D is still in custody.[74]

15.43

Where an order is made on the basis that the judge says that D can 'economise' on various outgoings, despite the evidence, unchallenged, showing D's outgoings to be more than his income, the order will not be just unless the judge identifies the basis on which the instalments ordered can be met, and the areas in which D can economise.[75]

---

69   *Pegley* [2012] EWCA Crim 2583, at [10]–[13].
70   *Pegley,* at [10].
71   *James v RSPCA* [2011] EWHC 1642 (Admin), at [15]–[17].
72   *R (Gray) v Aylesbury Crown Court* [2013] EWHC 500 (Admin), at [68]–[69].
73   *Wogui* [2013] EWCA Crim 1483, at [9]–[11].
74   *Wogui,* at [9]–[11].
75   *Richmond* [2013] EWCA Crim 2712, at [17]–[18].

Time to pay

15.44

As the Court noted in *Bow Street Magistrates' Court, ex p Mitchell*,[76] it used to be thought that the total sum by way of fines, costs and any compensation orders should be a sum which D would appear to be capable of paying within about 12 months.[77] However, since *Olliver and Olliver*[78] that period may in appropriate cases be extended to anything up to two or even three years.[79] Where there has been a complex investigation, such as a prosecution under the Copyright, Designs and Patents Act 1988, there is likely to be considerably greater expense in the investigation and presentation of the case by the prosecution, and thus a longer period will be needed to pay the level of expenses properly incurred.[80] Ultimately, the question for the court will always be circumstance-specific.[81]

Instalments

15.45

A costs order is enforced as if it had been adjudged to be paid on conviction in the magistrates' court as provided for by s 41 of the Administration of Justice Act 1970. However, the court has the power to allow an individual to pay by instalments as provided for by s 141 of the Powers of Criminal Courts (Sentencing) Act 2000.

Multiple defendants

15.46

Where there are several defendants it is usually appropriate to consider a reasonable estimate of costs as if each defendant was tried alone.[82] Where there is significant disagreement between parties about how long such individual trials would have taken, the court may not be able to use this method of calculation due to a lack of available evidence.[83] If this occurs the court will have to adopt a 'rough and ready' approach because detailed calculations are impractical.[84]

---

76   [2001] FSR 267.
77   *Ex p Mitchell*, at 268–269.
78   (1989) 11 Crim App R (S) 10.
79   *Olliver and Olliver*, at 15.
80   *Ex p Mitchell*, at 269.
81   *Guiness* [2009] EWCA Crim 1205, at [8].
82   *Harrison* (1993) 14 Cr App R (S) 419, at 421.
83   *Ronson and Parnes* (1992) 13 Cr App R (S) 153, at 156.
84   *Ronson and Parnes*, at 157.

15.47

However, ultimately it is the judge's discretion how apportionment is undertaken: an award of a greater proportion of costs against the principal defendant who stands to gain financially from the offences, and has the means to pay the amount ordered, will not be an improper use of the discretion in POA 1985, 18.[85]

15.48

In *Fresha Bakeries*,[86] the Court of Appeal distinguished *Ronson and Parnes*[87] and preferred the discretionary approach in *Harrison*,[88] that if the sentencing court concluded that any particular defendant among a number of defendants was more responsible than the others for the criminal conduct which led to the conviction, then it might be appropriate to order that defendant to pay a greater share of costs than he would have had to pay if he had been tried alone.[89] The sentencing judge was entitled to conclude that the corporate defendants bore a greater responsibility than the individual defendants for the overall breaches of the Act.[90] However the sentencing judge took too little account of the fact that the companies had no control over the proceedings brought against the individual defendants, and if those defendants had pleaded guilty when the companies tendered their pleas, the costs would have been significantly less.[91] The Court considered that the appropriate costs to be ordered against the two companies was £150,000, to be apportioned between those companies.

15.49

Where the majority of a trial concerned evidence against one D, who is impecunious, it is not fair to require other defendants to bear the full costs between them.[92]

15.50

When expressing costs figures, judges should make clear what sum is to be paid by each defendant, not simply give a global figure.[93] One D should not be held liable for the costs of a trial against a co-accused.[94]

---

85   *Harrison*, at 421.
86   [2002] EWCA Crim 1451.
87   See fn 84.
88   See fn 83.
89   *Fresha Bakeries*, at [27]–[28].
90   *Fresha Bakeries*, at [29].
91   *Fresha Bakeries*, at [29].
92   *Ronson and Parnes*, at 157.
93   *Durose* [2004] EWCA Crim 2188, at [2], [9]–[10].
94   *Vaitekunas* [2006] EWCA Crim 2922, at [6].

15.51

A joint and several order can properly be made,[95] but it will still require proper enquiry into D's means. If there is significant disparity in means, then an order specifying the amount to be paid by each is likely to be a fairer course.[96]

15.52

Where the prosecution apparently forgot to apply for costs against one co-defendant, and the judge then orders the full amount to be paid by the other co-defendant, the order is likely to be unfair and disproportionate.[97]

Interest

15.53

Interest cannot be awarded on costs as the power of the High Court under s 17 and s 18 of the Judgments Act 1838 to award interest on a judgment debt or order for costs applies only to civil proceedings; and in the absence of any relevant statutory provision, no interest can be awarded on costs to be paid out of central funds.[98]

Enforcement

15.54

In default of payment, imprisonment will be imposed, according to the scale as set out in Sch 4 to the Magistrates' Courts Act 1980.

Collection orders

15.55

As noted at 15.40, where D cannot pay a costs order at the date it is being made, but there is a real possibility that D will be able to do so at some point in the future (eg when a house in which they have an interest is sold) the correct solution is likely to be to make an application for costs, but not seek a collection order.

---

95   *Parish* [2010] EWCA Crim 2631, at [18]–[19].
96   *Parish*, at [22]–[23].
97   *Azam* [2010] EWCA Crim 512, at [19]–[20].
98   *Westminster City Council v Wingrove* [1991] 1 QB 652.

15.56

This occurred in *James v RSPCA*,[99] because the RSPCA requested the magistrates' court not to make such an order. As the court explained:[100]

'Para. 12(1) of Schedule 5 to the Courts Act 2003 required the court to make a collection order "unless it appears to the court that it is impracticable or inappropriate to make the order". The magistrates' court was satisfied that it was impracticable or inappropriate to make a collection order, given (a) the large amount and (b) the RSPCA's intention to enforce the order for "costs" as a civil debt. The RSPCA was entitled to do that by virtue of s 41(3) of the Administration of Justice Act 1970, which provided that sums required to be paid as a result of orders in criminal proceedings are enforceable in the High Court or the county court as if the sum was due as a result of a judgment of the High Court or the county court, though certain methods of enforcement such as the issue of a writ of fieri facie are excluded.'

Appeal

15.57

Appeal against an order for costs made by the magistrates is only by way of certiorari.[101] (Though if there has been an appeal against sentence the Crown Court may also review the costs figure imposed – see 15.28.) A case can be stated to the Divisional Court if the applicant wishes to argue that the level of costs awarded demonstrated an error of law or were *Wednesbury* unreasonable.[102] The Court has encouraged those aggrieved by magistrates' court costs orders to appeal by way of case stated, to ensure that a statement of agreed facts, and the findings made and their evidential base, are all before the court hearing the appeal.[103]

15.58

Where an appeal against a costs order made by the Crown Court is made to the Court of Appeal, the usual threshold of wrong in principle or manifestly excessive applies.[104] The appellant should put before the Court up-to-date evidence about their current financial situation.[105] The Court will not engage in matters of detailed calculation, only in questions of principle.[106] However,

---

99   [2011] EWHC 1642 (Admin).
100 *James v RSPCA*, at [12].
101 *Nottingham Justices, ex p Fohmann*, at 317.
102 *Blows v Herefordshire District Council* [2009] EWHC 666 (Admin).
103 *R (Boyce) v Horsham Magistrates' Court* [2014] EWHC 2462 (Admin), at [25].
104 *Hazell* [2009] EWCA Crim 2330, at [7].
105 *Suleman* [2006] EWCA Crim 2187, at [10]–[12].
106 *Macatonia* [2009] EWCA Crim 2516, at [14]–[16].

where there is a significant matter that is easily calculable that the Court thinks unjustified, it could allow the appeal and reduce the costs order by that amount (eg where it held that second counsel was not necessary).[107]

15.59

Where an order was made properly, based upon information then available as to D's means, the Court of Appeal will not allow an appeal against the order because D has fallen on unexpected financial hardship.[108] The proper forum for issues relating to payment of a costs order is the magistrates' court, which will be enforcing the order.[109]

Interaction with other orders

15.60

An order for costs should not be grossly disproportionate to any fine that D has received by way of sentence. The Court of Appeal has not been drawn on what ratio this entails, but in *Middleton v Cambridge Magistrates' Court*,[110] where D had been sentenced to a fine of £75 on each of two offences, a costs order for £6,871 was grossly disproportionate, and the matter remitted to the magistrates for them to make an appropriate costs order.

15.61

Where consideration of costs is adjourned until after contemplated confiscation proceedings, which are subsequently abandoned, the adjournment of the question of costs was not invalidated.[111] When the costs order is later made, it is a postponed part of the sentence, not a variation.[112]

15.62

In *Constantine*,[113] the Court of Appeal provided helpful guidance on the timing of costs and confiscation orders in relation to one another:[114]

'First, on the correct interpretation of sections 13–15 of the Proceeds of Crime Act 2002, the judge did not have the power to make a costs order against the appellant on 5 March 2009 once the prosecution instigated confiscation proceedings and the making of a confiscation

---

107 *Rahal*, at [15]–[16].
108 *Coleman* [2016] EWCA Crim 1665, at [25]–[26].
109 *Coleman*, at [19] and [39].
110 [2012] EWHC 2122 (Admin), at [20].
111 *Smart* [2003] EWCA Crim 258, at [22].
112 *Smart*, at [20]–[22].
113 [2010] EWCA Crim 2406.
114 *Constantine*, at [30].

order was postponed. Secondly, the judge was obliged to take account of the confiscation order before he made any order for costs against the defendant (including costs of the proceedings other than the confiscation proceedings). Therefore, thirdly, even though the prosecution impliedly asked the judge to make a costs order against the appellant at the hearing on 5 March 2009, the judge was, albeit perhaps unwittingly, correct not to make any order at that stage. Fourthly, we find that the judge plainly did not, implicitly, make an order that the appellant should not pay costs of the proceedings. Fifthly, although the judge should, in the normal course of things, have made the costs order at the end of the confiscation proceedings (as postponed) on 10 December 2009, a costs order could be made up to 28 days after that time. Sixthly, the judge had the power to adjourn part of the sentencing exercise, viz. the issue of costs of the proceedings other than the confiscation proceedings, on 10 December 2009, if it was necessary to do so. Seventhly, on a proper analysis of the facts, all the judge did on 10 December 2009 was to exercise his power to adjourn the final element in the sentencing exercise that the judge had to carry out, viz. whether or not to make a costs order as to the proceedings other than the confiscation proceedings. He had the power to adjourn that issue for more than the 28-day period mentioned in section 15(4) of the 2002 Act. Therefore, finally, the judge had the power to make the costs order he did on 4 February 2010.'

15.63

Where the court wishes to impose costs in addition to a fine, compensation and/or the victim surcharge but the offender has insufficient resources to pay the total amount, the order of priority is as follows (see Chapter 4 for further details):

(1)   compensation;

(2)   victim surcharge;

(3)   fine;

(4)   costs.

Private prosecutors

15.64

Private prosecutors should note that they can recover their costs from central funds.[115]

---

115 POA 1985, s 17(1).

15.65

However, this does not apply to public authorities, and others who are sometimes regarded as 'private prosecutors': POA 1985, s 17(2) sets out that no order under this section may be made in favour of:

- a public authority;[116] or

- a person acting:[117]

    – on behalf of a public authority;[118] or

    – in his capacity as an official appointed by such an authority.[119]

15.66

The definition of public authority is given in POA 1985, s 17(6):

- a police force within the meaning of POA 1985, s 3;[120]

- the Crown Prosecution Service or any other government department;[121]

- a local authority or other authority or body constituted for purposes of:[122]

    – the public service or of local government;[123] or

    – carrying on under national ownership any industry or undertaking or part of an industry or undertaking;[124] or

- any other authority or body whose members are appointed by Her Majesty or by any Minister of the Crown or government department or whose revenues consist wholly or mainly of money provided by Parliament.[125]

---

116 POA 1985, s 17(2)(a).
117 POA 1985, s 17(2)(b).
118 POA 1985, s 17(2)(b)(i).
119 POA 1985, s 17(2)(b)(ii).
120 POA 1985, s 17(6)(a).
121 POA 1985, s 17(6)(b).
122 POA 1985, s 17(6)(c).
123 POA 1985, s 17(6)(c)(i).
124 POA 1985, s 17(6)(c)(ii).
125 POA 1985, s 17(6)(d).

16 Slavery and Trafficking Prevention Orders (on conviction)

16.01

The Modern Slavery Act (MSA) 2015 gives a sentencing court the power to make a slavery and trafficking prevention order (STPO) both on conviction (this chapter) and on application (see Chapter 23). There is also the slavery and trafficking risk order (STRO) which can be made on a civil application (see Chapter 28).

Pre-conditions for an order

16.02

An STPO prohibits D from doing anything described in the order.[1]

16.03

A court may make an STPO against a defendant (D) whom it deals with in respect of a:

- conviction[2] for a slavery or human trafficking offence;[3,4]

- finding[5] that D is not guilty of a slavery or human trafficking offence by reason of insanity;[6] or

- finding[7] that D is under a disability and has done the act charged in respect of a slavery or human trafficking offence.[8]

16.04

The court may make the order only if it is satisfied that:

---

1 MSA 2015, s 17(1).
2 Which can include a conviction before MSA 2015, s 15 came into force – as provided for by s 15(5).
3 Defined by MSA 2015, s 15(3) as an offence listed in Sch 1 to the 2015 Act.
4 MSA 2015, s 15(1)(a).
5 Which can include a finding before MSA 2015, s 15 came into force – as provided for by s 15(5).
6 MSA 2015, s 15(1)(b).
7 Which can include a finding before MSA 2015, s 15 came into force – as provided for by s15(5).
8 MSA 2015, s 15(1)(c).

- there is a risk that D may commit a slavery or human trafficking offence;[9,10] and

- it is necessary to make the order for the purpose of protecting persons generally, or particular persons, from the physical or psychological harm which would be likely to occur if D committed such an offence.[11]

Content of an order

16.05

The only prohibitions that may be included are those which the court is satisfied are necessary for the purpose of protecting persons generally, or particular persons, from the physical or psychological harm which would be likely to occur if D committed a slavery or human trafficking offence.[12]

16.06

The order may prohibit D from doing things in any part of the UK, and anywhere outside the UK.[13]

Foreign travel prohibition

16.07

An STPO may contain an outright prohibition on travelling to any country outside the UK,[14] or travelling to any country outside the UK that is,[15] or is other than,[16] those named or described in the order.

16.08

Such a prohibition may last for no more than five years,[17] but can be renewed for additional periods of up to five years on application under s 20.[18]

16.09

If the STPO contains a prohibition on any travel outside the UK, it must require D to surrender all their passports at a police station specified in the order:

---

9   Defined by MSA 2015, s 15(3) as an offence listed in Sch 1 to the 2015 Act.
10 MSA 2015, s 15(2)(a).
11 MSA 2015, s 15(2)(b).
12 MSA 2015, s 17(2).
13 MSA 2015, s 17(3).
14 MSA 2015, s 18(2)(c).
15 MSA 2015, s 18(2)(a).
16 MSA 2015, s 18(2)(c).
17 MSA 2015, s 18(1).
18 MSA 2015, s 18(3).

- on or before the date when the prohibition takes effect;[19] or

- within a period specified in the order.[20]

16.10

Any passports surrendered must be returned as soon as reasonably practicable after the person ceases to be subject to an STPO containing a prohibition on any travel outside the UK,[21] unless it is a passport issued by or on behalf of authorities of a country outside the UK[22] or an international organisation,[23] if the passport has been returned to those authorities or organisation.

Requirement to provide name and address

16.11

As well as prohibitions, an STPO may require D to provide information,[24] if the court is satisfied that the requirement is necessary for the purpose of protecting persons generally, or particular persons, from the physical or psychological harm which would be likely to occur if D committed a slavery or human trafficking offence.[25]

16.12

From the day on which an STPO is served on D, they have three days to notify in the manner and to the person specified in the order, the relevant matters, namely:[26]

- D's name and, where D uses one or more other names, each of those names;[27] and

- D's home address.[28]

16.13

If while subject to the order, D:

- uses a name which has not been notified;[29] or

---

19 MSA 2015, s 18(4)(a).
20 MSA 2015, s 18(4)(b).
21 MSA 2015, s 18(5).
22 MSA 2015, s 18(6)(a).
23 MSA 2015, s 18(6)(b).
24 MSA 2015, s 19(1).
25 MSA 2015, s 19(2).
26 MSA 2015, s 19(3).
27 MSA 2015, s 19(4)(a).
28 MSA 2015, s 19(4)(b).
29 MSA 2015, s 19(5)(a).

- changes home address,[30]

they must, within three days beginning with the day on which D uses the name or changes home address,[31] in the manner and to the person specified in the order, notify of that.

16.14

Where the order requires D to notify the Director General of the National Crime Agency (NCA) ('the Director General'), an immigration officer or the Gangmasters and Labour Abuse Authority ('GLA Authority'), the Director General, the officer or the GLA Authority must give details of any notification to the chief officer of police for each 'relevant police area',[32] defined as:

- where D notifies a new name, the police area where the defendant lives;[33]

- where D notifies a change of home address, the police area where the defendant lives and (if different) the police area where D lived before the change of home address.[34]

Duration of an STPO

16.15

A prohibition contained in an STPO has effect:

- for a fixed period, specified in the order, of at least five years;[35] or

- until further order;[36]

except for prohibitions on foreign travel, which must be for a fixed period of five years or less.[37]

16.16

Some of its prohibitions may be specified to have effect until further order and some for a fixed period,[38] and an STPO may specify different periods for different prohibitions.[39]

---

30 MSA 2015, s 19(5)(b).
31 MSA 2015, s 19(6).
32 MSA 2015, s 19(7).
33 MSA 2015, s 19(8)(a).
34 MSA 2015, s 19(8)(b).
35 MSA 2015, s 17(4)(a).
36 MSA 2015, s 17(4)(b).
37 MSA 2015, s 18(1).
38 MSA 2015, s 17(5)(a).
39 MSA 2015, s 17(5)(b).

16.17

If a court makes an STPO against someone who is already subject to such an order (made by any court), the earlier order ceases to have effect.[40]

Renewal, discharge or variation of an STPO

16.18

An application for an order varying, renewing or discharging an STPO[41] should be made to the appropriate court:[42]

- where the Crown Court or the Court of Appeal made the STPO, the Crown Court;[43]

- where an adult magistrates' court made the order:[44]

  - that court;[45]

  - an adult magistrates' court for the area in which D lives;[46] or

  - where the application is made by a chief officer of police, any adult magistrates' court acting for a local justice area that includes any part of the chief officer's police area;[47]

- where a youth court made the order and D is under 18:[48]

  - that court;[49]

  - a youth court for the area in which D lives;[50] or

  - where the application is made by a chief officer of police, any youth court acting for a local justice area that includes any part of the chief officer's police area;[51]

- where a youth court made the order and D is 18 or over:[52]

  - an adult magistrates' court for the area in which D lives;[53] or

---

40 MSA 2015, s 17(6).
41 MSA 2015, s 20(1).
42 MSA 2015, s 20(10).
43 MSA 2015, s 20(10)(a).
44 MSA 2015, s 20(10)(b).
45 MSA 2015, s 20(10)(b)(i).
46 MSA 2015, s 20(10)(b)(ii).
47 MSA 2015, s 20(10)(b)(iii).
48 MSA 2015, s 20(10)(c).
49 MSA 2015, s 20(10)(c)(i).
50 MSA 2015, s 20(10)(c)(ii).
51 MSA 2015, s 20(10)(c)(iii).
52 MSA 2015, s 20(10)(d).
53 MSA 2015, s 20(10)(d)(i).

> – where the application is made by a chief officer of police, any adult magistrates' court acting for a local justice area that includes any part of the chief officer's police area.[54]

16.19

Where the appropriate court is the Crown Court, an application is to be made in accordance with rules of court,[55] and in any other case, by complaint.[56]

16.20

The application may be made by any of the following:

- the defendant;[57]

- the chief officer of police for the area in which the defendant lives;[58]

- a chief officer of police who believes that the defendant is in, or is intending to come to, that officer's police area;[59]

16.21

The court will hear the applicant,[60] and any other persons who could make the application should they wish to be heard.[61]

16.22

An order may be renewed, or varied so as to impose additional prohibitions on D or require D to provide their name and address, only if the court is satisfied that:

- there is a risk that D may commit a slavery or human trafficking offence;[62] and

- it is necessary to renew or vary the order for the purpose of protecting persons generally, or particular persons, from the physical or psychological harm which would be likely to occur if D committed such an offence.[63]

16.23

Any renewed or varied order may:

---

54 MSA 2015, s 20(10)(d)(ii).
55 MSA 2015, s 20(8)(a).
56 MSA 2015, s 20(8)(b).
57 MSA 2015, s 20(2)(a).
58 MSA 2015, s 20(2)(b).
59 MSA 2015, s 20(2)(c).
60 MSA 2015, s 20(3)(a).
61 MSA 2015, s 20(3)(b).
62 MSA 2015, s 20(4)(a).
63 MSA 2015, s 20(4)(b).

- contain only those prohibitions which the court is satisfied are necessary for that purpose;[64]

- require D to provide their name and address only if the court is satisfied that the requirement is necessary for that purpose.[65]

16.24

The court must not discharge an order (unless it contains a prohibition on foreign travel)[66] before the end of five years beginning with the day on which the order was made, without the consent of:

- D and the chief officer of police for the area where D lives;[67] or

- where the application is made by a chief officer of police, D and that chief officer.[68]

16.25

Where an immigration officer, the Director General or the GLA Authority makes an application under this section, the officer, the Director General or the GLA Authority must give notice of the application to the chief officer of police for:

- the police area where D lives;[69] or

- a police area which the immigration officer or the Director General believes D is in or is intending to come to.[70]

Appeals

16.26

D may appeal against the making of an STPO to the Crown Court[71] as if the order were a sentence passed on D for the offence[72] or as if D had been convicted of the offence and the order were a sentence passed on D for the offence.[73]

---

64 MSA 2015, s 20(5)(a).
65 MSA 2015, s 20(5)(b).
66 MSA 2015, s 20(7).
67 MSA 2015, s 20(6)(a).
68 MSA 2015, s 20(6)(b).
69 MSA 2015, s 20(9)(a).
70 MSA 2015, s 20(9)(b).
71 MSA 2015, s 22(2).
72 MSA 2015, s 22(1)(a).
73 MSA 2015, s 22(1)(b).

16.27

D may appeal against the renewal, discharge or variation, or the refusal to make such an order to the Crown Court,[74] unless the application had been made to the Crown Court, in which case appeal lies to the Court of Appeal.[75]

16.28

On an appeal to the Crown Court against the making of an order or variation or renewal, or refusal to vary or discharge, the court may make such orders as may be necessary to give effect to its determination of the appeal, and may also make such incidental or consequential orders as appear to it to be just.[76]

16.29

Any order made by the Crown Court on an appeal except an order directing the magistrates' court to re-hear the application,[77] is to be treated as if it were an order of the court from which the appeal was brought.[78]

Breach

16.30

A person who, without reasonable excuse:

- does anything they are prohibited from doing by an STPO;[79] or

- fails to comply with a requirement to surrender passports (MSA 2015, s 18(4));[80] or

- fails to provide their name and address (MSA 2015, s 19(1)),[81]

is liable on conviction:

- on indictment, to imprisonment for a term not exceeding five years;[82]

- summarily, to imprisonment for a term not exceeding six months, or a fine, or both.[83]

16.31

The court cannot give a conditional discharge in respect of a breach offence.[84]

---

74 MSA 2015, s 22(3)(b).
75 MSA 2015, s 22(3)(a).
76 MSA 2015, s 22(4).
77 MSA 2015, s 22(6).
78 MSA 2015, s 22(5).
79 MSA 2015, s 30(1).
80 MSA 2015, s 30(2)(a).
81 MSA 2015, s 30(2)(b).
82 MSA 2015, s 30(3)(a).
83 MSA 2015, s 30(3)(b).
84 MSA 2015, s 30(4).

17 Criminal Behaviour Orders

17.01

These orders (CBOs), created by the Anti-social Behaviour, Crime and Policing Act (ABCPA) 2014, are available only on conviction,[1] in addition to a sentence imposed in respect of the offence,[2] or a conditional discharge.[3]

17.02

CBOs are the successors to anti-social behaviour orders (ASBOs),[4] and an ASBO can still be imposed in relation to any offence for which the criminal proceedings began before 20 October 2014.[5] The Court of Appeal have concluded that a CBO can only be made in relation to offences *committed* after the 2014 Act came into force on 20 October 2014 (not simply where the date of proceedings or sentence occurred after 20 October 2014).[6] The transitional provisions cease to have effect on 20 October 2019, after which date a CBO may be made in relation to an offence committed at any time.[7] The Court has observed that the case law in relation to CBOs is not yet fully developed, but the jurisprudence has been clear that the imposition of CBOs, despite the very wide variety of offences which may fulfil Conditions 1 and 2 (see below), should only be done with consideration of whether the particular case merits such an order.[8]

17.03

Before a CBO can be imposed, two conditions must be met as outlined below.[9]

---

1   ABCPA 2014, s 22(1).
2   ABCPA 2014, s 22(6)(a).
3   ABCPA 2014, s 22(6)(b).
4   Crime and Disorder Act 1998, s 1C.
5   As provided for in the transitional provisions in ABCPA 2014, s 33.
6   *Simsek* [2015] EWCA Crim 1268, at [8]–[10].
7   ABCPA 2014, s 33(1) and (4).
8   *Khan* [2018] EWCA Crim 1472, at [19]–[20].
9   ABCPA 2014, s 22(2).

Condition 1

17.04

The first condition is that the court is satisfied, beyond reasonable doubt, that the offender has engaged in behaviour that caused or was likely to cause harassment, alarm or distress to any person.[10]

17.05

Repeated convictions for drug supply will meet this condition.[11] There is, however, no requirement for a sustained course of conduct, and a single conviction for defrauding an elderly vulnerable man will also suffice.[12]

Condition 2

17.06

The second condition is that the court considers that making the order will help in preventing the offender from engaging in such behaviour.[13]

17.07

This condition was subject to appellate scrutiny in *DPP v Bulmer*.[14] The District Judge had concluded that the terms sought by the prosecution would not help prevent the defendant (D) from engaging in further anti-social behaviour. This was because it took no action to address the root cause of the behaviour – her chronic alcoholism. Banning her from York would simply displace her behaviour elsewhere, and the police already had powers under s 24(1) of the Police and Criminal Evidence Act 1984, and s 27 of the Violent Crime Reduction Act 2006, to arrest someone whom they suspected was about to commit an offence, and to require D to leave a particular area and not return for 48 hours.[15] The judge formed the view that CBOs had shifted from the 'necessity and protection' rationale of ASBOs to a 'help and prevention' rationale,[16] with which the Administrative Court disagreed.[17]

17.08

The Court held that the use of 'consider' in Condition 2 means the court at first instance has a power and not a duty, but not that it is a matter of pure

---

10   ABCPA 2014, s 22(3).
11   *Browne-Morgan* [2016] EWCA Crim 1903, [2017] 1 Cr App R (S) 33, at [10].
12   *Janes* [2016] EWCA Crim 676, at [17].
13   ABCPA 2014, s 22(4).
14   [2015] EWHC (Admin) 2323.
15   *DPP v Bulmer*, at [14].
16   *DPP v Bulmer*, at [18].
17   *DPP v Bulmer*, at [48].

discretion. A factual analysis that is the result of a judge having 'plainly erred' will still be susceptible to challenge.[18]

17.09

Whilst a court can have regard to the other powers available to the police to deal with the offender, it must also consider whether those powers may be insufficient to permit necessary pre-emptive action where a person has a history of anti-social behaviour.[19] The District Judge's consideration of the power under the Violent Crime Reduction Act 2006 was erroneous, as that provision had been repealed.[20]

Interaction between the two conditions

17.10

Condition 2 makes no reference to the burden or standard of proof. It is concerned whether, once the gateway in Condition 1 has been passed, the court 'considers' that making the order will 'help in preventing' anti-social behaviour which caused or was likely to cause harassment, alarm or distress to any person. The inquiry under Condition 1 is a factual one whereas under Condition 2 it is one of judgment and evaluation.

17.11

For these reasons, the Court of Appeal has concluded that there is no requirement for proof beyond reasonable doubt in relation to Condition 2, even in the context of ASBOs where there was a requirement of necessity.[21] This did not, however, mean that ASBOs should be imposed lightly, without a proper degree of caution and circumspection.[22] In *DPP v Bulmer* the same was held to apply to CBOs.[23]

No necessity test

17.12

Whilst ASBOs had to be 'necessary', there is no such test for making a CBO,[24] lowering the threshold.

---

18   *DPP v Bulmer*, at [36].
19   *DPP v Bulmer*, at [44].
20   *DPP v Bulmer*, at [45].
21   *Boness* [2005] EWCA Crim 2395, at [16].
22   *McGrath* [2005] EWCA Crim 353, at [12].
23   *DPP v Bulmer*, at [35].
24   *DPP v Bulmer*, at [22].

17.13

Each condition contained in the CBO, however, must be proportionate.[25]

Procedure

17.14

A CBO can only be made on the application of the prosecution.[26]

17.15

Rule 3.3 of the Criminal Procedure Rules (CrimPR) requires advance notice to be served on D where there is to be an application for a CBO. However, failure to do so will not lead automatically to unfairness or render a resulting order invalid.[27]

Proceedings on an application for an order

17.16

The court may consider evidence from both the prosecution and defence,[28] regardless of whether it would have been admissible at trial for the offence(s) of which D has been convicted.[29]

17.17

The court may adjourn proceedings on an application for a CBO, even after sentencing the offender.[30] If the offender does not appear for any adjourned proceedings the court may:

- further adjourn the proceedings;[31]

- issue a warrant for the offender's arrest,[32] providing it is satisfied that D has had adequate notice of the time and place;[33] or

- hear the proceedings in the offender's absence,[34] providing the court is satisfied that the offender has:

---

25   *Abdi* [2017] EWCA Crim 2648, at [15].
26   ABCPA 2014, s 22(7).
27   *Asfi* [2016] EWCA Crim 1236, at [13]–[18].
28   ABCPA 2014, s 23(1).
29   ABCPA 2014, s 23(2).
30   ABCPA 2014, s 23(3).
31   ABCPA 2014, s 23(4)(a).
32   ABCPA 2014, s 23(4)(b).
33   ABCPA 2014, s 23(5).
34   ABCPA 2014, s 23(4)(c).

-   had adequate notice of the time and place of the adjourned proceedings;[35] and

-   been informed that if the offender does not appear for those proceedings the court may hear the proceedings in his or her absence.[36]

The provisions of Chapter 1 of Part 2 of the Youth Justice and Criminal Evidence Act (YJCEA) 1999 concerning special measures' directions in the case of vulnerable and intimidated witnesses applies to CBO proceedings in the magistrates' court or Crown Court[37] as it applies to criminal proceedings,[38] with the following exceptions:[39]

-   YJCEA 1999, s 17(4) to (7);[40]

-   YJCEA 1999, s 21(4C)(e);[41]

-   YJCEA 1999, s 22A;[42]

-   YJCEA 1999, s 27(10);[43]

-   YJCEA 1999, s 32.[44]

17.18

Rules of court made under or for the purposes of Chapter 1 of Part 2 of YJCEA 1999 apply to CBO proceedings:

-   to the extent provided by rules of court;[45] and

-   subject to any modifications provided by rules of court.[46]

17.19

Section 47 of the YJCEA 1999 (restrictions on reporting special measures directions etc) applies with any necessary modifications to a direction:

-   under s 19 of that Act as applied by this section;[47]

-   discharging or varying such a direction.[48]

---

35   ABCPA 2014, s 23(6)(a).
36   ABCPA 2014, s 23(6)(b).
37   ABCPA 2014, s 31(5).
38   ABCPA 2014, s 31(1).
39   ABCPA 2014, s 31(1)(a).
40   ABCPA 2014, s 31(2)(a).
41   ABCPA 2014, s 31(2)(b).
42   ABCPA 2014, s 31(2)(c).
43   ABCPA 2014, s 31(2)(d).
44   ABCPA 2014, s 31(2)(e).
45   ABCPA 2014, s 31(3)(a).
46   ABCPA 2014, s 31(3)(b).
47   ABCPA 2014, s 31(4)(a).
48   ABCPA 2014, s 31(4)(b).

17.20

Offences contrary to YJCEA 1999, s 49 committed by publishing any matter or report by an individual apply where special measures are put in place in CBO proceedings. Likewise, s 51 applies, which provides that where such an offence is committed by a body corporate with consent or connivance of an officer, both the officer and the body corporate are liable.[49]

Content of an order

17.21

A CBO:

- prohibits the offender from doing anything described in the order;[50]
- requires the offender to do anything described in the order[51]

for the purpose of preventing the offender from engaging in behaviour that is likely to cause harassment, alarm or distress to any person.

17.22

A CBO that includes a requirement must specify the person who is to be responsible for supervising compliance with the requirement, who may be an individual or an organisation.[52]

17.23

Before including a requirement, the court must receive evidence about its suitability and enforceability from the individual,[53] or an individual representing the organisation[54] who will be specified to supervise compliance.

17.24

Before including two or more requirements, the court must consider their compatibility with each other.[55]

17.25

It is the duty of a person specified to supervise compliance:

---

49   ABCPA 2014, s 31(4).
50   ABCPA 2014, s 22(5)(a).
51   ABCPA 2014, s 22(5)(b).
52   ABCPA 2014, s 24(1).
53   ABCPA 2014, s 24(2)(a).
54   ABCPA 2014, s 24(2)(b).
55   ABCPA 2014, s 24(3).

- to make any necessary arrangements in connection with the requirements for which the person has responsibility (the 'relevant requirements');[56]

- to promote the offender's compliance with the relevant requirements;[57]

- if the person considers that the offender:[58]

  - has complied with all the relevant requirements;[59] or

  - has failed to comply with a relevant requirement,[60]

  to inform the prosecution and the appropriate chief officer of police, being:

  - the chief officer of police for the police area in which it appears to the supervising person that the offender lives;[61] or

  - if it appears to that person that the offender lives in more than one police area, whichever of the relevant chief officers of police that person thinks it most appropriate to inform.[62]

17.26

All CBOs contain the following obligations on D, having effect as requirements of the order:

- D must keep in touch with the supervising person, in accordance with any instructions given by that person from time to time;[63]

- D must notify the person of any change of address.[64]

Acceptable terms

17.27

Case law on the acceptable terms of ASBOs is broadly applicable to CBOs,[65] though it should be noted that ASBOs could only contain prohibitions, whereas CBOs can contain positive requirements, as noted in *DPP v Bulmer*,[66] making the statutory language a little less clear.[67]

---

56 ABCPA 2014, s 24(4)(a).
57 ABCPA 2014, s 24(4)(b).
58 ABCPA 2014, s 24(4)(c).
59 ABCPA 2014, s 24(4)(c)(i).
60 ABCPA 2014, s 24(4)(c)(ii).
61 ABCPA 2014, s 24(5)(a).
62 ABCPA 2014, s 24(5)(b).
63 ABCPA 2014, s 24(6)(a).
64 ABCPA 2014, s 24(6)(b).
65 *DPP v Bulmer*, at [26].
66 *DPP v Bulmer*, at [12].
67 *DPP v Bulmer*, at [21].

17.28

A requirement prohibiting D from being in possession of drugs paraphernalia in public will be unnecessary, and susceptible to quashing on appeal, as possession is insufficient to cause distress – it is the use of such paraphernalia which would cause distress. However, such use would also be a criminal offence in its own right, and thus it is unnecessary to prohibit it in a CBO.[68]

17.29

Similarly, a prohibition on the possession of 'any herbal substance', where D had been convicted of possessing cannabis with intent to supply, exposed D to breach proceedings for the possession of many lawful substances which bore no relation to the indicted offences, and a prohibition on having with him self-sealing bags was also 'patently too wide'.[69]

17.30

It is permissible to include a prohibition on 'congregating in a public place in a group of two or more persons in a manner causing or likely to cause any person to fear for their safety' despite possible practical uncertainties,[70] and such terms have been upheld a number of times.[71]

17.31

Prohibitions and requirements in a CBO must, so far as practicable, avoid:

- any interference with times at which the offender normally works or attends school or any other educational establishment;[72]

- any conflict with the requirements of any other court order or injunction to which D may be subject.[73]

17.32

In *Khan*,[74] the Court of Appeal endorsed the guidance given in relation to ASBOs in the case of *Boness*. These are reproduced in full here for the assistance of practitioners:

'Because an ASBO must obviously be precise and capable of being understood by the offender, a court should ask itself before making an

---

68   *Simsek*, at [17], the Court of Appeal applying the decision in *Briggs* [2009] EWCA Crim 1477, citing para [15], which was a decision on the necessity of conditions of ASBOs.
69   *Simsek*, at [18].
70   *Browne-Morgan*, at [22]–[23].
71   *Boness* [2005] EWCA Crim 2395, at [79]–[80]; and *N v DPP* [2007] EWHC 883 (Admin), at [9]–[10].
72   ABCPA 2014, s 22(9)(a).
73   ABCPA 2014, s 22(9)(b).
74   [2018] EWCA Crim 1472, at [14]–[15].

order: "Are the terms of this order clear so that the offender will know precisely what it is that he is prohibited from doing?"[75]

17.33

The judgment then sets out further guidance on both the drafting and content of terms:

'[21] Home Office guidance suggests that prohibitions, should amongst other things:

- be reasonable and proportionate;

- be realistic and practical;

- be in terms which make it easy to determine and prosecute a breach.

[22] In the report of the working group set up under Thomas LJ there is a section which identifies elements of best practice adopted within the courts when dealing with the terms of an ASBO. Included amongst these elements are:

- the prohibition should be capable of being easily understood by the defendant;

- the condition should be enforceable in the sense that it should allow a breach to be readily identified and capable of being proved;

- exclusion zones should be clearly delineated with the use of clearly marked maps;

- individuals whom the defendant is prohibited from contacting or associating with should be clearly identified;

- in the case of a foreign national, consideration should be given to the need for the order to be translated.

[23] The report of the working group also provides examples of general prohibitions imposed by the courts which in their view were specific and enforceable, and could be incorporated in ASBOs in order to protect persons from a wide range of anti-social behaviour. These include conditions prohibiting the offender from:

- living anywhere other than a specified address without the permission of a nominated person;

---

75   *Boness*, at [19].

- entering an area edged in red on the attached map including both footways of any road which forms the boundary area;

- visiting a named individual unless accompanied by a parent or legal guardian;

- associating with a named individual in a public place;

- leaving his home between certain hours except in the case of emergency etc.'[76]

17.34

In *Khan*, the Court of Appeal observed that while a nationwide order or one of wide geographical extent might well be disproportionate if the restriction is a broad one, it might more readily be justified when the only prohibition is against associating in public with a named individual who is not a member of D's family.[77]

Duration

17.35

The duration of a CBO will depend upon the age of the defendant.

17.36

Where the CBO is made before D has reached 18, it must be for a fixed period of:

- not less than one year; and

- not more than three years.

17.37

Where D has reached 18 when the CBO is made, it must be for:

- a fixed period of not less than two years; or

- an indefinite period (so that the order has effect until further order).

17.38

A CBO must specify the period ('the order period') for which it has effect.

---

76   *Boness*, at [21]–[23].
77   *Khan*, at [23].

17.39

A CBO takes effect on the day it is made. If, on the day a new CBO is made the offender is subject to an existing CBO, the new order may be made so as to take effect on the day on which the existing order ceases to have effect.

17.40

A CBO may specify periods for which particular prohibitions or requirements have effect.

17.41

The level and number of repetitions of any conduct will influence the appropriate duration of such an order.[78]

Variation or discharge

17.42

A CBO may be varied or discharged by the court which made it on the application of:

- D;[79] or

- the prosecution.[80]

17.43

If an application by either D[81] or the prosecution[82] is dismissed, that party may make no further application without the consent of the court,[83] or the other party.[84]

17.44

The power to vary an order includes power to include an additional prohibition or requirement in the order, subject to the provisions of ABCPA 2014, s 24,[85] or to extend the period for which a prohibition or requirement has effect.[86]

---

78   *Janes*, at [20].
79   ABCPA 2014, s 27(1)(a).
80   ABCPA 2014, s 27(1)(b).
81   ABCPA 2014, s 27(2).
82   ABCPA 2014, s 27(3).
83   ABCPA 2014, s 27(2)(a), (b).
84   ABCPA 2014, ss 27(2)(b), 27(3)(b).
85   ABCPA 2014, s 27(5).
86   ABCPA 2014, s 27(4).

17.45

Where a CBO is made by a magistrates' court, the references in ABCPA 2014, s 27 to the court which made the order include a reference to any magistrates' court acting in the same local justice area as that court.[87]

The Crown Court does not have the power to vary a CBO made by a magistrates' court when the Crown Court is sentencing D for breach of the CBO.[88] Section 27(1) deals exclusively with variation and discharge of such orders and is clear that those procedures can only be undertaken by the court that made the CBO.[89] The Court was also clear that any attempt to use s 66 of the Courts Act 2003 for the Crown Court judge to sit as a District Judge to achieve that end would have been invalid, as that did not make the judge sitting in the Crown Court the magistrates' court which made the order or another in the same local justice area.[90]

Youths

17.46

The prosecution must find out the views of the local youth offending team[91] before applying for a CBO against a D who is under 18 on the date of application.[92]

17.47

Where a CBO is made against a D under 18,[93] s 39 of the Children and Young Persons Act 1933 applies (power to prohibit publication of certain matters),[94] but s 49 of that Act does not (restrictions on reports of proceedings in which children and young persons are concerned).[95]

---

87   ABCPA 2014, s 27(6).
88   *Potter* [2019] EWCA Crim 461.
89   *Potter*, at [5].
90   *Potter*, at [6].
91   Defined in ABCPA 2014, s 22(10) – (a) the youth offending team in whose area it appears to the prosecution that D lives, or (b) if it appears to the prosecution that D lives in more than one such area, whichever one or more of the relevant youth offending teams the prosecution thinks appropriate.
92   ABCPA 2014, s 22(8).
93   ABCPA 2014, s 23(7).
94   ABCPA 2014, s 23(8)(b).
95   ABCPA 2014, s 23(8)(a).

Review of orders

17.48

If D subject to a CBO will be under 18 at the end of a review period,[96] and the term of the order runs until the end of that period or beyond,[97] and the order is not discharged before the end of that period,[98] a review of the operation of the order must be carried out before the end of that period.

17.49

The 'review periods' are:

- the period of 12 months beginning with:

    - the day on which the CBO takes effect;[99] or

    - if during that period the order is varied under ABCPA 2014, s 27, the day on which it is varied (or most recently varied, if the order is varied more than once);[100]

- a period of 12 months beginning with:

    - the day after the end of the previous review period;[101] or

    - if during that period of 12 months the order is varied under s 27, the day on which it is varied (or most recently varied, if the order is varied more than once).[102]

17.50

A review under ABCPA 2014, s 28 is to be carried out by the chief officer of police for the police area in which the offender lives or appears to be living.[103] The chief officer may invite the participation in the review of any other person or body.[104]

17.51

The chief officer and council for the local government area in which D lives or appears to be living must cooperate in the carrying out of the review.[105] 'Local government area' means:

---

96   ABCPA 2014, s 28(1)(a).
97   ABCPA 2014, s 28(1)(b).
98   ABCPA 2014, s 28(1)(c).
99   ABCPA 2014, s 28(2)(a)(i).
100 ABCPA 2014, s 28(2)(a)(ii).
101 ABCPA 2014, s 28(2)(b)(i).
102 ABCPA 2014, s 28(2)(b)(ii).
103 ABCPA 2014, s 29(1).
104 ABCPA 2014, s 29(3).
105 ABCPA 2014, s 29(2).

- in relation to England, a district or London borough, the City of London, the Isle of Wight and the Isles of Scilly (the council for Inner and Middle Temples is the Common Council of the City of London);[106]

- in relation to Wales, a county or a county borough.[107]

17.52

A review under ABCPA 2014, s 28 must include consideration of:

- the extent to which the offender has complied with the order;[108]

- the adequacy of any support available to the offender to help him or her comply with it;[109]

- any matters relevant to the question whether an application should be made for the order to be varied or discharged.[110]

17.53

Those carrying out or participating in a review under this section must have regard to any relevant guidance issued by the Secretary of State under ABCPA 2014, s 32 when considering:

- how the review should be carried out;[111]

- what particular matters the review should deal with;[112]

- what action (if any) it would be appropriate to take as a result of the findings of the review.[113]

Interim CBOs

17.54

Where a court adjourns the hearing of an application for a CBO,[114] it may make an interim CBO that lasts until the final hearing of the application or until further order if the court thinks it just to do so.[115]

---

106 ABCPA 2014, s 28(4)(a).
107 ABCPA 2014, s 28(4)(b).
108 ABCPA 2014, s 28(3)(a).
109 ABCPA 2014, s 28(3)(b).
110 ABCPA 2014, s 28(3)(c).
111 ABCPA 2014, s 38(4)(a).
112 ABCPA 2014, s 38(4)(b).
113 ABCPA 2014, s 38(4)(c).
114 ABCPA 2014, s 26(1).
115 ABCPA 2014, s 26(2).

17.55

A court has the same powers as when making a full CBO,[116] except that ABCPA 2014, s 22(6)–(8) and s 25(3)–(5) do not apply in relation to the making of an interim order.[117]

Breach

17.56

A person who without reasonable excuse:

- does anything they are prohibited from doing by a CBO;[118] or

- fails to do anything they are required to do by a CBO,[119]

commits an offence.

17.57

A person guilty of breaching a CBO is liable:

- on summary conviction, to imprisonment for a period not exceeding six months or to a fine, or to both;[120]

- on conviction on indictment, to imprisonment for a period not exceeding five years or to a fine, or to both.[121]

17.58

A conditional discharge cannot be imposed for breach of a CBO.[122]

17.59

In proceedings for a breach offence, a copy of the original CBO, certified by the proper officer of the court which made it, is admissible as evidence of its having been made and of its contents to the same extent that oral evidence of those things is admissible in those proceedings.[123]

---

116 ABCPA 2014, s 26(4).
117 ABCPA 2014, s 26(3).
118 ABCPA 2014, s 30(1)(a).
119 ABCPA 2014, s 30(1)(b).
120 ABCPA 2014, s 30(2)(a).
121 ABCPA 2014, s 30(2)(b).
122 ABCPA 2014, s 30(3).
123 ABCPA 2014, s 30(4).

17.60

Where breach proceedings are brought against a D under 18,[124] ABCPA 2014, s 45 applies (restrictions on reports of proceedings in which children and young persons are concerned),[125] and if the court exercises its power to give a direction under that section it must give its reasons for doing so.[126]

17.61

Breaching a CBO often involves behaviour that is criminal in its own right, and a sentence for breach of a CBO will usually be consecutive to any other sentence imposed at the same time for criminality which occurred at or around the time of the breach.[127] Where the breach has followed a matter of days after the CBO was made, where the CBO was made to try to direct D away from criminal associates, that will be significant aggravation.[128] Overlap between the two, however, for example where behaviour that is inseparable from the commission of the new offence is itself a breach of a CBO, will need to be taken into account when sentencing, to respect totality.[129]

17.62

Section 49 of the Children and Young Persons Act 1933 does not apply to breach proceedings (restrictions on reports of proceedings in which children and young persons are concerned).[130]

---

124 ABCPA 2014, s 23(7).
125 ABCPA 2014, s 30(5)(b).
126 ABCPA 2014, s 30(6).
127 *Ezeh* [2017] EWCA Crim 1766, at [18].
128 *Reilly* [2017] EWCA Crim 2237, at [9].
129 *Moriarty* [2018] EWCA Crim 1590, at [19].
130 ABCPA 2014, s 30(5)(a).

PART 2

ORDERS ON ACQUITTAL/ AVAILABLE WITHOUT NEED FOR CONVICTION

18 Defence Costs Orders

18.01

The primary legislation for defence costs orders is s 16 of the Prosecution of Offences Act (POA) 1985. The statutory provisions are supplemented by the Costs in Criminal Cases (General) Regulations 1986,[1] the Practice Direction (Costs in Criminal Proceedings) 2015,[2] and Part 45 of the Criminal Procedure Rules. Detailed expositions on costs can be found in *Archbold* and dedicated texts. The intention of this chapter is to give practitioners a broad overview of the powers to award costs, as opposed to an in-depth examination of the specific figures and calculations.

Magistrates' court

18.02

Where an information laid before a magistrate for any area, charging any person with an offence, is not proceeded with,[3] or a magistrates' court dealing summarily with an offence dismisses the information,[4] that court or, where the information is not proceeded with, a magistrates' court for that area, may make an order in favour of the accused for payment to be made out of central funds in respect of his/her costs (a 'defendant's costs order' (DCO)).

Crown Court

18.03

Where a defendant (D) is not tried for an offence for which s/he has been indicted or sent for trial,[5] or D is tried on indictment and acquitted on any count on the indictment, the Crown Court may make a DCO in favour of the accused.[6]

---

1   SI 1986/1335.
2   [2015] EWCA Crim 1568.
3   POA 1985, s 16(1)(a).
4   POA 1985, s 16(1)(c).
5   POA 1985, s 16(2)(a).
6   POA 1985, s 16(2)(b).

18.04

Where D is convicted of an offence by a magistrates' court and appeals to the Crown Court as of right under s 108 of the Magistrates' Courts Act (MCA) 1980, and on appeal his/her conviction is set aside;[7] or a less severe punishment is imposed,[8] the Crown Court may make a DCO in favour of the accused.

Retrials

18.05

Where a person being retried is acquitted at retrial (presumably in either the magistrates' court or Crown Court; POA 1985, s 16(11) does not specify), the costs which may be ordered to be paid out of central funds shall include:

- any costs which, at the original trial, could have been ordered to be so paid under this section if s/he had been acquitted;[9] and

- if no order was made under this section in respect of his/her expenses on appeal, any sums for the payment of which such an order could have been made.[10]

Court of Appeal

18.06

The Court of Appeal may make a DCO where it:

- allows an appeal under Part I of the Criminal Appeal Act 1968 against:

  - conviction;[11]

  - a verdict of not guilty by reason of insanity;[12] or

  - a finding under the Criminal Procedure (Insanity) Act 1964 that the appellant is under a disability, or that s/he did the act or made the omission charged against him;[13]

- directs under s 8(1B) of the Criminal Appeal Act 1968 the entry of a judgment and verdict of acquittal;[14]

- on an appeal against conviction under that Part against conviction:

---

7   POA 1985, s 16(3)(a).
8   POA 1985, s 16(3)(b).
9   POA 1985, s 16(11)(a).
10   POA 1985, s 16(11)(b).
11   POA 1985, s 16(4)(a)(i).
12   POA 1985, s 16(4)(a)(ii).
13   POA 1985, s 16(4)(a)(iii).
14   POA 1985, s 16(4)(aa).

- — substitutes a verdict of guilty of another offence;[15]

- — in a case where a special verdict has been found, orders a different conclusion on the effect of that verdict to be recorded;[16] or

- — is of the opinion that the case falls within s 6(1)(a) or (b) of that Act (cases where the court substitutes a finding of insanity or unfitness to plead);[17]

- on an appeal against sentence under that Part, exercises its powers under s 11(3) of that Act (powers where the Court considers that the appellant should be sentenced differently for an offence for which he was dealt with by the court below);[18]

- allows, to any extent, an appeal under s 16A of that Act (appeal against order made in cases of insanity or unfitness to plead);[19]

- hears an appeal under s 9(11) of the Criminal Justice Act 1987, s 35(1) of the Criminal Procedure and Investigations Act 1996, or a prosecution appeal under Part 9 of the Criminal Justice Act 2003 (appeals against orders or rulings at preparatory hearings).[20]

Divisional Court/leave to appeal to Supreme Court/ hearings before the Supreme Court

18.07

A DCO may be made when:

- any proceedings in a criminal cause or matter are determined before a Divisional Court of the Queen's Bench Division;[21]

- the Supreme Court determines an appeal, or application for leave to appeal, from such a Divisional Court in a criminal cause or matter;[22]

- the Court of Appeal determines an application for leave to appeal to the Supreme Court under Part II of the Criminal Appeal Act 1968;[23] or

- the Supreme Court determines an appeal, or application for leave to appeal, under Part II of that Act.[24]

---

15   POA 1985, s 16(4)(b)(i).
16   POA 1985, s 16(4)(b)(ii).
17   POA 1985, s 16(4)(b)(iii).
18   POA 1985, s 16(4)(c).
19   POA 1985, s 16(4)(d).
20   POA 1985, s 16(4A).
21   POA 1985, s 16(5)(a).
22   POA 1985, s 16(5)(b).
23   POA 1985, s 16(5)(c).
24   POA 1985, s 16(5)(d).

Amount

18.08

The amount for which DCOs will be made has reduced radically since the Legal Aid, Sentencing and Punishment of Offenders Act (LASPOA) 2012. It means that the content of the next two paragraphs is subject to the limits set out in s 16A[25] (see 18.12), and the regulations bringing Part II of the 1985 Act into effect.[26]

18.09

A DCO orders payment out of central funds, to the person in whose favour the order is made, of such amount as the court considers reasonably sufficient to compensate him/her for any expenses properly incurred by him/her in the proceedings.[27]

18.10

Where the court considers that there are circumstances that make it inappropriate for the accused to recover the full amount, a DCO must be for the payment out of central funds of the lesser amount the court considers just and reasonable.[28]

18.11

Where the DCO is being made because an information laid is not proceeded with,[29] or because D is not tried for an offence for which s/he was indicted,[30] the words 'in the proceedings' are to be considered to mean 'in or about the defence'.[31]

Section 16A – limits from LASPOA 2012

18.12

LASPOA 2012 seriously curtailed a defendant's right to recover their 'legal costs', as set out above. These are defined as 'fees, charges, disbursements and other amounts payable in respect of advocacy services[32] or litigation services[33] including, in particular, expert witness costs.[34],[35]

---

25   POA 1985, s 16(6B)(a).
26   POA 1985, s 16(6B)(b).
27   POA 1985, s 16(6).
28   POA 1985, s 16(6A).
29   POA 1985, s 16(1)(a).
30   POA 1985, s 16(2)(a).
31   POA 1985, s 16(10).
32   Defined in POA 1985, s 16A(10) as any services which it would be reasonable to expect a person who is exercising, or contemplating exercising, a right of audience in relation to any proceedings, or contemplated proceedings, to provide.
33   Defined in POA 1985, s 16A(10) as amounts payable in respect of the services of an expert witness, including amounts payable in connection with attendance by the witness at court or elsewhere.
34   Defined in POA 1985, s 16A(10) as any services which it would be reasonable to expect a person who is exercising, or contemplating exercising, a right to conduct litigation in relation to proceedings, or contemplated proceedings, to provide.
35   POA 1985, s 16A(10).

18.13

What this means in effect is that costs like travel expenses remain recoverable as before,[36] but the extent to which defendants can reclaim expenses they have incurred in instructing a legal team privately have become much stricter. This has been the subject of much commentary in both the legal and wider press.[37] As illustrated in the exchange between counsel for the appellant and Elias LJ in *Ritchie*:[38] an appellant who privately-funds counsel for an appeal against sentence in the Court of Appeal, even where the appeal is successful, is not permitted to make any application for legal costs.[39]

18.14

This legislation has been challenged for incompatibility with Article 6 of the European Convention on Human Rights (ECHR) in *R (Henderson) v Secretary of State for Justice*.[40] In that case, D had been acquitted at a retrial in the Crown Court, the first jury having been hung. He had spent around £70,000 instructing solicitors and counsel. The judge trying the case refused an application for a DCO at the end of the trial on the basis that he had no jurisdiction to make such an order in light of Sch 7 to LASPOA 2012. No challenge could be made to that decision as it was an exercise of his jurisdiction in matters relating to trial on indictment (Senior Courts Act (SCA) 1981, s 29(3) as applied in *In Re Sampson*[41]).

18.15

The facts to which this challenge related occurred before Condition D (see 18.17) had been added as a qualifying factor in respect of legal costs, though by the time the application for judicial review was heard, Condition D was in place.[42] However, it is important to note that Condition D will not assist a defendant who did not apply for Legal Aid, and/or who was eligible but preferred to pay privately to secure solicitors or counsel of his choice, for example. The claimant in *Henderson* was such a person.[43] He would thus still not be permitted a DCO for any costs even with Condition D in place, as Condition D requires that D has applied for, but been refused, Legal Aid on the basis of their financial circumstances.

---

36 *Evans v Serious Fraud Office* [2015] EWHC 263 (QBD), at [86].
37 Eg writings by Nigel Evans MP on the cost of refuting false allegations made against him: https://www.theguardian.com/law/2018/dec/27/its-completely-wrong-falsely-accused-tory-mp-attacks-legal-aid-cuts.
38 *Ritchie* [2014] EWCA Crim 2114.
39 *Ritchie*, at [24]–[25].
40 [2015] EWHC 130 (Admin).
41 [1987] 1 WLR 194.
42 *Henderson*, at [14]–[15].
43 *Henderson*, at [16].

18.16

The Court held that there was no breach of Article 6 rights, as the unavailability of a DCO in those circumstances did not compromise the requirement of Article 6(3)(c) – that D has a right to defend him- or herself in person or through legal assistance of his/her own choosing; or if s/he has insufficient means to do so, to be given free legal assistance when the interests of justice so require.[44] In practical terms, therefore, all those facing criminal proceedings would be well-advised to make an application for Legal Aid, even where solicitors think it very likely to fail, on the basis that it means Condition D is capable of being fulfilled if they are later acquitted or the proceedings discontinued.

18.17

POA 1985, s 16A(1) provides that a DCO may not require the payment out of central funds of an amount that includes an amount in respect of the accused's legal costs, unless one of the following conditions is fulfilled:[45]

(1)   Condition A:

D is an individual and the order is made:

- by a magistrates' court when an information has not been proceeded with, or the information summarily dismissed (s 16(1));[46]

- by the Crown Court hearing an appeal from the magistrates' court (s 16(3));[47] or

- by the Court of Appeal having allowed an appeal against a verdict of not guilty by reason of insanity; a finding that the appellant is under a disability, or that s/he did the act or made the omission charged against them, or allows an appeal, to any extent, against an order made in cases of insanity or unfitness to plead (s 16(4)(a)(ii), (iii) or (d)).[48]

(2)   Condition B:

D is an individual and the legal costs were incurred in proceedings in a magistrates' court,[49] or on an appeal to the Crown Court from the magistrates' court.[50]

(3)   Condition C:

Legal costs were incurred in proceedings in the Supreme Court.[51]

---

44   *Henderson,* at [24].
45   POA 1985, s 16A(2).
46   POA 1985, s 16A(3)(a).
47   POA 1985, s 16A(3)(b).
48   POA 1985, s 16A(3)(c).
49   POA 1985, s 16A(4)(a).
50   POA 1985, s 16A(4)(b).
51   POA 1985, s 16A(5).

This exception cannot be removed or limited by regulations made under s 16A(7).

(4)   Condition D:

- the accused is an individual;[52]

- the order is made under s 16(2);[53]

- the legal costs were incurred in relevant Crown Court proceedings,[54] as defined by s 16A(11):

    - in respect of an offence for which the accused has been sent by a magistrates' court to the Crown Court for trial;

    - relating to an offence in respect of which a bill of indictment has been preferred by virtue of s 2(2)(b) of the Administration of Justice (Miscellaneous Provisions) Act 1933;

    - following an order by the Court of Appeal or the Supreme Court for a retrial;

    and

- the Director of Legal Aid Casework has made a determination of financial ineligibility (under LASPOA 2012, s 21)[55] in relation to the accused and those proceedings (and Condition D continues to be met if the determination is withdrawn).

18.18

Where a court makes a DCO requiring the payment out of central funds of an amount that includes an amount in respect of legal costs, the order must include a statement to that effect.[56]

18.19

Where, in a DCO, a court fixes an amount to be paid out of central funds that includes an amount in respect of legal costs incurred in proceedings in a court other than the Supreme Court, the latter amount must not exceed an amount specified by regulations made by the Lord Chancellor.[57]

---

52   POA 1985, s 16A(5A)(a).
53   POA 1985, s 16A(5A)(b).
54   POA 1985, s 16A(5A)(c).
55   POA 1985, s 16A(11).
56   POA 1985, s 16A(8).
57   POA 1985, s 16A(9) – however, the only regulations made under that section do not specify a figure as the limit.

18.20

When making a DCO, the court must fix the amount to be paid out of central funds in the order if it considers it appropriate to do so and the accused agrees the amount,[58] or if the court has ordered payment of the amount of expenses it considers properly incurred.[59]

18.21

Where the court does not fix the amount to be paid out of central funds in the order:

- it must describe in the order, if it considers it inappropriate for D to recover the full amount of expenses properly incurred by him in the proceedings, the level of consequent reduction to give an amount that the court considers reasonably sufficient to compensate D;[60] and

- the amount must be fixed by means of a determination made by or on behalf of the court in accordance with procedures specified in regulations made by the Lord Chancellor.[61]

Alternative routes to recovery of costs

Senior Courts Act 1981, s 28A

18.22

Where a case has been heard in the High Court (for example, by way of case stated), there is an additional possible route by which a successful appellant may claim their costs. This is s 28A(3) of SCA 1981, which deals with proceedings on a case stated by the magistrates' court or Crown Court. It provides that the High Court shall hear and determine the question arising on the case (or the case as amended) and shall:

- reverse, affirm or amend the determination in respect of which the case has been stated;[62] or

- remit the matter to the magistrates' court, or the Crown Court, with the opinion of the High Court;[63] and

- may make such other order in relation to the matter (including as to costs) as it thinks fit.

---

58 POA 1985, s 16(6C)(a).
59 POA 1985, s 16(6C)(b).
60 POA 1985, s 16(6D)(a).
61 POA 1985, s 16(6D)(b) – a reference to Costs in Criminal Cases (General) Regulations 1986, reg 7.
62 SCA 1981, s 28A(3)(a).
63 SCA 1981, s 28A(3)(b).

18.23

Practitioners should note that the Civil Procedure Rules govern all matters in the High Court, including criminal case stated hearings. Thus practitioners will need to abide by requirements for the service of skeletons/schedules within a given time frame as required by those Rules.

18.24

The Court in *Lord Howard of Lympne v DPP*,[64] held that s 28A of SCA 1981 was part of the 'civil' costs regime, and not the 'criminal' costs regime, which was found under POA 1985, ss 16 and 16A. The civil costs regime would only apply to criminal matters where there were 'exceptional circumstances'.[65] There were none in Lord Howard's case – it being a simple case stated with some 'procedural skirmishes' along the way,[66] and therefore the appellant was not entitled to recover any costs at all.

18.25

It should be highlighted, however, that there will sometimes be situations where a case that has been heard in the magistrates' court will nonetheless fulfil the exceptional circumstances needed to bring it under the civil costs regime of SCA 1981.

18.26

An example is the case of *Murphy v Media Protection Services Ltd*.[67] This was a private prosecution brought by a company retained by the FA Premier League to prosecute publicans who showed Sky broadcasts of Premier League matches without a licence. The offence for which D was prosecuted was one contrary to s 297(1) of the Copyright, Designs and Patents Act 1988. This is a summary-only, fineable-only offence. After her conviction before the magistrates, which was upheld on appeal, D appealed by way of case stated, and sought a reference to the European Court of Justice on free movement principles. Following that ruling, D succeeded in her appeal by way of case stated.

18.27

The Divisional Court held that these were exceptional circumstances.[68] They arose because the prosecution was to protect a private interest (the financial interest of the FA Premier League).[69] Furthermore, it was a test case and required substantial resources – it took a form reminiscent of a hearing in the Chancery

---

64   [2018] EWHC 100 (Admin).
65   *Lord Howard*, at [26]–[27] and [34]–[35].
66   *Lord Howard*, at [34].
67   [2012] EWHC 529 (Admin).
68   *Murphy*, at [15]–[19].
69   *Murphy*, at [17].

Division or Civil Division of the Court of Appeal – far away from the usual appeal against conviction for a summary offence.[70]

18.28

However, it cannot simply be assumed that because a case was originally brought under a particular section, or concerned a particular issue, that all cases of that type will then fall under the civil costs regime. *Hull and Holderness Magistrates' Court v Darroch*,[71] a case concerning the same underlying legislative regime, was held by the Divisional Court not to be an exceptional case, and thus an order under SCA 1981, s 28A was refused, on the bases that:[72]

'a) the only costs for our consideration are the costs below;

b) the proceedings below were not so unusual as to be exceptional. The hearing was a short one, lasting two days (followed by a short oral judgment);

c) although points of law were raised, the matter was conducted like many prosecutions with junior counsel on both sides. The mere fact that points of European law were raised did not, without more, take a case into the category of being an "exceptional" case or a "test" case. There was no reference to the Court of Justice of the European Union (CJEU);

d) Murphy, by contrast, was undoubtedly a "test case". Indeed it determined the copyright subsistence/"exclusive rights" issue sought to be re-argued by the Applicants (see paragraphs 43 and 44 of *Karen Murphy v Media Protection Services Ltd* [2007] EWHC 3091 (Admin));

e) whilst it might be said that the full appeal would have raised novel issues, that appeal has never proceeded. The costs of such an appeal are not before us;

e) equally, the fact that a non-party has a strong financial interest in the prosecution does not make it an "exceptional" situation entitling a defendant to secure a costs order against it. There was in addition a public interest being served (in terms of upholding and enforcing the criminal law).'

18.29

Darroch was appealed to the Court of Appeal (Civil Division), which held that it had no jurisdiction to hear the appeal, as an appeal from a case stated in the High Court lay to the Supreme Court, not the Court of Appeal.[73]

---

70 *Murphy*, at [15].
71 [2014] EWHC 4184 (Admin).
72 *Darroch*, (HC) at [39].
73 [2016] EWCA Civ 1220, at [22].

18.30

However, Sir Brian Leveson (PQBD), Hallett and Burnett LJJ went on to consider the merits of the case *obiter*. They disagreed with Stanley Burnton LJ's decision in *Murphy* that the Divisional Court did have power to make an order in respect of costs below:[74]

> 'In my judgment s 51 of the 1981 Act does not empower the High Court, on an appeal by way of case stated, or a claim for judicial review that seeks to quash convictions, to make a civil costs order in respect of costs incurred in the underlying criminal proceedings in the Crown Court or Magistrates' Court [...] the conclusion which confirmed the power of the High Court proceeded on a concession relating to s 51. In my view that concession was wrongly made.'

18.31

Applying *Wright v Bennett*,[75] his Lordship concluded that the term 'of and incidental to' does not include the proceedings from which an appeal is brought.[76]

Magistrates' Courts Act 1980, s 64

18.32

Section 64 of the MCA 1980 provides a very narrow power applicable only to magistrates' court proceedings, subject to any other Act enabling a magistrates' court to order a successful party to pay the other party's costs.[77] It applies where a claim was contested and failed, as opposed to s 52 of the Courts Act 1971 (see 18.59) which applies where a claim was made and 'not proceeded with'.[78] However, both sections apply materially identical criteria, and it can be assumed that case law principles relating to one relate equally to the other.

18.33

On hearing a complaint, a magistrates' court shall have power in its discretion to make such order as to costs:

- on making the order for which the complaint is made, to be paid by the defendant to the complainant;[79]

---

74   *Darroch,* (CA) at [25]–[26].
75   [1948] 1 KB 601 – this case concerned an earlier version of the same provision.
76   *Wright v Bennett,* at [29].
77   MCA 1980, s 64(5)
78   *Chief Constable of Warwickshire v MT* [2015] EWHC 2303 (Admin).
79   MCA 1980, s 64(1)(a).

- on dismissing the complaint, to be paid by the complainant to the defendant;[80]

as it thinks just and reasonable; but if the complaint is for an order for the variation of an order for the periodic payment of money, or for the enforcement of such an order, the court may, whatever adjudication it makes, order either party to pay the whole or any part of the other's costs.[81]

18.34

The Divisional Court has held that this is a wide power, and the courts would take a wide view of what constituted a complaint. For example, dismissal of an application for a closure order possessed the necessary characteristics and the successful D should have had her costs awarded against the police who applied for the order.[82]

Amount

18.35

The amount of any sum ordered to be paid shall be specified in the order, or order of dismissal, as the case may be.[83] The party claiming the costs must have sufficient material to present to the court to justify the sum being claimed.[84] The discretion of the magistrates or District Judge is a wide one, however, and there is no need to adjourn or refer to a taxing master, even in cases where the sum may be significant (such as in environmental cases).[85] The then-Judge J ruled that to set out a rigid framework to guide the discretion would not be appropriate.[86] There is no requirement that costs follow the event.[87] There is no power under MCA 1980, s 64 to award costs to a litigant in person for loss of time and trouble, even where they are self-employed and, in preparing the case, have consequently lost earnings.[88]

18.36

Regard must be had to the means of any individual against whom costs are awarded, otherwise the order will be susceptible to quashing.[89]

---

80 MCA 1980, s 64(1)(b).
81 MCA 1980, s 64(1)(b).
82 *R (Taylor) v Commissioner of Police for the Metropolis* [2009] EWHC 264 (Admin), at [52].
83 MCA 1980, s 64(2).
84 *R v West London Magistrates Court, ex p Kyprianou* [1993] 4 WLUK 174.
85 *R v Southend Stipendiary Magistrate, ex p Rochford DC* [1995] Env LR 1, at 5.
86 *Rochford DC*, at 6.
87 *Bradford MDC v Booth* (2000) 164 JP 485.
88 *North Yorkshire CC v Kind* [2000] 11 WLUK 373 (QBD – Admin).
89 *Carney v North Lincolnshire Council* [2016] EWHC 3726 (Admin).

Against which party?

18.37

In *Bradford MDC v Booth*,[90] Lord Bingham held that the proper approach to costs questions can be summarised in three propositions:[91]

'1.　Section 64(1) confers a discretion upon a magistrates' court to make such order as to costs as it thinks just and reasonable. That provision applies both to the quantum of the costs (if any) to be paid, but also as to the party (if any) which should pay them.

2.　What the court will think just and reasonable will depend on all the relevant facts and circumstances of the case before the court. The court may think it just and reasonable that costs should follow the event, but need not think so in all cases covered by the subsection.

3.　Where a complainant has successfully challenged before justices an administrative decision made by a police or regulatory authority acting honestly, reasonably, properly and on grounds that reasonably appeared to be sound, in exercise of its public duty, the court should consider, in addition to any other relevant fact or circumstances, both (i) the financial prejudice to the particular complainant in the particular circumstances if an order for costs is not made in his favour; and (ii) the need to encourage public authorities to make and stand by honest, reasonable and apparently sound administrative decisions made in the public interest without fear of exposure to undue financial prejudice if the decision is successfully challenged.'

18.38

The court must consider that if costs merely followed the event then there would be a chilling effect on public authorities.[92]

18.39

It must be noted, however, that it has been held that the judgment in *Booth* does not set out a checklist or test – instead it set out factors which the court should take into account. Where a police force has acted reasonably in detaining cash under the civil power in s 298 of the Proceeds of Crime (POCA) Act 2002, it will not be penalised in costs if the application is not ultimately successful.[93]

90　(2000) 164 JP 485.
91　*Booth*, at [23].
92　*R (Qin) v Commissioner of Police for the Metropolis* [2017] EWHC 2750 (Admin).
93　*R (Perinpanathan) v Westminster Magistrates Court* [2010] EWCA Civ 40.

Relying on an offence of which D has been acquitted will not be acting reasonably.[94]

18.40

Where the appellate court finds, as in *Powell*,[95] that the magistrates did not exercise their discretion properly in declining an appellant's application for costs the correct course is to remit the case to the magistrates for them to award costs in a just and reasonable amount.[96] Where the magistrates applied the wrong test by importing the qualifier 'necessarily' into its analysis of the local authority's conduct – 'we were not satisfied that the local authority had necessarily acted honestly, reasonably and properly in suspending the respondent's private hire licence'[97] – any resulting costs order would be quashed.[98]

18.41

Similarly, where the magistrates had regard to an irrelevant consideration in ordering which party was to pay costs, the order would be quashed.[99] Withholding D's costs because on a series of hypothetical facts he might have lost the appeal also led to the order being quashed.[100]

18.42

Where D has made an application to the court for return of property from the police under s 1(1) of the Police Property Act 1897 (as may happen where property has been forfeited, see 1.32) the magistrates have power to award costs on a complaint, which was the proper procedure, as opposed to an application.[101] Although the costs awarded against the police were not quashed, as the order made was within the court's jurisdiction, the court expressed 'a considerable degree of unease' that an order for costs should have been made against the police, as they have an exceptional role in such cases as custodians of the property in issue.[102] There is no power to make an order for costs against the police on a s 1(1) complaint if the matter has been determined in the police's favour.[103]

---

94   *Chief Constable of Sussex v Taylor* [2013] EWHC 1616 (Admin).
95   *Powell v Chief Executive of the City and County of Swansea* [2003] EWHC 2185 (Admin).
96   *Powell*, at [10]–[11].
97   *Milton Keynes Council v Edwards* [2004] EWHC 267 (Admin).
98   *Edwards*, at [15]–[17] and [24]–[26].
99   *R (Bristol Council) v Bristol Magistrates' Court* [2009] EWHC 625 (Admin).
100 *Ware v Hackney LBC* [2009] EWHC 1698 (Admin).
101 *R v Uxbridge Justices, ex p Commissioner of Police of the Metropolis* [1981] QB 829.
102 *R v Uxbridge Justices, ex p Commissioner of Police of the Metropolis*, at 848, confirmed by *R v Maidstone Magistrates' Court, ex p Knight* [2000] 6 WLUK 422 (QBD).
103 *R (Chief Constable of Northamptonshire) v Daventry Justices* [2001] EWHC 446 (Admin).

18.43

Similarly, a hearing following a complaint under MCA 1980, s 115 regarding a breach of the peace did not remove the magistrates' powers to make an order for costs.[104]

18.44

When deciding whether to award costs it is proper for a court to consider that D had to defend an unsubstantiated allegation, and in determining the amount it was proper to take into account that the prosecutor was a public authority.[105]

18.45

If D had brought the proceedings on themselves through their conduct, then even if they were successful, it could be proper to make an order against the successful party for costs.[106]

18.46

If a local authority has served a notice that it then wishes to withdraw on the day of hearing, the correct course is for the magistrates to quash the notice, and then consider whether to award the defendant their costs. For the correct procedure to be otherwise would mean that a local authority could undermine the statutory discretion to award costs by depriving D of a hearing.[107]

18.47

Where the Serious and Organised Crime Agency (SOCA – the forerunner to the National Crime Agency) had brought forfeiture proceedings under POCA 2002, s 298 and interested parties who claimed ownership of the money joined the proceedings under s 301, those interested parties became complainants within the meaning of MCA 1980, s 64 and could have costs awarded in their favour.[108]

Costs do not follow the event

18.48

If a local authority has acted conscientiously and reasonably in a licensing case, but the defendant has succeeded in part, then it will not be appropriate to order any costs against the local authority – any suggestion that the magistrates have erroneously applied the civil 'costs follow the event' principle may lead to the

---

104 *R v Coventry Magistrates' Court, ex p CPS* (1996) 160 JP 741.
105 *R (Swale BC) v Boulter* [2002] EWHC 2306 (Admin), at [26].
106 *Prasannan v Kensington and Chelsea RLBC* [2010] EWHC 319 (Admin), though this concerned the equivalent power under the Licensing Act 2003 – s 181(2).
107 *Prasannan*, at [23].
108 *R (Doherty) v Westminster Magistrates' Court* [2012] EWHC 2990 (Admin).

quashing of the order.[109] The starting point will be that there is to be no order for costs, providing the prosecuting body has acted reasonably.[110,111]

18.49

Close scrutiny of the local authority's conduct will be required to determine whether it was reasonable: where a District Judge found that the local authority had commenced its process without proper and full consideration of the legal question (in particular, at a late stage of proceedings the local authority had disclosed internal emails showing that it had not been certain of the legal position), but then declined to make an order against the local authority, it was held that he had erred in law.[112]

18.50

Similarly, in a hearing before the Solicitors' Disciplinary Tribunal, the Law Society was exercising a regulatory function, and was thus in a wholly different position to that in ordinary civil litigation. That meant that the starting point was that costs did not follow the event.[113]

18.51

In deciding to whom to award costs, the court must weigh up the need to avoid a chilling effect on public authorities with hardship faced by D.[114] Where the local authority had persisted with its case despite the non-attendance of all complainants at the magistrates' court hearing, it was appropriate for D to be awarded his costs.[115]

18.52

Equally, if the individual has not acted reasonably, for example refusing to meet with the council to discuss a litter problem, instead issuing proceedings, an order for costs against that individual will not be unreasonable.[116] In considering the behaviour of the parties, the court would only take into account events leading up to the bringing of the complaint to the court.[117]

18.53

Section 64 does not permit an award of costs in favour of or against third parties.[118]

---

109 *R (Cambridge City Council) v Alex Nestling Ltd* [2006] EWHC 1374 (Admin), at [13].
110 *Kialka v Home Office* [2015] EWHC 4143 (Admin).
111 *Woods v Sevenoaks DC* [2004] EWHC 1511 (Admin), at [36].
112 *Burdett v Devon County Council* [2016] 1 WLUK 128.
113 *Baxendale-Walker v Law Society* [2007] EWCA Civ 233, at [34].
114 *Luton BC v Zeb* [2014] EWHC 732 (Admin), at [20].
115 *Zeb*, at [21].
116 *Hemming MP v Birmingham City Council* [2015] EWHC 1472 (Admin).
117 *Hemming MP*, at [53]–[54].
118 *Wheeler v Norfolk County Council* [2014] EWHC 2232 (Admin), at [9]–[11].

Reasons

18.54

In *Crawley BC v Attenborough*,[119] the Divisional Court held that MCA 1980, s 64(1) was analogous to s 181 of the Licensing Act 2003, and the same principles applied.[120] Reasons are to be given as to why costs have or have not been awarded, but these need not be lengthy, lest they encourage satellite litigation as to costs.[121] There is no need for the behaviour of the prosecuting body to be unreasonable for costs to be awarded against it.[122]

18.55

If proper reasons for an award of costs are not given then the order will be susceptible to quashing.[123] Providing the basis upon which the decision to order, or not to order, costs was clear, and did not prejudice either party through its economy of expression, the order would be upheld.[124]

Enforcement

18.56

Costs ordered to be paid under MCA 1980, s 64 shall be enforceable as a civil debt.[125]

Appeal

18.57

There can be no appeal against an award of costs – MCA 1980, s 108 expressly omits costs from the scope of an appeal to the Crown Court against sentence. Unless the statute under which the proceedings were brought allowed for specific provisions as to costs, there would be no general right of appeal.[126] A challenge to quantum is a separate issue.

18.58

Where the aggrieved party states a case regarding the award of costs, it must do so within the 21-day period required by MCA 1980, s 111(2) – although the point has not been decided, the Divisional Court has indicated that it is

---

119 [2006] EWHC 1278 (Admin).
120 *Crawley BC v Attenborough*, at [8]
121 *Crawley BC v Attenborough*, at [11]
122 *Crawley BC v Attenborough*, at [13]
123 *Leeds City Council v Leeds District Magistrates* [2013] EWHC 1346 (Admin).
124 *Reigate and Banstead BC v Pawlowski* [2017] EWHC 1764 (Admin), at [34]–[35].
125 MCA 1980, s 64(3).
126 *R v Canterbury Crown Court, ex p Kent County Council* [1994] Env LR 192, at 195–196.

'highly probable' that the High Court does not have the power to extend the 21-day period.[127]

Courts Act 1971, s 52

18.59

Section 52 of the Courts Act (CA) 1971 is formulated in similar terms to MCA 1980, s 64, but applies only where the claim was made and not proceeded with.

18.60

It provides that where a complaint is made to a magistrate but the complaint is not proceeded with, a magistrates' court in that local justice area may make such order as to costs to be paid by the complainant to D as it thinks just and reasonable.[128] The indemnity principle – that no costs would be awarded in favour of a successful party except in respect of costs which the successful party was liable to pay – applies to costs orders made under CA 1971, s 52.[129]

18.61

There is no jurisdiction for the Crown Court to entertain an appeal against costs awarded under this section.[130]

18.62

Similarly to MCA 1980, s 64, CA 1971, s 52 does not follow the civil pattern, in which there is a strong presumption that the discontinuing party would pay the other party's costs. In *Chief Constable of Warwickshire Police v MT*,[131] the Divisional Court made clear that when a regulatory function was being exercised, a costs order would generally only be made on a withdrawal if the regulator's conduct justified it, for example, if no order for costs would result in substantial hardship for the other party, or if the regulatory function was exercised in bad faith or unreasonably.[132] In that case, an award of costs against the Chief Constable when he had justifiably withdrawn an application for a Sexual Harm Prevention Order on the basis of new information, was quashed.

---

127 *Chief Constable of Cleveland v Vaughan* [2009] EWHC 2831 (Admin), at [6].
128 CA 1971, s 52(3)(b).
129 *Manchester City Council v Manchester Magistrates' Court* [2009] EWHC 1866 (Admin), at [16] and [26].
130 *R v Lewes Crown Court, ex p Rogers* [1974] 1 WLR 196.
131 [2015] EWHC 2303 (Admin).
132 *Chief Constable of Warwickshire Police v MT*, at [31]

18.63

Magistrates were entitled to make an order under CA 1971, s 52 against the police, where proceedings were discontinued ten days before trial, on the basis that the CPS conducted the claim on behalf of the police, but the statutory scheme made the police liable for the conduct of the CPS in dealing with the claim.[133]

18.64

The power to make a costs order extends only to the particular complaint which is not proceeded with. Related matters brought successfully in earlier proceedings, such as detention and forfeiture of goods by the Customs and Excise Commissioner, were not eligible to be covered by such a costs order.[134]

18.65

Such an order shall specify the amount of the costs ordered to be paid.[135]

18.66

For the purpose of enforcement such an order shall be treated as if it were an order made under MCA 1980, s 64.[136]

---

133 *Chief Constable of Warwickshire v Young* [2014] EWHC 4213 (Admin), at [43].
134 *R v Dover Magistrates' Court, ex p Customs and Excise Commissioners* [1995] 11 WLUK 468.
135 CA 1971, s 52(4).
136 CA 1971, s 52(5).

19 Destruction Orders – Dangerous Dogs Act 1991 (on complaint)

19.01

Section 4B of the Dangerous Dogs Act (DDA) 1991 allows a destruction order to be made otherwise than on conviction in certain circumstances.

19.02

DDA 1991, s 5(1) gives a power to a police officer or officer of the local authority to seize any dog in a public place:

- that appears to be a dog to which s 1 applies when:

    - possession or custody of that breed is unlawful under s 1;[1]

    - possession or custody of that breed is lawful, but the animal is not both muzzled and on a lead;[2]

    (this power also applies if the dog is in a private place if dangerously out of control[3]);

- that appears to be a dog to which an order under s 2 applies and an offence against the order has been or is being committed;[4] or

- any dog which appears to be dangerously out of control.[5]

19.03

DDA 1991, s 5(2) provides that a magistrate, with reasonable grounds for believing the commission,[6] and evidence,[7] of any offence under any provision of the 1991 Act may issue a warrant for entry to search, and seize any dog or other thing found there which is evidence of the commission of such an offence.

---

1   DDA 1991, s 5(1)(a)(i).
2   DDA 1991, s 5(1)(a)(ii).
3   DDA 1991, s 5(1A).
4   DDA 1991, s 5(1)(b).
5   DDA 1991, s 5(1)(c).
6   DDA 1991, s 5(2)(a).
7   DDA 1991, s 5(2)(b).

19.04

Where a dog is seized under either the power in s 5(1) or (2) and it appears to a magistrate:

- that no person has been or is to be prosecuted for an offence under DDA 1991 or an order under s 2 in respect of that dog (whether because the owner cannot be found or for any other reason);[8] or

- that the dog cannot be released into the custody or possession of its owner without the owner contravening the prohibition in s 1(3),[9]

the magistrate MUST order destruction of the dog if it is a dangerous type unless it can be shown that it does not constitute a danger to public safety, and may order the destruction of the dog if it constitutes a danger to public safety.[10] Contingent destruction orders are also possible in the same circumstances as they are where there is an order made on conviction – see 14.13.[11] An individual who has never owned, possessed or been in charge of the dog does not have standing to intervene in such an application.[12]

19.05

When deciding whether the dog is such a danger, the magistrate must consider the temperament of the dog and its past behaviour,[13] and whether the owner of the dog, or the person for the time being in charge of it, is a fit and proper person to be in charge of the dog.[14] The magistrate may also consider any other relevant circumstances.[15]

19.06

DDA 1991, s 4B(2A) states that for the purposes of s 4B(2)(a), when deciding whether a dog would constitute a danger to public safety, the magistrate:

- MUST consider:

    - the temperament of the dog and its past behaviour;[16] and

    - whether the owner of the dog, or the person for the time being in charge of it, is a fit and proper person to be in charge of the dog;[17] and

- MAY consider any other relevant circumstances.[18]

---

8   DDA 1991, s 4B(1)(a).
9   DDA 1991, s 4B(1)(b).
10   DDA 1991, s 4B(2)(a).
11   DDA 1991, s 4B(5).
12   *Henderson v Commissioner of Police for the Metropolis* [2018] EWHC 666 (Admin), at [26]–[33].
13   DDA 1991, s 4B(2A)(a)(i).
14   DDA 1991, s 4B(2A)(a)(ii).
15   DDA 1991, s 4B(2A)(b).
16   DDA 1991, s 4B(2A)(a)(i).
17   DDA 1991, s 4B(2A)(a)(ii).
18   DDA 1991, s 4B(2A)(b).

19.07

For the purposes of DDA 1991, s 4B(2A), a court cannot make a finding that someone other than the owner, or the person in charge of the dog currently, is a fit and proper person to be in charge of it.[19] Such a person can also not be considered as part of the circumstances under s 4B(2A)(b).[20] Who is in charge of the dog at the time is a matter of fact, and will usually require the hearing of evidence for a determination to be made under s 4B(2A)(a)(ii).[21] It is unlikely that the requirements of that section will be met by someone who has never owned, possessed or met the dog in question, such as a member of the public who has heard about a seized dog and wishes to give it a home,[22] though the answer will depend on an evaluation of the facts, applying *Webb*.[23] If a person who is fit and proper and in charge of the dog can be identified, they cannot be compelled by the court to apply for the requisite certificate for a dog falling under s 1(3).[24] Being a 'fit and proper' person is not simply a moral question – it also covers practical ability to control the specific dog in question, bearing in mind its size and weight, in light of other likely demands on the handler's strength and attention, such as being a single parent to very young children.[25]

19.08

If the case is one in which releasing the dog to its owner would cause the owner to contravene DDA 1991, s 1(3), and destruction of the dog is not ordered, the magistrate shall order that, unless the dog is exempted from the prohibition in s 1(3) within two months[26] (capable of extension on application),[27] the dog shall be destroyed.[28] If the police believe that the exemption under s 4B has ceased to exist or apply, they cannot summarily destroy the dog – they must apply to the court for a destruction order, otherwise the destruction would be unlawful.[29] A contingent destruction order ceased to have effect once the dog became exempted within the specified requisite period.

19.09

If an order for destruction is made against an offender who is not the owner, the owner may appeal to the Crown Court.[30] The destruction shall not occur until

---

19 *Webb v Chief Constable of Avon and Somerset Constabulary v Secretary of State for Food, Environment and Rural Affairs* [2017] EWHC 3311 (Admin), at [77].
20 *Webb*, at [78].
21 *Webb*, at [101]. It was on the basis of this omission that the Divisional Court remitted the case to the Crown Court to determine that point (at [104]).
22 *Henderson v Commission of Police for the Metropolis* [2018] EWHC 666 (Admin).
23 *Henderson*, at [39].
24 *Webb*, at [98].
25 *R (Grant) v Sheffield Crown Court* [2017] EWHC 1678 (Admin), at [36]–[37] and [46]–[47].
26 DDA 1991, s 4B(5) applying s 4A(3).
27 DDA 1991, s 4B(5) applying s 4A(2).
28 DDA 1991, s 4B(3).
29 *R (Ali) v Chief Constable of Merseyside* [2014] EWHC 4772 (Admin), at [25].
30 DDA 1991, s 4B(4) applying s 4(2).

the time for giving notice of appeal against the conviction or order has ended.[31] If any appeal is instituted within that time, the dog shall not be destroyed until it has been determined or withdrawn.[32]

19.10

When making a destruction order, the court may appoint a person to destroy the dog and require the person with custody of the dog to deliver it up for that purpose.[33] To fail to do so is a summary-only offence under DDA 1991, s 4(8)(b), with a maximum punishment of a fine not exceeding level 5 on the standard scale.

31 DDA 1991, s 4B(4) applying s 4(3)(a).
32 DDA 1991, s 4B(4) applying s 4(3)(b).
33 DDA 1991, s 4B(4) applying s 4(4)(a).

20 Restraining Orders (on acquittal)

20.01

Section 5A of the Protection from Harassment Act (PHA) 1997 allows a court to make a restraining order even where a defendant (D) has been acquitted of the offences for which s/he was being tried.

20.02

The power is also available where D has been found 'not guilty by reason of insanity', this being a species of acquittal.[1] If the acquittal is later found to be unlawful, however (as where on appeal by way of case stated the Deputy District Judge was held to have acted unlawfully in dismissing the charge of his own motion without hearing any evidence) then the imposition of a restraining order on acquittal will also be unlawful.[2]

20.03

Where D is unfit to stand trial but is found 'to have committed the acts charged against him' under the Criminal Procedure (Insanity) Act 1964, the outcome was neither a conviction nor an acquittal, and consequently no restraining order under PHA 1997, s 5 or s 5A can be imposed.[3]

20.04

Although most commonly used in domestic violence cases, it is not confined to such cases.[4]

20.05

Any application must be considered by the court before which the offender was tried (PHA 1997 s 5A(1)).

20.06

Where the Crown Court allows an appeal against conviction,[5] or a case is remitted to the Crown Court from the Court of Appeal, the Court of Appeal

---

1   *R* [2013] EWCA Crim 591, at [12]–[15].
2   *DPP v Christou* [2015] EWHC 4157 (Admin), at [17].
3   *Chinegwundoh* [2015] EWCA Crim 109, at [21]–[26].
4   *Smith* [2012] EWCA Crim 2566, at [33]; *Young* [2012] EWCA Crim 363.
5   PHA 1997, s 5A(4)(a).

having allowed an appeal against conviction, for the Crown Court to consider whether to proceed under PHA 1997, s 5A,[6] the reference in s 5A(1) to 'a court before which a person is acquitted of an offence' is to be read as referring to that Crown Court.[7] This empowers the Crown Court to make a s 5A order when the case has been remitted.

Pre-requisites for making an order

20.07

The order can only be made if the court considers it:

- necessary;
- to protect a person from harassment;
- by the defendant.

20.08

If those criteria are fulfilled, then the court may make an order prohibiting the defendant from doing anything described in the order.

Necessary

20.09

An order will not be unnecessary because in the time between being bailed with conditions and the trial, D did not breach his bail conditions in relation to contact with the complainant.[8] To propose this overlooks the fact that breach of bail carries with it the prospect of the serious sanction of remand, which will be absent once the proceedings have come to an end.[9]

20.10

PHA 1997, s 5A is addressing a future risk – based on the evidence that the judge has in front of them about past conduct of D, on the balance of probabilities (see 20.23), might future conduct amount to harassment? If so, the order is necessary.[10]

---

6 PHA 1997, s 5A(3).
7 PHA 1997, s 5A(4)(b).
8 *Thompson* [2010] EWCA Crim 2955, at [12].
9 *Major* [2010] EWCA Crim 3016, at [16].
10 *Major*, at [16] (obiter).

20.11

The meaning of 'necessary' is not to be diluted when making an order on acquittal – it is prohibiting a person who has not committed any proven criminal offence from doing an act which is otherwise lawful, on pain of imprisonment, and thus is an interference with that person's autonomy which could be justified only when it is truly necessary for the protection of some other person.[11]

20.12

An order being 'appropriate' is not the same as it being 'necessary', and is not a sufficient threshold,[12] likewise whether an order can be 'reasonably imposed' is not the correct test.[13]

To protect a person from harassment

20.13

The victim need not be blameless in the events that led to the proceedings,[14] but if they instigated the confrontation then an order under PHA 1997, s 5A against the former defendant is unlikely to be necessary, especially if there have been no further incidents.[15] However, the victim must be identifiable – it is not permissible to make an order to prevent harassment of an unidentified and unidentifiable victim, or the world at large.[16]

20.14

The court must be satisfied that D is likely to pursue a course of conduct which amounts to harassment within the meaning of PHA 1997, s 1. Pursuit of a course of conduct requires intention. There must therefore be a basis for finding that there was a likelihood of intentional conduct by D involving mental or physical oppression of a victim by persistent interference or intimidation.[17]

20.15

There is no requirement that the anticipated behaviour be more than oppressive and unreasonable and potentially causing alarm or distress – it need not make

---

11 *Smith* [2012] EWCA Crim 2566, at [30].
12 *Jose* [2013] EWCA Crim 939, at [20].
13 *Howard* [2016] EWCA Crim 1906, at [16]–[17].
14 *Major*, at [13].
15 *Haque* [2014] EWCA Crim 832, at [13].
16 *Smith* [2012] EWCA Crim 2566, at [27]–[28] – D had been found not guilty by reason of insanity of criminal damage and interfering with the performance of the crew of an aircraft in flight. Not usually suffering from any psychiatric problems, he had suffered a short period of psychosis due to a concatenation of unusual factors, causing him to attempt to open the rear door of an aircraft, wrench remote controls from the seats of other passengers, and be abusive when restrained. A PHA 1997, s 5A order preventing him from flying on any domestic or international airline for three years was inappropriate, and quashed.
17 *Smith*, at [29].

the victim fear violence.[18] However, a general fear that a defendant will approach a complainant, for instance, with whom he had no previous or subsequent contact, whose pub he burgled in unusual circumstances, but in an isolated incident not likely to be repeated, having not specifically targeted it, is not sufficient to justify an order.[19]

20.16

An order under PHA 1997, s 5A is not to be used as a means of protecting the public against the possible effects of a hypothetical recurrence of transient mental illness.[20]

20.17

As a matter of principle, it is not required that there be evidence of previous incidents of harassment to justify a finding of what may be likely to happen in the future.[21] A single incident is unlikely to be able to give rise to a finding that in the future there will be a 'course of conduct', as required by PHA 1997, s 1 amounting to harassment.[22]

20.18

A single threatening letter will not suffice,[23] neither will one threat in a text message sent in breach of a non-molestation order that D had not read.[24] A judge making such an order will need to expressly apply his/her mind (and remarks when making the order) to the likelihood of D repeating previous relevant conduct, and what is required by the Act itself to establish harassment.[25]

Content of an order

20.19

It is necessary for any order to be tailored to the precise requirements of the individual case. In a case where D attempted to murder his seven-month-old daughter while suffering from extreme mental ill-health the Court emphasised that it is not to say that all relationship between father and daughter (and other siblings) should be cut off indefinitely, without regard to the possibilities of supervised or indirect contact.[26]

---

18 *Haque*, at [12].
19 *Taylor* [2017] EWCA Crim 2209, at [12], [22]–[25].
20 *Smith*, at [34].
21 *Jose*, at [21].
22 *R*, at [20].
23 *Haque* [2015] EWCA Crim 767, at [10].
24 *Frasle* [2015] EWCA Crim 1121, at [10]–[11].
25 *Jose*, at [20].
26 *R*, at [26].

20.20

The five-year duration of the order in that case, given the children's young ages, risked precluding any sensible resumption of a relationship between father and children, and these matters had to be addressed when making an order. The breadth of the order made in that case, extending to preventing contact between children who were not involved in the incident, demonstrated the difficulty of framing such an order in the context of a sentencing hearing in the Crown Court. The Family Court was better equipped to deal with relevant child protection concerns in such a case.

Duration of the order

20.21

The order may have effect for a specified period or until further order.[27] It will be in very rare circumstances that an order unlimited in time will be appropriate,[28] particularly where the complainant is not particularly vulnerable; the defendant is of good character; there have been no further incidents in the intervening months, and the terms of the order were broad.[29]

Procedure

20.22

Part 50 of the Criminal Procedure Rules (CrimPR) apply to applications for orders under PHA 1997, s 5A.[30] Judges must take care if they are going to exercise their discretion under CrimPR, r 50.9 to shorten the time frames provided, to ensure procedural fairness.[31]

20.23

The statute is silent as to the standard of proof to be applied to relevant evidence before an order is made, but as it is a civil order, the Court of Appeal has stated that the civil standard of proof applies.[32]

20.24

In proceedings under this section both the prosecution and the defence may lead, as further evidence, any evidence that would be admissible in proceedings

---

27 PHA 1997, s 5A(2) applying s 5(3).
28 *Howard*, at [17].
29 *Howard*, at [12] and [17].
30 *Kapotra* (often 'K') [2011] EWCA Crim 1843, at [9].
31 *Kapotra*, at [14].
32 *Major*, at [15].

for an injunction under PHA 1997, s 3,[33] which provides that a course of conduct amounting to harassment can also found a civil claim for damages, without time limit.[34]

20.25

When considering an application under PHA 1997, s 5A, the court must consider the evidence that was heard in the trial, including all contested evidence,[35] even though it led to an acquittal – this did not amount to going behind the jury's verdict.[36]

20.26

What should not be taken into account are matters such as an improper attitude shown by D towards the complainant; whether D was moral or immoral; cost to the public; saving of court time; saving the complainant from bringing civil proceedings, or that it was in the interests of D himself that there should be a restraining order.[37]

20.27

For a clear demarcation between the trial (which will have ended in an acquittal) and the making of the order in a context in which it is not a sentence, it has been suggested that the judge may want to consider adjourning until the next day.[38] This will allow full consideration of the evidence, and the reasons for making the order. It may also assist to reduce any appearance of going behind the jury's verdict.

20.28

Where the Crown has offered no evidence, and consequently the judge has not heard any evidence, and D does not concede that making the order is appropriate, an assessment will need to be made on the basis of statements alone.[39] For this to be done fairly, the court will need to consider adjourning for proper procedural safeguards to be adhered to, as set out in *Kapotra*:[40]

(1) The prosecution and/or the appellant in compliance with CrimPR, r 50.4(2) should have served notice in writing on the court officer and every other party identifying any evidence it wished the court to take account of, attaching to the notice any written statement which had not already been served.

---

33 PHA 1997, s 5A(2) applying s 5(3A).
34 PHA 1997, s 5(6), applying the provisions of the Limitation Act 1980, s 11(1A).
35 *Major*, at [13].
36 *Thompson*, at [12].
37 *Thompson*, at [9].
38 *Major*, at [18].
39 *Brough* [2011] EWCA Crim 2802, at [22].
40 [2011] EWCA Crim 1843, at [13]–[14].

(2) If any party sought to introduce hearsay evidence, it had to do so in compliance with CrimPR, r 50.6. by serving a notice in writing as required by r 50.6(1)(a), (b).

(3) Any party seeking the court's permission to cross-examine the maker of a hearsay statement had to comply with the procedural provisions of CrimPR, r 50.7.

Even if the judge was minded to exercise the discretion open to him or her under CrimPR, r 50.9, that decision itself had to bear in mind the fundamental principle underlying the Rules, namely that any person faced with the possible imposition of a restraining order should be given proper notice of what is sought, the evidential basis for the application and, in addition, be allowed a proper opportunity to address the evidence and make informed representations as to the appropriateness of such an order.

20.29

If this does not occur, it is likely that there will not be sufficient evidence before the court to found an evidential basis upon which a restraining order could be made.[41] A proper consideration of the issues may well require oral evidence from both the complainant and the (former) defendant.[42]

20.30

This will also be necessary where there has been alleged intimidating behaviour after the offence towards a witness. Simply taking submissions from counsel in accordance with their instructions will be insufficient – both parties will need to give evidence to illuminate the context and nature of the behaviour.[43]

20.31

The judge must state the factual basis for imposing the order.[44] Where the facts are disputed, the judge should state which are found to be proven, and which justified the making of the order – 'so this does not happen again' will not be sufficient.[45] Although a PHA 1997, s 5A order is not a sentence, the Court of Appeal has expressed the view that s 174(1) of the Criminal Justice Act 2003 applies to the making of such an order.[46]

---

41 *Kapotra*, at [15].
42 *Brough*, at [26]–[27].
43 *Hart* [2015] EWCA Crim 389, at [8]–[9].
44 *Major*, at [17].
45 *Lawrence* [2012] EWCA Crim 1164, at [11].
46 *Major*, at [18].

20.32

A failure to make clear the factual basis is liable to lead to the quashing of the order on appeal,[47] though detailed findings are not required where D consents to the making of the order.[48] Similar consequences will follow if D is not given the opportunity, him/herself or through counsel, to address the court on whether the order is necessary and well-founded.[49]

20.33

The consent of the defendant is not needed for an order under PHA 1997, s 5A (unlike for a bind over).[50] Where D does consent to the imposition of an order under s 5A (usually as part of a compromise between Crown and defence that if D accepts a restraining order, the Crown will offer no evidence on the charges) if s/he then wishes to challenge that order in the appellate court waiver of privilege will be required to enable the court to investigate why a restraining order, to which consent was apparently freely given, should be set aside.[51]

Variation and discharge

20.34

The prosecutor, D, or any other person mentioned in the order may apply to the court which made the order for it to be varied or discharged by a further order.[52]

20.35

Any person mentioned in the order is entitled to be heard on the hearing of an application for variation or discharge.[53] The same considerations apply as when an application is being made in respect of an order under PHA 1997, s 5 (see Chapter 11).

Offence of breach

20.36

If without reasonable excuse D does anything which they are prohibited from doing by an order under this section, they are guilty of an offence.[54] This offence is triable either way, and carries sentences of:

---

47 *Major*, at [19]–[20].
48 *Dennis* [2014] EWCA Crim 2331, at [14].
49 *Trott* [2011] EWCA Crim 2395, at [12].
50 *Major*, at [12].
51 *Dennis*, at [17].
52 PHA 1997, s 5A(2) applying s 5(4).
53 PHA 1997, s 5A(2) applying s 5(4A).
54 PHA 1997, s 5A(2) applying s 5(5).

- on conviction on indictment – to imprisonment for a term not exceeding five years, or a fine, or both;[55] or

- on summary conviction – to imprisonment for a term not exceeding six months, or a fine not exceeding the statutory maximum, or both.[56]

20.37

A court dealing with a person for an offence under this section may vary or discharge the order in question by a further order.[57]

20.38

Where D has a background of non-compliance, this will aggravate the sentence imposed for a breach.[58]

Appeal

20.39

A person made subject to a restraining order on acquittal has the same right of appeal against the order as if s/he had been convicted of the offence before the court which made the order,[59] and the order had been made under PHA 1997, s 5.60

---

55 PHA 1997, s 5A(2) applying s 5(6)(a).
56 PHA 1997, s 5A(2) applying s 5(6)(b).
57 PHA 1997, s 5A(2) applying s 5(7).
58 *Young (Justin James)* [2013] 11 WLUK 304.
59 PHA 1997, s 5A(5)(a).
60 PHA 1997, s 5A(5)(b).

21 Sexual Harm Prevention Orders (on application)

21.01

In addition to the power to make a Sexual Harm Prevention Order (SHPO) on conviction, s 103A of the Sexual Offences Act (SOA) 2003 creates a power for a court to make an SHPO on application from the chief officer of police. All pertinent issues concerning SHPOs on application have been covered in Chapter 9, and readers should refer to that chapter for assistance on effect, content, duration and other matters. Anything not explicitly addressed in this chapter applies to SHPOs on application in the same way as it does to those on conviction.

21.02

A chief officer of police or the Director General of the National Crime Agency[1] may by complaint to a magistrates' court[2] apply for an SHPO in respect of:

- a person who resides in the chief officer's police area;[3] or

- a person whom the chief officer believes is in that area or is intending to come to it.[4]

21.03

The application may be made to any magistrates' court acting for a local justice area that includes any part of a relevant police area,[5] or any place where it is alleged that the person acted in such a way as to give reasonable cause to believe that it is necessary for such an order to be made.[6]

---

1 If the application is made by the Director General of the National Crime Agency then they must as soon as practicable notify the chief officer of police for a relevant police area of the application (SOA 2003, s 103A(7)).
2 To be read as a Youth Court if the defendant (D) is under 18 (SOA 2003, s 103A(8)).
3 SOA 2003, s 103A(5)(a).
4 SOA 2003, s 103A(5)(b).
5 SOA 2003, s 103A(6)(a), as defined in s 103A(9) – (a) where the applicant is a chief officer of police, the officer's police area, or (b) where the applicant is the Director General, either (i) the police area where the person in question resides, or (ii) a police area which the Director General believes the person is in or is intending to come to.
6 SOA 2003, s 103A(6)(b).

Pre-conditions

21.04

For such an application to be made, it must appear to the chief officer or the Director General that:[7]

- the person is a qualifying offender;[8] AND

- the person has, since the appropriate date, acted in such a way as to give reasonable cause to believe that it is necessary for such an order to be made.[9]

'Qualifying offender'

21.05

A 'qualifying offender' is someone who, whether before or after the commencement of SOA 2003, Part II, in England and Wales,[10] or abroad:[11]

- has been convicted of an offence listed in SOA 2003, Sch 3[12] (other than at para 60) or in Sch 5 in England and Wales,[13] or has been convicted of a relevant offence (whether or not the person has been punished for it) in another country;[14]

- has been found not guilty of such an offence by reason of insanity,[15] or the equivalent of that finding abroad;[16]

- has been found to be under a disability and to have done the act charged against him in respect of such an offence,[17] or an equivalent finding abroad;[18]

- has been cautioned in respect of a relevant offence in England and Wales,[19] or abroad.[20]

---

7 SOA 2003, s 103A(4).
8 SOA 2003, s 103A(4)(a).
9 SOA 2003, s 103A(4)(b).
10 SOA 2003, s 103B(2).
11 SOA 2003, s 103B(3).
12 Per SOA 2003, s 103B(9) – when construing any reference to an offence listed in Sch 3, any condition subject to which an offence is so listed that relates (a) to the way in which the defendant is dealt with in respect of an offence so listed or a relevant finding (as defined by s 132(9)), or (b) to the age of any person, is to be disregarded.
13 SOA 2003, s 103B(2)(a).
14 SOA 2003, s 103B(3)(a).
15 SOA 2003, s 103B(2)(b).
16 SOA 2003, s 103B(3)(b).
17 SOA 2003, s 103B(2)(c).
18 SOA 2003, s 103B(3)(c).
19 SOA 2003, s 103B(2)(d).
20 SOA 2003, s 103B(3)(d).

'Relevant offence'

21.06

A 'relevant offence' is defined as an act which:[21]

- constituted an offence under the law in force in the country concerned;[22] and

- would have constituted an offence listed in SOA 2003, Sch 3 (other than at para 60) or in Sch 5 if it had been done in any part of the UK.[23]

21.07

It is taken that that second condition is met, unless, not later than the rules of court provide, D serves on the applicant a notice that:

- states on the facts as alleged with respect to the act concerned, the condition is not in D's opinion met;[24]

- shows grounds for that opinion;[25] and

- requires the applicant to prove that the condition is met.[26]

21.08

The court, if it thinks fit, may permit D to require the applicant to prove that the condition is met without service of a notice.[27]

21.09

It is important for practitioners to note the availability of an application by the police where D has only been cautioned in relation to a sexual offence. Where that has occurred, particular care will need to be taken about the proportionality of an SHPO, considering that the police have clearly accepted that a caution is an appropriate disposal. However, to receive a caution D must have admitted their guilt to the conduct for which the caution is administered, so this may become a delicate balancing act.

21.10

An SHPO on application can be made if it is proved on the application that D is a qualifying offender,[28] and the court is satisfied that D's behaviour

---

21 SOA 2003, s 103B(4).
22 SOA 2003, s 103B(4)(a).
23 SOA 2003, s 103B(4)(b).
24 SOA 2003, s 103B(6)(a).
25 SOA 2003, s 103B(6)(b).
26 SOA 2003, s 103B(6)(c).
27 SOA 2003, s 103B(7).
28 SOA 2003, s 103A(3)(a).

since the appropriate date makes it necessary to make an SHPO, for the purpose of:[29]

- protecting the public or any particular members of the public from sexual harm from D;[30] or

- protecting children or vulnerable adults generally, or any particular children or vulnerable adults, from sexual harm from D outside the UK.[31]

'Appropriate date'

21.11

Section 103B(1) defines *'appropriate date'* as, in relation to a qualifying offender, the date or (as the case may be) the first date on which the offender was convicted, found to have done the act, or cautioned (see 21.12).

Content

21.12

All provisions relating to content, effect and duration apply as they do to SHPOs made on conviction; see Chapter 9.

Notification requirements

21.13

On an application for an SHPO made by a chief officer of police, the court must make a notification order in respect of D (either in addition to or instead of an SHPO) if:

- the applicant invites the court to do so;[32] and

- it is proved that the conditions in SOA 2003, s 97(2)–(4) are met:[33]

  - **First condition**: under the law in force in a country outside the UK:

    (a) D has been convicted of a relevant offence (whether or not s/he has been punished for it);[34]

---

29 SOA 2003, s 103A(3)(b).
30 SOA 2003, s 103A(3)(b)(i).
31 SOA 2003, s 103A(3)(b)(ii).
32 SOA 2003, s 103G(6)(a).
33 SOA 2003, s 103G(6)(b).
34 SOA 2003, s 97(2)(a).

(b)   a court exercising jurisdiction under that law has made in respect of a relevant offence a finding equivalent to a finding that D is not guilty by reason of insanity;[35]

(c)   such a court has made in respect of a relevant offence a finding equivalent to a finding that D is under a disability and did the act charged against him/her in respect of the offence;[36] or

(d)   D has been cautioned in respect of a relevant offence.[37]

– **Second condition**:

(a)   the first condition is met because of a conviction, finding or caution which occurred on or after 1 September 1997,[38]

(b)   the first condition is met because of a conviction or finding which occurred before that date, but D was dealt with in respect of the offence or finding on or after that date, or has yet to be dealt with in respect of it;[39] or

(c)   the first condition is met because of a conviction or finding which occurred before that date, but on that date D was, in respect of the offence or finding, subject under the law in force in the country concerned to detention, supervision or any other disposal equivalent to any of those mentioned in SOA 2003, s 81(3) (read with s 81(6) and s 131)).[40]

– **Third condition**: the period set out in SOA 2003, s 82 (as modified by s 98(2) and (3)) in respect of the relevant offence has not expired.[41]

Breach

21.14

The provisions relating to breach are the same as those where the SHPO had been made following conviction.

---

35 SOA 2003, s 97(2)(b).
36 SOA 2003, s 97(2)(c).
37 SOA 2003, s 97(2)(d).
38 SOA 2003, s 97(3)(a).
39 SOA 2003, s 97(3)(b).
40 SOA 2003, s 97(3)(c).
41 SOA 2003, s 97(4).

Appeal

21.15

Appeal against an SHPO made on application lies to the Crown Court.[42]

21.16

On such an appeal the Crown Court may make such orders as may be necessary to give effect to its determination of the appeal, and may also make such incidental or consequential orders as appear to it to be just.[43]

21.17

Any order made by the Crown Court (other than an order directing that an application be re-heard by a magistrates' court) is for the purposes of SOA 2003, s 103E(9) or s 103F(5) (respectively) to be treated as if it were an order of the court from which the appeal was brought (and not an order of the Crown Court).[44]

---

42 SOA 2003, s 103H(1)(c).
43 SOA 2003, s 103H(4).
44 SOA 2003, s 103H(5).

22 Football Banning Orders (on complaint)

22.01

The definitions of phrases in this chapter are the same as those set out in Chapter 13 and are not repeated here.

22.02

Prosecutors are able to apply for a 'civil' football banning order (FBO) on complaint to a magistrates' court[1] on behalf of the relevant chief officer,[2] (of police;[3] or of the British Transport Police Force[4]) or the DPP.[5] In *Gough v Chief Constable of Derbyshire Constabulary*,[6] the Court of Appeal upheld the decision of the Divisional Court that FBOs do not involve criminal penalties and are thus civil in character, as no conviction is needed for an order under s 14B of the Football Spectators Act (FSA) 1989, and the requirement in s 14A for a relevant conviction is 'no more than a gateway criterion'.[7]

22.03

If there is insufficient evidence to prosecute a football-related offence or the defendant is acquitted, it may still be possible to apply for an order under FSA 1989, s 14B. Prosecutors should engage with police officers to establish whether there is enough evidence to support the complaint, and defence advocates should be aware of this possibility.

22.04

Such an application can be made if it appears to any of those individuals that the respondent (R) has at any time caused or contributed to any violence or disorder in the UK or elsewhere.[8]

---

1   FSA 1989, s 14B(3).
2   FSA 1989, s 14B(1)(a).
3   FSA 1989, s 14B(1A)(a).
4   FSA 1989, s 14B(1A)(b).
5   FSA 1989, s 14B(1)(b).
6   [2001] EWHC 554 (Admin).
7   *Gough*, Laws LJ at [42](2).
8   FSA 1989, s 14B(2).

Pre-conditions for making an order under FSA 1989, s 14B

22.05

The court MUST make an order if it is satisfied by the applicant that:[9]

- R has at any time caused or contributed to any violence or disorder in the UK or elsewhere;[10] and

- there are reasonable grounds to believe that an order would help to prevent violence or disorder at or in connection with any regulated football matches.

22.06

The magistrates' court may take into account the following matters (among others), so far as they consider it appropriate to do so, in determining whether to make an order under FSA 1989, s 14B:[11]

- any decision of a court or tribunal outside the UK;[12]

- deportation or exclusion from a country outside the UK;[13]

- removal or exclusion from premises used for playing football matches, whether in the UK or elsewhere;[14]

- conduct recorded on video or by any other means.[15]

22.07

The magistrates' court may not take into account anything done by R prior to ten years before the application under FSA 1989, s 14B(1), except circumstances ancillary to a conviction.[16,17]

22.08

Before taking into account any conviction for a relevant offence, where a court stated under:[18]

- FSA 1989, s 14A(3) (relating to FBOs on conviction);

---

9   FSA 1989, s 14B(4).
10 FSA 1989, s 14B(4)(a).
11 FSA 1989, s 14C(4).
12 FSA 1989, s 14C(4)(a).
13 FSA 1989, s 14C(4)(b).
14 FSA 1989, s 14C(4)(c).
15 FSA 1989, s 14C(4)(d).
16 FSA 1989, s 14C(5) – 'circumstances ancillary to a conviction' has the same meaning as it has for the purposes of s 4 of the Rehabilitation of Offenders Act 1974 (effect of rehabilitation), and does not prejudice anything in that Act (s 14C(6)).
17 FSA 1989, s 14C(5)(a).
18 FSA 1989, s 14C(5)(b).

- FSA 1989, s 15(2A) (relating to restriction orders – now repealed); or

- s 30(3) of the Public Order Act 1986 (relating to domestic football banning orders – now repealed),

that it was not satisfied that there were reasonable grounds to believe that making an FBO on conviction would help prevent violence or disorder at or in connection with any regulated football matches, the magistrates' court must consider the reasons given in the statement.

22.09

If the criteria are met, the court is to make the order, and there is no discretion as to its form or provisions outside of those stipulated by the statute in FSA 1989, s 14G.[19]

22.10

If an order is made, the provisions of FSA 1989, s 14G (additional requirements) apply equally to orders under s 14B (see 13.77 ff).

Period of order

22.11

The minimum length of an order on complaint is three years, and the maximum is five years.[20]

Procedure

22.12

The provisions of FSA 1989, s 14E apply equally to an FBO on complaint as they do on conviction (see 13.52 ff).

22.13

It should be noted that there are no directly applicable disclosure requirements in relation to an application under FSA 1989, s 14B, as they are civil proceedings.[21] Therefore hearsay (providing it complied with the Civil Evidence Act 1995) and compilation evidence was held to be permissible, the only question being whether it was fair to admit the material.[22]

---

19 *Commissioner of Police for the Metropolis v Thorpe* [2016] EWHC 3339 (Admin), at [12]–[13].
20 FSA 1989, s 14F(5).
21 *Newman v Commissioner of Police of the Metropolis* [2009] EWHC 1642 (Admin), at [34].
22 *Newman*, at [35]–[44].

Standard of proof

22.14

In *Gough v Chief Constable of Derbyshire Constabulary*,[23] the Court of Appeal upheld Laws LJ's judgment in the Divisional Court that FBOs were civil in nature. However, the Court made the following observations about the application of the civil standard of proof in cases of this kind:[24]

> 'It does not follow from this that a mere balance of probabilities suffices to justify the making of an order. Banning orders under section 14B fall into the same category as antisocial behaviour orders and sex offenders' orders. While made in civil proceedings they impose serious restraints on freedoms that the citizen normally enjoys. While technically the civil standard of proof applies, that standard is flexible and must reflect the consequences that will follow if the case for a banning order is made out. This should lead the Magistrates to apply an exacting standard of proof that will, in practice, be hard to distinguish from the criminal standard — see *B v Chief Constable of Avon and Somerset Constabulary [2001] 1 WLR 340* at p.354 and *R (McCann) v Manchester Crown Court [2001] 1 WLR 1084* at p.1102.
>
> Thus the necessity in the individual case to impose a restriction upon a fundamental freedom must be strictly demonstrated. The first thing that has to be proved under section 14B(4)(a) is that the respondent has caused or contributed to violence or disorder in the United Kingdom or elsewhere. Mr Pannick conceded that the standard of proof of this is practically indistinguishable from the criminal standard.'

22.15

This does not sit entirely comfortably, however, with the law following *Re B*[25] (Baroness Hale giving the leading opinion). In that case it was made clear that there is one standard of proof in proceedings outside of criminal courts, even where criminal conduct is alleged, and that standard of proof is the balance of probabilities.

22.16

The Court in *Gough* also considered what threshold of evidence should be required before an application to travel abroad during a control period was permitted, and concluded:[26]

---

23 [2002] EWCA Civ 351.
24 *Gough*, at [90]–[91].
25 [2008] UKHL 35.
26 *Gough*, at [95].

'We have drawn attention above to the requirement of "special circumstances" as a precondition to granting an applicant permission to go abroad during a prescribed period. This is not a helpful phrase. Were it to be interpreted so that permission was only granted in extraordinary circumstances, it would not satisfy the Community requirement of necessity. Individuals subject to banning orders may have reasons for going abroad during prescribed periods that are perfectly ordinary and cannot naturally be described as "special circumstances". Provided that the reason for going abroad is other than attendance at the prescribed match, there can be no justification for refusing permission. When considering whether there are "special circumstances" the FBOA [Football Banning Orders Authority], or on appeal the Magistrates, should do no more than satisfy themselves on balance of probabilities that this is the true position. This should not be something that is difficult to prove, for the bona fide prospective traveller is likely to be in a position to produce some evidence of the proposed trip.'

Football Spectators Act 1989, s 21B – summary measures – reference to court

22.17

During a control period in relation to a regulated football match outside the UK, or an external tournament,[27] if a constable in uniform has reasonable grounds for suspecting that:[28]

- a person who is a British citizen;[29]

- whom s/he has encountered;

- has at any time caused or contributed to any violence or disorder in the UK or elsewhere;[30] and

- the officer has reasonable grounds to believe that making a banning order would help to prevent violence or disorder at or in connection with any regulated football matches

the officer may detain that person until s/he has decided whether to issue a notice under FSA 1989, s 21B,[31] providing that period is not longer than four hours,[32] or six if authorised by an officer of inspector rank or above.[33]

---

27 FSA 1989, s 21A(1).
28 FSA 1989, s 21A(1)(a).
29 FSA 1989, s 21C(1).
30 FSA 1989, s 14B(4)(a).
31 FSA 1989, s 21A(2).
32 FSA 1989, s 21A(3).
33 FSA 1989, s 21A(3).

22.18

Where the constable is authorised by an officer of at least the rank of inspector to do so,[34] s/he may give the person a written notice requiring him/her:[35]

- to appear before a magistrates' court at a time, or between the times, specified in the notice,[36] which must be within 24 hours of:

  - the giving of the notice;[37] or

  - the person's detention under s 21A(2),[38]

  whichever is earlier;[39]

- not to leave England and Wales before that time (or the later of those times);[40] and

- if the control period relates to a regulated football match outside the UK or to an external tournament which includes such matches, to surrender his/her passport to the constable,[41,42]

and must state the grounds referred to in s 21A(1).

22.19

For the purposes of FSA 1989, s 14B, the notice is to be treated as an application for an FBO made by complaint by the constable (s 14B(1)) and is to have effect as if the references to the relevant chief officer were references to that constable.[43]

22.20

A constable may arrest a person to whom s/he is giving such a notice if s/he has reasonable grounds to believe that it is necessary to do so to secure compliance with the notice.[44] When a person appears before the magistrates as a result of a FSA 1989, s 21B notice, whether under arrest or not, the court can remand him/her.[45] If s/he is bailed, then the following conditions can be attached:

- not to leave England or Wales before his/her court appearance;[46] and

---

34 FSA 1989, s 21B(1).
35 FSA 1989, s 21B(2).
36 FSA 1989, s 21B(2)(a).
37 FSA 1989, s 21B(3)(a).
38 FSA 1989, s 21B(3)(b).
39 FSA 1989, s 21B(3).
40 FSA 1989, s 21B(2)(b).
41 FSA 1989, s 21B(2)(c).
42 FSA 1989, s 21B(6) requires that any passport surrendered by a person under this section must be returned to him in accordance with directions given by the court.
43 FSA 1989, s 21B(4).
44 FSA 1989, s 21B(5).
45 FSA 1989, s 21C(3).
46 FSA 1989, s 21B(4)(a).

- if the control period relates to a regulated football match outside the UK or to an external tournament which includes such matches, to surrender his/her passport to a police constable, if s/he has not already done so.[47]

22.21

If, on his/her appearance before the court, the application for an FBO under FSA 1989, s 14B is refused, the court may order compensation from central funds of up to £5,000[48] be paid to the subject of the application if it is satisfied:

- that the notice should not have been given;

- that s/he has suffered loss as a result of the giving of the notice; and

- that, having regard to all the circumstances, it is appropriate to order the payment of compensation in respect of that loss.

22.22

A refusal to pay compensation can be appealed to the Crown Court,[49] but there is no appeal against the amount of the order where compensation is awarded.[50]

22.23

Failure to comply with a FSA 1989, s 21B notice is an offence, and liable on summary conviction to imprisonment for no longer than six months and/or a fine not exceeding level 5.[51]

22.24

The Practice Direction (Court of Appeal (Criminal Division)): Costs in Criminal Proceedings[52] applies.

Remand/bail

22.25

If the magistrates' court adjourns proceedings on an application under FSA 1989, s 14B, it may remand R.[53] Alternatively, if given bail, the court has a discretion to require R to:

---

47 FSA 1989, s 21B(4)(b).
48 FSA 1989, s 21D(3).
49 FSA 1989, s 21D(2).
50 FSA 1989, s 21D(3).
51 FSA 1989, s 21C(2).
52 [2015] EWCA Crim 1568.
53 FSA 1989, s 14B(5).

- not leave England and Wales before his/her next appearance before the court;[54] and

- surrender his/her passport to a police constable, if within the control period of a regulated football match outside of the UK, or an external tournament containing such matches.[55]

Termination

22.26

The provisions of FSA 1989, s 14H apply equally to an FBO on complaint as they do on conviction (see 13.87 ff).

Appeals

22.27

An appeal lies to the Crown Court against the making,[56] or dismissal of an application for,[57] an order under FSA 1989, s 14B.

22.28

On such appeal the Crown Court:

- may make any orders necessary to give effect to its determination of the appeal;[58] and

- may also make any incidental or consequential orders which appear to it to be just.[59]

22.29

An order of the Crown Court made on appeal (other than one directing the application be re-heard by a magistrates' court) is to be treated for the purposes of Part II of FSA 1989 as if it were an order of the magistrates' court from which the appeal was brought.[60]

---

54 FSA 1989, s 14B(6)(a).
55 FSA 1989, s 14B(6)(b).
56 FSA 1989, s 14D(1).
57 FSA 1989, s 14D(1A).
58 FSA 1989, s 14D(2)(a).
59 FSA 1989, s 14D(2)(b).
60 FSA 1989, s 14D(3).

Human rights

22.30

An order under FSA 1989, s 14B is capable of engaging Article 8 of the European Convention on Human Rights, but not merely because it is in mandatory terms. The protection under Article 8 is confined to the private sphere of a person's existence and does not extend to involvement in sporting activities as a spectator that necessarily have a public element.[61]

Offence of breach

22.31

The provisions of FSA 1989, s 14J apply equally to an FBO on complaint as they do on conviction (see 13.95).

---

61 *Commissioner of Police for the Metropolis v Thorpe* [2016] EWHC 3339 (Admin), at [18]–[23].

23 Slavery and Trafficking Prevention Orders (on application)

23.01

The power to make slavery and trafficking prevention orders (STPOs) is provided by s 15 of the Modern Slavery Act (MSA) 2015. Where explanations of definitions are not provided, readers should refer to Chapter 16 on STPOs on conviction.

23.02

A magistrates' court may make an STPO against a person (D) on an application by:

- a chief officer of police;[1]
  - in respect of someone who:
    - (a) lives in the officer's police area;[2] or
    - (b) who the officer believes is in that area or intending to come in to it;[3]
- an immigration officer;[4]
- the Director General of the National Crime Agency ('Director General');[5]
- the Gangmasters and Labour Abuse Authority ('GLA Authority').[6]

Pre-conditions

23.03

The court may make the order only if it is satisfied that two conditions are met:

- D is a relevant offender;[7] and

---

1 MSA 2015, s 15(1)(a).
2 MSA 2015, s 15(4)(a).
3 MSA 2015, s 15(4)(b).
4 MSA 2015, s 15(1)(b).
5 MSA 2015, s 15(1)(c).
6 MSA 2015, s 15(1)(d).
7 MSA 2015, s 15(2)(a).

- since D first became a relevant offender, they have acted in a way which means that the condition in MSA 2015, s 15(3) is met,[8] including at a time before this section came into force.[9]

D is a 'relevant offender'

23.04

'Relevant offender' is defined in MSA 2015, s 16.

23.05

D will be a relevant offender if s/he has, in the UK or elsewhere, at any time:[10]

- been convicted of a slavery or human trafficking (or equivalent)[11] offence;[12]

- been the subject of a finding of a court that s/he is not guilty of a slavery or human trafficking (or equivalent)[13] offence by reason of insanity;[14]

- been the subject of a finding of a court that s/he is under a disability and has done the act charged against him/her in respect of a slavery or human trafficking (or equivalent)[15] offence;[16] or

- been cautioned in respect of a slavery or human trafficking (or equivalent)[17] offence.[18]

23.06

An 'equivalent offence' means an act which is punishable under the law of another country, however described in that law[19] which:

- constituted an offence under the law of the country concerned;[20] and

- would have constituted a slavery or human trafficking offence under the law of England and Wales if it had been done in England and Wales, or by a UK national, or as regards the UK.[21]

---

8   MSA 2015, s 15(2)(b).
9   MSA 2015, s 15(9).
10 MSA 2015, s 16(7).
11 MSA 2015, s 16(3)(a).
12 MSA 2015, s 16(2)(a).
13 MSA 2015, s 16(3)(b).
14 MSA 2015, s 16(2)(b).
15 MSA 2015, s 16(3)(c).
16 MSA 2015, s 16(2)(c).
17 MSA 2015, s 16(3)(d).
18 MSA 2015, s 16(2)(d).
19 MSA 2015, s 16(5).
20 MSA 2015, s 16(4)(a).
21 MSA 2015, s 16(4)(b).

23.07

Where D is alleged to have committed an equivalent offence elsewhere, the act is to be taken to constitute a slavery or human trafficking offence under the law of England and Wales if it had been done in England and Wales, or by a UK national, or as regards the UK unless:

- not later than provided by rules of court, D serves on the applicant a notice which states that in D's opinion the condition is not met, shows the grounds for that opinion, and requires the applicant to prove that the condition is met;[22] or

- the court permits D to require the applicant to prove that the condition is met without service of such a notice.[23]

23.08

The Magistrates' Courts (Modern Slavery Act 2015) Rules 2015[24] make further provision regarding challenging equivalency under this provision.

Condition in Modern Slavery Act 2015, s 15(3) is met

23.09

The condition in MSA 2015, s15(3) is that, since D became a relevant offender, s/he has acted in such a way that:

- there is a risk that D may commit a slavery or human trafficking offence;[25] and

- it is necessary to make the order for the purpose of protecting persons generally, or particular persons, from the physical or psychological harm which would be likely to occur if D committed such an offence.[26]

Procedure

23.10

An application under MSA 2015, s 15 is to be made by complaint by those listed at 23.02. It may be made to any magistrates' court acting for a local justice area that includes:

---

22 MSA 2015, s 16(6)(a).
23 MSA 2015, s 16(6)(b).
24 SI 2015/1478.
25 MSA 2015, s 15(3)(a).
26 MSA 2015, s 15(3)(b).

- any part of a relevant police area;[27] or

- any place where it is alleged that D acted in a way that means there is a risk that D may commit a slavery or human trafficking offence, and it is necessary to make the order for the purpose of protecting persons generally, or particular persons, from the physical or psychological harm which would be likely to occur if D committed such an offence.[28]

23.11

Where D is under 18, a reference in this section to a magistrates' court is to be taken as referring to a youth court (subject to any rules of court made under MSA 2015, s 32).[29]

23.12

Where an immigration officer, the Director General, or the GLA Authority makes an application under this section, the officer, Director General or GLA Authority must give notice of the application to the chief officer of police for a relevant police area, meaning:[30]

- where the applicant is a chief officer of police, the officer's police area;[31]

- where the applicant is an immigration officer, the Director General or the GLA Authority, the police area where D lives or a police area which the officer, Director General or the GLA Authority believes D is in or is intending to come to.[32]

Content

23.13

The same provisions apply to an STPO on application as to one on conviction.

Variation, renewal and discharge

23.14

The relevant provisions are exactly the same as for an order made on conviction, save for there being four additional people who can apply where an order has been made under MSA 2015, s 15:

---

27 MSA 2015, s 15(5)(a).
28 MSA 2015, s 15(5)(b).
29 MSA 2015, s 15(6).
30 MSA 2015, s 15(7).
31 MSA 2015, s 15(8)(a).
32 MSA 2015, s 15(8)(b).

- where the order was made on an application under s 15 by a chief officer of police, that officer;[33]

- where the order was made on an application under s 15 by an immigration officer, an immigration officer;[34]

- where the order was made on an application under s 15 by the Director General, the Director General;[35]

- where the order was made on an application under s 15 by the GLA Authority, the GLA Authority.[36]

Interim slavery and trafficking prevention orders

23.15

Where an application for an STPO under MSA 2015, s 15 has not been determined,[37] an application for an interim STPO may be made by the same complaint as the main application,[38] or by the same person and to the same court as the main application.[39]

23.16

The court may make the order if it considers it just to do so.[40]

23.17

An interim STPO prohibits D from the activities described in the order,[41] within or outside the UK,[42] or in any part of it.[43]

23.18

The order may (as well as imposing prohibitions on the defendant) require the defendant to comply with MSA 2015, s 19(3)–(6), which require that:

- From the day on which an STPO is served on D, they have three days to notify in the manner and to the person specified in the order, the relevant matters, namely:[44]

---

33 MSA 2015, s 20(2)(d).
34 MSA 2015, s 20(2)(e).
35 MSA 2015, s 20(2)(f).
36 MSA 2015, s 20(2)(g).
37 MSA 2015, s 21(1).
38 MSA 2015, s 21(2)(a).
39 MSA 2015, s 21(2)(b).
40 MSA 2015, s 21(3).
41 MSA 2015, s 21(4).
42 MSA 2015, s 21(4).
43 MSA 2015, s 21(5).
44 MSA 2015, s 19(3).

    −   D's name and, where D uses one or more other names, each of those names;[45] and

    −   D's home address.[46]

- If while subject to the order, D:

    −   uses a name which has not been notified;[47] or

    −   changes home address,[48]

they must, within three days beginning with the day on which D uses the name or changes home address,[49] in the manner and to the person specified in the order, notify of that.

23.19

If the interim STPO does impose such requirements, those subsections apply as if references to an STPO were to an interim STPO.

23.20

An interim STPO has effect only for a fixed period, specified in the order[50] and ceases to have effect, if it has not already done so, on the determination of the main application.[51]

23.21

The applicant or the defendant may by complaint apply to the court that made the interim STPO for the order to be varied, renewed or discharged,[52] and an interim STPO can be appealed to the Crown Court.[53]

Appeal

23.22

STPOs made on application[54] and interim STPOs,[55] may be appealed to the Crown Court.

---

45 MSA 2015, s 19(4)(a).
46 MSA 2015, s 19(4)(b).
47 MSA 2015, s 19(5)(a).
48 MSA 2015, s 19(5)(b).
49 MSA 2015, s 19(6).
50 MSA 2015, s 21(7)(a).
51 MSA 2015, s 21(7)(b).
52 MSA 2015, s 21(8).
53 MSA 2015, s 22(2).
54 MSA 2015, s 22(1)(c).
55 MSA 2015, s 22(2).

23.23

On an appeal against an STPO made on application, the Crown Court may make such orders as may be necessary to give effect to its determination of the appeal and may also make such incidental or consequential orders as appear to it to be just.[56]

23.24

Any order made by the Crown Court on such an appeal is, for the purposes of MSA 2015, s 20(10) (variation etc) or s 21(8) (interim STPOs), to be treated as if it were an order of the court from which the appeal was brought.[57]

Breach

23.25

A person who, without reasonable excuse:

- does anything they are prohibited from doing by an STPO;[58] or
- does anything they are prohibited from doing by an interim STPO;[59]
- fails to comply with a requirement to surrender passports (MSA 2015, s 18(4));[60] or
- provide their name and address (MSA 2015, s 19(1) or s 21(6)),[61]

is liable on conviction:

- on indictment – to imprisonment for a term not exceeding five years;[62]
- summarily – to imprisonment for a term not exceeding six months, or a fine, or both.[63]

23.26

The court cannot give a conditional discharge in respect of a breach offence.[64]

---

56 MSA 2015, s 22(4).
57 MSA 2015, s 22(5).
58 MSA 2015, s 30(1)(a).
59 MSA 2015, s 30(1)(b).
60 MSA 2015, s 30(2)(a).
61 MSA 2015, s 30(2)(b).
62 MSA 2015, s 30(3)(a).
63 MSA 2015, s 30(3)(b).
64 MSA 2015, s 30(4).

24 Serious Crime Prevention Orders (on application to the High Court)

24.01

This chapter sets out the ways in which an application to the High Court for a serious crime prevention order (SCPO) under the Serious Crime Act (SCA) 2007 is different to an application made to the Crown Court on conviction. Where the same provisions apply to both sorts of orders, readers are referred to Chapter 10.

24.02

The High Court may make an SCPO if:

- it is satisfied that a person (D) has been involved in serious crime (whether in England and Wales or elsewhere);[1] and

- it has reasonable grounds to believe that the order would protect the public by preventing, restricting or disrupting involvement by the person in serious crime in England and Wales.[2]

Pre-requisite 1 – involved in serious crime, whether in England and Wales or elsewhere

24.03

D has been involved in serious crime in England and Wales if he has:

- committed a serious offence in England and Wales;[3]

- facilitated the commission by another person of a serious offence in England and Wales;[4] or

---

1   SCA 2007, s 1(1)(a).
2   SCA 2007, s 1(1)(b).
3   SCA 2007, s 2(1)(a).
4   SCA 2007, s 2(1)(b).

- conducted him- or herself in a way that was likely to facilitate the commission by him- or herself or another person of a serious offence in England and Wales (whether or not such an offence was committed).[5]

24.04

Involvement (ie that which is ongoing, as opposed to in the past, as in s 2(1)) in serious crime is any one or more of those acts listed at 24.03, with the same definitions applying.[6]

24.05

D has been involved in serious crime elsewhere than in England and Wales if s/he:

- has committed a serious offence in a country outside England and Wales;[7]

  - this means an offence (however described, providing it is an act punishable under the law)[8] under the law of a country outside England and Wales which, at the time when the court is considering the application or matter in question would be an offence under the law of England and Wales if committed in or as regards England and Wales;[9] and either:

    (a) would be an offence which is specified, or falls within a description specified, in Part 1 of Sch 1 to SCA 2007 if committed in or as regards England and Wales;[10] or

    (b) is conduct which, in the particular circumstances of the case, the Court considers to be sufficiently serious to be treated for the purposes of the application or matter as if it was specified in Sch 1, Part 1;[11]

- has facilitated the commission by another person of a serious offence in a country outside England and Wales;[12] or

- has conducted him- or herself in a way that was likely to facilitate the commission by him- or herself or another person of a serious offence in a country outside England and Wales (whether or not such an offence was committed).[13]

---

5 SCA 2007, s 2(1)(c).
6 SCA 2007, s 2(3)(a)–(c) .
7 SCA 2007, s 2(4)(a).
8 SCA 2007, s 2(7).
9 SCA 2007, s 2(5)(a).
10 SCA 2007, s 2(5)(b)(i).
11 SCA 2007, s 2(5)(b)(ii).
12 SCA 2007, s 2(4)(b).
13 SCA 2007, s 2(4)(c).

Pre-requisite 2 – making the order would prevent/ restrict/disrupt 'involvement in serious crime'

24.06

See 10.13 ff.

Standard of proof

24.07

Proceedings before the High Court are civil,[14] and the civil standard of proof is said to apply.[15] However, see 10.23 ff on this, where case law has held that the standard of proof to be applied is the criminal standard.

Content, duration and other matters

24.08

An SCPO made under this section may contain such prohibitions, restrictions or requirements;[16] and such other terms;[17] as the Court considers appropriate for the purpose of protecting the public by preventing, restricting or disrupting involvement by the person concerned in serious crime in England and Wales. For more details on particular content issues, see 10.26, and for the safeguards applying to the Court's powers under this section,[18] see 10.36. The same provisions relating to orders against different types of organisations (eg corporations (see 10.29) and partnerships (see 10.47)) and duration also apply.

Opportunity to make representations

24.09

The High Court must, on an application by a person, give the person an opportunity to make representations in proceedings before it about:

- the making of an SCPO if it considers that the making of the order would be likely to have a significant adverse effect on that person;[19]

- the variation of an SCPO if it considers that:

---

14 SCA 2007, s 35(1).
15 SCA 2007, s 35(2).
16 SCA 2007, s 1(3)(a).
17 SCA 2007, s 1(3)(b).
18 SCA 2007, s 1(4).
19 SCA 2007, s 9(1).

–   the variation of the order;[20] or

–   a decision not to vary it;[21]

would be likely to have a significant adverse effect on that person;

• the discharge of an SCPO if it considers that

–   the discharge of the order;[22] or

–   a decision not to discharge it,[23]

would be likely to have a significant adverse effect on that person.

Variation

24.10

SCA 2007, s 17(1) provides that the High Court may, on an application under this section, vary an SCPO in England and Wales if it has reasonable grounds to believe that the terms of the order as varied would protect the public by preventing, restricting or disrupting involvement by the person who is the subject in serious crime in England and Wales.

24.11

An application for the variation of an SCPO may be made by the relevant applicant authority;[24] D subject to the order;[25] or any other person.[26]

24.12

The Court must not entertain an application by D unless it considers that there has been a change of circumstances affecting the order.[27]

24.13

The Court must not entertain an application by any other person unless it considers that:

• the person is significantly adversely affected by the order;[28] AND

---

20 SCA 2007, s 9(2)(a).
21 SCA 2007, s 9(2)(b).
22 SCA 2007, s 9(3)(a).
23 SCA 2007, s 9(3)(b).
24 SCA 2007, s 17(3)(a) – which will be the Director of Public Prosecutions or the Director of the Serious Fraud Office where there has been a conviction.
25 SCA 2007, s 17(3)(b)(i).
26 SCA 2007, s 17(3)(b)(ii).
27 SCA 2007, s 17(4).
28 SCA 2007, s 17(5)(a).

- the person has, on an application under SCA 2007, s 9, been given an opportunity to make representations;[29] or has made an application otherwise than under s 9[30] in earlier proceedings in relation to the order and there has been a change of circumstances affecting the order,[31,32] OR

- the person has not made an application of any kind in earlier proceedings in relation to the order,[33] and it was reasonable in all the circumstances for them not to have done so,[34] AND

- the application is not for the purpose of making the order more onerous on the person who is the subject of it.[35]

24.14

A variation on an application by the relevant applicant authority may include an extension of the period during which the order, or any provision of it, is in force (subject to the original limits imposed by SCA 2007, s 16(2) and (4)(b)).[36]

Discharge of SCPOs

24.15

On application by the relevant applicant authority,[37] D subject to the order,[38] or any other person,[39] the High Court may discharge an SCPO.[40]

24.16

The High Court must not entertain an application by D unless it considers that there has been a change of circumstances affecting the order.[41]

24.17

The High Court must not entertain an application by any other person unless it considers that:[42]

---

29 SCA 2007, s 17(6)(a)(i).
30 SCA 2007, s 17(6)(a)(ii).
31 SCA 2007, s 17(6)(b).
32 SCA 2007, s 17(6).
33 SCA 2007, s 17(7)(a).
34 SCA 2007, s 17(7)(b).
35 SCA 2007, s 17(5)(c).
36 SCA 2007, s 17(8).
37 SCA 2007, s 18(2)(a).
38 SCA 2007, s 18(2)(b)(i).
39 SCA 2007, s 18(2)(b)(ii).
40 SCA 2007, s 18(1).
41 SCA 2007, s 18(3).
42 SCA 2007, s 18(4).

- the person is significantly adversely affected by the order;[43] AND

- the person has, on an application under SCA 2007, s 9, been given an opportunity to make representations;[44] or has made an application otherwise than under s 9[45] in earlier proceedings in relation to the order and there has been a change of circumstances affecting the order;[46,47] OR

- the person has not made an application of any kind in earlier proceedings in relation to the order,[48] and it was reasonable in all the circumstances for them not to have done so.[49]

Appeal

24.18

An appeal may be made to the Court of Appeal in relation to a decision of the High Court:

- to make an SCPO;[50]

- to vary, or not, an SCPO;[51] or

- to discharge, or not, an SCPO,[52]

by any person who was given an opportunity to make representations in the proceedings concerned by virtue of SCA 2007, s 9.

24.19

This power does not prejudice the rights of other persons to make appeals, by virtue of SCA 2007, s 16 in relation to any judgments or orders of the High Court about SCPOs.[53]

Breach

24.20

The same provisions apply as to SCPOs on conviction (see 10.83 ff).

---

43 SCA 2007, s 18(4)(a).
44 SCA 2007, s 18(5)(a)(i).
45 SCA 2007, s 18(5)(a)(ii).
46 SCA 2007, s 18(5)(b).
47 SCA 2007, s 18(5).
48 SCA 2007, s 17(7)(a).
49 SCA 2007, s 17(7)(b).
50 SCA 2007, s 23(1)(a).
51 SCA 2007, s 23(1)(b).
52 SCA 2007, s 23(1)(c).
53 SCA 2007, s 23(2).

PART 3

ORDERS AVAILABLE ONLY FOR YOUNG OFFENDERS

25 Reparation Orders

25.01

Reparation orders[1] are created by s 73 of the Powers of Criminal Courts (Sentencing) Act (PCC(S)A) 2000, and are available only on conviction for young offenders under the age of 18 for an offence for which the sentence is not fixed by law.[2] If the court does not make a reparation order in a case where it has power to do so it has to give reasons.[3]

Effect of an order

25.02

Such an order may require the defendant (D) to make reparation (other than by compensation)[4] as specified in the order to:

- one or more people specified in the order;[5] or
- the community at large,[6]

who are identified by the court as a victim of the offence or affected by it.

Pre-conditions for the making of an order

25.03

The court shall not make a reparation order if it proposes to sentence D to:

- a custodial sentence;[7] or
- a youth rehabilitation order (YRO);[8] or
- a referral order.[9]

---

1   PCC(S)A 2000, s 73(2).
2   PCC(S)A 2000, s 73(1).
3   PCC(S)A 2000, s 73(8).
4   PCC(S)A 2000, s 73(3).
5   PCC(S)A 2000, s 73(1)(a).
6   PCC(S)A 2000, s 73(1)(b).
7   PCC(S)A 2000, s 73(4)(a).
8   PCC(S)A 2000, s 73(4)(b).
9   PCC(S)A 2000, s 73(4)(b).

25.04

The court shall not make a reparation order if D has a current YRO unless when it makes the reparation order it revokes the YRO.[10] Written notice of the revocation must be supplied to the parties as required by Sch 2, para 24 to the Criminal Justice and Immigration Act 2008.[11]

25.05

Before making a reparation order, a court shall obtain and consider a written report by an officer of a local probation board, provider of probation services, social worker of a local authority or a member of a youth offending team (YOT) indicating:

- the type of work that is suitable for the offender;[12] and

- the attitude of the victim(s) to the requirements proposed to be included in the order.[13]

25.06

The court shall not make a reparation order unless it has been notified by the Secretary of State that arrangements for implementing such orders are available in the area proposed to be named in the order under PCC(S)A 2000, s 74(4) and the notice has not been withdrawn.[14]

Contents of an order

25.07

Requirements specified in a reparation order are to be commensurate with the seriousness of the offence, or the combination of the offence and one or more offences associated with it.[15]

25.08

However, a reparation order shall not require the offender:

- to work for more than 24 hours in aggregate;[16] or

- to make reparation to any victim or person affected without the consent of that person.[17]

---

10 PCC(S)A 2000, s 73(4A).
11 PCC(S)A 2000, s 73(4B).
12 PCC(S)A 2000, s 73(5)(a).
13 PCC(S)A 2000, s 73(5)(b).
14 PCC(S)A 2000, s 73(6).
15 PCC(S)A 2000, s 74(2).
16 PCC(S)A 2000, s 74(1)(a).
17 PCC(S)A 2000, s 74(1)(b).

25.09

Requirements specified in the order shall, as far as practicable, avoid:

- any conflict with the offender's religious beliefs;[18] and

- any interference with times at which he normally works or attends school or any other educational establishment.[19]

25.10

A reparation order shall name the local justice area in which it appears to the court making or amending a reparation order that the offender resides or will reside.[20]

25.11

Any reparation required by a reparation order:

- shall be made under the supervision of the responsible officer;[21] and

- shall be made within a period of three months from the date of the making of the order.[22]

25.12

Under the PCC(S)A 2000, 'responsible officer', in relation to an offender subject to a reparation order, means one of the following who is specified in the order:

- an officer of a local probation board or provider of probation services:[23]

    - who must be an officer acting in the local justice area named in the order;[24]

- a social worker of a local authority:[25]

    - who must be a social worker of the local authority within whose area it appears the offender does or will reside;[26] or

- a member of a YOT:[27]

    - who must be a member of the YOT established by the local authority within whose area it appears the offender does or will reside.[28]

---

18 PCC(S)A 2000, s 74(3)(a).
19 PCC(S)A 2000, s 74(3)(b).
20 PCC(S)A 2000, s 74(4).
21 PCC(S)A 2000, s 74(8)(a).
22 PCC(S)A 2000, s 74(8)(b).
23 PCC(S)A 2000, s 74(5)(a).
24 PCC(S)A 2000, s 74(6) and (6A).
25 PCC(S)A 2000, s 74(5)(b).
26 PCC(S)A 2000, s 74(7)(a).
27 PCC(S)A 2000, s 74(5)(c).
28 PCC(S)A 2000, s 74(7)(b).

Amendment, revocation etc

25.13

Paragraph 5 of Sch 8 to PCC(S)A 2000 addresses revocation or amendment hearings. If while a reparation order is in force, it appears to the relevant court, on the application of the responsible officer or the offender, that it is appropriate to do so, the court may:

- make an order revoking the reparation order;[29] or

- make an order amending it:[30]

  - by cancelling any provision included in it;[31] or

  - by inserting in it (additionally or in substitution) any provision which could have been included in the order if the court had then had power to make it and were exercising the power.[32]

25.14

Where an application for the revocation of a reparation order is dismissed, no further application for its revocation shall be made except with the consent of the relevant court,[33] which is:

- a youth court acting in the local justice area named in the order;[34] or

- in the case of an application made both under Sch 8, para 5 and under Sch 8, para 2(1), the youth court for the area where D lives.[35]

25.15

Any amendments or revocations must be made with D present at court,[36] except for:

- revoking the reparation order;[37]

- cancelling a requirement included in the reparation order;[38]

- altering the name of any area in the reparation order;[39]

- changing the responsible officer.[40]

---

29 PCC(S)A 2000, Sch 8, para 5(1)(a).
30 PCC(S)A 2000, Sch 8, para 5(1)(b).
31 PCC(S)A 2000, Sch 8, para 5(1)(b)(i).
32 PCC(S)A 2000, Sch 8, para 5(1)(b)(ii).
33 PCC(S)A 2000, Sch 8, para 5(3).
34 PCC(S)A 2000, Sch 8, para 5(4)(a).
35 PCC(S)A 2000, Sch 8, para 5(4)(b).
36 PCC(S)A 2000, Sch 8, para 6(1).
37 PCC(S)A 2000, Sch 8, para 6(9)(a).
38 PCC(S)A 2000, Sch 8, para 6(9)(b).
39 PCC(S)A 2000, Sch 8, para 6(9)(c).
40 PCC(S)A 2000, Sch 8, para 6(9)(d).

25.16

Where the responsible officer makes an application to a court concerning breach, or revocation or amendment of a reparation order he may bring the offender before the court; and a court shall not make an order (except for those in 25.15) unless the offender is present before the court.[41]

25.17

Without prejudice to any other power to issue a summons or warrant apart from Sch 8, para 6(2), the court to which an application is made may issue a summons or warrant for the purpose of securing the attendance of the offender.[42]

25.18

Section 55(3) and (4) of the Magistrates' Courts Act (MCA) 1980 (which among other things restrict the circumstances in which a warrant may be issued) applies with the necessary modifications to such a warrant, but as if in s 55(3) after the word 'summons' there were inserted the words 'cannot be served or'.[43]

25.19

Where the offender is arrested in pursuance of a warrant and cannot be brought immediately before the court to which the warrant directs the offender be brought ('the relevant court'), the person in whose custody he is:

- may make arrangements for his detention in a place of safety[44] for a period of not more than 72 hours from the time of the arrest (and it shall be lawful for him to be detained in pursuance of the arrangements);[45] and

- shall within that period bring him before a youth court.[46]

25.20

When he is brought before a youth court other than the relevant court, the youth court may:

- direct that he be released forthwith;[47] or

- remand him to local authority accommodation,[48] providing he is under 18.[49]

---

41 PCC(S)A 2000, Sch 8, para 6(1).
42 PCC(S)A 2000, Sch 8, para 6(2).
43 PCC(S)A 2000, Sch 8, para 6(3).
44 PCC(S)A 2000, Sch 8, para 6(4) – having the same definition as in the Children and Young Persons Act 1933.
45 PCC(S)A 2000, Sch 8, para 6(4)(a).
46 PCC(S)A 2000, Sch 8, para 6(4)(b).
47 PCC(S)A 2000, Sch 8, para 6(5)(a).
48 PCC(S)A 2000, Sch 8, para 6(5)(b).
49 As per PCC(S)A 2000, Sch 8, para 6(7).

25.21

Where an application is made to a court to revoke or amend a reparation order, the court may remand (or further remand) the offender to local authority accommodation if:

- a warrant has been issued for the purpose of securing the attendance of the offender at court;[50] or

- the court considers that remanding (or further remanding) him will enable information to be obtained which is likely to assist the court in deciding whether and, if so, how to exercise its powers to revoke or amend the reparation order.[51]

25.22

However, where the offender is 18 or over when he is brought before a youth court other than the relevant court, or is aged 18 or over when the relevant court could exercise its powers to remand D to local authority accommodation, he shall not be remanded to local authority accommodation but may instead be remanded:

- to a remand centre, if the court has been notified that such a centre is available for the reception of persons under Sch 8, para 6(7);[52] or

- to a prison, if there has been no notification that a remand centre is available.[53]

25.23

A court remanding an offender to local authority accommodation shall designate, as the authority who are to receive him, the local authority for the area in which the offender resides or, where it appears to the court that he does not reside in the area of a local authority, the local authority specified by the court[54] and in whose area the offence or an offence associated with it was committed.[55]

Power to remand

25.24

PCC(S)A 2000, Sch 8, para 6A addresses procedural matters relating to breach, revocation or amendment hearings.

---

50 PCC(S)A 2000, Sch 8, para 6(6)(a).
51 PCC(S)A 2000, Sch 8, para 6(6)(b).
52 PCC(S)A 2000, Sch 8, para 6(7)(a).
53 PCC(S)A 2000, Sch 8, para 6(7)(b).
54 PCC(S)A 2000, Sch 8, para 6(8)(a).
55 PCC(S)A 2000, Sch 8, para 6(8)(b).

25.25

The youth court[56] may adjourn any hearing relating to the breach, revocation or amendment of a reparation order.[57] Where it does, it may:

- direct that the offender be released forthwith;[58] or

- remand the offender.[59]

25.26

Where the court remands the offender:

- it must fix the time and place at which the hearing is to be resumed;[60] and

- that time and place must be the time and place at which the offender is required to appear or be brought before the court by virtue of the remand.[61]

25.27

Where the court adjourns but does not remand the offender:

- it may fix the time and place at which the hearing is to be resumed;[62] but

- if it does not do so, it must not resume the hearing unless it is satisfied that the offender,[63] their parent or guardian if the offender is under 14,[64] a local authority[65] with parental responsibility[66,67] and the responsible officer,[68] have had adequate notice of the time and place for the resumed hearing.[69]

25.28

The powers of a youth court under Sch 8, para 6A may be exercised by a single justice of the peace, notwithstanding anything in MCA 1980,[70] and when that occurs, it is this paragraph that applies to the adjournment in place of MCA 1980, s 10.[71] This only applies to breach, revocation or amendment hearings.[72]

---

56 PCC(S)A 2000, Sch 8, para 6A(1).
57 PCC(S)A 2000, Sch 8, para 6A(2).
58 PCC(S)A 2000, Sch 8, para 6A(2)(a).
59 PCC(S)A 2000, Sch 8, para 6A(2)(b).
60 PCC(S)A 2000, Sch 8, para 6A(3)(a).
61 PCC(S)A 2000, Sch 8, para 6A(3)(b).
62 PCC(S)A 2000, Sch 8, para 6A(4)(a).
63 PCC(S)A 2000, Sch 8, para 6A(5)(a).
64 PCC(S)A 2000, Sch 8, para 6A(5)(b).
65 PCC(S)A 2000, Sch 8, para 6A(7) – as defined in s 7 of the Criminal Justice and Immigration Act 2008.
66 PCC(S)A 2000, Sch 8, para 6A(7) – as defined in s 3 of the Children Act 1989.
67 PCC(S)A 2000, Sch 8, para 6A(6).
68 PCC(S)A 2000, Sch 8, para 6A(5)(c).
69 PCC(S)A 2000, Sch 8, para 6A(4)b).
70 PCC(S)A 2000, Sch 8, para 6A(8).
71 PCC(S)A 2000, Sch 8, para 6A(9)(a).
72 PCC(S)A 2000, Sch 8, para 6A(9)(b).

Appeals against orders made on breach, or on applications to revoke or amend

25.29

These are dealt with in PCC(S)A 2000, Sch 8, para 7.

25.30

The offender may appeal to the Crown Court against:

- any order made when dealing with D for a breach of a requirement of a reparation order, or any order dealing with amendment or revocation except an order which could have been made in his absence (by virtue of PCC(S)A 2000, Sch 8, para 6(9));[73]

- the dismissal of an application to revoke a reparation order.[74]

Breach

25.31

PCC(S)A 2000, Sch 8, para 2 makes provision for dealing with breaches of requirements of a reparation order.

25.32

Breach proceedings are brought on the application of the responsible officer, where the offender has failed to comply with any requirement included in the order.[75]

25.33

Any proceedings for breach of a reparation order must take place in:

- a youth court acting in the local justice area in which the offender resides;[76] or

- if it is not known where the offender resides, a youth court acting in the local justice area named in the order.[77]

---

73 PCC(S)A 2000, Sch 8, para 7(1)(a).
74 PCC(S)A 2000, Sch 8, para 7(1)(b).
75 PCC(S)A 2000, Sch 8, para 2(1).
76 PCC(S)A 2000, Sch 8, para 2(1)(a).
77 PCC(S)A 2000, Sch 8, para 2(1)(b).

25.34

If the court is satisfied that there has been a breach, whether or not it revokes or amends the order under PCC(S)A 2000, Sch 8, para 5(1),[78] it may:

- order the offender to pay a fine of an amount not exceeding £1,000;[79] or

- if the reparation order was made by a magistrates' court, revoke the order and deal with the offender, for the offence in respect of which the order was made, in any way in which he could have been dealt with for that offence by the court which made the order if the order had not been made;[80] or

- if the reparation order was made by the Crown Court, commit him in custody or release him on bail until he appears before the Crown Court.[81]

25.35

If the court commits the offender, it shall send to the Crown Court a certificate signed by a justice of the peace giving:

- particulars of the offender's breach;[82] and

- such other particulars of the case as may be desirable;[83]

and that certificate is admissible as evidence of the breach before the Crown Court.

25.36

Where, having been committed, the offender is brought or appears before the Crown Court,[84] and the breach is proven or admitted,[85] that court may deal with him for the offence in respect of which the order was made in any way in which it could have dealt with him for that offence if it had not made the order. It must also revoke the reparation order if it is still in force.[86]

25.37

A fine imposed for breach under para 2 is deemed to be a sum adjudged to be paid by a conviction.[87]

---

78 PCC(S)A 2000, Sch 8, para 2(2)(a).
79 PCC(S)A 2000, Sch 8, para 2(2)(a)(i).
80 PCC(S)A 2000, Sch 8, para 2(2)(b).
81 PCC(S)A 2000, Sch 8, para 2(2)(c).
82 PCC(S)A 2000, Sch 8, para 2(3)(a).
83 PCC(S)A 2000, Sch 8, para 2(3)(b).
84 PCC(S)A 2000, Sch 8, para 2(4)(a).
85 PCC(S)A 2000, Sch 8, para 2(4)(b).
86 PCC(S)A 2000, Sch 8, para 2(5).
87 PCC(S)A 2000, Sch 8, para 2(6).

25.38

When dealing with an offender for breach under para 2, a court shall take into account the extent to which he has complied with the requirements of the reparation order.[88]

25.39

Where a reparation order has been made on appeal, it shall be deemed:

- if it was made on an appeal brought from a magistrates' court, to have been made by that magistrates' court;[89]

- if it was made on an appeal brought from the Crown Court or from the Criminal Division of the Court of Appeal, to have been made by the Crown Court,[90]

and, in relation to a reparation order made on appeal, para (2)(b) shall have effect as if the words 'if the order had not been made' were omitted and para 2(4) above shall have effect as if the words 'if it had not made the order' were omitted.

---

88 PCC(S)A 2000, Sch 8, para 2(7).
89 PCC(S)A 2000, Sch 8, para 2(8)(a).
90 PCC(S)A 2000, Sch 8, para 2(8)(b).

PART 4

CIVIL ORDERS MADE BY CRIMINAL COURTS

26 Violent Offender Orders

26.01

Violent offender orders (VOOs) are a standalone civil order available only on complaint by the chief of police for the relevant area. They were created by s 98 of the Criminal Justice and Immigration Act (CJIA) 2008.

26.02

A VOO is an order made in respect of a qualifying offender (see 26.03 ff) which contains such prohibitions, restrictions or conditions authorised by s 102 as the court making the order considers necessary for the purpose of protecting the public from the risk of serious violent harm caused by the offender.[1]

Pre-condition 1 – 'qualifying offender'

26.03

These orders can only be made in respect of 'qualifying offenders',[2] as defined in CJIA 2008, s 99.

26.04

A qualifying offender is aged 18 or over,[3] AND:

- has been convicted of a specified offence;[4] AND either received:
  - a custodial sentence of at least 12 months;[5] OR
  - a hospital order (with or without restriction);[6]
- has been found not guilty of a specified offence by reason of insanity[7] AND the court made a hospital order (with or without restriction),[8] or a supervision order;[9]

---

1   CJIA 2008, s 98(1)(a).
2   CJIA 2008, s 100(2)(a).
3   CJIA 2008, s 99(1).
4   CJIA 2008, s 99(2).
5   CJIA 2008, s 99(2)(a)(i).
6   CJIA 2008, s 99(2)(a)(ii).
7   CJIA 2008, s 99(2)(b).
8   CJIA 2008, s 99(3)(a).
9   CJIA 2008, s 99(3)(b).

- has been found to be under a disability and to have done the act charged in respect of a specified offence[10] AND the court made a hospital order (with or without restriction),[11] or a supervision order;[12]

- has been convicted in another jurisdiction of a relevant offence[13] (that being an offence in that jurisdiction,[14] however described,[15] which would have constituted a specified offence, or murder, in England and Wales[16]); AND either received by way of sentence:

  - a sentence of imprisonment or other detention for at least 12 months;[17] OR

  - an order equivalent to a hospital order (with or without restriction) or a supervision order;

- a court exercising jurisdiction under that law has made a finding equivalent to a finding that the person was not guilty by reason of insanity in respect of a relevant offence and has made an order equivalent to a hospital order (with or without restriction) or supervision order;[18] or

- such a court has made a finding equivalent to a finding that the person was under a disability and did the act charged in respect of a relevant offence, and has made an order equivalent to a hospital order (with or without restriction) or a supervision order.[19]

26.05

The requirement that the offence would be a specified offence in England and Wales is to be taken as fulfilled unless, not later than rules of court may provide,[20] the offender serves on the applicant a notice:[21]

- denying that, on the facts as alleged with respect to the act in question, the condition is met;[22]

- giving the reasons for denying that it is met;[23] and

- requiring the applicant to prove that it is met.[24]

---

10   CJIA 2008, s 99(2)(c).
11   CJIA 2008, s 99(3)(a).
12   CJIA 2008, s 99(3)(b).
13   CJIA 2008, s 99(4)(a).
14   CJIA 2008, s 99(5)(a).
15   CJIA 2008, s 99(6).
16   CJIA 2008, s 99(5)(b).
17   CJIA 2008, s 99(4)(a)(i).
18   CJIA 2008, s 99(4)(b).
19   CJIA 2008, s 99(4)(c).
20   Or without notice, if the court thinks fit – CJIA 2008, s 99(8).
21   CJIA 2008, s 99(7).
22   CJIA 2008, s 99(7)(a).
23   CJIA 2008, s 99(7)(b).
24   CJIA 2008, s 99(7)(c).

26.06

If the offender wishes to serve such a notice on the applicant, the offender must do so no later than three days before the hearing date for the application.[25]

Protecting the public

26.07

'Protecting the public from the risk of serious violent harm caused by a person' is a reference to protecting the public in the UK,[26] or any particular members of the public in the UK,[27] from a current risk of serious physical or psychological harm caused by that person committing one or more specified offences.

Specified offence

26.08

A 'specified offence' is:

- manslaughter;[28]

- an offence under s 4 of the Offences Against the Person Act (OAPA) 1861 (soliciting murder);[29]

- an offence under OAPA 1861, s 18 (wounding with intent to cause grievous bodily harm);[30]

- an offence under OAPA 1861, s 20 (malicious wounding);[31]

- attempting to commit murder or conspiracy to commit murder;[32] or

- a relevant service offence,[33] being any offence under:

   - Army Act 1955, s 70;[34] or

   - Air Force Act 1955, s 70;[35] or

   - Naval Discipline Act 1957, s 42;[36] or

---

25 Magistrates' Courts (Violent Offender Orders) Rules 2009 (SI 2009/2197), r 4.
26 CJIA 2008, s 98(2)(a).
27 CJIA 2008, s 98(2)(b).
28 CJIA 2008, s 98(3)(a).
29 CJIA 2008, s 98(3)(b).
30 CJIA 2008, s 98(3)(c).
31 CJIA 2008, s 98(3)(d).
32 CJIA 2008, s 98(3)(e).
33 CJIA 2008, s 98(3)(f).
34 CJIA 2008, s 98(4)(a)(i).
35 CJIA 2008, s 98(4)(a)(ii).
36 CJIA 2008, s 98(4)(a)(iii).

- Armed Forces Act 2006, s 48 (attempts, conspiracy etc of any of those offences)[37] of which the corresponding civil offence (within the meaning of the section in question) is a specified offence as defined above; and

- any offence under s 42 of the Armed Forces Act 2006 in respect of which the corresponding offence under the law of England and Wales is a specified offence as defined above.

Pre-condition 2 – behaviour giving reasonable cause to believe order necessary

26.09

As well as being a qualifying offender, the person must have 'since the appropriate date, acted in such a way as to give reasonable cause to believe that it is necessary for a violent offender order to be made in respect of the person'.[38]

26.10

The appropriate date is the date (or, as the case may be, the first date) on which the person was convicted of a specified offence and received either a custodial sentence of at least 12 months,[39] or a hospital order (with or without restriction),[40] or had been convicted of and received the equivalent outside of the UK,[41] whether that date fell before or after the commencement of VOOs.[42]

Procedure for application

26.11

A chief officer of police may, by complaint to a magistrates' court, apply for a VOO in respect of a person who resides in the chief officer's police area,[43] or who the chief officer believes is in, or is intending to come to, that area,[44] if it appears to the chief officer that the pre-conditions set out above are met.

---

37 CJIA 2008, s 98(5).
38 CJIA 2008, s 100(2)(b).
39 CJIA 2008, s 99(2)(a).
40 CJIA 2008, s 99(2)(b).
41 CJIA 2008, s 99(4).
42 CJIA 2008, s 100(5).
43 CJIA 2008, s 100(1)(a).
44 CJIA 2008, s 100(1)(b).

26.12

An application under this section may be made to any magistrates' court whose commission area includes any part of the applicant's police area,[45] or any place where it is alleged that the person acted in such a way as to give reasonable cause to believe that it is necessary for a VOO to be made in respect of the person.[46]

26.13

An application shall be in the form provided in para 1 of Sch 1 to the Magistrates' Courts (Violent Offender Orders) Rules 2009.[47]

26.14

A magistrates' court may not begin hearing an application for a VOO[48] unless it is satisfied that the subject of the proposed order[49] has been given notice of the application,[50] and the time and place of the hearing,[51] a reasonable time before the hearing.

26.15

The court must hear both the applicant,[52] and the person (P) regarding whom the application is made (if they wish to be heard),[53] before deciding whether the pre-conditions set out above are met. The court can only make an order if they are met.[54]

26.16

When deciding whether it is necessary to make such an order, the court must have regard to whether P would, at any time when such an order would be in force, be subject under any other enactment to any measures that would operate to protect the public from the risk of such harm.[55]

26.17

A VOO may be applied for and made at any time,[56] but may not be made so as to come into force at any time when P:

---

45   CJIA 2008, s 100(3)(a).
46   CJIA 2008, s 100(3)(b).
47   As required by r 2(1)(a).
48   CJIA 2008, s 105(1)(a).
49   CJIA 2008, s 105(3)(a) and (b).
50   CJIA 2008, s 105(2)(a).
51   CJIA 2008, s 105(2)(b).
52   CJIA 2008, s 101(2)(a).
53   CJIA 2008, s 101(2)(b).
54   CJIA 2008, s 101(3)(a) and (b).
55   CJIA 2008, s 101(4).
56   CJIA 2008, s 101(6).

- is subject to a custodial sentence imposed in respect of any offence;[57]

- is on licence for part of the term of a custodial sentence;[58] or

- is subject to a hospital order or a supervision order made in respect of any offence.[59]

Content of an order

26.18

Any VOO made shall be in the form provided in para 1 of Sch 2 to the Magistrates' Courts (Violent Offender Orders) Rules 2009.[60]

26.19

A VOO may contain prohibitions, restrictions or conditions preventing the offender from doing the following, (in Scotland and Northern Ireland as well as England and Wales):[61,62]

- going to any premises, or other place, at all or at particular times, as specified in the order;[63,64]

- attending any specified event;[65]

- having any, or any specified description of, contact with any specified individual.[66]

26.20

If one of the requirements is notification, this is dealt with in some detail both in CJIA 2008, ss 107–112, and supplemented by the Criminal Justice and Immigration Act 2008 (Violent Offender Orders) (Notification Requirements) Regulations 2009.[67]

---

57   CJIA 2008, s 101(5)(a).
58   CJIA 2008, s 101(5)(b).
59   CJIA 2008, s 101(5)(c).
60   As required by r 2(2).
61   CJIA 2008, s 102(2).
62   CJIA 2008, s 102(1).
63   CJIA 2008, s 102(4) defines 'specified' as matters specified in the order.
64   CJIA 2008, s 102(1)(a).
65   CJIA 2008, s 102(1)(b).
66   CJIA 2008, s 102(1)(c).
67   SI 2009/2019.

Duration

26.21

A VOO must last for at least two years, but not more than five years, as specified in the order (unless renewed or discharged under CJIA 2008, s 103).[68]

Application for variation, renewal or discharge

26.22

Any variation in a VOO is subject to r 3(2) of the Magistrates' Courts (Violent Offender Orders) Rules 2009,[69] which requires that an application shall be made in writing and shall specify the reason why the applicant believes the court should vary, discharge or renew the order.

26.23

An application for variation or discharge,[70] or renewal for five years or less[71] may be made by:

- the offender;[72]

- the chief officer of police who applied for the order;[73]

- (if different) the chief officer of police for the area in which the offender resides;[74] and

- (if different) a chief officer of police who believes that the offender is in, or is intending to come to, his police area.[75]

26.24

Such an application is by complaint to the appropriate magistrates' court, which means the magistrates' court that made the order or (if different), the magistrates' court for the area in which the offender resides,[76] or any magistrates' court whose area includes any part of the police area of the chief officer who made the application.[77]

---

68   CJIA 2008, s 98(1)(b).
69   According to r 3(1)(a).
70   CJIA 2008, s 103(1)(a).
71   CJIA 2008, s 103(2)(b).
72   CJIA 2008, s 103(2)(a).
73   CJIA 2008, s 103(2)(b).
74   CJIA 2008, s 103(2)(c).
75   CJIA 2008, s 103(2)(d).
76   CJIA 2008, s 103(3)(a).
77   CJIA 2008, s 103(3)(b).

26.25

A magistrates' court may not begin hearing such an application for discharge, variation or renewal of a VOO[78] unless it is satisfied that the subject[79] has been given notice of the application,[80] and the time and place of the hearing,[81] a reasonable time before the hearing.

26.26

The court will hear the applicant,[82] and any other person with the power to apply who wishes to be heard,[83] before it makes an order varying, renewing or discharging the VOO as it considers appropriate.

26.27

A VOO may only be renewed,[84] or varied,[85] so as to impose additional prohibitions, restrictions or conditions on the offender, if the court considers that it is necessary to do so for the purpose of protecting the public from the risk of serious violent harm caused by the offender. Any renewed or varied order may contain only such prohibitions, restrictions or conditions as the court considers necessary for this purpose.

26.28

A court may not discharge a VOO before the end of two years beginning with the date on which it came into force unless consent to its discharge is given by the offender and the chief officer of police (either who made the application,[86] or for the area where the offender resides[87]).

Appeals

26.29

The subject of a VOO,[88] or interim VOO,[89] can appeal to the Crown Court against the making of the order, or the making[90] or refusal[91] of variation, renewal or discharge.

---

78 CJIA 2008, s 105(1)(c).
79 CJIA 2008, s 105(3)(a) and (b).
80 CJIA 2008, s 105(2)(a).
81 CJIA 2008, s 105(2)(b).
82 CJIA 2008, s 103(4)(a).
83 CJIA 2008, s 103(4)(b).
84 CJIA 2008, s 103(5)(a).
85 CJIA 2008, s 103(5)(b).
86 CJIA 2008, s 103(7)(a).
87 CJIA 2008, s 103(7)(b).
88 CJIA 2008, s 106(1)(a).
89 CJIA 2008, s 106(1)(b).
90 CJIA 2008, s 106(2)(a).
91 CJIA 2008, s 106(2)(b).

26.30

On an appeal, the Crown Court may make such orders as may be necessary to give effect to its determination of the appeal;[92] and may also make such incidental or consequential orders as appear to it to be just.[93]

Interim VOOs

26.31

Such orders are available where an application for a VOO has not yet been determined.[94] An application shall be in the form provided in para 1 of Sch 1 to the Magistrates' Courts (Violent Offender Orders) Rules 2009.[95]

26.32

An application may be made:

- by the complaint by which the main application is made;[96] or

- if the main application has already been made to a court, by means of a further complaint made to that court by the person making the main application.[97]

26.33

A magistrates' court may not begin hearing such an application for an interim VOO[98] unless it is satisfied that the person to be the subject of the proposed order[99] has been given notice of the application,[100] and the time and place of the hearing,[101] a reasonable time before the hearing.

26.34

If it appears to the court that:

- the person to whom the main application relates (P) is a qualifying offender,

- if the court were determining that application, it would be likely to make a VOO, and

---

92 CJIA 2008, s 106(3)(a).
93 CJIA 2008, s 106(3)(b).
94 CJIA 2008, s 104(1).
95 As required by r 2(1)(b).
96 CJIA 2008, s 104(2)(a).
97 CJIA 2008, s 104(2)(b).
98 CJIA 2008, s 105(1)(b).
99 CJIA 2008, s 105(3)(a) and (b).
100 CJIA 2008, s 105(2)(a).
101 CJIA 2008, s 105(2)(b).

- that it is desirable to act before that application is determined, with a view to securing the immediate protection of the public from the risk of serious violent harm caused by P,

the court may make an interim VOO in respect of P that contains such prohibitions, restrictions or conditions as it considers necessary for the purpose of protecting the public from the risk of such harm.

26.35

An interim VOO may not be made so as to come into force at any time when P:

(a)   is subject to a custodial sentence for any offence;[102]

(b)   is on licence for part of the term of such a sentence;[103] or

(c)   is subject to a hospital order or a supervision order for any offence.[104]

26.36

An interim VOO has effect only for such period as is specified in the order,[105] and ceases to have effect, if it has not already done so,[106] when a VOO comes into force if the main application succeeds,[107] or when the main application is refused or withdrawn.[108]

26.37

Any variation in an interim VOO is subject to the provisions of CJIA 2008, s 103 (except s 103(7)),[109] and r 3(2) of the Magistrates' Courts (Violent Offender Orders) Rules 2009, which require that an application shall be made in writing and shall specify the reason why the applicant believes the court should vary, discharge or renew the order.

26.38

Any interim VOO shall be in the form provided in para 1 of Sch 3 to the Magistrates' Courts (Violent Offender Orders) Rules 2009.[110]

---

102 CJIA 2008, s 104(5)(a).
103 CJIA 2008, s 104(5)(b).
104 CJIA 2008, s 104(5)(c).
105 CJIA 2008, s 104(6)(a).
106 CJIA 2008, s 104(6)(b).
107 CJIA 2008, s 104(7)(a).
108 CJIA 2008, s 104(7)(b).
109 CJIA 2008, s 104(8).
110 As required by r 2(3).

Breach

26.39

If a person fails, without reasonable excuse, to comply with any prohibition, restriction or condition contained in a VOO[111] or interim VOO[112] they commit an offence.

26.40

Proceedings for an offence of breach may be commenced in any court having jurisdiction in any place where the person charged with the offence resides or is found.[113]

26.41

If a person fails, without reasonable excuse, to comply with CJIA 2008, ss 108(1), 109(1) or (6)(b), 110(1) or 112(4),[114] or any requirement imposed by regulations made under s 111(1),[115] the person commits an offence.

26.42

If the offence is failure to comply with CJIA 2008, ss 108(1), 109(1) or 110(1),[116] or any requirement imposed by regulations made under s 111(1),[117] the offence is committed on the day on which the person first fails, without reasonable excuse, to comply with the provision/requirement, and continues throughout any period during which the failure continues. However, a person must not be prosecuted more than once in respect of the same failure.[118]

26.43

If a person notifies to the police, in purported compliance with CJIA 2008, ss 108(1), 109(1) or 110(1),[119] or any requirement imposed by regulations made under s 111(1),[120] any information which the person knows to be false, the person commits an offence.

---

111 CJIA 2008, s 113(1)(a).
112 CJIA 2008, s 113(1)(b).
113 CJIA 2008, s 113(8).
114 CJIA 2008, s 113(2)(a).
115 CJIA 2008, s 113(2)(b).
116 CJIA 2008, s 113(4)(a).
117 CJIA 2008, s 113(4)(b).
118 CJIA 2008, s 113(5).
119 CJIA 2008, s 113(3)(a).
120 CJIA 2008, s 113(3)(b).

26.44

The penalty for any breach is:

- on summary conviction – imprisonment for a term not exceeding 12 months,[121] or a fine not exceeding the statutory maximum, or both;[122]

- on conviction on indictment – imprisonment for a term not exceeding five years, or a fine, or both.[123]

---

121 CJIA 2008, s 113(7)(a).
122 CJIA 2008, s 113(6)(a).
123 CJIA 2008, s 113(6)(b).

27 Sexual Risk Orders

27.01

Sexual risk orders (SROs) are provided for in s 122A of the Sexual Offences Act (SOA) 2003.

Making the application

27.02

These orders do not require the commission of any offence before they can be made. The legislation is in similar terms to that for sexual harm prevention orders (SHPOs).[1] However the only mechanism, as no offence has been committed, is by application to a magistrates' court by a chief officer of police or the Director General of the National Crime Agency (NCA).[2] If the Director General makes the application, they must as soon as practicable notify the chief officer of police for the relevant police area.[3]

27.03

A chief officer of police may make an application in respect of a person who resides in their police area,[4] or whom the officer believes is intending to come into it.[5]

27.04

'Relevant police area' is defined is SOA 2003, s 122B(3). Where the applicant is a chief officer of police, it refers to the officer's police area.[6] Where the applicant is the Director General of the NCA, it applies to the police area where the person in question resides,[7] or a police area which the Director General believes the person is in or is intending to come to.[8]

---

1 See Chapters 9 and 21.
2 SOA 2003, s 122A(1).
3 SOA 2003, s 122A(5).
4 SOA 2003, s 122A(3)(a).
5 SOA 2003, s 122A(3)(b).
6 SOA 2003, s 122B(3)(a).
7 SOA 2003, s 122B(3)(b)(i).
8 SOA 2003, s 122B(3)(b)(ii).

27.05

The application may be made to any magistrates' court acting for a local justice area that includes any part of a relevant police area,[9] or any place where it is alleged that the person acted in a way mentioned in the condition for making the order.[10]

27.06

Where the subject of the application is a youth, such an application is to be made to the youth court,[11] other than in prescribed circumstances as set out in SOA 2003, s 122K. The first of these is that rules of court may provide that an SRO application can be made to the youth court where the subject is over 18 if an application to the youth court has been made, or is to be made, under that section against a person aged under 18,[12] and the youth court thinks that it would be in the interests of justice for the applications to be heard together.[13] The second is that rules of court may, in relation to a person turning 18 after proceedings under SOA 2003, ss 122A, 122D or 122E have begun, determine circumstances in which the proceedings may or must remain in the youth court;[14] and may make provision for the transfer of the proceedings from the youth court to a magistrates' court that is not a youth court (including provision applying s 122E with modifications).[15]

27.07

The Secretary of State must issue,[16] and may revise,[17] guidance to chief officers of police and to the Director General of the NCA in relation to the exercise by them of their powers with regard to SROs and interim SROs. This must be published.[18] As at December 2018 no such guidance has been published.

Criteria for making an order

27.08

The single condition to be met before an SRO can be made is:[19]

'that the defendant has, whether before or after the commencement of this Part, done an act of a sexual nature as a result of which there is

9   SOA 2003, s 122A(4)(a).
10   SOA 2003, s 122A(4)(b).
11   SOA 2003, s 122B(2).
12   SOA 2003, s 122K(1)(a)(i).
13   SOA 2003, s 122K(1)(a)(ii).
14   SOA 2003, s 122K(1)(b)(i).
15   SOA 2003, s 122K(1)(b)(ii).
16   SOA 2003, s 122J(1).
17   SOA 2003, s 122J(2).
18   SOA 2003, s 122J(3).
19   SOA 2003, s 122A(2).

reasonable cause to believe that it is necessary for a sexual risk order to be made.'

27.09

That requirement for necessity of the order will be fulfilled where the court is satisfied that the defendant (D) has, whether before or after the commencement of Part 2 of the SOA 2003, done an act of a sexual nature as a result of which it is necessary to make such an order for the purpose of:[20]

- protecting the public or any particular members of the public from harm from D; or

- protecting children or vulnerable adults generally, or any particular children or vulnerable adults, from harm from D outside the UK.

27.10

Although it is a civil application, the criminal standard of proof applies to the behaviour that is required before the order can be made.[21]

27.11

'Harm' means physical or psychological harm caused by D doing an act of a sexual nature.[22]

27.12

It is noteworthy that for the purposes of an SRO, 'child' refers to those under 18, and 'vulnerable adult' means a person aged 18 or over whose ability to protect themselves from physical or psychological harm is significantly impaired through physical or mental disability or illness, through old age or otherwise.[23]

27.13

The Family Court has emphasised that SROs have an important role to play where there are insufficient concerns to justify the High Court invoking its inherent jurisdiction to make an injunctive order to protect children within an area from the sexual risk posed by an individual. In *London Borough of Redbridge v SNA*,[24] Hayden J departed from the most recent such case as at that time,[25] which had been decided before the legislation on SROs came into force:[26]

---

20 SOA 2003, s 122A(6).
21 *Commissioner of Police for the Metropolis v Ebanks* [2012] EWHC 2368 (Admin), a judgment regarding the forerunner to the SRO, the Risk of Sexual Harm Order (RSHO), under SOA 2003, s 123.
22 SOA 2003, s 122B(1).
23 SOA 2003, s 122B(1).
24 [2015] EWHC 2140 (Fam).
25 *Birmingham City Council v Riaz* [2014] EWHC 4247 (Fam).
26 *LB Redbridge v SNA*, at [47]–[48].

'When Keehan J heard the arguments in the Birmingham case these provisions had not come into force and accordingly, the protection that they offer was, at that stage, not available. I have been told by Mr Lefteri that an application has been made to a Magistrates' Court in respect of SNA. It is believed that the conditions for the making of such an order are met. That will ultimately be a matter for the Magistrates' Court. It would seem therefore, that the protection contemplated in this application may, in due course, be available. Recognising this from the outset Mr Lefteri sought orders in this Court in an attempt to "hold the ring" until orders have been made in the criminal courts.

There are sound reasons why the criminal courts are the correct venue to consider the making of these orders. Firstly, and most obviously, Parliament, after proper scrutiny, has carefully defined the scope and ambit of the provisions. Secondly, notwithstanding the considerable advancements made in achieving much greater levels of transparency in the Family Court, a judge sitting in this jurisdiction will invariably have to protect the identity of the child and in order to do so, preserve, by a side wind, the anonymity of a perpetrator.'

27.14

Following that case, a later decision by Keehan J highlighted the use to which SROs could be put, and reiterated the importance of collaborative multi-agency approaches in protecting young people from sexual exploitation.[27]

Content of an SRO

27.15

An SRO:[28]

- prohibits D from doing anything described in the order;
- has effect for a fixed period (not less than two years) specified in the order or until further order.

27.16

Only prohibitions necessary for the following purposes are permissible under an SRO:

- protecting the public or any particular members of the public from harm from D;[29] or

---

27   *Birmingham City Council v SK* [2016] EWHC 310 (Fam), at [10], [47]–[49].
28   SOA 2003, s 122A(7).
29   SOA 2003, s 122A(9)(a).

- protecting children or vulnerable adults generally, or any particular children or vulnerable adults, from harm from D outside the UK.[30]

27.17

Advocates will therefore have to take care to ensure that the prohibitions are proportionate when considered against the fact that no offence has been proven.

27.18

Different prohibitions may run for different periods of time.[31]

27.19

An SRO may contain a prohibition on foreign travel. It is likely that the considerations when imposing such a restriction are akin to those articulated by the appellate courts on many occasions relating to travel restriction orders.[32]

27.20

If someone is made subject to an SRO, any existing RSHO or foreign travel order ceases to have effect unless the court orders otherwise.[33]

Foreign travel prohibition

27.21

A prohibition on foreign travel may be phrased as:[34]

- a prohibition on travelling to any country outside the UK named or described in the order;

- a prohibition on travelling to any country outside the UK other than a country named or described in the order; or

- a prohibition on travelling to any country outside the UK.

27.22

Any prohibition on foreign travel contained in an SRO must not be for a period of more than five years,[35] but it can be extended by subsequent periods, each of no more than five years.[36]

---

30 SOA 2003, s 122A(9)(b).
31 SOA 2003, s 122A(8).
32 See Chapter 12.
33 SOA 2003, s 136ZB.
34 SOA 2003, s 122C(2).
35 SOA 2003, s 122C(1).
36 SOA 2003, s 122C(3).

27.23

An SRO that contains a prohibition on travelling to any country outside of the UK must require D to surrender all of their passports at a police station specified in the order on or before the date when the prohibition takes effect,[37] or within a period specified in the order.[38]

27.24

Any passports surrendered must be returned as soon as reasonably practicable after the person ceases to be subject to such a prohibition (unless they are subject to an equivalent prohibition under another order). However, this requirement of return does not apply to a passport issued by or on behalf of the authorities of a country outside the UK if the passport has been returned to those authorities;[39] or a passport issued by or on behalf of an international organisation if the passport has been returned to that organisation.[40]

27.25

For these purposes, 'passport' means:[41]

(a)   a UK passport within the meaning of the Immigration Act 1971;

(b)   a passport issued by or on behalf of the authorities of a country outside the UK, or by or on behalf of an international organisation;

(c)   a document that can be used (in some or all circumstances) instead of a passport.

27.26

Where a court makes an SRO in relation to a person who is already subject to such an order (made by any court), the earlier order ceases to have effect.[42]

Renewal and variation

27.27

Any of the following people may apply to the appropriate court for variation, renewal or discharge of an SRO:[43]

•   the defendant;[44]

---

37   SOA 2003, s 122C(4)(a).
38   SOA 2003, s 122C(4)(b).
39   SOA 2003, s 122C(6)(a).
40   SOA 2003, s 122C(6)(b).
41   SOA 2003, s 122C(7).
42   SOA 2003, s 122A(10).
43   SOA 2003, s 122D(1).
44   SOA 2003, s 122D(2)(a).

- the chief officer of police for the area in which D resides;[45]

- a chief officer of police who believes that D is in, or is intending to come to, that officer's police area;[46]

- where the order was made on an application by a chief officer of police, that officer.[47]

27.28

An order may be renewed or varied so as to impose additional prohibitions on D only if it is necessary to do so for the purpose of:[48]

(a) protecting the public or any particular members of the public from harm from D; or

(b) protecting children or vulnerable adults generally, or any particular children or vulnerable adults, from harm from D outside the UK.

27.29

'The appropriate court' means:[49]

(a) *where an adult magistrates' court made the SRO:* that court, any adult magistrates' court for the area in which the defendant resides or, where the application is made by a chief officer of police, any adult magistrates' court acting for a local justice area that includes any part of the chief officer's police area;

(b) *where a youth court made the order and D is under the age of 18:* that court, a youth court for the area in which D resides or, where the application is made by a chief officer of police, any youth court acting for a local justice area that includes any part of the chief officer's police area;

(c) *where a youth court made the order and D is aged 18 or over:* an adult magistrates' court for the area in which D resides or, where the application is made by a chief officer of police, any adult magistrates' court acting for a local justice area that includes any part of the chief officer's police area.

Discharge

27.30

The court must not discharge an order before the end of two years beginning with the day on which the order was made, without the consent of D and the

---

45   SOA 2003, s 122D(2)(b).
46   SOA 2003, s 122D(2)(c).
47   SOA 2003, s 122D(2)(d).
48   SOA 2003, s 122D(4).
49   SOA 2003, s 122D(7).

chief officer of police who applied for the order,[50] or, if the application was not made by such an officer, the chief officer for the area in which D resides.[51]

Interim SROs

27.31

An interim SRO may only be made where an application for a substantive SRO has not been determined.[52] An interim order has effect only for a fixed period, specified in the order,[53] and ceases to have effect, if it has not already expired, on the determination of the main application.[54]

27.32

The court has a power, not a duty, and may only make the order 'if it considers it just to do so'.[55]

27.33

An application for an interim order:

- may be made within the complaint by which the main application is made;[56] or

- may be made after the main application to the same court by the person who has made that main application.[57]

27.34

The applicant or the defendant may by complaint apply to the court that made the interim SRO for variation, renewal or discharge.[58]

Appeals

27.35

SOA 2003, s 122G provides that any appeal against the making of an SRO,[59] an interim SRO,[60] or the making, or refusal, of a variation, renewal or discharge[61]

---

50 SOA 2003, s 122D(5)(a).
51 SOA 2003, s 122D(5)(b).
52 SOA 2003, s 122E(1).
53 SOA 2003, s 122E(4)(a).
54 SOA 2003, s 122E(4)(b).
55 SOA 2003, s 122E(3).
56 SOA 2003, s 122E(2)(a).
57 SOA 2003, s 122E(2)(b).
58 SOA 2003, s 122E(5).
59 SOA 2003, s 122G(1)(a).
60 SOA 2003, s 122G(1)(b).
61 SOA 2003, s 122G(1)(c).

is to the Crown Court. The Crown Court may make such orders as may be necessary to give effect to its determination of the appeal, as well as any incidental or consequential orders that appear just.[62]

27.36

Any order made by the Crown Court on an appeal against an SRO or interim SRO is for the purposes of SOA 2003, s 122D(7) or s 122E(5) to be treated as if it were an order of the court from which the appeal was brought (and not an order of the Crown Court).[63]

Breach

27.37

Breach of a full or interim SRO,[64] as well as its forerunners as listed in the statute,[65] is an offence[66] punishable by:

- on summary conviction – imprisonment for a term not exceeding six months, or a fine, or both;[67]

- on conviction on indictment – imprisonment for a term not exceeding five years.[68]

27.38

In whichever court a person is convicted of breach of an SRO, the court cannot impose a conditional discharge as the sentencing disposal.[69]

27.39

Where a person fails to comply with a prohibition on foreign travel under SOA 2003, s 122C(4), there is a defence of reasonable excuse.[70] There are no statutory defences available to breaches of other prohibitions under an SRO, though arguments about ability to comply (such as those seen in cases on SHPOs)[71] may sensibly be thought to apply equally to SROs.

---

62 SOA 2003, s 122G(2).
63 SOA 2003, s 122G(3).
64 SOA 2003, s 122H(1)(a) and (b).
65 SOA 2003, s 122H(1)(c)–(f).
66 SOA 2003, s 122H(3).
67 SOA 2003, s 122H(3)(a).
68 SOA 2003, s 122H(3)(b).
69 SOA 2003, s 122H(4).
70 SOA 2003, s 122H(2).
71 See Chapter 9.

27.40

If D is:

- convicted;[72]

- found not guilty by reason of insanity;[73]

- found to have done the act whilst under a disability;[74] or

- cautioned[75]

in respect of breaching an SRO[76] (or a RSHO),[77] s/he becomes subject to notification requirements[78] as follows:

- *already a relevant offender:*[79] ceases to be subject to the notification requirements of Part II of the SOA 2003 while the SRO,[80] or interim SRO[81] (as renewed from time to time) has effect;

- *not already a relevant offender:*[82] notification requirements apply to them from the date that they become a 'relevant offender'[83] (ie the date of conviction/finding/caution) until the SRO,[84] or interim SRO[85] (as renewed) ceases to have effect.

27.41

In relation to the latter category, it is entirely possible that a person who is subject to an SRO will not have been convicted of, or cautioned for, any offence – the rationale for an SRO is to bite before the commission of offences. Therefore, counsel must be alive to a client who will become subject to the notification requirements for the first time as a result of conviction for breach of an SRO. For some offenders, the notification requirements will duplicate requirements of the SRO, and consequently an application to discharge or vary the SRO might be necessary.

---

72   SOA 2003, s 122I(1)(a).
73   SOA 2003, s 122I(1)(b).
74   SOA 2003, s 122I(1)(c).
75   SOA 2003, s 122I(1)(d).
76   SOA 2003, s 122I(2)(a).
77   SOA 2003, s 122I(2)(a).
78   SOA 2003, s 122I(4)(a).
79   SOA 2003, s 122I(3)(b).
80   SOA 2003, s 122I(6)(a).
81   SOA 2003, s 122I(6)(b).
82   SOA 2003, s 80(2).
83   As defined in SOA 2003, s 80(2).
84   SOA 2003, s 122I(6)(a).
85   SOA 2003, s 122I(6)(b).

Interaction between SROs and notification requirements

27.42

Where an SRO or interim SRO is made, the subject of it must, within three days beginning with the date of service of the order, notify the police of the following information (unless the person is subject to the notification requirements of SOA 2003, Part 2 on that date):[86]

- the person's name and, where the person uses one or more other names, each of those names;[87]

- the person's home address.[88]

27.43

If the subject of the SRO is not subject to notification requirements and uses a name which has not been notified under this section (or under any other provision of SOA 2003, Part 2), or changes home address, they must notify the police of that name or new home address within three days starting with the date of the change.[89]

27.44

In line with SOA 2003, s 87, a person gives notification under s 122F(1)[90] or 122F(3)[91] by:

- attending at such police station in his/her local police area as the Secretary of State may by regulations prescribe or, if there is more than one, at any of them;[92] and

- giving an oral notification to any police officer, or to any person authorised for the purpose by the officer in charge of the station.[93]

27.45

A person giving a notification under SOA 2003, s 122F(3):[94]

- in relation to a prospective change of home address;[95] or

- in relation to premises at which s/he has resided or stayed, for a qualifying period, in the UK the address of which has not been notified to the police

---

86   SOA 2003, s 122F(1).
87   SOA 2003, s 122F(2)(a).
88   SOA 2003, s 122F(2)(b).
89   SOA 2003, s 122F(3)(b).
90   SOA 2003, s 122F(4)(a).
91   SOA 2003, s 122F(4)(b).
92   SOA 2003, s 87(1)(a).
93   SOA 2003, s 87(1)(b).
94   SOA 2003, s 122F(4)(b).
95   SOA 2003, s 87(2)(a).

under s 122F(1) or (3),[96] may give the notification at a police station in his/her local area if the change in home address had already occurred or if the address of those premises were his/her home address.

27.46

Any notification under SOA 2003, s 122F(3) must be acknowledged, in writing, in such form as the Secretary of State may direct.[97]

27.47

Where a notification is given under SOA 2003, s 122F(1)[98] or 122F(3),[99] the relevant offender must, if requested to do so by the police officer or person referred to in s 122F(1)(b), allow the officer or person to take their fingerprints,[100] and/or[101] photograph any part of them,[102] to verify their identity.[103]

---

96   SOA 2003, s 87(2)(a).
97   SOA 2003, s 122F(3).
98   SOA 2003, s 122F(4)(a).
99   SOA 2003, s 122F(4)(b).
100 SOA 2003, s 87(4)(a).
101 SOA 2003, s 87(4)(c).
102 SOA 2003, s 87(4)(b).
103 SOA 2003, s 87(5).

28 Slavery and Trafficking Risk Orders

28.01

Slavery and trafficking risk orders (STROs) are created by s 23 of the Modern Slavery Act (MSA) 2015. Where explanations of definitions are not provided, readers should refer to Chapter 16 – material from that chapter is not repeated here, except where it is given under a different section number of the Act.

Applicants

28.02

A magistrates' court may make an STRO against a person (D) on an application by:

- a chief officer of police:[1]
    - in respect of someone who:
        - (a) lives in the officer's police area;[2] or
        - (b) who the officer believes is in that area or intending to come in to it;[3]
- an immigration officer;[4]
- the Director General of the National Crime Agency ('the Director General');[5]
- the Gangmasters and Labour Abuse Authority ('GLA Authority').[6]

---

1   MSA 2015, s 23(1)(a).
2   MSA 2015, s 23(3)(a).
3   MSA 2015, s 23(3)(b).
4   MSA 2015, s 23(1)(b).
5   MSA 2015, s 23(1)(c).
6   MSA 2015, s 23(1)(d).

Pre-condition for making order

28.03

The court may make the order only if it is satisfied that D has acted in a way, at any time,[7] which means that:

- there is a risk that D will[8] commit a slavery or human trafficking offence;[9] and

- it is necessary to make the order for the purpose of protecting persons generally, or particular persons, from the physical or psychological harm which would be likely to occur if the defendant committed such an offence.[10]

Procedure

28.04

An application under this section is to be made by complaint by those listed at 28.02. It may be made to any magistrates' court acting for a local justice area that includes:

- any part of a relevant police area;[11] or

- any place where it is alleged that the defendant acted in a way that means there is a risk that the defendant will commit a slavery or human trafficking offence, and it is necessary to make the order for the purpose of protecting persons generally, or particular persons, from the physical or psychological harm which would be likely to occur if the defendant committed such an offence.[12]

28.05

Where the defendant is under 18, a reference in this section to a magistrates' court is to be taken as referring to a youth court (subject to any rules of court made under MSA 2015, s 32).[13]

28.06

Where an immigration officer, the Director General or the GLA Authority makes an application under this section, the officer, Director General or

---

7   Including before this section came into force – MSA 2015, s 23(8).
8   This being one difference to an STPO on application, where the requirement is 'may'.
9   MSA 2015, s 23(2)(a).
10   MSA 2015, s 23(2)(b).
11   MSA 2015, s 23(4)(a).
12   MSA 2015, s 23(4)(b).
13   MSA 2015, s 23(5).

GLA Authority must give notice of the application to the chief officer of police for a relevant police area, meaning:[14]

- where the applicant is a chief officer of police, the officer's police area;[15]

- where the applicant is an immigration officer, the Director General or the GLA Authority, the police area where the defendant lives or a police area which the officer, Director General or the GLA Authority believes the defendant is in or is intending to come to.[16]

Content of an STRO

28.07

An STRO prohibits D from doing anything described in the order.[17]

28.08

The only prohibitions that may be included are those which the court is satisfied are necessary for the purpose of protecting persons generally, or particular persons, from the physical or psychological harm which would be likely to occur if D committed a slavery or human trafficking offence.[18]

28.09

The order may prohibit D from doing things in any part of the UK, and anywhere outside the UK.[19]

Foreign travel prohibition

28.10

An STRO may contain an outright prohibition on travelling to any country outside the UK,[20] or travelling to any country outside the UK that is,[21] or is other than,[22] those named or described in the order.

---

14 MSA 2015, s 23(6).
15 MSA 2015, s 23(7)(a).
16 MSA 2015, s 23(7)(b).
17 MSA 2015, s 24(1).
18 MSA 2015, s 24(2).
19 MSA 2015, s 24(3).
20 MSA 2015, s 25(2)(c).
21 MSA 2015, s 25(2)(a).
22 MSA 2015, s 25(2)(b).

28.11

Such a prohibition may last for no more than five years,[23] but can be renewed for additional periods of up to five years on application under MSA 2015, s 27.[24]

28.12

If the STRO contains a prohibition on any travel outside the UK, it must require D to surrender all their passports at a police station specified in the order:

- on or before the date when the prohibition takes effect;[25] or

- within a period specified in the order.[26]

28.13

Any passports surrendered must be returned as soon as reasonably practicable after the person ceases to be subject to an STRO containing a prohibition on any travel outside the UK,[27] unless it is a passport issued by or on behalf of authorities of a country outside the UK[28] or an international organisation,[29] if the passport has been returned to those authorities or organisation.

Requirement to provide name and address

28.14

As well as prohibitions, an STRO may require D to provide information,[30] if the court is satisfied that the requirement is necessary for the purpose of protecting persons generally, or particular persons, from the physical or psychological harm which would be likely to occur if D committed a slavery or human trafficking offence.[31]

28.15

From the day on which an STRO is served on D, they have three days to notify in the manner and to the person specified in the order, the relevant matters, namely:[32]

---

23   MSA 2015, s 25(1).
24   MSA 2015, s 25(3).
25   MSA 2015, s 25(4)(a).
26   MSA 2015, s 25(4)(b).
27   MSA 2015, s 25(5).
28   MSA 2015, s 25(6)(a).
29   MSA 2015, s 25(6)(b).
30   MSA 2015, s 26(1).
31   MSA 2015, s 26(2).
32   MSA 2015, s 26(3).

- D's name and, where D uses one or more other names, each of those names;[33] and

- D's home address.[34]

28.16

If, while subject to the STRO, D:

- uses a name which has not been notified;[35] or

- changes home address,[36]

they must, within three days beginning with the day on which D uses the name or changes home address,[37] in the manner and to the person specified in the order, notify that fact.

28.17

Where the order requires D to notify the Director General, an immigration officer or the GLA Authority, the Director General, the officer or the GLA Authority must give details of any notification to the chief officer of police for each 'relevant police area',[38] defined as:

- where D notifies a new name, the police area where the defendant lives;[39]

- where D notifies a change of home address, the police area where D lives and (if different) the police area where D lived before the change of home address.[40]

Duration of an STRO

28.18

A prohibition contained in an STRO has effect:

- for a fixed period, specified in the order, of at least two years;[41] or

- until further order;[42]

---

33   MSA 2015, s 26(4)(a).
34   MSA 2015, s 26(4)(b).
35   MSA 2015, s 26(5)(a).
36   MSA 2015, s 26(5)(b).
37   MSA 2015, s 26(6).
38   MSA 2015, s 26(7).
39   MSA 2015, s 26(8)(a).
40   MSA 2015, s 26(8)(b).
41   MSA 2015, s 24(4)(a).
42   MSA 2015, s 24(4)(b).

- except for prohibitions on foreign travel, which must be for a fixed period of five years or less.[43]

28.19

Some of its prohibitions may be specified to have effect until further order and some for a fixed period,[44] and an STRO may specify different periods for different prohibitions.[45]

28.20

If a court makes an STRO against someone who is already subject to such an order (made by any court), the earlier order ceases to have effect.[46]

Appeal

28.21

Appeal lies to the Crown Court against the making of:

- an STRO;[47]

- variation, renewal or discharge of an order, or refusal thereof, under MSA 2015, s 27.[48]

28.22

The Crown Court may make such orders as may be necessary to give effect to its determination of the appeal, and may also make such incidental or consequential orders as appear to it to be just.[49]

28.23

An order made by the Crown Court on an appeal against the making of an STRO or an interim STRO is to be treated for the purposes of MSA 2015, s 27(8) or 28(8) (respectively) as if it were an order of the court from which the appeal was brought,[50] unless it is an order directing that an application be reheard by a magistrates' court.[51]

---

43   MSA 2015, s 25(1).
44   MSA 2015, s 24(5)(a).
45   MSA 2015, s 24(5)(b).
46   MSA 2015, s 24(6).
47   MSA 2015, s 29(1)(a).
48   MSA 2015, s 29(1)(c).
49   MSA 2015, s 29(2).
50   MSA 2015, s 29(3).
51   MSA 2015, s 29(4).

Variation, discharge and renewal

28.24

An application for an order varying, renewing or discharging an STRO[52] should be made to the appropriate court:[53]

- where an adult magistrates' court made the order:[54]
    - that court;[55]
    - an adult magistrates' court for the area in which the defendant lives;[56] or
    - where the application is made by a chief officer of police, any adult magistrates' court acting for a local justice area that includes any part of the chief officer's police area;[57]

- where a youth court made the order and the defendant is under 18:[58]
    - that court;[59]
    - a youth court for the area in which the defendant lives;[60] or
    - where the application is made by a chief officer of police, any youth court acting for a local justice area that includes any part of the chief officer's police area;[61]

- where a youth court made the order and the defendant is 18 or over:[62]
    - an adult magistrates' court for the area in which the defendant lives;[63] or
    - where the application is made by a chief officer of police, any adult magistrates' court acting for a local justice area that includes any part of the chief officer's police area.[64]

28.25

The application may be made by any of the following:

---

52 MSA 2015, s 27(1).
53 MSA 2015, s 20(10).
54 MSA 2015, s 27(8)(a).
55 MSA 2015, s 27(8)(a)(i).
56 MSA 2015, s 27(8)(a)(ii).
57 MSA 2015, s 27(8)(a)(iii).
58 MSA 2015, s 27(8)(b).
59 MSA 2015, s 27(8)(b)(i).
60 MSA 2015, s 27(8)(b)(ii).
61 MSA 2015, s 27(8)(b)(iii).
62 MSA 2015, s 27(8)(c).
63 MSA 2015, s 27(8)(c)(i).
64 MSA 2015, s 27(8)(c)(ii).

- the defendant;[65]

- the chief officer of police for the area in which D lives;[66]

- a chief officer of police who believes that D is in, or is intending to come to, that officer's police area;[67]

- where the order was made on an application under MSA 2015, s 23 by a chief officer of police, that officer;[68]

- where the order was made on an application under s 23 by an immigration officer, an immigration officer;[69]

- where the order was made on an application under s 23 by the Director General, the Director General;[70]

- where the order was made on an application under s 23 by the GLA Authority, the GLA Authority.[71]

28.26

The court will hear the applicant,[72] and any other persons who could make the application, should they wish to be heard.[73]

28.27

An order may be renewed, or varied so as to impose additional prohibitions on D or require D to provide their name and address, only if the court is satisfied that:

- there is a risk that D may commit a slavery or human trafficking offence;[74] and

- it is necessary to renew or vary the order for the purpose of protecting persons generally, or particular persons, from the physical or psychological harm which would be likely to occur if D committed such an offence.[75]

28.28

Any renewed or varied order may:

---

65 MSA 2015, s 27(2)(a).
66 MSA 2015, s 27(2)(b).
67 MSA 2015, s 27(2)(c).
68 MSA 2015, s 27(2)(d).
69 MSA 2015, s 27(2)(e).
70 MSA 2015, s 27(2)(f).
71 MSA 2015, s 27(2)(g).
72 MSA 2015, s 27(3)(a).
73 MSA 2015, s 27(3)(b).
74 MSA 2015, s 27(4)(a).
75 MSA 2015, s 27(4)(b).

- contain only those prohibitions which the court is satisfied are necessary for that purpose;[76]

- require D to provide their name and address only if the court is satisfied that the requirement is necessary for that purpose.[77]

28.29

The court must not discharge an order (unless it contains a prohibition on foreign travel)[78] before the end of two years beginning with the day on which the order was made, without the consent of:

- D and the chief officer of police for the area where D lives;[79] or

- where the application is made by a chief officer of police, D and that chief officer.[80]

28.30

Where an immigration officer, the Director General or the GLA Authority makes an application under MSA 2015, s 27, the officer, the Director General or the GLA Authority must give notice of the application to the chief officer of police for:

- the police area where D lives;[81] or

- a police area which the immigration officer or the Director General believes D is in or is intending to come to.[82]

Interim STROs

28.31

Where an application for an STRO has not been determined,[83] an application for an interim STRO may be made by the same complaint as the main application,[84] or by the same person and to the same court as the main application.[85]

28.32

The court may make the order if it considers it just to do so.[86]

---

76   MSA 2015, s 27(5)(a).
77   MSA 2015, s 27(5)(b).
78   MSA 2015, s 20(7).
79   MSA 2015, s 27(6)(a).
80   MSA 2015, s 27(6)(b).
81   MSA 2015, s 27(7)(a).
82   MSA 2015, s 27(7)(b).
83   MSA 2015, s 28(1).
84   MSA 2015, s 28(2)(a).
85   MSA 2015, s 28(2)(b).
86   MSA 2015, s 28(3).

28.33

An interim STRO prohibits D from the activities described in the order,[87] within or outside the UK,[88] or in any part of it.[89]

28.34

The order may (as well as imposing prohibitions on the defendant) require the defendant to comply with MSA 2015, s 26(3)–(6), which require that from the day on which an STRO is served on D, they have three days to notify the relevant matters in the manner and to the person specified in the order, namely:[90]

- D's name and, where D uses one or more other names, each of those names;[91] and

- D's home address.[92]

28.35

If while subject to the interim STRO, D:

- uses a name which has not been notified;[93] or

- changes home address,[94]

they must, within three days beginning with the day on which D uses the name or changes home address,[95] in the manner and to the person specified in the order, notify that fact.

28.36

If the interim STRO does contain those requirements, MSA 2015, s 26(3)–(6) apply as if references to an STRO were to an interim STRO.

28.37

An interim STRO has effect only for a fixed period, specified in the order[96] and ceases to have effect, if it has not already done so, on the determination of the main application.[97]

---

87 MSA 2015, s 28(4).
88 MSA 2015, s 28(4).
89 MSA 2015, s 28(5).
90 MSA 2015, s 26(3).
91 MSA 2015, s 26(4)(a).
92 MSA 2015, s 26(4)(b).
93 MSA 2015, s 26(5)(a).
94 MSA 2015, s 26(5)(b).
95 MSA 2015, s 26(6).
96 MSA 2015, s 28(7)(a).
97 MSA 2015, s 28(7)(b).

28.38

The applicant or D may by complaint apply to the court that made the interim STRO for the order to be varied, renewed or discharged,[98] and an interim STRO can be appealed to the Crown Court.[99]

Breach

28.39

A person who, without reasonable excuse:

- does anything he is prohibited from doing by an STRO;[100] or

- does anything he is prohibited from doing by an interim STRO;[101] or

- fails to comply with a requirement to surrender passports (MSA 2015, s 25(4));[102] or

- fails to provide his name and address (MSA 2015, s 26(1) or 28(6));[103]

is liable on conviction:

- on indictment – to imprisonment for a term not exceeding five years;[104]

- summarily – to imprisonment for a term not exceeding six months, or a fine, or both.[105]

28.40

The court cannot give a conditional discharge in respect of a breach offence.[106]

---

98   MSA 2015, s 28(8).
99   MSA 2015, s 29(1)(b).
100 MSA 2015, s 30(1)(c).
101 MSA 2015, s 30(1)(d).
102 MSA 2015, s 30(2)(a).
103 MSA 2015, s 30(2)(b).
104 MSA 2015, s 30(3)(a).
105 MSA 2015, s 30(3)(b).
106 MSA 2015, s 30(4).

29 Closure Orders

29.01

Closure orders allow a court to put conditions on who can be present within premises (residential or commercial) where there are concerns about nuisance or anti-social behaviour associated with that address. For a closure order to be made there must first have been a closure notice. The process for the two is therefore unusually intertwined. However, notices are not generally within the scope of this book and, as the case law below demonstrates, although a closure notice must have been issued before there can be a closure order, the magistrates making the order need not concern themselves with the validity of the notice. For that reason, this chapter does not cover closure notices.

29.02

The power to make a closure order is found within Part 4, Chapter 3 of the Anti-social Behaviour, Crime and Policing Act (ABCPA) 2014.

Application

29.03

Whenever a closure notice is issued under ABCPA 2014, s 76, an application must be made to a magistrates' court for a closure order (unless the notice has been cancelled under s 78).[1] However, the magistrates should not consider the validity or otherwise of a closure notice when considering an application for a closure order.[2] The link between the closure notice and a closure order is that an application for the latter cannot be made without the former having been issued; there is nothing in the statute that requires the magistrates to go beyond confirming that a closure notice has been issued.[3]

29.04

An application for a closure order must be made:

- by a constable, if the closure notice was issued by a police officer;[4]

---

1   ABCPA 2014, s 80(1).
2   *R (Qin) v Commissioner of Police for the Metropolis* [2017] EWHC 2750 (Admin), at [54], citing a review of authorities decided under the predecessor in the Anti-social Behaviour Act 2003.
3   *R (Qin)*, at [57].
4   ABCPA 2014, s 80(2)(a).

- by the authority that issued the closure notice, if the notice was issued by a local authority.[5]

29.05

The application must be heard by the magistrates' court not later than 48 hours (Christmas Day being disregarded)[6] after service of the closure notice.[7] The speed with which the legislation requires these steps to be taken has been recognised by the Court of Appeal (Civil Division) as indicative of the serious effect that the behaviour leading to such orders has on victims.[8]

Making the order

29.06

The court may make a closure order if it is satisfied that:

- a person has engaged, or (if the order is not made) is likely to engage, in disorderly, offensive or criminal behaviour on the premises;[9] or

- the use of the premises has resulted, or (if the order is not made) is likely to result, in serious nuisance to members of the public;[10] or

- there has been, or (if the order is not made) is likely to be, disorder near those premises associated with the use of those premises,[11]

and that the order is necessary to prevent the behaviour, nuisance or disorder from continuing, recurring or occurring.

Duration

29.07

A closure order is an order prohibiting access to the premises for a period specified in the order, which must not exceed three months.[12]

---

5   ABCPA 2014, s 80(2)(b).
6   ABCPA 2014, s 80(4).
7   ABCPA 2014, s 80(3).
8   *Harris v Hounslow LBC* [2017] EWCA Civ 1476, at [2], [3] and [17].
9   ABCPA 2014, s 80(5)(a).
10   ABCPA 2014, s 80(5)(b).
11   ABCPA 2014, s 80(5)(c).
12   ABCPA 2014, s 80(6).

Extension

29.08

At any time before the expiry of a closure order, an application may be made to a magistrate, by complaint, for an extension (or further extension) of the order's duration.[13]

29.09

Such an application can be made:

- where the closure order was made on the application of a constable, by a police officer of at least the rank of inspector;[14]

- where the closure order was made on the application of a local authority, by that authority.[15]

29.10

A police officer or local authority may make an application under this section only if satisfied on reasonable grounds that it is necessary for the period of the order to be extended to prevent the occurrence, recurrence or continuance of:

- disorderly, offensive or criminal behaviour on the premises;[16]

- serious nuisance to members of the public resulting from the use of the premises;[17] or

- disorder near the premises associated with the use of the premises,[18]

and also satisfied that the appropriate consultee has been consulted about the intention to make the application.[19]

29.11

The 'appropriate consultee' means:

- the local authority, in the case of an application by a police officer;[20]

- the chief police officer for the area in which the premises are situated, in the case of an application by a local authority.[21]

---

13   ABCPA 2014, s 82(1).
14   ABCPA 2014, s 82(2)(a).
15   ABCPA 2014, s 82(2)(b).
16   ABCPA 2014, s 82(3)(a).
17   ABCPA 2014, s 82(3)(b).
18   ABCPA 2014, s 82.
19   ABCPA 2014, s 82(3)(c).
20   ABCPA 2014, s 82(4)(a).
21   ABCPA 2014, s 82(4)(b).

29.12

Where an application is made under ABCPA 2014, s 82, the magistrate may issue a summons directed to:

- any person on whom the closure notice was served under ABCPA 2014, s 79;[22] or

- any other person who appears to the magistrate to have an interest in the premises but on whom the closure notice was not served,[23]

requiring the person to appear before the magistrates' court to respond to the application.

29.13

If a summons is issued a notice stating the date, time and place of the hearing of the application must be served on the persons to whom the summons is directed.[24]

29.14

If the magistrates' court is satisfied that the extension will prevent the occurrence, recurrence or continuance of the behaviour listed above in 29.10, it may make an order extending (or further extending) the closure order by three months or less.[25] A closure order may not be extended such that it lasts for more than six months.[26]

Content

29.15

A closure order may prohibit access:

- by all persons, or by all persons except those specified, or by all persons except those of a specified description;[27]

- at all times, or at all times except those specified;[28]

- in all circumstances, or in all circumstances except those specified.[29]

---

22   ABCPA 2014, s 82(5)(a).
23   ABCPA 2014, s 82(5)(b).
24   ABCPA 2014, s 82(6).
25   ABCPA 2014, s 82(7).
26   ABCPA 2014, s 82(8).
27   ABCPA 2014, s 80(7)(a).
28   ABCPA 2014, s 80(7)(b).
29   ABCPA 2014, s 80(7)(c).

29.16

A closure order:

- may be made in respect of the whole or any part of the premises;[30]
- may include provision about access to a part of the building or structure of which the premises form part.[31]

29.17

The court must notify the relevant licensing authority if it makes a closure order in relation to premises with a premises licence in force.[32]

Discharge

29.18

At any time before the expiry of a closure order, an application may be made to a magistrate, by complaint, for the order to be discharged.[33]

29.19

Those entitled to make an application under this section are:

- a constable, where the closure order was made on the application of a constable;[34]

- the authority that applied for the closure order, where the order was made on the application of a local authority;[35]

- a person on whom the closure notice was served under ABCPA 2014, s 79;[36]

- anyone else who has an interest in the premises but on whom the closure notice was not served.[37]

29.20

Where a person other than a constable[38] or the local authority which applied for the order,[39] makes an application under this section for the discharge of an

---

30   ABCPA 2014, s 80(8)(a).
31   ABCPA 2014, s 80(8)(b).
32   ABCPA 2014, s 80(9).
33   ABCPA 2014, s 83(1).
34   ABCPA 2014, s 83(2)(a).
35   ABCPA 2014, s 83(2)(b).
36   ABCPA 2014, s 83(2)(c).
37   ABCPA 2014, s 83(2)(d).
38   ABCPA 2014, s 83(3).
39   ABCPA 2014, s 83(5)(b).

order that was made on the application of a constable,[40] or a local authority[41] the magistrate may issue a summons directed to the applicant local authority or a constable considered appropriate by the magistrate requiring him or her to appear before the magistrates' court to respond to the application.[42]

29.21

If a summons is issued, a notice stating the date, time and place of the hearing of the application must be served on:

- the constable to whom the summons is directed [43] or the local authority which made the application;[44]

- any person on whom the closure notice was served under ABCPA 2014, s 79 and anyone else who has an interest in the premises but on whom the closure notice was not served.[45,46]

29.22

The magistrates' court may not make an order discharging the closure order unless satisfied that the closure order is no longer necessary to prevent the occurrence, recurrence or continuance of:

- disorderly, offensive or criminal behaviour on the premises;[47]

- serious nuisance to members of the public resulting from the use of the premises;[48] or

- disorder near the premises associated with the use of the premises.[49]

Temporary closure orders

29.23

Where an application for a closure order has been made to a magistrates' court,[50] but the court does not make the order, it can nevertheless order that the closure notice continues in force for a specified further period of not more than 48 hours, if it is satisfied that:

---

40 ABCPA 2014, s 83(3).
41 ABCPA 2014, s 83(5)(a).
42 ABCPA 2014, s 83(3).
43 ABCPA 2014, s 83(4)(a).
44 ABCPA 2014, s 83(6)(a).
45 ABCPA 2014, s 83(4)(b).
46 ABCPA 2014, s 83(6)(b).
47 ABCPA 2014, s 83(7)(a).
48 ABCPA 2014, s 83(7)(b).
49 ABCPA 2014, s 83(7)(c).
50 ABCPA 2014, s 81(1).

- the use of particular premises has resulted, or (if the notice is not continued) is likely soon to result, in nuisance to members of the public;[51] or

- there has been, or (if the notice is not continued) is likely soon to be, disorder near those premises associated with the use of those premises,[52]

and that the continuation of the notice is necessary to prevent the nuisance or disorder from continuing, recurring or occurring.

29.24

The court may adjourn the hearing of the application for a period of up to 14 days to enable:

- the occupier of the premises;[53]

- the person with control of or responsibility for the premises;[54] or

- any other person with an interest in the premises,[55]

to show why a closure order should not be made. If it does so, it may order that the closure notice continues in force until the end of the period of the adjournment.[56]

Costs

29.25

A local policing body or a local authority that incurs expenditure through clearing, securing or maintaining premises in respect of which a closure order is in force may apply to the court that made the order for an order under s 88.[57]

29.26

On such an application the court may make whatever order it thinks appropriate for the reimbursement (in full or in part) by the owner or occupier of the premises of that expenditure.[58]

---

51   ABCPA 2014, s 81(2)(a).
52   ABCPA 2014, s 81(2)(b).
53   ABCPA 2014, s 81(3)(a).
54   ABCPA 2014, s 81(3)(b).
55   ABCPA 2014, s 81(3)(c).
56   ABCPA 2014, s 81(4).
57   ABCPA 2014, s 88(1).
58   ABCPA 2014, s 88(2).

29.27

An application for an order under this section may not be heard unless it is made before the end of the period of three months starting with the day on which the closure order ceases to have effect.[59]

29.28

An order under this section may be made only against a person who has been served with the application for the order.[60]

29.29

An application under this section must also be served on:

- the local policing body for the area in which the premises are situated, if the application is made by a local authority;[61]

- the local authority, if the application is made by a local policing body.[62]

29.30

Where an application for a closure order has been made, but not granted, providing the police authority has acted reasonably in the public interest in making the closure notice, a refusal to award costs against the police is reasonable.[63] (For further guidance on costs, see Chapters 15 and 18.)

Compensation

29.31

A person who claims to have incurred financial loss in consequence of a closure notice or a closure order may apply to the appropriate court for compensation, that being:

- the magistrates' court that considered the application for a closure order; unless[64]

- the closure order was made or extended by an order of the Crown Court on an appeal under ABCPA 2014, s 84, in which case the appropriate court is the Crown Court.[65]

---

59   ABCPA 2014, s 88(3).
60   ABCPA 2014, s 88(4).
61   ABCPA 2014, s 88(5)(a).
62   ABCPA 2014, s 88(5)(b).
63   *R (Qin)*, at [78]–[84]; *Beard v Devon and Cornwall Constabulary* [2017] WLUK 338.
64   ABCPA 2014, s 90(2)(a).
65   ABCPA 2014, s 90(2)(b).

29.32

An application under ABCPA 2014, s 90 may not be heard unless it is made before the end of three months starting with whichever of the following is applicable:

- the day on which the closure notice was cancelled under s 78;[66]

- the day on which a closure order was refused[67] (this is the day on which the magistrates' court decided not to make a closure order,[68] unless the Crown Court dismissed an appeal against a decision not to make a closure order, in which case it is that day);[69]

- the day on which the closure order ceased to have effect.[70]

29.33

On an application under ABCPA 2014, s 90, the court may order the payment of compensation out of central funds[71] if it is satisfied:

- that the applicant is not associated with the use of the premises, or the behaviour on the premises, on the basis of which the closure notice was issued or the closure order made;[72]

- if the applicant is the owner or occupier of the premises, that the applicant took reasonable steps to prevent that use or behaviour;[73]

- that the applicant has incurred financial loss in consequence of the notice or order;[74] and

- that having regard to all the circumstances it is appropriate to order payment of compensation in respect of that loss.[75]

29.34

Because compensation is awarded out of central funds, the approach to it is not the same as to whether an award of costs should be made,[76] as there can be no financial prejudice caused to the party whose actions led to the award of compensation. This means there can be no 'chilling' effect caused to public bodies applying for closure orders. It is incorrect to start from the point that there will be no compensation – the correct approach is simply to consider the

---

66   ABCPA 2014, s 90(3)(a).
67   ABCPA 2014, s 90(3)(b).
68   ABCPA 2014, s 90(4)(a).
69   ABCPA 2014, s 90(4)(b).
70   ABCPA 2014, s 90(3)(c).
71   Per ABCPA 2014, s 90(6) – 'central funds' has the same meaning as in enactments providing for the payment of costs.
72   ABCPA 2014, s 90(5)(a).
73   ABCPA 2014, s 90(5)(b).
74   ABCPA 2014, s 90(5)(c).
75   ABCPA 2014, s 90(5)(d).
76   *R (Qin)*, at [43].

matters in ABCPA 2014, s 90(5).[77] If that is not done, the refusal to make an award will be susceptible to challenge.[78]

Access to other premises

29.35

Where:

- access to premises is prohibited or restricted by, or as a result of, a final or temporary closure order, or an extension thereto, at first instance or on appeal to the Crown Court;[79]

- those premises are part of a building or structure;[80] and

- there is another part of that building or structure that is not subject to the prohibition or restriction,[81]

an occupier or owner of that other part may apply to the appropriate court for an order under ABCPA 2014, s 87.

29.36

The appropriate court is:

- the magistrates' court,[82] except where the order has been made on appeal to the Crown Court under ABCPA 2014, s 84, when it is the Crown Court;[83]

- the Crown Court, in the case of an order under s 84.

29.37

Notice of an application under ABCPA 2014, s 87 must be given to:

- whatever constable the court thinks appropriate;[84]

- the local authority;[85]

- a person on whom the closure notice was served under ABCPA 2014, s 79;[86]

---

77 *R (Qin)*, at [45].
78 *R (Qin)*, at [46]–[47].
79 ABCPA 2014, s 87(1)(a).
80 ABCPA 2014, s 87(1)(b).
81 ABCPA 2014, s 87(1)(c).
82 ABCPA 2014, s 87(2)(a).
83 ABCPA 2014, s 87(2)(b).
84 ABCPA 2014, s 87(3)(a).
85 ABCPA 2014, s 87(3)(b).
86 ABCPA 2014, s 87(3)(c).

- anyone else who has an interest in the premises but on whom the closure notice was not served.[87]

29.38

On an application under ABCPA 2014, s 87, the court may make whatever order it thinks appropriate in relation to access to any part of the building or structure: it does not matter whether provision has been made under s 80(8)(b).[88]

Appeals

29.39

Any appeal against a closure order lies to the Crown Court[89] and must be made within 21 days beginning with the date of the decision to which it relates.[90] On appeal the Crown Court may make whatever order it thinks appropriate.[91]

29.40

The Crown Court must notify the relevant licensing authority if it makes a closure order in relation to premises in respect of which a premises licence is in force.[92]

29.41

An appeal against a decision to make or extend a closure order may be made by:

- a person on whom the closure notice was served under ABCPA 2014, s 79;[93]

- anyone else who has an interest in the premises but on whom the closure notice was not served.[94]

29.42

A constable[95] or a local authority[96] may appeal against a decision not to:

- make a closure order applied for by a constable[97] or that authority;[98]

---

87   ABCPA 2014, s 87(3)(d).
88   ABCPA 2014, s 87(4).
89   ABCPA 2014, s 84(4).
90   ABCPA 2014, s 84(5).
91   ABCPA 2014, s 84(6).
92   ABCPA 2014, s 84(7).
93   ABCPA 2014, s 84(1)(a).
94   ABCPA 2014, s 84(1)(b).
95   ABCPA 2014, s 84(2).
96   ABCPA 2014, s 84(3).
97   ABCPA 2014, s 84(2)(a).
98   ABCPA 2014, s 84(3)(a).

- extend a closure order made on the application of a constable[99] or that authority;[100]

- (under ABCPA 2014, s 81) order the continuation in force of a closure notice issued by a constable[101] or that authority.[102]

Breach

29.43

There are three ways in which a closure order can be breached, each of which is an offence contrary to ABCPA 2014, s 86:

- A person who without reasonable excuse remains on or enters premises in contravention of a closure notice (including a temporary closure order).[103]

- A person who without reasonable excuse obstructs a person serving a closure notice (under ABCPA 2014, s 79) or enforcing a closure order (under s 85(1)).[104]

A person guilty of an offence under either of these subsections is liable on summary conviction to imprisonment for a period not exceeding three months,[105] or a fine,[106] or both.

- A person who without reasonable excuse remains on or enters premises in contravention of a closure order.[107]

A person guilty of an offence under this subsection is liable on summary conviction to imprisonment for a period not exceeding 51 weeks,[108] or to a fine,[109] or to both.

29.44

As the Criminal Justice Act 2003, s 281(5) has not yet come into force, the reference to 51 weeks is to be read as six months. No date has yet been appointed for its commencement. When it does come into force, it will require the reference to be read faithfully to the drafting, as 51 weeks.[110]

---

99 ABCPA 2014, s 84(2)(b).
100 ABCPA 2014, s 84(3)(b).
101 ABCPA 2014, s 84(2)(c).
102 ABCPA 2014, s 84(3)(c).
103 ABCPA 2014, s 86(1).
104 ABCPA 2014, s 86(3).
105 ABCPA 2014, s 86(4)(a).
106 ABCPA 2014, s 86(4)(b).
107 ABCPA 2014, s 86(2).
108 ABCPA 2014, s 86(5)(a).
109 ABCPA 2014, s 86(5)(b).
110 ABCPA 2014, s 86(6).

Index

[all references are to paragraph number]